LOS CABOS

NIKKI GOTH ITOI

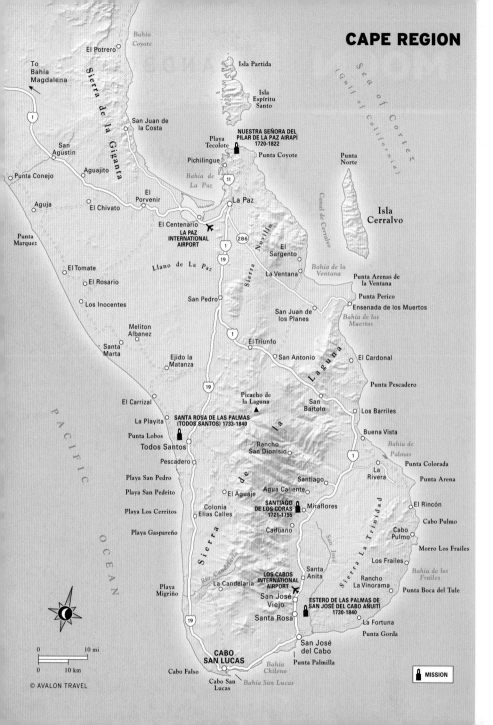

CAPE REGION

Bahía Coyote

El Potrero

Sierra de la Giganta

To Bahía Magdalena

San Juan de la Costa

Isla Partida

Isla Espíritu Santo

NUESTRA SEÑORA DEL PILAR DE LA PAZ AIRAPÍ 1720-1822

Playa Tecolote

Punta Coyote

Pichilingue

Punta Norte

San Agustín

Aguajito

El Porvenir

Bahía de La Paz

La Paz

Sea of Cortez (Gulf of California)

Punta Conejo

El Chivato

El Centenario

LA PAZ INTERNATIONAL AIRPORT

Isla Cerralvo

Canal de Cerralvo

Aguja

Punta Marquez

El Tomate

El Rosario

Los Inocentes

Llano de La Paz

San Pedro

El Sargento

La Ventana

Bahía de la Ventana

Punta Arenas de la Ventana

Sierra Novillo

San Juan de los Planes

Punta Perico

Ensenada de los Muertos

Bahía de los Muertos

Meliton Albanez

Santa Marta

Ejido la Matanza

El Triunfo

San Antonio

El Cardonal

Punta Pescadero

El Carrizal

Picacho de la Laguna ▲

San Bartolo

Los Barriles

La Playita

SANTA ROSA DE LAS PALMAS (TODOS SANTOS) 1733-1840

Buena Vista

Bahía de Palmas

Punta Lobos

Todos Santos

Pescadero

Rancho San Dionisio

Sierra de la Laguna

La Rivera

Punta Colorada

Punta Arena

Playa San Pedro

Playa San Pedrito

El Aguaje

Agua Caliente

Santiago

El Rincón

Cabo Pulmo

Playa Los Cerritos

Colonia Elias Calles

SANTIAGO DE LOS CORAS 1721-1795

Miraflores

Cabo Pulmo

Playa Gaspareño

Caduaño

Morro Los Frailes

Los Frailes

Bahía de los Frailes

Sierra La Trinidad

Río Candelaria

La Candelaria

LOS CABOS INTERNATIONAL AIRPORT

Santa Anita

Rancho La Vinorama

Punta Boca del Tule

Playa Migriño

San José Viejo

Santa Rosa

ESTERO DE LAS PALMAS DE SAN JOSÉ DEL CABO AÑUITÍ 1730-1840

Río San José

La Fortuna

Punta Gorda

CABO SAN LUCAS

San José del Cabo

Punta Palmilla

PACIFIC OCEAN

Cabo Falso

Bahía Chileno

Cabo San Lucas

Bahía San Lucas

0   10 mi
0   10 km

© AVALON TRAVEL

■ **MISSION**

Contents

DISCOVER
Los Cabos

Once upon a time, the typical Cabo visitor chose this destination for one reason: to catch big fish. These days, any number of pastimes might inspire a journey to the southern tip of the Baja Peninsula. At Los Cabos International Airport, retirees mingle with tipsy spring breakers. Newlyweds wait in line with artists and anglers. And scuba divers roll bags full of gear through the crowd.

What brings them all to a remote peninsula that early explorers thought to be an island? Miles of white-sand beaches and a tropical-desert climate, luxury resorts with championship golf courses, protected marine preserves, and the promise of an eco-adventure. Surfing, kayaking, and snorkeling are among the most popular activities. Kiteboarding, golfing, mountain biking, and conservation work are possible, too.

Increasingly, travelers are discovering cultural attractions. Local chefs are shaping a distinctive *bajacaliforniano* cuisine, and the art districts in San José del Cabo and Todos Santos are thriving. Meanwhile, historic ghost towns and the state capital of La Paz offer opportunities to experience Baja California's colonial past.

Los Cabos is more than the sum of its culture and history, however. In the last decade, dozens of local, national, and international organizations

have teamed up to protect its fragile ecosystem. Together they are working to protect sea turtle habitats; rescue whales, sharks, and dolphins that get caught in commercial fishing nets; promote sustainable fishery management; clean up beaches; and teach local residents to be ecotourism guides. From Cabo San Lucas to La Paz, their efforts are making a difference.

Longtime Baja travelers will tell you that Cabo has changed--that it's not the offbeat destination it once was. In many ways, they are right. As one of the most popular, fastest-growing, and most expensive destinations in Mexico, Los Cabos is more upscale and Americanized than ever. Although they may pine for the days of deserted beaches, these seasoned travelers still return year after year to enjoy the beautiful scenery and relaxed pace of life. There are many dimensions to this ever-changing destination, and it's become much more than an angler's paradise. With a sense of adventure and willingness to explore, you're sure to discover a part of Los Cabos that captures your imagination.

Planning Your Trip

▶ WHERE TO GO

Once just a quiet fishing village at the tip of Baja California, Los Cabos today encompasses two cape towns and a tourist corridor all wrapped up into one destination.

San José del Cabo

The original Cabo is an authentic town with a history that goes back to mission times. It has a historic art district, fine dining, boutique hotels, and a more traditional Mexican culture. This is a great location for surfing and sportfishing.

The Corridor

Along the Corridor that connects the two towns, luxury resorts pamper guests with every amenity imaginable, and designer golf courses abound. Beaches are not private, but finding access can be a challenge.

Cabo San Lucas

This "Cabo" entertains the young and young at heart in a uniquely Americanized fashion. The action centers around a busy marina district and crowded beach called Playa El Médano.

Todos Santos and the West Cape

Along the Pacific coast, a rugged shoreline extends from Cabo San Lucas north to the funky artist community of Todos Santos, a crossroads for painters, sculptors, yoga students, surfers, and early retirees. Experienced surfers camp out here for weeks on end, hoping to catch the perfect wave. Development is on the rise, but the West Cape remains the least-developed stretch of coastline on either side of the peninsula south of La Paz.

the Gulf coast near Cabo Pulmo

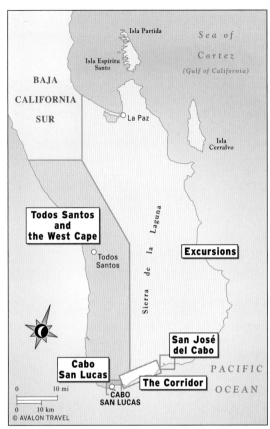

roads, *panga* boats, and *palapa* restaurants. The Sea of Cortez offers secluded beaches, steady winds, abundant game fish, a living coral reef, and days of 30-meter visibility underwater.

Farther north, Los Barriles is the most developed town between La Paz and San José del Cabo, with services for anglers, kiteboarders, and divers.

In the Sierra de la Laguna, hikers, mountain bikers, and horseback riders experience more rugged terrain. The silver mining ghost towns of El Triunfo and San Antonio hold hidden treasures, like a piano museum and a cactus sanctuary.

By contrast, La Paz, the capital of Baja California Sur, is an authentic Mexican city with a strong mainland influence. White-sand beaches along the Pichilingue Peninsula invite relaxation, while the protected islands offshore support a rare and fragile ecosystem.

Southeast of La Paz, Bahía de la Ventana is a stunning and remote bay that serves kiteboarders and windsurfers in the windy winter months, and scuba divers, snorkelers, sportfishers, and stand-up paddlers in the calmer summer months.

Beyond La Ventana, Bahía de los Muertos is a *panga*-lined bay that still holds the ruins of the abandoned Ensenada de los Muertos.

Excursions

If you have the time to venture outside of the immediate Los Cabos vicinity, there are many more adventures to try. The East Cape holds intrigue for travelers with a passion for water sports and a willingness to rough it. Here, Cabo Pulmo is defined by solar power, dirt

► WHEN TO GO

Southern Baja is warm year-round, and the desert climate means very little precipitation except during late summer and early fall. The best travel season depends on your activity of choice. Anglers and scuba divers prefer summer, when the game fish are running and the Sea of Cortez reaches its warmest temperatures. The air on land can be intolerably hot this time of year. Head to the Pacific coast if you need to cool off. Surfers flock to

view of the mountains near Cabo Pulmo

beaches on the Pacific in winter to catch the north swell, and they choose the Corridor or the East Cape when the summer swell rolls in from the south. Winter brings gray whales to the shallow birthing lagoons along the Pacific. It's also the windy season for kiteboarders and windsurfers.

Places book up in Los Cabos and La Paz during Christmas and around New Year's Day and also for the week before Easter (Semana Santa). In March Cabo San Lucas fills with college students on spring break. La Paz fills up in November during the Baja 1000 off-road race.

▶ BEFORE YOU GO

Passports and Other Documents

Anyone traveling by air, land, or sea from the United States, Canada, Mexico, Central and South America, the Caribbean, and Bermuda is required to present a valid passport. Citizens of the United States or Canada (or of 42 other designated countries in Europe and Latin America, plus Singapore) who are visiting Mexico as tourists do not need a visa. They must, however, obtain validated tourist cards, called *formas migratorias turistas,* or FMTs, available at any Mexican consulate or Mexican tourist office, for flights to Mexico and any border crossings. The tourist card is valid for 180 days and must be used within 90 days of issue. It expires when you exit the country. If you are planning to enter and leave Mexico more than once during your trip, you can ask for a multiple-entry tourist card, which is available at Mexican consulates. In 1999 the Mexican government instituted a tourist fee (currently around US$25-30), which is factored into your airfare if you fly but must be paid separately at a bank in Mexico if you cross the border by land or sea.

Transportation

Buy round-trip airfare to Los Cabos International Airport (SJD) or arrange to

view from Secrets Marquis Los Cabos, The Corridor

arrive by land or by sea. Reserve a rental car for pickup at the airport or plan to take a shuttle or taxi into town and use public transportation to get around. Buy street maps for the larger towns and topo maps if you are planning to explore the mountains. If you are driving your own vehicle, bring two copies of your Mexican auto liability insurance policy, plus road maps and at least a basic auto repair kit.

Best of Los Cabos

Ready for a getaway? Travelers based in the western United States can reach Los Cabos by air in a matter of hours, and there are easy connections from elsewhere in North America as well. Choose a home base in high-energy Cabo San Lucas or sophisticated San José del Cabo (30 minutes apart by car) or in the exclusive atmosphere of the Corridor that connects the two. Once settled, you'll have white-sand beaches, water sports, restaurants, shops, and galleries all within easy reach of your hotel.

Day 1

Start your first day in Los Cabos on the plaza in downtown San José. Walk to the French Riviera for breakfast. If it's a Saturday, head to the San José del Cabo Mercado Organico for organic produce; otherwise, pack up a beach bag and walk or drive to Playa California in front of the Zona Hotelera. Spend the morning relaxing at the beach, and later, grab lunch at the Baja Blue Bar and Grille. In the afternoon, return to the plaza to browse the galleries, shops, and restaurant menus in the historic art district *(distrito del arte)*. If it's Thursday, the galleries will stay open late for the evening Art Walk. When the mood strikes, order a homemade tamale from Tamales Doña Nina on the plaza. Or savor the tastes of "BajaMed" cuisine at one of San José's stylish restaurants, such as La Panga Antigua, Tequila Restaurant, or Don Sanchez Restaurant.

Round off your evening at the Baja Brewing Company, where you can enjoy made-in-Baja brews along with live music.

Day 2

Drive to The Container Bar-Restaurant at the Puerto Los Cabos Marina for brunch. Relax on the beach by the harbor, or walk through the cactus garden in the marina. Later, head back through town to snorkel the rock reefs at Bahía Chileno or Bahía Santa María, looking for green moray eels, spotted eagle rays, and schools of tropical fish; or catch some waves at Playa Costa Azul. Plan for a late lunch at Mi Ensalada I or Mama Mia near the beach. Book a sunset horseback-riding tour along Playa California. Head into Cabo San Lucas for dinner at Hacienda Cocina y Cantina and enjoy the legendary Cabo nightlife at Cabo Wabo or the Passion Club and Lounge at ME Cabo.

spa with a view at Los Colobris in Todos Santos

stormy day on the East Cape

sunset over Bahia La Paz

Day 3

Head out for a day at sea. You might choose sportfishing from La Playita, surfing at Playa Costa Azul, or scuba diving in the Bahía San Lucas with Manta or Eagle Divers, both based in Cabo San Lucas. If you want to stay on land, browse the many home decor shops in San José or sign up for a massage at one of the luxurious spas at the Westin Resort & Spa Los Cabos, Las Ventanas al Paraíso, or Esperanza Resort.

For dinner, head to Flora Farms for a menu of organic dishes, made with produce that is grown right there on the property. Afterward, head to the Tropicana Bar and Grill on Boulevard Mijares for regional Mexican music or the rooftop bar at Shooters Bar & Grill for a livelier scene.

Day 4

On your last full day, soak in the sun at Playa del Amor, where you can book a snorkeling tour around Pelican Rock. Spend the late afternoon browsing the shops in Plaza Bonita and the Puerto Paraíso mall, and head to the rooftop Baja Brewing Company at Cabo Villas for drinks and a sunset view. In the evening, enjoy Argentinian-style grilled steak at Patagonia or shellfish at Maro's Shrimp House, followed by live jazz at Edith's before you head out.

Options

Travelers with more than four days could head north along the Gulf coast to explore remote beaches along the East Cape, or north along the Pacific coast to visit the artist colony of Todos Santos and the Baja California Sur state capital of La Paz. For either of these excursions, an overnight stay is recommended.

shrimp served in a stone bowl at Maro's Shrimp House

stunning view from a cliff walk in Todos Santos

Best Beaches

For most travelers, a Los Cabos trip is all about getting in the water, or at least digging toes in the sand. There are hundreds of miles of beaches to explore—most of them white-sand. Some are steps away from hotels, shops, and restaurants; others are completely remote and off the grid. Here is a sampling of the best.

PLAYA CALIFORNIA (PAGE 27)

This popular beach fronts the hotel zone in San José del Cabo. The longest beach in San José del Cabo is easy to access and offers plenty of space for relaxing in the sand and peaceful beach walks. Swimming is not advised.

LA PLAYITA (PAGE 27)

Outside San José del Cabo, La Playita is a small beach on a protected harbor inside the Puerto Los Cabos marina. The area around the beach has the feel of a small seaside village and there is a roped off swimming area that is great for children.

PLAYA COSTA AZUL (PAGE 27)

Just outside San José del Cabo, this is a good place to learn to surf. Several shops offer lessons and rentals.

PLAYA EL BLEDITO (PAGE 60)

A breakwater creates a protected cove for swimmers and snorkelers at Playa El Bledito, also known as Tequila Cove. This is hands-down the best beach in Los Cabos for families.

PLAYA EL MÉDANO (PAGE 80)

The busiest of Los Cabos beaches fronts a row of resorts and hotels within walking distance from downtown Cabo San Lucas. People come here for sunbathing, water activities, and partying.

FINISTERRA (LAND'S END) (PAGE 91)

The end of the road in Baja comes at the granite rock formations that culminate at El Arco, Cabo San Lucas's signature arch. A quick boat ride will bring you into perfect view of the site and proximity to a nearby sea lion colony.

PLAYA DEL AMOR (PAGE 81)

At the southernmost tip of the cape, Lover's Beach offers a rare opportunity to experience the Pacific Ocean and the Sea of Cortez from

Finisterra (Land's End)

baby sea turtles heading for the sea

Playa del Amor (Lover's Beach)

the very same location. Bring your snorkeling gear and a picnic lunch.

PLAYA SOLMAR (PAGE 81)
A strong undertow makes this beach unsuitable for swimming, but it remains ideal for escaping the crowds at Médano. Just sit back, soak up the sun, enjoy the ocean breeze, and keep your eyes open for whales.

PLAYA LOS CERRITOS (PAGE 112)
The West Cape's most popular beach has great beginner waves—and sometimes more advanced surf. A handful of businesses provide food and accommodations, and even massage on the beach.

PLAYA LA SIRENITA (PAGE 190)
You have to hike to get to the best snorkeling on the East Cape, but the rock formations and protected coves are well worth the effort.

PLAYA BALANDRA (PAGE 204)
The best beach for swimming and snorkeling near La Paz is located on the Pichilingue Peninsula. The famous Mushroom Rock balances just offshore, and the shallow water is great for kids.

oyster harvest on the Gulf coast

palapas along Playa California

Best Snorkeling and Scuba Diving

The southern Sea of Cortez offers tropical conditions for diving and snorkeling, with drift diving over a living coral reef, sea lion colonies, dozens of islands, secluded coves, and white-sand beaches. The most popular dive destinations in the region are near La Paz, Cabo Pulmo, and in the Bahía San Lucas.

PLAYA EL BLEDITO (PAGE 62)

Kids and adults who are comfortable swimming and snorkeling in deep water will enjoy exploring the rocks in this protected harbor in front of the Hilton Los Cabos resort.

BAHÍAS CHILENO AND SANTA MARÍA (PAGE 62)

Playa Chileno, the most accessible public beach on the Corridor, offers protected snorkeling along a rock reef. Playa Santa María is a smaller bay nearby, also with swimming and snorkeling.

PLAYA DEL AMOR AND PELICAN ROCK (PAGES 81 AND 82)

The rocky shoreline near Playa del Amor is an easy place to look for fish—the rocks are teeming with wildlife. Just offshore, Pelican Rock is another good snorkeling site.

BAHÍA SAN LUCAS (PAGE 82)

In Cabo San Lucas, scuba diving sites are just a short boat ride away. A deep submarine canyon just 45 meters offshore offers exciting underwater topography for experienced divers. The canyon is known for its "sand falls," streams of falling sand channeled between rocks along the canyon walls.

LAND'S END (PAGE 82)

A popular dive from Cabo San Lucas begins in the surge under a sea lion colony on the Sea of Cortez side of Land's End and concludes with an underwater swim around to the Pacific side.

PULMO REEF SYSTEM (PAGE 190)

Along the East Cape, the hard coral reef in Cabo Pulmo Bay has the best snorkeling anywhere in Southern Baja. Best of all, you can access it from shore.

wetsuits for rent in Cabo Pulmo

CABO PULMO NATIONAL PARK
www.eastcapeadventures.com

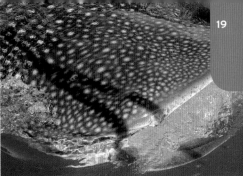

mama and baby whales near Cabo San Lucas

whale shark

PLAYA LA SIRENITA (PAGE 190)

You have to hike to reach this hidden beach just south of Cabo Pulmo, but the views above and below the water are well worth the effort.

BAHÍA DE LOS FRAILES (PAGE 191)

The rocky point at the north end of this bay is home to a wide variety of fish and marine creatures. The seafloor drops rapidly here into a submarine canyon, which can bring larger pelagics close to shore.

BALANDRA BAY (PAGE 204)

With its signature Mushroom Rock and sandy bottom, the shallow Balandra Bay is a delight for novice snorkelers and a popular stop for guided boat trips out of La Paz.

ISLA ESPÍRITU SANTO (PAGE 207)

The uninhabited islands and seamounts offshore from La Paz harbor some of the most exciting underwater topography and the largest marine creatures in the sea. An advanced dive site called El Bajo is famous for its summer population of giant manta rays and, in summer, schooling hammerhead sharks.

Bahía de Los Frailes

snorkeling stand at Cabo Pulmo

Best Adventure Sports

Sea Kayaking

PLAYA EL MÉDANO (PAGE 84)
Rent a kayak at Playa El Médano and paddle over to Playa del Amor instead of taking a water taxi.

ESTERO SAN JOSÉ (PAGE 37)
Look for birds in the estuary that separates the San José hotel zone from the Puerto Los Cabos marina.

CABO PULMO (PAGE 189)
Explore a living hard coral reef, from above.

ISLANDS OFF LA PAZ (PAGE 212)
Pack your snorkeling gear and paddle the secluded coves of uninhabited islands just offshore from the capital city of Baja California Sur.

Kiteboarding

BAHÍA DE LA VENTANA (PAGE 229)
La Ventana generally provides more consistent conditions and a safe place for beginners to learn, with rustic accommodations in a more remote setting.

LOS BARRILES (PAGE 178)
The stronger winds at Los Barriles appeal to advanced kiters and sailors. Los Barriles also is more developed as a tourist town, with a broader mix of accommodations and restaurants.

Surfing

PLAYA COSTA AZUL (PAGE 30)
Most of the waves in the immediate Los Cabos region break near Playa Costa Azul, just outside San José del Cabo. When summer's south swells roll in, experienced surfers wait for a turn at Zippers and The Rock, while beginners can usually handle the waves at Playa Acapulquito, the next cove to the west.

TODOS SANTOS AND THE WEST CAPE (PAGE 116)
At Playa Los Cerritos, beginners appreciate the sandy bottom and can learn to stand up on the whitewater on the inside. Closer to Todos Santos, the cobblestone point at Punta San Pedro breaks on both north and south swells. Surfers looking for big waves head to Playa La Pastora north of Todos Santos. You can rent boards and buy gear at two shops in Todos Santos or at the beach at Los Cerritos.

Kayakers on Balandra Bay near La Paz

Zip Lines

WILD CANYON ADVENTURES (PAGE 63)

This adventure park has 10 zip lines and a bungee jump, in a canyon near Playa El Tule along the Corridor.

CABO ADVENTURES (PAGE 63)

Cabo Adventures offers zip-line experiences about one-hour north of San José del Cabo. These are among the longest, highest, and fastest zip lines in southern Baja. Set in the UNESCO-protected biosphere, the scenery is not to be missed.

CANOPY COSTA AZUL ECO-ADVENTURE (PAGE 63)

Near Playa Palmilla, this option for zip line tours is ideal if you don't want to travel too far off the beaten path for your day of adventure. It is set in an ecological sanctuary just outside of San Jose del Cabo. Brake systems here are controlled by pulleys, not your hands, which makes zip lining easier and more efficient.

ATV Rides

WILD CANYON ADVENTURES (PAGE 63)

This eco-adventure park offers ATV rides along the canyon floor, beneath its popular zip line and bungee jump.

WEST CAPE (PAGE 117)

Several outfitters based in Cabo San Lucas lead ATV tours to the West Cape region, near Todos Santos. Migriño Beach and Candelaria are the most popular destinations.

Horseback Riding

PLAYA CALIFORNIA (PAGE 34)

Ride from the estuary to Playa Costa Azul, or anywhere in between. Outfitters walk the beach in the afternoons. Book on the spot, or reserve for the next day.

PACIFIC BEACHES (PAGE 88)

Outfitters based on Playa El Médano can arrange scenic rides along the Pacific beaches of Cabo San Lucas.

TODOS SANTOS (PAGE 117)

Todos Santos Eco Adventures leads horseback rides along the remote beaches of Todos Santos.

Thrill-seekers who prefer to stay on land can enjoy the desert scenery by ATV.

horseback riding near Todos Santos

Best for Romance

There are many opportunities for romance in Los Cabos, whether you are celebrating a wedding, a 50th anniversary, or just a date night away from the kids.

Accommodations

Some of the most romantic accommodations in Los Cabos include Zoëtry Casa del Mar Los Cabos on the Corridor, Casa Natalia in San José del Cabo, and Pueblo Bonito Pacifica in Cabo San Lucas. Cliffside Capella Pedregal would also make for a fantastic honeymoon stay. The Bungalows bed-and-breakfast also has a honeymoon suite. Near Todos Santos on the West Cape, Rancho Pescadero is a top pick for its private setting, small size, and attentive service.

Sunsets

Stroll along Playa California or the Estero San José, grab drinks at Hacienda Cocina y Cantina in Cabo San Lucas or The Container Bar-Restaurant at Puerto Los Cabos, or book a sunset cruise out to El Arco and watch the sun melt into the Pacific Ocean.

Eats

Many resorts offer candlelight dinners for two by the beach. For other intimate dining experiences, try Flora Farms near Puerto Los Cabos, Deckman's at Playa Costa Azul, or El Farallón in Cabo San Lucas. In La Paz, Las Tres Virgenes is a good choice for creative cuisine in a garden setting.

Spas

Some of the most romantic spa experiences in Baja are to be found at Las Ventanas al Paraíso and Desire Resort & Spa Los Cabos. At Las Ventanas, couples can enjoy specialized spa treatments, including the Romance Ritual for Two, which begins with a foot soak, full-body exfoliation, and massage. It culminates with aromatherapy and a rose petal bath for two. At Desire, couples can enjoy sensual and erotic massages in a clothing-optional resort.

Shopping

Browse contemporary art in the galleries of San José del Cabo and Todos Santos, shop for a Mexican fire opal in one of San José's jewelry shops, or pick up a bottle of made-in-Baja wine at La Europea or the Mercado Santa Carmela along the Corridor.

a deluxe room at the Pueblo Bonito Pacifica

Best Nightlife

From super-luxe lounges to wild nightclubs, there's something for everyone in Cabo San Lucas, the city that parties from dusk till dawn.

PLAYA EL MÉDANO CLUBS
(PAGES 96 AND 103)
A trend-setter in beach club experiences, Nikki Beach is based at the ME Cabo resort. Nearby, The Office and Billygan's Island have similar offerings.

TWO-FOR-ONE DRINKS AT THE
NOWHERE BAR (PAGE 94)
This bar along the marina is a popular place to start the night's frivolities.

NIGHTLY DANCE SHOWS AT THE
GIGGLING MARLIN (PAGE 94)
Hang upside down like a hooked marlin at this mainstay on the party circuit in Cabo.

LIVE MUSIC AT CABO WABO (PAGE 95)
One of the town's oldest nightclubs, Cabo Wabo is owned by Sammy Hagar, who makes an appearance from time to time.

DANCE TILL YOU DROP AT
EL SQUID ROE (PAGE 95)
This club serves up massive margaritas and other drinks, two at a time. Balloons and confetti rain down from above as the music pounds all night long.

SEE AND BE SEEN AT PASSION
CLUB AND LOUNGE (PAGE 96)
The super chic head to the Passion Club at the ME Resort on Médano Beach. During daytime hours it serves as an uber-trendy bar and lounge, and then morphs into a dance club at night when the beach party crowd is ready to move indoors.

CRAFT BEERS AT THE BAJA
BREWING CO. (PAGE 96)
Baja's only artisanal brewery has several outposts in Los Cabos. Find them in downtown San José del Cabo, at Playa El Médano, and in the Puerto Paraíso mall.

CUBAN CIGARS AT LA CASA
DEL HABANO (PAGE 93)
Cigar aficionados will want to check out the walk-in humidor and sit at one of a few tables inside.

the swanky Passion Club and Lounge at the ME Resort

Best Local Culture

Despite a strong American influence, Los Cabos offers a number of opportunities to experience the local culture through its art, food, and history.

SAN JOSÉ DEL CABO MERCADO ORGANICO (PAGE 49)
The seasonal farmers market in San José offers a chance to taste the local harvest and browse handicrafts made by local artists.

WEEKLY ART WALKS (PAGE 37)
On Thursday evenings, galleries in the historic art district of San José stay open late for visitors to browse their exhibits.

FLORA FARMS (PAGE 38)
This sustainable farm and restaurant outside of San José offers garden tours as well as tasty meals.

WIRIKUTA DESERT BOTANICAL GARDEN (PAGE 38)
Inside the Puerto Los Cabos marina, this new park holds more than 1,500 kinds of desert plants.

PABELLÓN CULTURAL DE LA REPÚBLICA (PAGE 90)
Cabo San Lucas has a new cultural pavilion that hosts music, lectures, films, and other programs.

MUSEO DE HISTORIA NATURAL CABO SAN LUCAS (PAGE 90)
In the heart of Cabo San Lucas, this small museum documents the origins of the Los Cabos region.

COOKING CLASSES (PAGES 69 AND 124)
Rancho Pescadero, Las Ventanas al Paraíso, Esperanza Resort, and other resorts offer culinary programs for guests who want to experience the local cuisine and hone their cooking skills.

TODOS SANTOS HISTORIC DISTRICT (PAGE 120)
A side trip to the West Cape leads to a collection of colonial buildings and another gathering place for working artists.

the new Pabellón Cultural de la República in Cabo San Lucas

SAN JOSÉ DEL CABO

San José del Cabo boasts a historic downtown with an attractive plaza and church as well as many restored colonial buildings. Its growing art district holds a handful of well-respected galleries, representing artists from all over Mexico as well as some from the United States.

© PAUL ITOI

HIGHLIGHTS

LOOK FOR ◖ TO FIND RECOMMENDED SIGHTS, ACTIVITIES, DINING, AND LODGING.

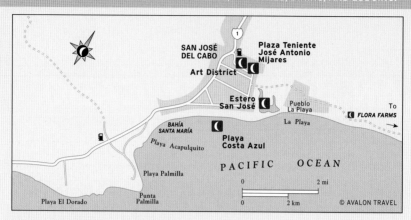

◖ **Playa Costa Azul:** Catch the waves, take a surf lesson, or just watch the action from a beachfront table at Zippers (page 27).

◖ **Plaza Teniente José Antonio Mijares:** Town life centers around this cobblestone plaza in front of an elegant 1940 church built on the site of the original Jesuit mission (page 36).

◖ **Art District:** Historic adobe buildings in the *distrito del arte* house contemporary art galleries. More than a dozen galleries participate in Thursday evening Art Walks, which draw visitors

and locals alike (page 36).

◖ **Estero San José:** This large estuary, home to hundreds of species of birds, connects the Pacific Ocean to an underground river that flows out of the sierra (page 37).

◖ **Flora Farms:** This working sustainable farm community outside of San José is a farm, ranch, restaurant, teaching center, and market all in one. Book a tour of the gardens before your meal (page 38).

The newer part of town includes a nine-hole golf course and beachfront hotel zone (the Zona Hotelera). There is also a busy commercial area along the Carretera Transpeninsular (Highway 1). The town is the municipal seat for Los Cabos. Many expats, especially artists, have taken up residence in San José in recent years, but for the most part they seem committed to restoring and preserving their adopted community of Josefinos, and so far the town retains an authentic Mexican feel.

The new Puerto Los Cabos marina has brought power, Internet, and a modern sewage system to the village at La Playita. But with these amenities come the noise and mess of constant construction, threats to coastal wildlife, higher prices, and increasing traffic congestion. In many ways, San José is becoming unaffordable for the local residents whose families have lived here for generations.

PLANNING YOUR TIME

In a couple of days, you can easily explore the main sections of downtown San José and sample a few restaurants, plus have time for the beach. Add extra days for any special activities, such as scuba diving, fishing, or mountain biking. The drive from San José del Cabo to Cabo San Lucas along the Corridor takes about 30-45 minutes.

ORIENTATION
Four main areas in the town of San José del Cabo are of interest to visitors. The **Centro Historico** (Central Historic District) extends several blocks from the mission church and plaza through the present-day art district. At the shoreline, a newer hotel zone, **Zona Hotelera,** fronts the beach along Playa California. At the west end of town, where San José del Cabo meets the Los Cabos Corridor, **Playa Costa Azul** has a surf culture all its own. And if you head east of town, across the new bridge to the north side of the estuary, you'll reach San José's new marina **Puerto Los Cabos,** the village of Pueblo La Playa, and the little beach known as La Playita.

Beaches

ZONA HOTELERA
Playa California/Playa Hotelera
Most of the newer resorts in San José line this long and exposed stretch of sand, which extends from the estuary to Playa Costa Azul. A few vendors sell crafts and snacks, and some of the hotels have restaurants that are open to the public, but the surf is rough here, so you won't see any of the water-sports outfitters that hang around the swimmable beaches in Los Cabos. Ideal for peaceful beach walks, Playa California is the longest beach in San José del Cabo and has a variety of services for visitors, including beachfront bars and restaurants, horseback riding, and vendors selling *artesanias* and refreshments.

◖ PLAYA COSTA AZUL
On the outskirts of San José, under a lookout point on the Transpeninsular Highway (Carretera Transpeninsular, or Highway 1) near kilometers 28 and 29, somewhat protected Plaza Costa Azul attracts surfers, beachcombers, and occasionally swimmers who walk from the condo complexes that front the beach. This is the closest surfing beach to downtown San Jose. When the swell rolls in, it can be a great place for surfers and spectators alike. For travelers coming from San José, there is an unmarked exit ramp just after Deckman's restaurant and before the wide arroyo. Turn left off the ramp and park in the sandy lot that divides Mira Vista condos and Zippers restaurant.

PUERTO LOS CABOS
La Playita
Outside of San José, adjoining the Puerto Los Cabos marina, this tiny beach has a roped-off swimming area in the harbor suitable for kids (stand-up paddling rentals may be available), a small play structure for children, fish cleaning stations, a few restaurants, and public restrooms. Although it is now part of a new and very large harbor, La Playita retains the feel of a small seaside village.

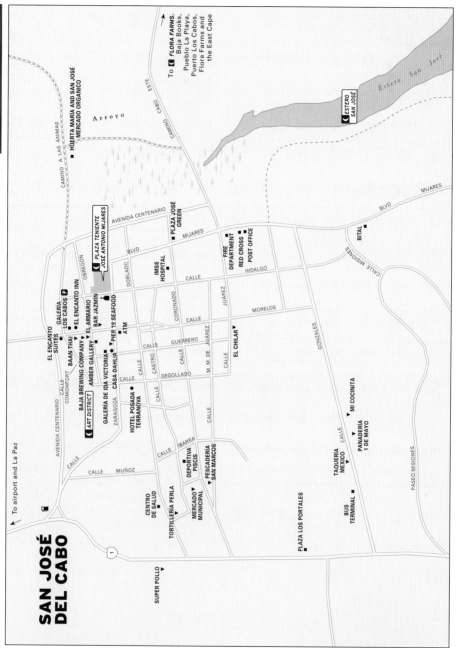

SAN JOSÉ DEL CABO

To airport and La Paz

SUPER POLLO

CENTRO DE SALUD

TORTILLERÍA PERLA

MERCADO MUNICIPAL

PESCADERÍA SAN MARCOS

DEPORTIVA PISCIS

HOTEL POSADA TERRANOVA

GALERÍA DE IDA VICTORIA

CASA DAHLIA

ART DISTRICT

BAJA BREWING COMPANY

AMBER GALLERY

EL ENCANTO SUITES

BAAN THAI

EL ARMARIO

PIER 19 SEAFOOD

ATM

GALERIA LOS CABOS

EL ENCANTO INN

BAR JAZMÍN

PLAZA TENIENTE JOSÉ ANTONIO MIJARES

PLAZA JOSÉ GREEN

HUERTA MARIA AND SAN JOSÉ MERCADO ORGANICO

CAMINO A LAS ANIMAS

Arroyo

CAMINO CABO ESTE

To FLORA FARMS, Baja Books, Pueblo La Playa, Puerto Los Cabos, Flora Farms and the East Cape

Estero San José

ESTERO SAN JOSÉ

AVENIDA CENTENARIO

MIJARES

BLVD

DOBLADO

OBREGÓN

IMSS HOSPITAL

CALLE

JUAREZ

CORONADO

CALLE

GUERRERO

CALLE

CASTRO

DEGOLLADO

CALLE

M. M. DE JUAREZ

EL CHILAR

MORELOS

FIRE DEPARTMENT

RED CROSS

POST OFFICE

HIDALGO

GONZALES

CALLE MISIONES

BITAL

BLVD

MIJARES

MI COCINITA

TAQUERÍA MEXICO

PANADERÍA 1 DE MAYO

CALLE

PASEO MISIONES

BUS TERMINAL

PLAZA LOS PORTALES

CALLE MUÑOZ

CALLE IBARRA

CALLE ZARAGOZA

CALLE COMONFORT

AVENIDA CENTENARIO

CALLE

1

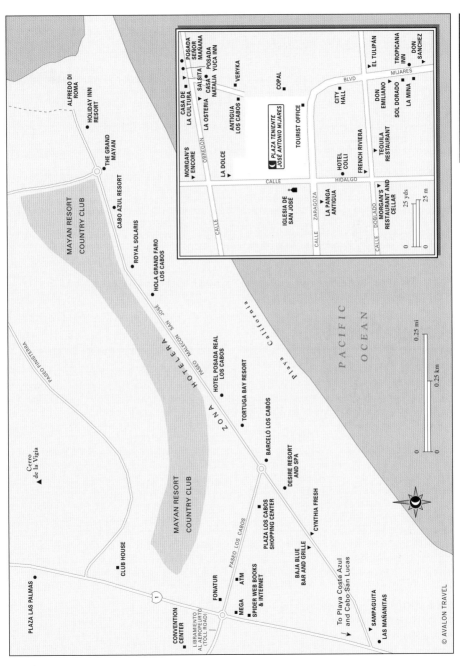

© AVALON TRAVEL

THE BEST DAY IN SAN JOSÉ DEL CABO

A perfect day in San José revolves around art and food. Plan your trip on a Thursday to coincide with the weekly evening **Art Walk** or on a Saturday to experience the organic farmers market in the morning.

Start the day with a freshly baked pastry at the **French Riviera** or homemade granola and an espresso drink at **Café Calafia.** Stroll over to the plaza and enjoy the cool morning air. If it's a Saturday in the high season, cross the plaza and Calle Obregón and make your way to the **San José del Cabo Mercado Organico** to sample the seasonal harvest and view local products for sale.

Other days of the week, follow Boulevard Mijares to the **Estero San José and Playa California** looking for birds and other coastal wildlife around the estuary. Alternatively, drive or cab to **Playa Costa Azul** with your beach gear. Rent a surfboard or take a lesson from an instructor at the **Costa Azul Surf Shop.** Spend the middle of the day splashing in the waves. And when you get hungry, walk up to the *palapa* restaurant and order a plate of tacos and a *limonada natural* at **Zippers.**

Head back to your hotel in the afternoon for a siesta and a break from the sun. Plan a late lunch or early dinner at **Flora Farms** (reservations recommended). Sign up in advance for an informative tour of the farm and gardens before you dine. Savor the local flavors—from carrot and beet margaritas to roast chicken and homemade pasta dishes. Stay to enjoy the live music, or head back to town for the weekly Art Walk (Thursdays only), when galleries stay open late serving tastes of wine and tequila. When the galleries close, the party moves to the **Baja Brewing Company** until late.

Water Sports

SNORKELING AND SCUBA DIVING

San José visitors must head to the East Cape, the Corridor, or Cabo San Lucas for suitable snorkeling and diving sites.

Puerto Los Cabos

Expert divers who are comfortable in strong currents and choppy seas and interested in exploring the offshore Gordo Banks seamounts may be able to hire a *panga* from La Playita; however, be aware that even groups of experienced dive instructors have run into complications when attempting to turn an angler into a dive-boat captain for the day. The safer approach is to book a trip through one of the PADI-certified dive shops in Cabo San Lucas.

SURFING AND STAND-UP PADDLING (SUP)
Playa Costa Azul

Summer is the peak season for catching waves in Los Cabos, but good-sized swells occasionally roll through as late as mid-November. Playa Costa Azul has three of the best-known breaks anywhere in Southern Baja. Enter from a sandy beach but beware the rocks at low tide. You can scope out the scene from a lookout on the Carretera Transpeninsular before taking the plunge. Longboarders and beginner surfers favor the Playa Acapulquito (Old Man's) reef break, in front of the Cabo Surf Hotel. Directly below the lookout, The Rock is another right. Localism is alive and well at Zippers, but only when the waves are pounding. The rest of the time you can easily paddle out to enjoy this short and fast break. Just flash a smile and be prepared to wait your turn.

There are many lesser-known breaks along the Corridor that break on different sized swells, plus a handful of breaks on the East Cape.

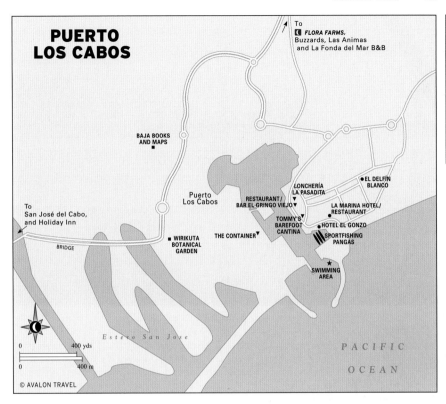

PUERTO LOS CABOS

To
◖ FLORA FARMS,
Buzzards, Las Animas
and La Fonda del Mar B&B

BAJA BOOKS
AND MAPS

Puerto
Los Cabos

LONCHERÍA
LA PASADITA

EL DELFÍN
BLANCO

To
San José del Cabo,
and Holiday Inn

RESTAURANT /
BAR EL GRINGO VIEJO

LA MARINA HOTEL/
RESTAURANT

BRIDGE

TOMMY'S
BAREFOOT
CANTINA

HOTEL EL GONZO

WIRIKUTA
BOTANICAL
GARDEN

THE CONTAINER

SPORTFISHING
PANGAS

SWIMMING
AREA

Estero San Jose

PACIFIC
OCEAN

0   400 yds
0   400 m

© AVALON TRAVEL

EQUIPMENT AND LESSONS

Several shops near Playa Costa Azul rent boards and other equipment. The **Cabo Surf Shop** (Carr. Transpeninsular km 28, tel. 624/172-6188, U.S. tel. 858/964-5117, www. cabosurfshop.com), located at the Cabo Surf Hotel, offers private or group instruction on Playa Acapulquito through the **Mike Doyle Surf School** (8am-6pm daily, until 7pm in summer, group rate US$75 pp for two hours, private lessons US$95/hour) as well as board rentals. Drop-ins are welcome. The **Costa Azul Surf Shop** (Carr. Transpeninsular km 28, Plaza Costa Azul, tel. 624/142-2771, www.costaazul.aguazulmedia.com, 8am-7pm Mon.-Sat., 9am-5pm Sun.) rents short boards, hybrids, and longboards to experienced surfers, as well as beginner boards with rubber fins, and offers lessons. Stop in for beach umbrellas, beach

chairs, and snorkeling gear, too. You can also rent boards right on the beach, next to Zippers restaurant. Here, instructor Pedro Capiz (tel. 624/158-9960) offers lessons to kids and adults.

If you want to try stand-up paddling near San José, contact **Baja Waterman** at Playa Costa Azul (Carr. Transpeninsular km 29, Mon.-Sat. 7:30am-6pm, Sun. 10am-3pm) for rental boards and private or group lessons. Instructors offer guided tours of the estuary, and the shop has beach equipment and accessories for sale.

FISHING

Whether you're a seasoned veteran or you've never fished a day in your life, there are plenty of options near San José. For newbies, your captain and crew will find the right spot for the day, rig up the bait, and handle boating the

© PAUL ITOI

heading out for a day at sea

fish. All you have to do is reel and smile for the picture. Later, top off the day by taking your fresh catch to a local restaurant to have it prepared to your liking.

Fishing boats for hire fall under two general categories: *pangas* and cruisers. Cruisers are the larger boats you'll see in the marina slips. They're often equipped with tuna towers, enclosed cabins, a bathroom, and other amenities. *Pangas* are the ubiquitous open launches, powered by outboard motor and sometimes featuring a sunshade and center console. If you see a *panga* with a newer four-stroke outboard, center console, sunshade, and mounted radio, jump in—you've got a winner. The fish don't care what kind of boat you're in, but the cruisers can handle the larger game fish and a non-fishing passenger in comfort.

Don't forget to pack a hat, sunglasses, sunscreen, water, food, waterproof camera, sandals, and a windbreaker. Take motion sickness medicine the night before and morning of the trip if you are prone to seasickness (or if you aren't sure).

There are a few extra costs to factor into the planning: Tips for the captain and fish-cleaning crew are the norm. About 20 percent of the cost of the trip is standard. Live bait is often not included in the cost of the *panga,* so expect to pay US$20 per boat. Fishing licenses cost US$8 a day or US$20 a week. You do not need a fishing license to fish from the shore. Licenses can be purchased online through the state tourism office at www2.ebajacalifornia. gob.mx/Pesca.

For tackle, bait, and fishing books, head to **Deportiva Piscis** (Castro and Green, 1 block south of the Mercado Municipal, tel. 624/142-0332, 8am-7pm daily).

Zona Hotelera

All hotels in the Zona Hotelera can arrange guided fishing trips. Well-known **Francisco's Fleet** (formerly Victor's Sportfishing, toll-free U.S. tel. 800/521-2281, www.jigstop.com) is based at Palmilla Beach on the Corridor. A six-hour super-*panga* trip for two or three people costs US$195; bring your own food and drinks.

Puerto Los Cabos

Gordo Banks Pangas (Puerto Los Cabos, tel./fax 624/142-1147, toll-free U.S. tel. 800/408-1199, www.gordobanks.com) launches out of La Playita and rents 22-foot *pangas* for US$210 (six hours, 1-3 anglers) or 23-foot super-*pangas* for US$250 (six hours, 1-3 anglers) and cruisers for US$380-470. **Jaime Castro** (Puerto Los Cabos, cell tel. 624/154-9110, U.S. tel. 858/922-3355, US$200-280 per boat) runs *panga* fishing charters by day and manages the kitchen at Buzzard's by night. Boats depart at 6am daily from B dock at the La Playita marina and return at noon. Bait, lunch, drinks, and fishing license cost extra. Reserve online.

Hiking and Biking

San José is a fairly urban area, and as such there is little hiking to be found within the town limits; however, many local outfitters offer trips to nearby trails. For example, **High Tide Los Cabos** (Arambura s/n Zazata, tel. 624/142-0424, www.hightideloscabos.com) offers a waterfall hike to Fox Canyon, one hour north of Cabo San Lucas. **Cabo Adventures** (U.S. tel. 888/526-2238, www.cabo-adventures.com) also organizes a long list of activities and tours, including desert mountain biking rides.

ZONA HOTELERA
Easy Walks and Hikes
Beach walks along the length of **Playa California** are the next best thing to a self-guided wilderness hike. You might also explore the estuary by foot at sunrise or sundown to catch the shorebirds in action.

Biking
Cycling has come to San José, inspired in part by the first Ironman Los Cabos triathlon, which took place in March 2013. **Sportia Specialized Concept Store** (Plaza El Pescador 15, Paseo San José, also known as Paseo Malecón, tel. 624/130-7159, info@sportia.mx, hours vary) opened in the Zona Hotelera to serve the needs of local residents and visiting cyclists.

Consider the traffic, uneven road surface, road debris, and lack of shoulders or bike lanes before you plan a road riding trip. In many ways, mountain biking the dirt roads along the East Cape and West Cape areas of the peninsula is more satisfying.

Golf and Tennis

Most of the now world-famous golf courses are located in the Corridor between San José and Cabo San Lucas; however, San José proper has a few courses of its own.

ZONA HOTELERA
Centrally located in the hotel zone, the **Punta Sur Golf Course** (tel. 624/142-0905, US$130/18 holes) is the oldest course in Los Cabos and makes a convenient and affordable option for beginners and intermediate players. The course was designed by M. Shedjnan and funded by Fonatur, Mexico's tourism foundation. Discounted twilight rates (US$70) begin at 2pm The clubhouse is on the south side of the Carretera Transpeninsular, between Paseo de los Cabos and Paseo Finisterra.

Most of the major resorts in Los Cabos have tennis facilities, but if you are looking for courts in San José proper, your best bets are at Posada Real Los Cabos, Holiday Inn Resort Los Cabos, Royal Solaris Los Cabos Hotel, and Worldmark Coral Baja Resort.

PLAYA COSTA AZUL

At kilometer 119, **Club Campestre San José Golf** (tel. 624/173-9400, www.clubcampestresan-jose.com, US$130-170) is an 18-hole, par-71 course designed by Jack Nicklaus. The course resides in the foothills of the Sierra de la Laguna mountains and overlooks the Sea of Cortez.

PUERTO LOS CABOS

Puerto Los Cabos Golf Club (Paseo de los Pescadores s/n, Puerto Los Cabos, tel. 624/105-6441, US tel. 877/795-8727, reservations1@questrogolf.com, www.puertoloscabos.com/golf/php) also has a signature golf course, with nine holes designed by Jack Nicklaus and nine holes designed by Greg Norman. The course has a full service clubhouse. Caddies cost US$50 per person. Taylor Made rentals cost US$55, US$35 for kids.

Adventure Sports and Tours

Most hotels have an activity desk with a binder full of brochures advertising guided tours, excursions, and recreational activities. You can choose from whale-watching cruises, snorkeling tours, ATV tours, horseback rides, sunset cruises, and more. Hotels generally do not charge an additional fee when they book these activities for their guests. A note for the environmentally aware: Ecotours have over-taken spas as the latest marketing tool for companies looking to earn a share of your tourist dollars. This means just about every operator will tell you they offer eco-some-thing. This does not necessarily mean that every hotel and outfitter in business follows a safe and low-impact approach with their trips and has experienced guides who really understand the fragile Baja ecosystem. Do some homework before you book: Understand where the business buys its supplies, how it supports the local community, what materi-als it reuses and recycles, and what kind of training it requires of its guides. Emergency training and environmental education should be top considerations.

ZONA HOTELERA

Here are a few of the larger and better-known outfitters: **Camino Aventura** (Paseo del Malecón, tel. 624/105-8413, www.cami-noaventura.mx, 9am-6pm daily) organizes horseback rides along the estuary and beach (US$35/hour, US$65/2 hours). **Rancho Tours** (tel. 624/143-5464, www.ranchotours.com) leads walking tours of La Paz and Todo Santos for US$69 per person, as well as glass-bottom boat tours and ATV rides near Cabo San Lucas. **Baja Wild Outfitters** (tel. 624/172-6300, www.bajawild.com) in San José leads a vari-ety of adventure trips, including kayaking, snorkeling, surfing, hiking, ATV, Jeep safa-ris, whale-watching, and turtle-release pro-grams. Half-day trips range US$70-85, and all-day trips are US$110-650, depending on the activity. Group and multisport packages are available.

Spas and Yoga

CENTRO HISTORICO

Ixchel Salon & Spa (Morelos 133, tel. 624/142-2330, www.elencantoinn.com/Spa/Archivos/Spa.html, 9am-7pm Mon.-Sat., 10am-6pm Sun.), inside the El Encanto Inn, offers a full menu of treatments, including massages (50 min. for US$70), facials (50 min. for US$80), manicures, and pedicures. In addition, La Tropicana Inn offers a full list of massage and other wellness therapies on-site.

On the north side of the highway (opposite side from the downtown area), **Baja Wellness** (Navarette and Chamizal, tel. 624/145-2801, www.bajawellness.com, 8am-10pm Mon.-Sun.) offers a range of holistic services, including yoga, massage, alphabiotics, LaStone therapy, a *temazcal* sweat lodge, Watsu, and meditation.

ZONA HOTELERA

Cabo Azul has a full-service spa called **PAZ** (Malecón s/n, Fonatur, tel. 624/163-5100, www.caboazulresort.com/PAZ), where a 50-minute massage runs US$120, manicures and pedicures start at US$45, and body treatments like "Draining Onyx" cost US$170-215. In addition, the Hola Grand Faro, The Grand Mayan, and other resorts have on-site spas that are open to the public.

Behind the Mega supermarket, the **Mex Sun Day Spa and Beauty Salon** (Plaza Garuffi 21/22, tel. 624/151-4507, www.mexsunspa.com, 9am-7pm Mon.-Fri., 9am-5pm Sun.) has a wide range of spa services available. Treatments include manicures, pedicures, massages (US$30-165), facials (60 min. for US$60), laser treatments (US$35 per session), waxing, and a variety of hair treatments.

PUERTO LOS CABOS

A spa opened in early 2013 at **Hotel El Ganzo** (Blvd. Tiburon s/n, La Playita, tel. 624/104-9000, U.S. tel. 855/835-4269, www.elganzo.com, US$250) in the Puerto Los Cabos marina. Details were not yet available at press time.

PLAYA COSTA AZUL

The **Sea Spa & Salon** at the Cabo Surf Hotel (www.seaspacabo.com, daily 8am-8pm) offers treatments for nails, hair, and body. Types of massage include Thai, Swedish, reflexology, Damiana, warm stone, and deep tissue. There are three treatment rooms available, and the spa uses all natural products. Walk-ins are welcome.

CHAMIZAL

San José now has about a half dozen yoga studios, but some instructors seem to come and go each season. Caryl Leffel teaches yoga classes at her own studio, **Mi Cielo Azul** (tel. 624/137-3278, www.kaleidoscopeyoga.com, US$10-25 per class), located in the Chamizal neighborhood, above Guacamaya's Restaurant.

The yoga center at **Raices y Brazos** (Navarrete and Chamizal, tel. 624/142-3794, www.raicesybrazos.com) offers a wide range of yoga styles and intensities for all levels, ages, and body types. Sessions are available daily and start at US$10. The center also offers dance and meditation courses. **Baja Wellness** (Navarette and Chamizal, tel. 624/145-2801, www.bajawellness.com, 8am-10pm Mon.-Sun.) offers consultations and beginning classes as well as more advanced, private sessions in a variety of styles.

Yoga instructor Natasha Grbich teaches courses through **Transformative Wellness** (San Vicente La Choya, tel. 624/105-6089, www.transformativewellness.com, 8am-10am Tues.-Thurs., US$10 per session). She offers sessions in Jivamukli and Hatha styles for teachers and more advanced yoga practitioners. Many of the larger resorts offer their own yoga classes for guests, as do Casa Natalia and El Encanto Inn.

Sights

CENTRO HISTORICO
◖ Plaza Teniente José Antonio Mijares

The center of all the action in San José is a wide brick plaza with a white gazebo-like structure in the middle. On the west side of the plaza, where the original mission once stood, is the 1940 Iglesia San José. Opposite the church, a relatively new fountain has a continuous light show at night. And behind it a row of statues pays tribute to important leaders in Mexican history. Mature trees provide ample shade, while street performers entertain adults and children alike. Restaurants and shops line the plaza on Calles Zaragoza, Hidalgo, and Obregón and Boulevard Mijares. At sundown a handful of food carts open for business. A nice alternative to a formal sit-down meal is to sample a taste of each: tamales, empanadas, *paletas* (popsicles), and more. Town festivals take place here, including events every Sunday evening during the Christmas season.

Misión San José del Cabo Añuiti

The Jesuit mission (1730-1840) at San José was founded in 1730 when Padre Nicolas Tamarál traveled south from La Purísima and baptized more than 1,000 indigenous people in the first year.

The current church, painted a creamy yellow color, was built in 1940 with two symmetrical towers and a mosaic over the main entrance, which depicts the murder of Padre Tamarál by the Pericú who rose up against him. The church holds regular worship services for the people of San José.

Palacio Municipal (City Hall)

This striking 1831 building on Boulevard Mijares just off the plaza has a neoclassical facade and a tower with a wrought-iron balcony and large clock. In the 19th century the building housed the municipal council for San José. Today it contains local government offices.

◖ Art District (Distrito del Arte)

About a dozen of the historic adobe buildings in downtown San José have been converted into fine-art studios and galleries representing artists from all over Mexico and Central and

THE BIG DIG

San José del Cabo's new Puerto Los Cabos marina has set some records in terms of its size and scale. Its 430 slips can accommodate yachts up to 180 feet long. When complete, the facility will be the largest marina in all of Mexico, with more than 21,000 linear feet of dock space at a price tag of US$50 million.

To form the protected harbor, construction crews shuttled 400,000 tons of granite blasted from a local quarry, with individual capstones weighing 60 tons apiece. They also removed some 650,000 cubic meters of earth from the site. Dump trucks were on the move six days a week for eight months straight to get the job done.

The new marina puts yachts and sportfishing boats one hour closer to Banco Gorda than the Cabo San Lucas marina, with a supposedly easier approach to navigate.

Puerto Los Cabos has also opened Wirikuta Desert Botanical Garden to honor more than 1,500 varieties of desert plants from around the world. A million or so plants are available for purchase for private gardens or as personal gifts.

To round off recent changes to the marina, the 72-room Hotel El Ganzo opened its doors to guests in December 2012.

THE MEXICAN-AMERICAN WAR

In a rarely documented chapter of the Mexican-American War (1846-1848), a group of 20 U.S. marines from the sloop *Portsmouth* briefly occupied the city of San José from barracks in a former mission building, which is now preserved as the town's Casa de la Cultura. The U.S. forces were given a nine-pounder carronade (a type of cannon) and 75 carbines to hold the town against about 150 Mexican insurgents. When Mexican lieutenant José Antonio Mijares attempted to invade the barracks and capture the cannon in 1847, he failed and was shot by the marines, but the heroic effort earned him a place in local history. Boulevard Mijares and Plaza Mijares are both named in his honor.

A 21-day siege of the U.S. forces' barracks in San José took place in early 1848, even as U.S. president James K. Polk was claiming victory in the Californias. The Americans were eventually rescued by a party of 102 men from the sloop *Cyane*. In the end, the Treaty of Guadalupe Hidalgo, signed on February 2, 1848, did not give the United States possession of Baja California. The U.S. forces that had held the garrison withdrew 18 months after the conflict had begun. Many expressed disappointment in the outcome, believing that the United States had abandoned its promise to take lower California under its wing and left its supporters at the mercy of their own government.

After the Mexican-American War and a short-lived mining era, San José experienced a period of agriculture in the 1930s. The mission church was rebuilt in 1940, and San José began to attract its first sportfishing tourists in the 1960s.

South America as well as the United States. Most of the galleries are concentrated in the blocks between Calles Guerrero and Hidalgo and Calles Zaragoza and Comonfort. On display are stone sculptures, paintings, photography, pottery, and jewelry. On Thursday evenings, the galleries stay open late for the weekly **Art Walk** (5pm-9pm Nov.-June). This is an unguided opportunity to visit the galleries at your own pace. Some serve refreshments, and some allow you to watch the artists at work in their studios. Recognizing the appeal of the district, the town decided to invest in an infrastructure upgrade in 2012. The old cobblestone streets got a facelift and wires were to be buried underground as part of the project.

Casa de la Cultura (Cultural Center)

U.S. marines stayed in this mission-era building just off the plaza in 1847-1848, during the Mexican-American War. Today the blue and green building hosts art exhibits as well as music, dance, and theater performances. The Cultural Center is located on Calle Obregón at the end of Boulevard Mijares, on the north side of the plaza. The building is open to the public 9am-8pm Monday-Saturday. Call 624/142-2960 for a schedule of events.

ZONA HOTELERA

San José's government-designated hotel zone encompasses more than 1,600 hectares that parallel the coastline from the Estero San José to Playa Costa Azul. To date, about a dozen large resorts and several condo complexes are complete, including the Royal Solaris Los Cabos Hotel, The Grand Mayan Los Cabos, and Cabo Azul Resort. As more properties have opened for business, Paseo de San José has become a busy thoroughfare, with several car rental offices and a few new shops and restaurants. Condos and vacation homes surround a nine-hole golf course, now owned by The Grand Mayan. You can walk the beach all the way from the estuary to the surf break known as Zippers at Playa Costa Azul, but swimming is generally not a good idea, as the undertow is strong most of the year.

C Estero San José

The Río San José, the largest source of

freshwater in Southern Baja, originates in the Sierra de la Laguna, travels about 48 kilometers (much of it underground), and empties into a long, narrow estuary that measures 50 hectares. Sebastián Vizcaíno called the estuary Bahía San Bernabé. At the mouth of the river, a sandbar encloses a lagoon ringed by towering tlaco palms and marsh grasses, which form a sanctuary for more than 200 species of birds.

Unfortunately, this fragile ecosystem is shrinking in size and biodiversity as the town of San José grows, the water table lowers, and the Puerto Los Cabos marina and development encroaches on the preserve.

To reach the estuary, walk or drive to the northeast end of the Zona Hotelera and park outside the Holiday Inn resort. Walk toward the beach and you'll see the estuary on the left.

PUERTO LOS CABOS

Once an isolated fishing village frequented only by *panga* fishers and adventurous travelers, Pueblo La Playa and its sandy beach, **La Playita,** are now linked to San José del Cabo via a paved road and bridge across the wide arroyo that separates the two.

The 800-hectare Puerto Los Cabos project includes a US$50 million marina designed to accommodate luxury mega-yachts, as well as a couple of designer golf courses, five-star accommodations, and beachfront lots that are selling for US$6-8 million. At the entrance to the marina, the **Wirikuta Desert Botanical Garden** and nursery holds some 1,500 types of desert plants. It is becoming a popular place

for event receptions and other formal gatherings. Closer to the water, the Cactus Garden Sculpture Park is an inviting green space with colorful wrought-iron figures of plants from the Baja desert. Elsewhere around the property are more bronze sculptures by surrealist Leonora Carrington. Puerto Los Cabos also has a signature golf course, with nine holes designed by Jack Nicklaus and nine holes designed by Greg Norman.

The harbor is open for business and the Hotel El Ganzo opened in December 2012. Pueblo La Playa has Internet access, paved streets with curbs, and a new, modern sewage system in the works. A *panga* marina and beachfront park features a play structure for kids; a roped-off, protected swimming area; clean restrooms; and the fanciest fish-cleaning tables found anywhere in Baja.

To reach La Playita, turn east off Boulevard Mijares onto Calle Juárez. Follow this four-lane road over the bridge and watch the signs at each roundabout.

🄲 FLORA FARMS

Beyond the marina, in an area known as Las Animas, **Flora Farms** (tel. 624/355-4564, www.flora-farms.com) is a modern-day farm that has evolved over a decade into a multifaceted culinary attraction. The owners grow organic vegetables, raise hormone-free livestock (at a different location), and offer informative tours of the property. There is also a small grocery stand, and a popular restaurant often hosts live music in the evenings.

Shopping

From souvenirs to collectible furnishings, you can find a little of everything along the streets of San José. And unlike in Cabo San Lucas, here you can browse at a leisurely pace without worrying about aggressive shop owners encouraging you to make a purchase.

CENTRO HISTORICO
Arts, Crafts, and Souvenirs
A handicraft market has opened on Boulevard Mijares near Plaza La Misión. About a dozen vendors sell reasonably priced arts and crafts, including hammocks, handmade toys for children, T-shirts, ceramics, sombreros, and more. Another handful of vendors sell inexpensive arts and crafts along the north side of Boulevard Mijares, between Calles Coronado and Juárez. These stands are open 11am-9pm daily. For better selection and quality, at higher

© LAUREN SWIFT

unique amber jewelery for sale in the Art District

prices, check out the shops that are closer to Plaza Mijares and the art district.

Antigua Los Cabos (Mijares 5, tel. 624/146-9933, antiguabcs@yahoo.com, 9am-9pm Mon.-Sat., 11am-4pm Sun.) has some antiques as well as handmade rugs, folk art, ceramics, and tequilas. **Sol Dorado** (Mijares 33, across from the Tropicana, tel. 624/142-1950) is a multilevel store filled with ceramics, glassware, ironworks, mirrors, and furnishings. For large or fragile items, the store ships via DHL (fully insured). It will also deliver purchases to your hotel for US$10-85, depending on the location. The smaller **Mejicanisimo** (Zaragoza 8, tel. 624/142-3090, 9am-10pm Mon.-Fri., till 9:30pm Sat., 10am-8pm Sun.) next to the plaza, has much of the same.

Cinthya Castro stocks **El Armario** (corner of Morelos and Obregón, tel. 624/105-2989, elarmario@gmail.com, 8am-8pm Mon.-Sat.) with an artistic mix of ceramics, paintings, locally made Baja Desert soaps, and other crafts made in Mexico.

Jewelry
Several stores sell high-quality Mexican fire opals and other gemstones. Ask to see the opals in natural light—the more "fire," the higher the price. If you don't see what you want, ask to see individual stones. Most stores offer 24-hour turnaround for custom settings, but don't plan your pickup time to the minute or you may be late to catch your flight home.

Martha Rodriguez at **El Rincón del Ópalo** jewelry factory (Mijares 6, tel. 624/142-2566, rincon_del_opalo@hotmail.com, 9am-9pm Mon.-Sat., 10am-2pm Sun.) can help you choose a stone and setting in a pleasant gallery off the main plaza. **Jewelry Factory** (Mijares 5, tel. 624/142-6394, 9am-8pm daily), on the plaza next to Antigua Los Cabos, has some of the highest-quality jewels in town, and service to match. **La Mina** (Mijares 33, tel. 624/143-3747, www.joyerialamina.com, 9am-8pm daily) displays costume jewelry on the porous walls of a small cave and has a second location in Cabo San Lucas.

Fine Art

San José has a thriving art district that is home to about 20 galleries, many of them first-rate. Galleries tend to be run by expats, but the artists are a fairly even mix of Mexicans and foreigners. Run by a graduate of the Parsons School of Design in New York City and a full-time Los Cabos resident, the three-story **Galería de Ida Victoria** (Guerrero 1128, tel. 624/142-5772, www.idavictoriaarts.com, 10am-7pm Mon-Fri.) shows original paintings, photography, sculpture, and other works of art in a three-level gallery. State-of-the-art lighting and hanging systems were custom designed for the space.

Galería Arenas (Obregón 10, tel. 624/142-4969, vicjorge71@hotmail.com, 10am-2pm and 4pm-8pm Mon.-Sat.) has original Mexican pottery.

Amber Gallery (Obregón 18, tel. 624/105-2332, www.amberart.net, 10am-2pm and 6pm-8pm daily) features the work of artist Ronsai, who travels to Chiapas, where amber is mined by hand, to select raw stones to make jewelry, sculptures, and perfume bottles. The most unusual part of his collection features perfectly preserved fossils of various flowers and insects such as cockroaches, crickets, spiders, and termites.

Muvezi Gallery (Obregón 20, tel. 624/157-2428, www.muvezi.com, 10am-2pm and 4pm-8pm Mon.-Tues., 10am-9pm Wed.-Fri., 11am-8pm Sat.-Sun.) specializes in fine African sculpture, with a focus on the art of Shona sculptors in Zimbabwe. The gallery supports 200 Shona sculptors with income and materials in exchange for the opportunity to share their art globally.

In 2011, **Ivan Guaderrama Art Gallery** (Obregón 20, tel. 624/189-1144, www.ivanguaderrama.com) opened its doors. Twenty-eight-year-old artist and owner Ivan Guaderrama

entrance to the Galería de Ida Victoria

© IDA GUSTAVSON

shares his spiritual art and sculpture in the labyrinthine gallery that contains his studio and brims with color, emphasizing the soul, spirit, and mind.

If you are looking for contemporary Mexican folk art, a visit to **Paquime Gallery** (Obregón 17, tel. 624/105-6360, www.paquimegallery.com, 10am-2pm and 5pm-9pm daily) is in order. The gallery specializes in sculpture and pottery from the Mata Ortiz village, the Huichol art of Francisco Bautista, and contemporary paintings from Mexican artists.

Home Decor

Second-home owners looking to furnish their new condos and villas with authentic Mexican design elements will find just about everything they need in San José. For a rustic look, head to **Galería Los Cabos** (Hidalgo north of Obregón, tel. 624/142-0044, 9am-8pm Mon.-Fri.), which has some antiques as well as rattan pieces and barrel-back chairs made by local crafters. **Casa Paulina** (Morelos at the corner of Comonfort, tel. 624/142-5555, www.casapaulina.com, 11am-7:30pm Mon.-Fri., 11am-3pm Sat.), across from El Encanto Suites, is a beautiful store to browse, even if you aren't in the market to buy. It has wood and upholstered pieces as well as ceramics and other decorative items displayed on two levels. **Adobe Design** (Plaza San José, Carr. Transpeninsular km 32, tel. 624/114-4976) carries furniture and interior design materials for both antique and modern home styles.

Deportiva Piscis (Castro, tel. 624/142-0332, 8am-7pm daily), on the south side of Calle Castro near the Mercado Municipal, has fishing tackle, bait, and fishing-related books and gear.

PLAYA COSTA AZUL
Sporting Goods

On the north side of the Carretera Transpeninsular in a small shopping plaza, the **Costa Azul Surf Shop** (Carr. Transpeninsular km 28, tel. 624/142-2771, www.costaazul.aguazulmedia.com, 8am-7pm Mon.-Sat.,

9am-5pm Sun.) has board rentals and surf and snorkel maps. You can also have your board repaired after a rough day in the water.

The **Cabo Surf Shop** (Carr. Transpeninsular km 28, tel. 624/172-6188, www.cabosurfshop.com, 8am-8pm daily), located at the Cabo Surf Hotel, offers board rentals. **Baja Waterman,** also at Playa Costa Azul (Carr. Transpeninsular km 29, tel. 624/172-6110, www.bajawaterman.com, 7:30am-6pm Mon.-Sat., 10am-3pm Sun.) has stand-up paddling rental boards (US$20/1-2 hours, US$25/3-5 hours, US$30/full day), surf lessons (US$50/lesson), snorkeling gear, and beach clothing and accessories for sale.

PUERTO LOS CABOS
Bookstores

The most comprehensive selection of English-language titles related to Baja California anywhere on the peninsula is to be found at **Baja Books and Maps** (Camino a La Playa, La Choya, tel. 624/165-5596, U.S. fax 415/962-0588, 10am-6pm Mon.-Sat.) in the pueblo of La Choya on the way to La Playita. Owner Jim Tolbert is a distributor of English-language books to shops throughout the central and southern peninsula. He also sells inventory online at www.bajabooksandmaps.com. A true bibliophile, Jim is a wealth of information on all things Baja.

The gift shop at **Buzzard's** (Laguna Hills, U.S. tel. 951/302-1735, www.buzzardsbar.com) has a few books for sale as well.

ZONA HOTELERA

San José's hotel zone is a relatively new addition to the tourism infrastructure of the town; as such, shopping is not well developed in the area at this time. Aside from a bike shop and furniture store across from the Hola Grand Faro, there is little that you can stroll to from your hotel, aside from the Mega supermarket complex, where you can find sunglasses, beachwear, and the like. Vendors do walk the beach selling *artesanías* (crafts), and the more authentic shops of downtown San José are just a short car ride away.

Bookstores

At the conveniently located **Spider Web** (tel. 624/105-2048, bajabookcenter@yahoo.com. mx, 9am-6pm Mon.-Sat.), you can trade used paperback books and browse a limited selection of new titles. Used pocket fiction books cost US$3. There are a few PCs available for Internet access (US$4/hour). The store is on an alley just west of the Mega shopping plaza.

Nightlife and Entertainment

San José nightlife is low-key compared to the famous clubs in Cabo San Lucas, where you can dance the night away, but there are a handful of places where you can enjoy a few drinks and listen to live music.

NIGHTLIFE
Centro Historico
Baja Brewing Company (Morelos 1227, btwn. Comonfort and Obregón, tel. 624/144-3805, www.bajabrewingcompany.com, 8am-1am daily, mains US$10-15) quickly became a popular watering hole when it opened next to Baan

© LAUREN SWIFT

a pint of Baja Blonde

Thai in December 2007. As the only brewery in Baja California Sur, it crafts eight different artisanal beers, including the popular Baja Blonde and Cactus Wheat brews, and you'll find them on menus as far north as Loreto. Order a brewtender and get five pints for the price of four, conveniently served from a mini-tap at your table. The brewery uses its barley, yeast, and beer to make a delicious pizza dough. Spicy chicken wings are another crowd pleaser.

Just off the plaza, **Tropicana Bar and Grill** (Mijares 30, tel. 624/142-1580, 8am-midnight Sun.-Thurs., till 2am Fri.-Sat.) has been a mainstay among gringos for many years. It continues to play regional Mexican music 6:30pm-8:30pm Wednesday-Monday.

Morgan's Restaurant and Cellar (Hidalgo and Doblado, tel. 624/142-3825, morgans@ prodigy.net.mx, 6pm-11pm daily) frequently has live jazz. Canadian-owned **Shooters Bar & Grill** (Doblado and Mijares, tel. 624/146-9900, noon-midnight Mon.-Fri., noon-2am Sat.-Sun.), above Tulipán Restaurant, is an open-air rooftop bar with seating in plastic chairs and usually jazz music.

Less than a block from the plaza on Boulevard Mijares, **Don Sanchez** (Mijares s/n, Eclipse, tel. 624/142-2444, www.donsanchezrestaurant.com, 5pm-11pm daily) is a multi-level affair set in a historic building that was remodeled in 2012. Its extensive wine list features mostly labels from the Guadalupe Valley in Northern Baja. Enjoy a glass—or more—in the comfortable shade of the lower-level courtyard. You'll be tempted to stay for dinner, too.

Zona Hotelera
Behind the Mega shopping center, the **Baja**

Blue Bar and Grille (formerly the Rusty Putter, Paseo del Malecón, tel. 624/142-4546, lunch and dinner daily, bar open until 11pm nightly, later on weekends) is a large sports bar and restaurant with live music on weekends, plus satellite TV and an 18-hole miniature golf course.

Playa Costa Azul

Near Playa Costa Azul on the north side of the highway, **Deckman's** (Carr. Transpeninsular km 29, tel. 624/172-6269, www.deckmans. com, breakfast-late night Tues.-Sun.) opens its bar at 5pm daily for tapas and signature drinks. The blackberry mojito, for example, comes garnished with a daisy made out of lime. This is also a great place to try some of the fabulous wines from Baja Norte. Across the street and a little farther west, **Zippers** (Carr. Transpeninsular km 28.5, tel. 624/172-6162, 11am-11pm daily) plays oldies for the baby-boomer crowd on Friday and Saturday nights.

Puerto Los Cabos

In Las Animas, northeast of town, **Flora Farms** (tel. 624/355-4564, www.flora-farms.com) has live music Tuesday through Saturday nights, often classic guitar.

EVENTS
Centro Historico

On weekend evenings during the high season, you can almost always find a fiesta in progress at Plaza Mijares, complete with music, dancing, cotton candy, toys, mimes, and piñatas.

The weekly **Art Walk** on Thursday evenings (5pm-9pm) has become a town-wide celebration during the high season, with wine and food served at many of the galleries. The streets close to traffic, and Cuban dancers sometimes perform in front of the Centro Cultural. When the galleries close, the party moves to the Baja Brewing Company, which stays open late.

San José celebrates the **feast day of its patron saint** on March 19, a day of more music, dancing, food, games, and a parade.

On June 1, San José celebrates the annual **Día de la Marina,** a national day of honor for the Mexican navy, with great fanfare, including a fishing tournament, carnival, music, and even a greased pig.

Food

For many travelers, San José del Cabo has become a culinary destination. At least one new and notable eatery opens every high season. Renowned chefs from Baja, mainland Mexico, and the United States are using local foods and, in many cases, organic ingredients to prepare creative interpretations of traditional Mexican cuisine. From the organic farmers market to fresh tortillas and *carnitas* (braised pork) by the kilo, you can find it all in and around the streets of San José.

CENTRO HISTORICO
Traditional and Contemporary Mexican

One of the trailblazers in this gourmet trend was **Tequila Restaurant** (Doblado 1011, west of Mijares, tel. 624/142-1155, www.

tequilarestaurant.com, dinner daily, mains US$20 and up). The setting is cozy, and the menu suggests Asian, Mexican, and Mediterranean influences—a fusion that food writers now call "BajaMed." Popular dishes include tequila shrimp, beef tenderloin *guajillo,* and lobster deep-fried in a wonton skin. The restaurant cooks with organic produce, and the tequila menu is, of course, top-notch. Cigar aficionados will appreciate the walk-in humidor.

Next to the plaza, **La Panga Antigua** (Zaragoza 20, tel. 624/142-4041, www.la-panga.com, lunch and dinner daily, mains US$20) offers colonial ambience, with a courtyard, lounge bar, and wine cellar. Chef Jacabo Turquie is a graduate of the Culinary Institute of America, and he prepares a menu of contemporary Mexican cuisine with a focus on seafood. Sample dishes include seared scallops with dry chile oil saffron risotto, asparagus tips, and bell peppers. The catch of the day comes drizzled with cilantro oil over mashed potatoes with *huitlacoche* (corn truffle). Enjoy the attentive service of an experienced staff.

In the art district, **Restaurant Bar Jazmín** (Zaragoza and Obregón, tel. 624/142-1760, 7am-10pm daily, mains US$13-40) serves *huachinango* (whole red snapper) and *carne asada a la tampiqueña* (grilled beef "Tampico" style) on sizzling hot platters. The atmosphere is casual, and the menu includes *licuados* (fruit smoothies) and *chilaquiles* (salsa or mole over crisp tortilla triangles) for breakfast and *tortas* (Mexican sandwiches), tacos, and fajitas for lunch and dinner. Credit cards, including American Express, are accepted. We've heard complaints of incorrect charges at check time. Take a second look at the bill before you pay.

If you don't mind the strip-mall setting, **Habaneros Gastro Grill and Tequila Bar** (Mijares in Plaza La Misión, tel. 624/142-2626, www.habanerosgastrogrill.com, 11am-10pm Mon.-Sat., lunch mains US$7-15, dinner mains US$10-30) has some creative Mexican fusion dishes in store. Try the chipotle tequila barbecue baby-back ribs or Cajun filet mignon with grilled prickly pear ratatouille. The Shrimp Extravaganza consists of seven different preparations, including coconut, Parmesan, gingered tequila tamarind, and "frazzled." The Sushizza blends the flavors of sushi rice, cream cheese, and tamarind. Choose from 120 different kinds of tequila to go with your meal.

Chef Tadd Chapman has opened **◖ Don Sanchez Restaurant** (Blvd. Mijares s/n, Edificio Eclipse Loc. 1 and 3, tel. 624/142-2444, 11am-11pm daily, mains US$15-35) on Boulevard Mijares, a few doors down from the Tropicana. Fresh salsa is made to order at your table, so you can get it as spicy, or not, as you like it. Main dishes fuse together a variety of flavors from around the world. Start with the Organic Aztec Salad of baby greens, strawberry chipotle vinaigrette, strawberries,

dining in historic San José del Cabo

© NIKKI GOTH ITOI

ceramics on display at La Osteria

grilled quince, pine nuts, goat cheese, quinoa, and fresh herbs. Or try the tempura oysters, served with a mango relish, ginger, and tamarind ponzu sauce. For main courses, the Baja Cioppino is a seafood lover's delight. And the filet *sous vide* is a six-ounce cut of grass-fed beef from Sonora seasoned with garlic, rosemary, olive oil, sea salt, and pepper. Gluten-free dishes are labeled on the menu. Aside from the creative cuisine, the real reason to visit is the wine. The cellar at Don Sanchez is stocked with more than 300 labels, many of them from small-production vineyards in the wine country of Northern Baja.

An art district option for straightforward Mexican is **Salsita Cocina y Cantina** (Obregón 1732, tel. 624/142-6787, 7:30am-11pm daily, mains US$10-20), in a pretty aqua and white building just behind the plaza and a block from the Cultural Center. Order shrimp tacos, tamales, enchiladas, *carne en su jugo* (beef slow-cooked in its juice), and chiles rellenos.

The owner of Salsita Cocina y Cantina has opened another eatery across the street with a tapas theme that's aimed to appeal to local residents. **La Osteria** (Obregón 1907, tel. 624/146-9696) opened its courtyard doors in October 2012, serving small plates such as a crostini platter, Mexican cheese plate, and chopped salad for US$7-10.

New American and contemporary Mexican themes shape the menu at **《 H Restaurant** (Obregón 1505, tel. 624/105-2974), a small eatery with just 10 tables, located in a two-story colonial in the historic art district. That translates into starters such as tortilla chowder and entrées such as seafood cannelloni and flounder encrusted in sunflower seeds. Chef Luis Herrera Thatcher is originally from Mexico City, trained at the prestigious Culinary Institute of America in Hyde Park, New York, and has recent experience as executive chef at Club Golf de Querencia and the Club Ninety Six beach club.

Also in the art district, a long-popular Cabo San Lucas restaurant, **Mi Casa** (Obregón 19, tel. 624/146-9263, www.micasarestaurant. com, mains US$20), runs a second location in

© NIKKI GOTH ITOI

Mi Casa's popular location in San José del Cabo

San José. Start with stuffed clams or the traditional tortilla soup and then move on to *cochinita pibil* (pork marinated in a strongly acidic citrus juice and roasted while wrapped in banana leaves) or the signature *mole poblano* (a complex Mexican sauce made of more than 20 ingredients, featuring a combination of *ancho, pasilla, mulato,* or chipotle peppers). The courtyard setting is a plus. Wines are generally overpriced here.

First-time visitors to San José del Cabo often grab a sidewalk table at the **Tropicana Bar and Grill** (Mijares 30, tel. 624/142-1580, 8am-10:30pm daily, mains US$10-23) for their first meal. They can take in the scene on Boulevard Mijares as they down their first *limonada* (lemonade), cerveza, or margarita. Inside and in the garden dining area behind the building, a regular clientele visits the restaurant for American-style fare and nightly live music and dancing. The menu is vast; the prices are for tourists.

American and International

Named for the large tulip tree growing in the center of the restaurant, **El Tulipán** (The Tulip Tree, Doblado at Mijares, tel. 624/146-9900, lunch and dinner daily, mains US$10-20), below Shooters Bar, serves casual fare such as burgers, steaks, salads, and pasta dishes. Booth seating and the varied menu make it a good place for kids.

Regulars praise the lamb dishes at **Baan Thai** (Morelos and Comonfort, tel. 624/142-3344, www.bajabaanthai.com, noon-10pm Mon.-Sat., 4pm-10pm Sun., mains US$10-25). You can also order pad thai, wok-tossed salmon, and an assortment of curries. In business for many years, this restaurant draws patrons from the East Cape and beyond for a refreshing change from everyday Mexican cooking.

Dinner at **Morgan's Restaurant and Cellar** (Hidalgo and Doblado, tel. 624/143-3825, morgans@prodigy.net.mx, 6pm-midnight daily, dinner till 10pm only, closed Sept., mains US$20 and up) begins with a basket of home-made bread. Wines from around the world complement the menu of Mediterranean entrées. Steaks come with heirloom veggies and foie gras butter. Coconut shrimp are as tasty as the red meat. A meal here is about sitting around the flaming grill in a warm and rustic patio setting.

Morgan's Encore (Morelos and Obregón, tel. 624/142-4737, 6pm-11pm daily, dinner till 10pm only, closed Sept., mains US$20-40), near the El Encanto Inn, is more intimate, but it can accommodate large groups in its main open-air dining area. The menu includes lobster ravioli, seared scallops, grilled fish, shrimp fettuccine, and spaghetti and meatballs. Consider ordering a couple of creative starters for your main meal.

In the plaza behind the Casa Paulina interior design store, **Voila! Bistro** (Plaza Paulina on Morelos and Comonfort, tel. 624/130-7569, www.voila-events.com, lunch and dinner daily, mains US$10-30) serves a few wines by the glass as well as soup, salads, and entrées like halibut in a mussel sauce and sea bass encrusted with pistachio and macadamia nuts. The jalapeno margarita is a memory-maker.

You can watch the staff make your personal, thin-crust pizza from a patio table at **La Dolce Ristorante Italiano & Pizzeria** (Plaza Mijares, Hidalgo and Zaragoza, tel. 624/142-6621, www.ladolcerestaurant.com, 1pm-11pm Tues.-Sun., mains US$10-20). The menu includes bruschetta to start and tiramisu to finish. This place has been around for years and continues to please with friendly service and reasonable prices.

In Plaza La Misión, chef/owner Pasquale Matera and his wife, Alicia, serve thin-crust pizza, osso buco, and other Italian delights at **Pasquales Pizzeria and Ristorante** (Plaza La Misión, Loc. 6, tel. 624/142-0496, www.pasqualesristorante.com.mx, noon-11pm Mon.-Fri., 2pm-11pm Sat.-Sun., mains US$9-18).

Many restaurants in San José serve excellent seafood. **Pier 19 Seafood & Bar** (Zaragoza s/n, btwn. Morelos and Guerrero, tel. 624/130-7453, www.pier19.mx, 11am-5pm lunch, 6pm-11pm dinner) is one that stakes its reputation on it. The owners were brave enough to open during the depths of the global recession. The raw oyster bar is reason enough to give it a try.

Ceviche and *aguachile* (ceviche in a watery, chile-based broth) are not to be missed. Live music plays on Wednesday nights.

Breakfast, Ice Cream, and Cafés

It's hard to resist the strong coffee and sweet pastries once you've discovered the **French Riviera** (corner of Hidalgo and Doblado, tel. 624/142-3350, www.frenchrivieraloscabos.com, 8am-11pm daily, breakfast mains US$5-10, lunch mains US$10-15). Order to go from the counter or grab a table for a full breakfast. Early risers note: Though the posted hours say the place opens at 7:30am and the staff will let you wander in and take a seat, you likely won't get served even a cup of coffee until they are fully ready, closer to 8am.

In the art district, **Casa Dahlia Gallery** (Morelos btwn. Obregón and Zaragoza, tel. 624/142-2129, www.casadahlia.com, 10am-3pm and 6pm-9pm Mon.-Fri., 10am-3pm Sat.) serves coffee and tea in a pleasant garden behind a 100-year-old adobe building and has wireless Internet.

Next to the store of the same name, **El Armario Café** (corner of Morelos and Obregón, tel. 624/105-2989, elarmario@gmail.com, 10am-8pm Mon.-Sat.) offers reasonably priced light fare, such as yogurt with fresh fruit and granola for US$2 and a baguette sandwich with chips and *limonada* for US$5.

AGUAS FRESCAS

Ladled out of large glass jars, refreshing *aguas frescas* are made of still water infused with fresh fruit and sweetened with sugar. Popular flavors include **fresa** (strawberry), **jamaica** (hibiscus flower), **melón** (cantaloupe), and **sandía** (watermelon). Although technically not an *agua fresca*, **horchata,** rice milk flavored with cinnamon and sugar, is often served alongside the fruit drinks. Look for *aguas frescas* at *taquerías* (casual restaurants), *licuado* stands, and Mexican restaurants all over Southern Baja.

Breakfast is a good value at the understated **Posada Terranova** (Degollado, south of Zaragoza, tel. 624/142-0534, 7am-10pm daily, mains US$5-18), a family-run restaurant inside the hotel of the same name. It has indoor and outdoor tables, and the menu covers all the basics of Mexican food.

Roughly across from the Casa de la Cultura, **Café Calafia** (Blvd. Mijares 2, tel. 624/130-7145, cafecalifia@yahoo.com.mx, Mon.-Sat. 7:30am-9:30pm, breakfast mains $2-5) is an espresso and coffee bar that also prepares fresh fruit juices, frappes, homemade granola, salads, panini, and desserts.

La Michoacana, on Zaragoza opposite the church, is the place to go for *paletas* (popsicles) and other frozen treats. There is another location on Doblado at the intersection with the highway.

Taquerías and Street Food

Cheap eats are clustered around the **Mercado Municipal** and close to the highway, near **Calle Doblado.** Try any of the *loncherías* (food stands) near the market (6am-6pm Mon.-Sat., 6am-4pm Sun.). Or order *tortas* (Mexican sandwiches) and *comida corrida* (fixed-price lunch) at **Mi Cocinita** (Gonzales, south of Panadería 1 de Mayo, tel. 624/142-6660, 8am-5pm Mon.-Sat., mains US$5), a cute place with plastic tables and floral tablecloths. The staff here speaks English.

At **Taquería Erika** (Doblado at Carr. Transpeninsular, no tel., lunch and dinner daily), two *tacos al pastor* (marinated pork tacos) cost about US$2.50.

Longtime favorite **Taquería Rossy** (tel. 624/145-6755, tacos US$1) is on the Carretera Transpeninsular, near the light for Calle Pescador.

Adventurous eaters head to **Taquería El Ahorcado** (Pescadores and Marinos, tel. 624/172-2093, 6pm-midnight Tues.-Sun., mains US$5-10), in the Chamizal neighborhood across the Carretera Transpeninsular, for beef-tongue tacos and a full menu of creative quesadillas. It's known among gringos as The Hangman and is famous for its eclectic decor.

Bring your own beer and enjoy live music while you dine.

In the Chamizal neighborhood, **◖ Las Guacamayas** (Calle Marinos at Pescadores, Col. Chamizal, 624/109-5993, dinner daily, mains US$8-12), off Calle Doblado on the north side of the Carretera Transpeninsular, upholds its reputation for outstanding *tacos al pastor* (marinated pork tacos). Huge stone bowls *(molcajetes)* filled with flank steak and avocado are another treat. For *carnitas* (heavily seasoned pork that is braised slowly until it can be pulled apart easily), **El Michoacano** (tel. 624/146-9848), across the street from Banorte, gets top marks from local expats. This is a chain with five small cantina-style eateries located around the Los Cabos region. Order one taco at a time, or by the kilo. Cash only.

Near the bus terminal, **Taquería México** (González s/n at Profesores, Col. 1 de Mayo, tel. 624/128-8953, 1pm-close Mon.-Fri., 4pm-close Sat.-Sun., mains US$4-12) draws a crowd of local gringos for lunch under a large *palapa* roof with at least a dozen ceiling fans that keep the air moving on warm days. Sit at plastic tables and chairs beside a busy street and order a plate of tacos or a super burrito, Mexican-style hamburger, *papas rellenas* (stuffed potatoes), or an entire *huachinango* (red snapper). This restaurant has a few large round tables that work well for a large group.

When the sun goes down, a handful of street carts roll onto Plaza Mijares. The longest line tends to form at **◖ Tamales Doña Nina.** Order them *de pollo* with *salsa verde* (green salsa) or *de rajas* (with poblano peppers) with cheese. Don't miss the sweet rice for dessert. Empanadas, tacos, and cups of *elote* (corn kernels) dusted with chili powder and a squeeze of lime are also popular evening fare.

Groceries

For an authentic food shopping experience, the small **Mercado Municipal** (between Calles Castro and Coronado in the west part of town, no tel., dawn to dusk daily) has separate stands for meat, fish, produce, and crafts. There is a *tortillería* that makes corn tortillas next door

EATING HEALTHY IN LOS CABOS

Since the early days of Baja exploration, tacos, cerveza, and tequila have anchored the diets of expat travelers. But in recent years, the global trend toward healthy, local, fresh, and minimally processed foods has reached Los Cabos. Farmers markets are now a weekend ritual in San José, Todos Santos, and La Paz. San José has its own working sustainable farm and ranch called Flora Farms, just beyond the Puerto Los Cabos marina.

A few resorts, such as Las Ventanas al Paraíso and Rancho Pescadero, source much of their produce from their own organic gardens on-site. Restaurants like Deckman's and Las Tres Virgenes are taking culinary creativity to new heights. There are many ways to experience this exciting culinary trend. Sign up for a cooking class, shop the farmers markets, attend one of the annual culinary festivals, or simply enjoy a memorable meal.

You can also pick up healthy eats to go at these markets:

- **Flora Farms,** San José del Cabo
- **Mercado Santa Carmela,** Punta Ballena, Corridor
- **Tutto Bene!,** Cabo San Lucas
- **Pura Vida,** Todos Santos
- **Sabores de México,** La Paz

---

on Calle Castro (no tel., opens daily at 5am) and another that makes flour tortillas across the street.

On Calle Gonzalez, near the Corona supermarket and down the street from the bus terminal, **Panadería 1 de Mayo** (no tel.) has freshly baked breads and pastries with the usual tray-and-tong service.

If you're in town on a Saturday in the winter, head to the ⟨ **San José del Cabo Mercado Organico** (Huerta Maria, Camino a las Animas, www.sanjomo.com, 9am-3pm Sat.), which draws some 50 vendors, many from as far away as La Paz and Todos Santos. They gather at a site located off the road to La Playita. In addition to fresh produce, you can buy cheese, ice cream, bread, books, and leather goods. There is usually music along with rotating themes such as alternative medicine and ecofriendly living. Look for a sign and dirt trail on Avenida Centenario, behind the Yuca Inn. It's about a five-minute walk from the plaza.

ZONA HOTELERA

Options for dining out are limited in the hotel zone, given all the new construction. Plaza El Misión on Boulevard Mijares, between the hotel zone and downtown San José, is the next closest option for a few cafés and restaurants.

American

Near the Mega shopping center, **Baja Blue Bar and Grille** (formerly the Rusty Putter, Paseo del Malecón, tel. 624/142-4546, lunch and dinner daily, bar open until 11pm nightly, later on weekends) serves a wide range of Mexican and pub-style dishes.

Organic

An option for healthy fare is between Desire Resort and Las Mañanitas condos: **Cynthia Fresh Organic Restaurant** (Plaza Caracol, Zona Hotelera, tel. 624/155-5874, Mon.-Sat. 11:30am-9pm). Stop in for lunch, dinner, coffee, or drinks and occasional live music. The menu includes fresh salads, wraps, paninis, and pasta dishes, as well as a vegetarian options. Cash only.

Groceries

These days, the best place to stock up on food and other supplies is the **Mega supermarket** (tel. 624/142-4524), at the intersection of Paseo Los Cabos and the Carretera Transpeninsular. Choose from a full array of Mexican and American brands, decent produce, and a wide selection of cheeses and meats. There is a well-stocked pharmacy, and those traveling with youngsters will find all manner of supplies,

© NIKKI GOTH ITOI

Fresh vegetables can be found at most local markets.

from pacifiers to bouncy seats. In the adjoining plaza are a Telcel store, surf shop, public restrooms, and numerous fast-food options. Beware the timeshare reps who pose as grocery store clerks and offer to help you find your way around the store.

PUERTO LOS CABOS
Mexican

On the road to La Playita, near the sportfishing *panga* area, **Tommy's Barefoot Cantina** (tel. 624/142-3774, www.tommysbarefootcantina. com, noon-10pm Thurs.-Tues., mains US$7-30) is owned by the gregarious TJ, originally from the San Francisco Bay Area; he entertains a well-heeled clientele with a slice of the old Baja. The menu consists of fresh seafood, American-style beef, and Mexican staples. This is a good place to go in the afternoon, when the fishing boats return with their catch. There is also live music and dancing on the weekends during the high season.

The friendly husband-and-wife team that previously ran Mariscos El Puerto has moved a few doors closer to the beach to open **La Marina Restaurant** (hotel tel. 624/142-4166, 9am-5pm Tues.-Sun., mains US$5-10). The same colorful checked tablecloths are now clustered on a shaded patio next to the La Marina Inn lobby. Ceiling fans keep the air moving on hot afternoons. On a recent visit, the wahoo filet was extremely overcooked, but the *arrachera* (skirt steak) tacos, served with the same signature tray of fresh condiments, were fantastic. The restaurant and hotel are located across from the *panga* marina, next to Tommy's Barefoot Cantina.

For a quick bite to eat in La Playita, order a *torta* (Mexican sandwich) or some tacos at **La Pasadita** (no tel., mains US$3-5), next to Lilly's salon on the way to the beach. The decor is barebones—a *palapa* roof with a dirt floor and live chickens running about—but the food is tasty and cheap. La Pasadita is open for dinner only, and days vary; if you see the sand in front of the restaurant hosed down, that's a likely sign it will be open for business that evening.

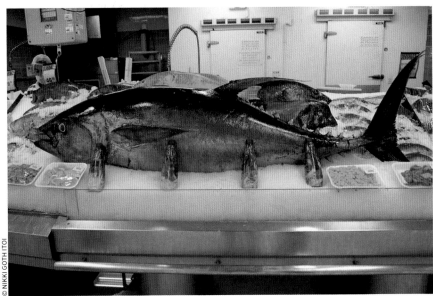
© NIKKI GOTH ITOI
fresh seafood for sale at the Mega supermarket

At the main Puerto Los Cabos Marina (not to be confused with the *panga* fishing area at La Playita), **The Container Bar-Restaurant** (tel. 624/160-2733, 8am-11pm Tues.-Sun., mains US$3-7) is a refurbished shipping container with a wooden deck that is perched on a hillside with nice views of the marina below. It has a full bar, and margaritas cost US$8. Prices are in U.S. dollars. Follow Boulevard Juárez over the bridge and take the first right turn into the marina and stay on this dirt road up and over the hill until you see the marina and restaurant on your left.

Hotel El Ganzo (Blvd. Tiburon s/n, La Playita, tel. 624/104-9000, U.S. tel. 855/835-4269, www.elganzo.com) opened an upscale restaurant in January 2013 on the lower level of the hotel. Staff were still working out the kinks at press time.

Beyond Puerto Los Cabos on the lower part of the East Cape, **Buzzard's Bar and Grill** (Laguna Hills, U.S. tel. 951/302-1735, www.buzzardsbar.com, 8am-8:30pm Mon.-Sat., 9am-2:30pm Sun., mains US$10-20) makes a tasty platter of coconut shrimp as well as a popular eggs Benedict for Sunday brunch. Dinner entrées are served all day, but the side dishes may not be ready until 5:30pm. To find Buzzard's from downtown San José del Cabo, follow the road to La Playita and turn left at the first traffic circle, following the coastal road (it reaches the coast at Buzzard's) and signs for Laguna Hills.

Organic

A unique dining experience in Southern Baja involves an excursion to Las Animas, just beyond the edge of town, where the road to the East Cape begins. At a bend in the dirt road, **《 Flora Farms** (tel. 624/355-4564, www.flora-farms.com) is a working organic farm that has been practicing sustainable agriculture for more than a decade and raises its own hormone-free chicken, pigs, and cattle on a 150-acre ranch nearby.

In recent years, the farm has evolved to include a field kitchen, bar, grocery counter, and "culinary cottages" for rent. For those

© PAUL ITOI

the restaurant at Flora Farms

who wish, the visit begins with an informative farm tour, after which you'll be good and ready to eat. Settle at a table in the open-air dining patio and enjoy live music in the evening. The bar menu puts a healthy spin on classic cocktails: Dare to try the ginger beet or carrot margarita (served in a mason jar, of course). Pasta night involves five courses for US$38 per person; kids are half price. Á la carte entrées include roast chicken (US$30) and wood-fired pizza. Reservations are recommended for dinner.

Tuesday through Saturday, breakfast is served 9am-11am, lunch 11am-3pm, and dinner 5pm-9:30pm; Sunday brunch is served 10am-2:30pm. Closed Monday. To get to Flora Farms, follow Benito Juárez east from Boulevard Mijares (at the traffic circle) across the bridge to Puerto Los Cabos. Follow signs through four more traffic circles, toward La Playita, Punta Gorda, and the East Cape. After the fourth traffic circle, turn left at the cement plant onto a dirt road. Head uphill and follow the signs to the farm and parking lot. The restaurant has detailed driving directions as well as a map on its website.

PLAYA COSTA AZUL
Mexican

For casual, beachfront dining, head to **Zippers** (Carr. Transpeninsular km 28.5, tel. 624/172-6162, 11am-10pm daily, mains US$10-20), where you can watch surfers try to catch the waves out front while you dine under the shade of a *palapa* roof. The menu is a mix of Mexican and pub fare. A small play structure entertains younger kids, and the Wi-Fi is free.

When you've had enough tacos for one trip, try **Mi Ensalada I** (Carr. Transpeninsular km 29.5, tel. 624/142-0236, 7am-10pm daily) for healthier fare. Mi Ensalada serves sandwiches and salads made of mostly organic ingredients. Sit inside or out on the shaded patio while you enjoy a latte and update your Facebook wall. **Mi Ensalada II** is a corner café at the end of Plaza La Misión on Boulevard Mijares. It serves the same menu at the same reasonable prices. Either location makes a convenient stop for one last meal before your flight home.

Italian

Mama Mia, at the Worldmark Coral Baja resort (Carr. Transpeninsular km 29.4, tel. 624/142-3939, lunch and dinner daily, mains US$7-14) offers casual beachfront dining with friendly and attentive service. Juicy burgers come with grilled onions and lots of pickles. Chicken fajitas are accompanied by the requisite basket of warm tortillas and a healthy serving of guacamole. The menu features many organic ingredients.

Seafood

Standout cuisine awaits at █ **Deckman's** (Carr. Transpeninsular km 29, Costa Azul, tel. 624/172-6269, www.deckmans.com), on the highway across from the white and blue, Greek-style Mykonos condos at Playa Costa Azul. The food here is top-notch: You might start with an amuse-bouche of tuna tartar with a blackberry mojito, then proceed to the five- or seven-course tasting menu for US$55/US$75 without wine pairings. Chef Drew reveals his Georgia roots with dishes that feature barnacles, mussels, frogs legs, quail, and short ribs. Guests can choose among three sizes for every dish on the menu, depending on how hungry you are and how many dishes you want to try.

Parking here can be daunting: If there are no spots right in front of the restaurant, U-turn at the exit ramp for Zippers and do a full circle back to Deckman's, parking parallel along the highway just before the restaurant. Limited parking is available in a small dirt area across the highway, but crossing here is not recommended, especially at night. If you cannot find a safe place to park, double park at the restaurant and ask the wait staff to help. In the off-season, Drew and his team head to the Baja wine country to run a restaurant at the Mogor Badan Winery in the Guadalupe Valley.

NEAR THE AIRPORT
Seafood

█ **Mariscos Mazatlán II** (Carr. Transpeninsular km 35, tel. 624/143-8565, 11am-10pm daily, mains US$10-14), near Soriana on the way to the airport, is a favorite among expats for fresh fish at reasonable prices in a non-touristy atmosphere. Look for an orange and blue *palapa*-roof building with outdoor seating on the west side of the Carretera Transpeninsular. There is also a sister location in Cabo San Lucas.

Groceries

A half kilometer north of town on the east side of the Carretera Transpeninsular, **Soriana** (tel. 624/142-6132) is a Walmart-style store with everything from beach towels to deli meats. If you are heading directly to the East Cape, this is a good place to stock up on supplies for the week.

Information and Services

TOURIST ASSISTANCE

The Baja Sur **state tourism office** (tel. 624/146-7600, www.loscabos.gob.mx) has a location near the plaza at Boulevard Mijares 1413.

POST OFFICES

The *correos* (post office) has moved to the new Plaza Cabo Ley (Paseo de los Misiones) on the west side of the Carretera Transpeninsular (8am-5pm Mon.-Fri.). **Mail Boxes Etc.** has a local branch in Plaza Las Palmas (Carr. Transpeninsular km 31, tel. 624/142-4355, fax 624/142-4360).

INTERNET ACCESS

Next to the Mega shopping center, on an alley just off the Carretera Transpeninsular, **Spider Web** (tel. 624/105-2048) has a few computers connected to the Internet. Rates are US$1 for

15 minutes (US$4 per hour). Most people use Wi-Fi at their hotel or a nearby café.

EMERGENCY SERVICES

For emergencies, dial 066. The main **centro de salud** (hospital, tel. 624/142-2770) is located on Calle Doblado between Colegio Militar and Márquez de León.

An **AmeriMed hospital** has opened in Plaza Cabo Ley (Paseo de los Misiones s/n, tel. 624/105-8550, 24 hours). For medical assistance, visit the **Walk-in MediClinic** (Carr. Transpeninsular km 28, tel. 624/130-7011) in the El Zalate Plaza. The facility has an emergency room, lab, pharmacy, and ambulance. Two other options are **BlueMedicalNet** (tel. 624/104-3911), which operates a clinic in the Plaza Misión, next to HSBC Bank, and **Médica Los Cabos** (Zaragoza 128, tel. 624/142-2770), near the Pemex station. All will respond to emergencies 24/7.

BANKS

There are ATMs aplenty in San José, with numerous options downtown, behind the Mega, and in several plazas in between. Several scams have been reported in recent years at ATMs in the supermarkets and other non-bank locations. It's always safer to withdraw your pesos at an official branch location.

CANADIAN CONSULATE

The office of the **Canadian consulate** (Mijares near Juárez, tel. 624/142-4333, www. canadainternational.gc.ca/mexico-mexique, 9am-1pm Mon.-Fri.). is on the second floor of Plaza José Green.

VETERINARIANS

San José has a number of respected veterinarians, should your pet need attention during your travels. One is usually available at the **Chiapas feed store** (Prolongación Av. Providencia, tel. 624/142-1095). **Veterinaria las Palmas Felipe Martinez** (Carr. Transpeninsular km 32.5, tel. 624/142-2928) comes highly recommended. If you fall in love with one of Baja's stray animals, it may be possible to bring it home, as long as it is in good health and you can show proof of a rabies vaccinations at least 30 days prior to entry into the United States. Talk to a local vet and then contact your airline for more information.

CLASSES

Eduardo Satorno offers Spanish-language instruction online or in person to individuals and groups through **Spanish in Cabo** (tel. 624/146-9975, www.spanishincabo.com). He offers classes via Skype, for those who want to brush up before or after a trip. Survival Spanish is a 30-hour course that teaches the basics in a series of 90-minute sessions. Situational Spanish courses (starting at US$85 per person) focus on vocabulary needed for grocery shopping, restaurants, and conversation around the home. These courses can be completed in one week.

Getting There and Around

GETTING THERE

The majority of Los Cabos visitors arrive by air, but you'll meet many who have traveled by car, boat, or bicycle, or even on foot. Public transportation by bus is also a possibility. Once you've arrived, you can do without a car if you plan to stay at an all-inclusive resort or at a hotel in town. Rent a car if you want to take a day trip to the East Cape or Todos Santos.

By Air

Los Cabos International Airport (SJD, Carr. Transpeninsular km 44, tel. 624/146-5111, http://aeropuertosgap.com.mx/english/airports/loscabos-airport) serves San José del Cabo and Cabo San Lucas. Additional airport information is available at www.sjdloscabosairport.com, but this is not the official airport website.

A shuttle *(colectivo)* into the San José area runs US$13 per person. A private taxi from the airport to San José del Cabo costs US$50 for up to four passengers.

By Car

Most of the big auto rental agencies have desks at Los Cabos International Airport as well as offices in or near San José.

If you're driving yourself, there are two ways to reach the towns along the Los Cabos Corridor from the airport: Follow signs for the Carretera Transpeninsular (Highway 1) south through town, passing through several stoplights before you reach the town of San José. Alternatively, if you don't mind paying a toll of about US$2.25 (MEX$28), you can exit the airport onto the *quota,* a fast four-lane road with no exits until you enter San José at the junction of Paseo Los Cabos and the Mega grocery store plaza. If you pick up a rental car off-site, you'll have to return to the terminal to get to the toll road. The roundabout at the intersection with the Carretera Transpeninsular can be an intimidating entry into town, especially if you are trying to go left into downtown San José. Wait for a break in the traffic or turn right and go about 1.6 kilometers to the *Retorno* sign. Exit right and then turn left under the highway and left again to reenter the highway heading back toward San José.

By Bus

San José's **main bus terminal** is on Calle González near the Carretera Transpeninsular. **Aguila** (tel. 624/143-5020, www.autotransportesaguila.com) and **Autotransportes de Baja California** (ABC, www.abc.com.mx) offer frequent service to and from La Paz via Todos Santos (shorter distance/fewer stops, US$20) and Los Barriles (longer distance/more stops, US$15). A few buses a day from La Paz continue on to the ferry terminal on the Pichilingue Peninsula. Schedules and fares are posted online, and you can purchase tickets in advance online.

By Sea

The nearest ferry service to the mainland operates between La Paz and Mazatlán. You can book tickets in La Paz or online through **Baja Ferries** (tel. 612/123-0208, 612/123-6600, or 800/122-1414, www.en.bajaferries.com).

The new **Marina at Puerto Los Cabos** (Paseo de los Pescadores, Col. La Playa, tel. 624/105-6028, www.marinapuertoloscabos.com) is open and designed to hold up to 500 boats, including the largest luxury yachts.

GETTING AROUND

By Bus

The **main bus station** is on Calle González (tel. 624/142-1100), near the Carretera Transpeninsular. About six buses a day go to Cabo San Lucas (US$2-3). The Flecha Verde and Estrella de Oro bus lines run hourly connections to Cabo San Lucas. Another option is the municipal Subur Cabo buses that connect San José and San Lucas. These buses stop at many places along the Carretera Transpeninsular, including near the Worldmark Coral Baja Resort at Playa Costa Azul, and the fare is only a few pesos (less then US$2). Buses run until 10pm most nights.

By Car

You can do without a car if you plan to stay at an all-inclusive resort or a downtown hotel. Rent a car if you want the convenience of being able to drive yourself into town from a more remote location or if you plan to take a day trip to the East Cape or Todos Santos. Most of the big auto rental agencies have desks at Los Cabos International Airport as well as offices in or near town (many have opened locations along the hotel zone). Note: When renting in Mexico, you must buy Mexican liability insurance (typically about US$25/day). On business days, expect heavy traffic getting into San José in the morning from points north and out of town in the evening.

RV SERVICE AND SUPPLIES

Those who drive their own home on wheels depend on **Wahoo RV Center** (Calle Misión de Mulegé, tel./fax 624/142-3792, www.wahoorv.com, 8am-1pm and 2:30pm-6pm Mon.-Fri., 8am-1pm Sat.), near the CFE electric utility office in Colonia Chula Vista, off the Carretera Transpeninsular (turn west between the Super Pollo and the turnoff for the Pemex station), for RV parts and accessories as well as maintenance and repair services. It has DirecTV satellite dishes and a dump station.

By Taxi and Shuttle

Except during the hottest months, San José is pleasant to explore on foot. As congestion increases around the plaza, it is a convenience to leave the car behind. Cabs are available on Boulevard Mijares near the plaza, at the bus station, and along the Paseo del Malecón in the Zona Hotelera (US$4-6 from the Zona Hotelera to the plaza downtown or from downtown to Puerto Los Cabos, about US$40-50 from town to Los Cabos airport or to Cabo San Lucas). Call 624/142-0401 or 624/142-0105 for pickups.

THE CORRIDOR

In between San José del Cabo and Cabo San Lucas, a 29-kilometer stretch of beautiful coastline has evolved from a no-man's land into a luxury resort corridor. In front of and in between the resort properties are sandy beaches, hidden coves, and exposed rocky points. Gaining access to many of these prime coastal areas becomes more difficult by the year as new hotels go up. Although builders

© NIKKI GOTH ITOI

THE CORRIDOR

HIGHLIGHTS

LOOK FOR ◖ TO FIND RECOMMENDED SIGHTS, ACTIVITIES, DINING, AND LODGING.

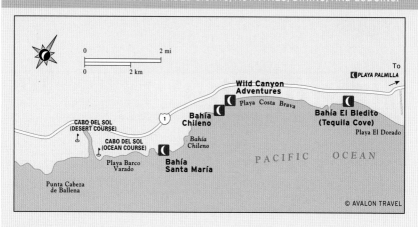

© AVALON TRAVEL

◖ **Playa Palmilla:** Fishing, swimming, and snorkeling all are possible at this small beach near the One&Only Palmilla resort (page 60).

◖ **Playa El Bledito (Tequila Cove):** The best beach in Los Cabos for families is protected by a breakwater and located in front of the Hilton Los Cabos resort (page 60).

◖ **Bahía Chileno:** The Corridor's most popu-

lar and accessible beach offers safe swimming and good snorkeling (page 60).

◖ **Bahía Santa María:** Tour boats bring dozens of snorkelers at a time to this protected bay (page 60).

◖ **Wild Canyon Adventures:** Thrill seekers head to the zip line and bungee jump at this adventure park near Playa El Tule (page 63).

may discourage the public from attempting to visit the beach by installing gates and security guards, they cannot legally prohibit access entirely. You may have to ask permission to pass or park at the highway and walk, but you should be able to get to the beach, one way or another.

There aren't really separate towns along the Corridor; instead, the area is divided into several *fraccionamientos,* or districts for development, each containing several resorts, golf courses, spas, and the like. At kilometer 19.5 of the Carretera Transpeninsular (Highway 1), the Cabo Real development presides over scenic Bahía El Bledito and comprises the Secrets Marquis Los Cabos, Hilton Los Cabos, Meliá Cabo Real, Zoëtry Casa del Mar, and Casa del Mar Condos as well

as the renowned Cabo Real Golf Course and the Jack Nicklaus-designed El Dorado Golf Club. Stretching between kilometer 10 and kilometer 20, Cabo del Sol consists of the Sheraton Hacienda del Mar and Fiesta Americana Grand resorts and the Cabo del Sol golf course.

Driving along the Corridor is easy compared to driving around the rest of Baja. The Carretera Transpeninsular is a four-lane highway between San José and San Lucas, with a mix of paved and dirt roads running perpendicular into the resorts and developments. Off-ramps are still the exception rather than the rule, so in some cases, you may have to pass your destination and make a U-turn to get to the other side of the road.

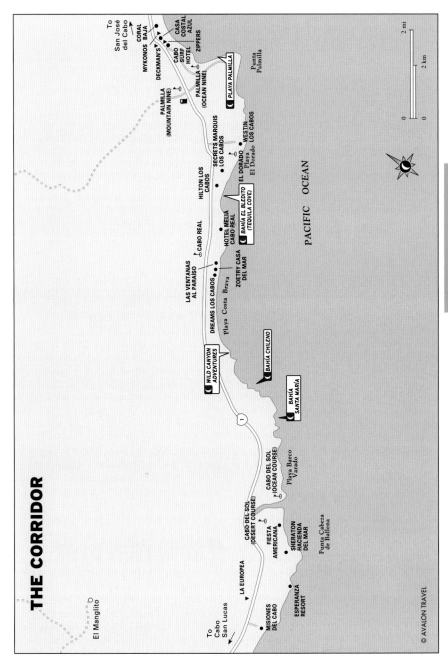

THE CORRIDOR

To
San José
del Cabo

CORAL
BAJA

CASA
COSTA
AZUL

MYKONOS

CABO
SURF
HOTEL

DECKMAN'S

ZIPPERS

PALMILLA
(OCEAN NINE)

PALMILLA
(MOUNTAIN NINE)

PLAYA PALMILLA

Punta
Palmilla

SECRETS MARQUIS
LOS CABOS

WESTIN
LOS CABOS

HILTON LOS
CABOS

EL DORADO   Playa
El Dorado

CABO REAL

HOTEL MELIÁ
CABO REAL

BAHÍA EL BLEDITO
(TEQUILA COVE)

ZOETRY CASA
DEL MAR

LAS VENTANAS
AL PARAÍSO

PACIFIC   OCEAN

DREAMS LOS CABOS

Playa Costa Brava

WILD CANYON
ADVENTURES

BAHÍA CHILENO

BAHÍA
SANTA MARÍA

CABO DEL SOL
(OCEAN COURSE)

Playa Barco
Varado

1

CABO DEL SOL
(DESERT COURSE)

FIESTA
AMERICANA

SHERATON
HACIENDA
DEL MAR

Punta Cabeza
de Ballena

LA EUROPEA

To
Cabo
San Lucas

MISIONES
DEL CABO

ESPERANZA
RESORT

El Manglito

2 mi

2 km

0

0

© AVALON TRAVEL

THE CORRIDOR

THE BEST DAY IN THE CORRIDOR

The Corridor is a resort paradise, and the best day you can plan is one where you never have to leave sight of your hotel. Whether you choose the Westin, Hilton, Sheraton, or another property, order a **leisurely breakfast** on the pool deck and then plan a **horseback ride, long beach walk,** game of **tennis,** or round of **golf** before it gets too hot. Return to grab a chaise lounge by the **pool** and order a cold drink, or bring a blanket to the beach with a **picnic lunch.**

In the afternoon, try a **cooking class, spa treatment, yoga class,** or other organized activity on-site. Or simply relax with a book on your private balcony or patio and scan the ocean for wildlife sightings.

Dinner at any of the resort's signature restaurants will be a culinary adventure in Mexican fusion cuisine made of fresh, seasonal ingredients, many of them grown in Los Cabos. For a romantic evening, ask for a candlelight dinner for two on the beach.

Evening entertainment could include live music, dancing, performances, bonfires, baby turtle releases, and more. When you are ready to retire for the night, your room is just a few short steps away.

Beaches

Pristine sunbathing beaches are the primary reason why so many high-end resorts have decided to build along the Corridor. To find the most easily accessible beaches, look for blue and white signs that say *Acceso a Playa,* with an image of a snorkel and mask or a swimmer. (Some signs have just the picture and not the words.) Ocean swimmers should be aware that strong undertows and rocks make many of these beaches unsafe for wading and bodysurfing. Playas Chileno and Santa María are two exceptions. You may also be able to get in at Playa Palmilla.

◖ PLAYA PALMILLA

The beautifully landscaped access road may trick you into thinking that Playa Palmilla (km 26) is private. At the moment, it's not. It does serve as the main beach for several upscale resorts, but it has a good-sized public parking lot, several *palapas* for shade, and plenty of sand to go around. The beach is pleasant for swimming or snorkeling. Palmilla is also the only place along the Corridor where you can watch the fishing *pangas* launch the old-fashioned way—without a paved boat launch or dock.

◖ PLAYA EL BLEDITO (TEQUILA COVE)

In front of the Hilton and Meliá resorts in Cabo Real, a breakwater protects swimmers from the pounding surf. This is hands-down the best beach in Los Cabos for families. You can rent personal watercraft on the beach (a safety concern for swimmers), or simply enjoy the bodysurfing, snorkeling, and swimming. The Hilton no longer offers day passes for use of its pool and facilities, but you may be able to arrange a visit if you call ahead of time. Parking is difficult if you aren't staying at one of the resorts. You may be able to park in the lot for guests and walk through the resort to get to the beach. Otherwise, it's best to take a bus or cab.

◖ BAHÍA CHILENO AND BAHÍA SANTA MARÍA

If you want to swim and snorkel during your stay in Los Cabos, chances are someone will direct you to one of these two accessible beaches on the Corridor. Construction is in progress around both of these bays, so access may change as yet more golf courses and resorts go up. Many land and sea tours bring groups of

Kids love to play in the sand at Playa El Bledito.

tourists to these bays because they are protected from the surf and have rocky points that attract a variety of marine life. Both have ample parking in dirt lots, though you may have to pay a few dollars to the security guard monitoring the lot. Shade and commercial services are lacking at both locations, though vendors seem to come and go each season. There are public restrooms at Chileno (km 14) and sometimes snorkeling rentals at Santa María (km 12). Both of these beaches can get crowded with shoulder-to-shoulder snorkelers when the tour boats come in mid-morning to mid-afternoon. It's best to get an early start if you'd like to have the bay to yourself. Playa Chileno has an exit ramp from a new stretch of the highway, which has moved inland to give way to a new development.

PLAYA LAS VIUDAS (WIDOWS BEACH)

At kilometer 12.5, between the now-demolished Twin Dolphin and up-and-running Fiesta Americana resorts, a shallow bay with rocky points offers secluded snorkeling and swimming, when conditions are calm. Access may be changing due to on-again/off-again construction. Look for a dirt road at kilometer 12.5, between Cabo del Sol and Playa Santa Maria. The sand can get deep, but most vehicles seem able to traverse the access road.

Water Sports

Each of the major resorts can book scuba diving tours; the dive shops themselves are located in Cabo San Lucas or at Cabo Pulmo on the East Cape. Here are some suggestions for places you can snorkel independently, or with a guide.

SNORKELING AND SCUBA DIVING

Punta Palmilla (km 27) can be a good spot to put on your mask and fins. A zebra eel slithered about in broad daylight during a recent snorkel here.

Bahías Santa María (5-18 meters) and **Chileno** (9-21 meters) both have rocky reefs for underwater exploration. Due to the crowds, sea life near the shore is limited compared to what you'll see in protected marine parks elsewhere on the peninsula. These two bays are best suited for snorkeling or shallow beginner dives. Offshore from Bahía Santa María, a site called the **Blowhole** (12-30 meters) features a wall dive where divers often see giant mantas, sea turtles, and schooling jacks and grouper.

Playa El Bledito, in front of the Hilton Los Cabos, has some decent snorkeling along the rocks that make up the jetty.

SURFING AND STAND-UP PADDLING (SUP)

Late summer storms bring a strong south swell to the Los Cabos coast, and several breaks offer fairly consistent rides. When the sea is calm, stand-up paddling is possible at a couple of the more protected beaches.

Playa Costa Azul on the outskirts of San José has the most popular and dependable surf breaks in the area. The right point break at Punta Palmilla (km 27) may be worth the long paddle on a super big day. This is also a suitable place to launch your stand-up paddling (SUP) board. Playa El Bledito near the Hilton resort is more protected for SUP due to the breakwater. Rentals are usually available on the beach.

El Tule is a dependable right at kilometer 16, near Chileno Bay and close to the Cabo Real resorts.

Close to Cabo San Lucas, **Monuments** breaks left over a rock reef located below the Misiones del Cabo condo complex at the west end of Playa Cabo Bello. Expect a crowd on good days, and beware the rocks and urchins.

FISHING

Well-known **Francisco's Fleet** (formerly Victor's Sportfishing, toll-free U.S. tel. 800/521-2281, www.jigstop.com), based at Palmilla Beach on the Corridor, can arrange guided fishing trips. A six-hour super-*panga* trip for two or three people costs US$195; bring your own food and drinks.

Hiking, Biking, and Adventure Tours

HIKING

A number of Los Cabos outfitters offer guided hikes in wilderness areas that are located outside the tourist area. For example, **High Tide Los Cabos** (Arambura s/n Zazata, San José del Cabo, tel. 624/142-0424, www.hightideloscabos.com) offers a waterfall hike to Fox Canyon, one hour north of Cabo San Lucas. **Cabo Adventures** (U.S. tel. 888/526-2238, www.cabo-adventures.com) also organizes a long list of activities and tours, including desert mountain biking rides. A typical tour includes round-trip transportation from your hotel to a trailhead along the West Cape or East Cape, water and snacks, and a guide. Hikes may be in coastal or mountain areas. The activity desk at most resorts can book these trips for guests.

BIKING

The first annual Ironman Los Cabos triathlon event in 2013 introduced cyclists to the roads in Los Cabos. Starting in the fall of 2012, they could be seen training along the Transpeninsular Highway. Two high-end cycling shops have opened to meet the specialized needs of this new kind of visitor.

Mountain biking is limited within the Corridor region; however, several outfitters based in San José del Cabo and Cabo San Lucas offer trips to nearby wilderness areas with trails into the foothills of the Sierra de la Laguna.

In the San José hotel zone, across from the Hola Grand Faro, **Sportia Los Cabos** (Plaza el Pescador Local 16-18, Col. Campo de Golf Zona Hotelera, tel. 624/130-7159, info@sportia.mx) was the official bike shop for the Ironman event. Owners David Alvarez, Alvarez Toño, and Jaime Cadaval were instrumental in getting the Ironman brand to consider a race in Los Cabos. They sell road bikes and accessories, offer guided tours, and are leading the charge to get a bike lane added to the highway between San José and San Lucas.

In the same plaza that has the Vinoteca wine shop and Crossfit Los Cabos, **Cabo Bike** (Plaza Paseo Los Arcos, Local B8, Carr. Transpeninsular km 6.5, Col. Cabo Bello, tel. 624/172-2332, www.cabobike.com) sells road bikes, mountain bikes, recreational bikes, and triathlon gear. Rentals were not offered at press time but may be available in the future. This store has a second location in La Paz.

ADVENTURE SPORTS AND TOURS
⟨ Wild Canyon Adventures

Located near Playa El Tule along the Corridor, this is one of the newest and most popular eco-friendly activity parks in Los Cabos. Prepare yourself for an extreme outback experience, whichever ride you choose. There are 10 zip lines, the longest 815 meters (tandem rides are possible), a bungee jump, ATV tours, and camel rides. The staff here genuinely seems to enjoy what they do.

The day begins with a pickup at your hotel and shuttle ride to the park. Tours run at 9am, noon, and 3pm, and each one lasts about three and a half hours. Most of the activities cost US$95 per person, and the transportation is included. Discounts may be offered by timeshare sales people around town, but you will have to sit through a two- to three-hour sales pitch in order to save a small percentage off the standard park fee.

Wild Canyon Adventures has an office in Cabo San Lucas (Blvd. Marina 20, Loc. 6, tel. 624/144-4433, www.wildcanyon.com.mx). You can also buy tickets online.

Other Zip Line and ATV Tours

Cabo Adventures offers **Outdoor Zip Line Adventure** (Blvd. Paseo de la Marina, Lote 7a, Cabo San Lucas, tel. 624/173-9500, www.cabo-adventures.com) about one hour north of San José del Cabo.

Near Playa Palmilla, **Canopy Costa Azul Eco-Adventure** (tel. 624/105-9312, www.

costaazulziplines.com) is another option for zip line tours.

Desertica (Carr. Transpeninsular km 61.8, tel. 624/146-9601, www.desertica.com.mx, US$35) has brought its amusement-park style of outdoor entertainment to Baja, with canopy tours on eight different zip lines, plus trails for ATVs, buggies, and horses. Four-hour tours begin at 9am, noon, and 3pm daily (minimum age seven and maximum weight 250 pounds).

You can also tour the backroads of Baja in a fleet of Hummers with **Baja Outback** (tel. 624/142-9200, www.bajaoutback.com, US$135-183 pp). Single- and multiday tours go to Todos Santos, Santiago, Rancho La Verdad, and Rancho Antares (between Cabo Pulmo and Los Frailes).

Golf

Designer golf courses have popped up all over Southern Baja, luring players away from the competition in Arizona and California. Jack Nicklaus, Robert Trent Jones II, Tom Fazio, Tom Weiskopf, and Roy Dye all have had a hand in shaping the Los Cabos golf experience.

Gray water irrigates most of these courses, but even so, keeping all those fairways groomed and green in a desert environment doesn't come cheap: Greens fees average US$250 for 18 holes. Discounted twilight rates begin at 2pm, earlier in summer. Rates typically include tax, use of a golf cart and driving range, bottled water, and club service, and prices may vary according to the travel season and day of the week.

Jack Nicklaus was the mastermind behind the arroyo, mountain, and ocean courses at the **One&Only Palmilla** (Carr. Transpeninsular km 26, Palmilla, tel. 624/144-5250, US$200 for 18 holes), which form the center of a 384-hectare resort community. Most of its 27 holes have views of the ocean. Palmilla is known for a 440-yard, par-4 Mountain Five hole, which challenges the golfer to a long drive across two desert arroyos. Callaway rental clubs cost US$55. The clubhouse here may not be as extensive or luxurious as those of other courses, but guests say the Palmilla offers the most bang for your buck.

Open since 1989, the 18-hole, par-72 **Cabo Real Golf Course** (Carr. Transpeninsular km 19.5, Cabo Real, tel. 624/144-0040, toll-free U.S. tel. 877/795-8727, www.caboreal.com, US$180-280 for 18 holes) covers 6,400 meters with three oceanfront holes. Guests of the Westin Los Cabos, Meliá Cabo Real, and Casa del Mar resorts get 10 percent off the greens fees. King Cobra-brand golf club rentals are US$50.

Jack Nicklaus designed the world-renowned 18-hole, par-72 **El Dorado Golf Club** (Carr. Transpeninsular km 19.5, Cabo Real, tel. 624/144-5450, US$280 for 18 holes) with an oceanfront driving range and clubhouse. Although it was initially designed as a public course, the El Dorado has now gone private, and four of the nine original oceanfront holes have been converted into home sites.

The golf community at **Cabo del Sol** (Carr. Transpeninsular km 10.5, Cabo del Sol, tel. 624/145-8200, toll-free U.S. tel. 877/703-4394) includes two separate courses, with more in the plans. The ocean course (US$265-350) was designed by Jack Nicklaus and opened in 1994. Built to preserve a natural look and feel, the course extends from a kilometer and a half of oceanfront property, with 7 of the 18 holes on the water. This is the only course in Mexico named to the 2011 *Golf Magazine* Top 100 Courses in the World list (#100) and one of only two courses in Mexico on the *Golf Digest* list of 100 courses outside the United States (#54). The adjacent desert course (US$165-220) was designed by Tom Weiskopf, his first anywhere in Mexico. TaylorMade clubs at either course rent for US$65. Guests of the Fiesta Americana and Sheraton resorts in Cabo del Sol receive a 10 percent discount.

Palo blanco trees, *cardón* cacti, and other desert flora form the backdrop for a challenging **18-hole course designed by Roy Dye** (Palo Blanco 501, tel. 624/143-4653 or 624/143-4654, toll-free U.S. tel. 888/298-1132, www.golfincabo.com). Enjoy stunning views of Bahía Cabo San Lucas, including the rock formations at Land's End. Winter greens fees are US$105-204; summer rates are lower. The adjacent **Los Cabos Golf Resort** (tel. 624/145-7100 or 877/496-1367) has rooms with kitchenettes starting at US$235. The largest units have three bedrooms and full kitchens.

Spas and Yoga

If you've come to Los Cabos to relax and rejuvenate, bodywork such as a massage, facial, wrap, or pedicure may top your must-do list for the trip. Many local resorts provide the option to have a massage under a tent on the beach or in an on-site treatment room in a European-style spa with steam rooms, whirlpools, and saunas. Signature treatments often involve oils and fragrances from plants growing in the nearby desert.

THE SPA AT THE WESTIN LOS CABOS

The Spa at the Westin Los Cabos (Carr. Transpeninsular km 22.5, tel. 624/142-9000, toll-free U.S. tel. 800/598-1864, www.starwoodhotels.com) is a standout for its heavenly body wraps, which include a chocolate wrap (US$128/50 minutes), aromatic mud treatment (US$128/50 minutes), and a celestial wrap (US$128/50 minutes). Massages average US$128 for 50 minutes, and special massages are offered for both golfers and pregnant women. A full range of skin care and beauty services are also available.

SECRETS MARQUI LOS CABOS

The **Secrets Marquis Los Cabos** (Carr. Transpeninsular km 21.5, tel. 624/144-2000, toll-free U.S. tel. 877/238-9399, www.secretsresorts.com/marquis-los-cabos) boasts a gorgeous 929-square-meter spa with six additional massage tents on the beach. A 50-minute facial runs US$100-115; deep-tissue, Shiatsu, Thai, or sports massage services are US$115-125 for 50 minutes; mud therapy treatments are US$115 for 50 minutes; and body scrubs are US$79 for 25 minutes. Nonguests can use the spa facilities (steam room, whirlpool tubs, and spa swimming pool) without reserving a treatment for US$25.

ONE&ONLY SPA AT PALMILLA

The **One&Only Spa at Palmilla** (Carr. Transpeninsular km 27, tel. 624/146-7000, toll-free U.S. tel. 866/382-4166, www.palmilla.oneandonlyresorts.com/spa.aspx) offers a range of treatments, from ancient techniques to cutting-edge spa technologies. Amenities include separate male and female relaxation areas, unisex outdoor relaxation garden, plunge pool, outdoor rain show, aromatherapy steam room, sauna, private villas, beauty salon, finishing studio, fitness center, and outdoor oceanside *palapas* for massage, meditation, yoga, and other wellness activities. Unique treatments include the Celebration of Life massage, a 1-hour 45-minute treatment choreographed to whale sounds and using salts harvested from the lagoons of Baja; the Palmilla Chocolate Synergy, which employs a blend of massage techniques with an herbal compress and chocolate oil; and the two-hour Holistic Body Ritual, which begins with a full body exfoliation followed by a body wrap, aromatherapy massage, and a scalp massage.

SUEÑOS DEL MAR

Sueños del Mar (Carr. Transpeninsular km 19.5, tel. 624/145-7700, toll-free U.S. tel.

800/227-9621, www.zoetryresorts.com/casadelmar) at the Zoëtry Casa del Mar resort in Cabo Real offers massages, facials, body treatments, and more. Prices start at US$85 for a 25-minute massage. Treatments range from skin analysis and personalized facials to a full holistic ritual.

SPA OASIS

Consistent with its reputation for treating families well, the Hilton Los Cabos's **Spa Oasis** (Carr. Transpeninsular km 19.5, U.S. tel. 877/354-1399, SpaOasis@Hilton.com) offers a special menu of spa services for kids and teens, including packages for groups of youngsters as well as for parents and their children. At the **Cabo Kids Oasis** kids can relax with their friends and enjoy a massage, reflexology, mani-pedi, or ice cream foot treatment. Services run US$15-45. A Teen Jacuzzi Party includes hair/makeup and virgin cocktails. A Best Friends Forever (BFF) party adds a few more treatments to the list. Adults, too, enjoy the full menu of bodywork, wraps, aquatherapies, salon services, and wellness care rituals in the main spa.

THE SPA AT LAS VENTANAS

In 2011, Las Ventanas al Paraíso overhauled **The Spa at Las Ventanas** (Carr. Transpeninsular km 20, tel. 624/144-2800, toll-free U.S. tel. 888/767-3966,www.rosewoodhotels.com/en/lasventanas/services_such/spa, spa open 8am-8pm daily, fitness center open 6am-8pm daily). Updates included doubling the former number of indoor-outdoor treatment cabanas, adding duet suites for couples, furnishing private terraces, building a solarium, creating a full-service beauty salon, and planting 45 new areca and date palms. The spa offers a "Four Elements" menu inspired by the ancient healers of Baja, which draws upon the different powers of earth, air, water, and fire. Some of the unique treatments offered here include the Holistic Twilight Ceremony, an energy cleansing ritual that begins at sunset; it is accented with sage smoke, shaman prayers, and the music of crystal bowls, followed by

a 90-minute massage. Fusion Massage uses a customized combination of aromatherapy and massage techniques like Thai, lomilomi, deep tissue, stone, shiatsu, and pindasweda. The Spa Pod Reawakening Experience is a multi-sensory hydro spa system that integrates steam, chromatherapy, LED light, water reflexology, vibratory massage, and aromatherapy.

SOMMA WINESPA

Housed at the Fiesta Americana Grand, the unique **SOMMA WineSpa** (Carr. Transpeninsular km 10.3, Cabo del Sol, tel. 624/145-6200, toll-free U.S. tel. 800/343-7821, www.fiestamericanagrand.com) is perhaps the only spa in Cabo to use the benefits of wine in its treatments, a technique called "vinotherapy." SOMMA WineSPA uses regional wines and wines from the Mediterranean to infuse many of its treatments. It also serves fresh fruit and tea to all guests—featuring the frozen, sugared grapes that visitors rave about. Other natural elements include chocolate, olive oil, coconut oil, avocado, lavender, hot stones, and bamboo. Any spa treatment also comes with free use of the fitness facilities.

THE SPA AT MARBELLA SUITES EN LA PLAYA

The Spa at Marbella Suites en La Playa (Carr. Transpeninsular km 17, tel. 624/144-1060, www.marbellasuites.com/explore/spa) is home to the newly renovated full-service Spa at Marbella Suites. Services like massages (US$55/hour) and manicures/pedicures are offered beachside or in the indoor facility. The spa is smaller than those you will find at larger resorts, and offers fewer treatments (the most exotic you'll find here is the hot rock massage), but readers report that you can't beat the idyllic setting and the hospitable staff.

CACTUS SPA

At the Sheraton Hacienda del Mar, visitors will find the peaceful **Cactus Spa** (Carr. Transpeninsular km 10.5, Cabo del Sol, tel. 624/145-8000, ext. 4080-4086, spahacienda2@sheraton.com, 9am-8pm daily). Amenities

Get a massage by the sea at The Spa at Esperanza Resort.

include body wraps, Vichy shower, three facial treatment rooms, six massage treatment rooms, beauty salon, Jacuzzi, sauna, cold and warm tubs, fitness center, indoor/outdoor relaxation areas, and boutique. Unique treatments include a Green Coffee Body Wrap (US$160/80 minutes), De-Stress Hydro Massage (US$63/25 minutes), Deep Tissue Massage (US$150/50 minutes), and an Oxygen Facial (US$140/50 minutes). The spa also offers specialized packages for newlyweds, couples, and men; full body treatments; and fragrance rituals.

THE HACIENDA SPA

The Hacienda Spa (Carr. Transpeninsular km 7.3, tel. 624/163-5555, www.haciendaencantada.com/spa.php, 9am-8pm Mon.-Sat., until 5pm Sun.) indulges visitors in body treatments (US$70-130), massages (US$65-185), facials (US$60-120), and salon services (US$10-115). The Hacienda Spa is also one of few to offer *temazcal* treatments, a small chamber heated by red-hot stones splashed with water infused with medicinal herbs.

THE SPA AT ESPERANZA RESORT

Indoor steam caves and waterfalls, plus holistic treatments using local fruits and vegetation, make **The Spa at Esperanza Resort** (Carr. Transpeninsular km 7, Manzana 10, Punta Ballena, tel. 624/145-6400, toll-free U.S. tel. 866/311-2226, www.esperanzaresort. com, 9am-8pm daily) an experience that is not to be missed. Ninety-minute treatments cost US$235-250 and use natural ingredients like aloe, desert clay, sea greens, tropical fruit, and various alcohols.

Shopping

There is surprisingly little shopping to be found along the Corridor between San José and San Lucas, aside from one shopping plaza near Palmilla and a handful of big box stores near Cabo San Lucas, along with the requisite resort gift shops. To find the good stuff at reasonable prices, you need to head into town.

SHOPPING CENTERS

For jewelry, clothing, antiques, and home furnishings, head to the upscale **Shoppes at Palmilla** (Carr. Transpeninsular km 27.5, Palmilla, tel. 624/144-6999, www.lastiendasdepalmilla.com), on the north side of the Carretera Transpeninsular at the Palmilla Resort exit. Here, the eclectic **Galeria Pez Gordo** (tel. 624/144-5292, www.pezgordoloscabos.com, 10am-8pm Mon.-Sat., 10am-2pm Sun.) represents more than 40 contemporary artists based in Baja and throughout Mexico. Works range from oil and acrylic to wax, collage, and photography.

CLOTHING AND JEWELRY

Several clothing boutiques and jewelers are also located in the plaza. For example, **Casa**

Vieja Boutique (tel. 624/144-6161, Mon.-Fri. 11am-7pm, Sat. 11am-6pm) is a high-end shop with apparel and jewelry made by well-known Mexican and Latin American designers.

The boutique at the One&Only Palmilla offers designer resort wear, arts and crafts, and Mexican hand-embroidered linens.

The jewelry shop at the Sheraton Hacienda del Mar has an attractive display of designs for sale.

HOME FURNISHINGS

Antigua de Mexico (tel. 624/144-6121, www.antiguademexico.com, Mon.-Fri. 10am-7pm, Sat. 10am-6pm) is a fun place to browse for home furnishings. Its main showroom and factory are located on the mainland in Guadalajara.

ARTS AND CRAFTS

At kilometer 16, across from the Marbella Suites Hotel, the **Regional Center of Popular Arts and Crafts** (9am-6pm Thurs.-Tues.) has a small glassblowing factory and several artisan workshops. Prices here are lower than what you'll find in San José or San Lucas.

Nightlife and Entertainment

Most of the hotels along the Corridor have nightly music of some kind—though some of it can be pretty cheesy. The Secrets Marquis, Westin, Dreams, and Esperanza resorts host musicians and vocalists from time to time. A few of the Corridor resorts host cooking classes and other events that draw in the foodie crowd. Otherwise, you can also venture into town for more options.

Golf tournaments, surf competitions, and the like draw visitors for destination events. The first annual Baja Film Festival took place in November 2012, and the first

Ironman Los Cabos triathlon brought elite athletes to town in March 2013. Visit Baja.com for up-to-date event listings across the Los Cabos region.

BARS

All the major resorts have at least one bar or lounge for evening entertainment; a few offer unique touches.

At **La Cantina Sports Bar** (Westin Resort & Spa, Carr. Transpeninsular km 22.5, tel. 624/142-9000, www.westinloscabos.com) evenings begin with a frozen margarita and light appetizers, and end with cheering on your favorite team on the big-screen televisions.

For a more elegant experience, try **Bar La Suerta** (Sheraton Hacienda del Mar, Carr. Transpeninsular km 10.5, Cabo del Sol, tel. 624/145-8000, www.sheratonhaciendadelmar.com), where you can sample hundreds of varieties of tequila late into the night.

CULINARY EVENTS

Esperanza Resort (Carr. Transpeninsular km 7, Manzana 10, Punta Ballena, tel. 624/145-6400, toll-free U.S. tel. 866/311-2226, www.esperanzaresort.com) offers a diverse menu of food-related activities. **Cooking classes** provide the opportunity to join executive chef Gonzalo Cerda in the kitchen for interactive sessions filled with tips and techniques of the trade. Each session concludes with a luncheon of dishes prepared with the chef.

Esperanza also offers **Tequila Tastings** of more than 100 varieties of Mexican tequila. The master *tequilero* provides information about the historical origins of the tequilas and how each is created. Each tasting includes six tequilas to sample. If you prefer wine to tequila, consider Esperanza's **Mexican Wine Journey** through the wine region of Northern Baja. Tastings include distinctive local wines and the history of winemaking in the country.

On Saturday mornings at **Las Ventanas al Paraíso** (Carr. Transpeninsular km 20, tel. 624/144-2800, toll-free U.S. tel. 888/767-3966, www.rosewoodhotels.com/en/lasventanas), guests can join a one-hour cooking class conducted by one of the resort's chefs. If you are already confident in your skills, you can compete in an Iron Chef-type program, challenging executive chef Fabrice Guisset by preparing a dish of your own in the Herb Garden demo kitchen. If the meal earns top marks, the dish gets added to the menu for one week. Anyone who participates gets a free shot of tequila.

Also available at Las Ventanas al Paraíso is a **Men in White** evening, for those looking for an especially romantic culinary experience. With the guidance of executive chef Fabrice Guisset, you will prepare a gourmet meal for your significant other, to be served in the resort's Herb Garden kitchen, while dressed in chef's "whites." Dinner will be served by a private waiter at a candlelit table.

The **One&Only Palmilla** (Carr. Transpeninsular km 27, tel. 624/146-7000, toll-free U.S. tel. 866/829-2977, www.oneandonlyresorts.com) also hosts cooking classes in its outdoor Herb Garden kitchen. Cooking demonstrations are led by visiting Mexican chefs and resort experts. Each class begins with a tour of the garden and ends with a meal paired with a Mexican wine or tequila.

A nutrition expert is on-site at **Zoëtry Casa del Mar** (Carr. Transpeninsular km 19.5, tel. 624/145-7700, toll-free U.S. tel. 800/227-9621, www.zoetryresorts.com/casadelmar) to provide weekly workshops to interested parties.

RESORT ENTERTAINMENT

Head to **Las Ventanas al Paraíso** (Carr. Transpeninsular km 20, tel. 624/144-2800, toll-free U.S. tel. 888/767-3966, www.rosewoodhotels.com/en/lasventanas) on Friday nights for **BBQ Las Ventanas,** featuring a four-course tasting menu of barbecue cuisine. Available at the Sea Grill from 6:30pm, the barbecue includes a starter, seafood course, meat course, and dessert.

Every Thursday and Friday evening, Las Ventanas al Paraíso also prepares an exclusive **Taste of Baja** dinner. This includes a special, five-course tasting menu served in La Cava wine cellar. The sommelier selects the appropriate fine wine to accompany each course. Dinner begins at 7:30pm, and seating is limited to 14 guests.

Each Thursday **Esperanza Resort** (Carr. Transpeninsular km 7, Manzana 10, Punta Ballena, tel. 624/145-6400, toll-free U.S. tel. 866/311-2226, www.esperanzaresort.com) hosts **Mexicanismo at La Palapa,** a traditional Mexican fiesta complete with regional foods, live music, and a fireworks display. Visitors can also browse the outdoor marketplace selling souvenirs, jewelry, and crafts from local vendors.

Esperanza Resort also hosts a weekly **Fish**

Market at La Palapa on Friday, where guests can select a catch of the day fresh from local waters and have it prepared by the resort chef into a traditional British fish and chips meal or *a la talla* (Mexican style).

On Saturdays, Sundays, and Tuesdays from sunset to midnight, Esperanza resort hosts its **Barefoot Bar on the Beach at La Palapa,** featuring food, margaritas, music, and beer buckets.

Food

Most restaurants along the Corridor are tucked inside full-service resorts. Expect to pay at least US$100 for two (without drinks) at most of the restaurants in this section. Here are a few standalone eateries and some of the resort standouts.

SEAFOOD AND INTERNATIONAL

At the Cabo Surf Hotel, **7 Seas** (Carr. Transpeninsular km 28, tel. 624/142-2676, www.7seasrestaurant.com, 7am-10pm daily, lunch mains US$7-13, dinner mains US$15-30) serves breakfast, lunch, and dinner under an open-air *palapa.* The dinner menu features Mexican, Mediterranean, and seafood entrées with a decent wine list. Seafood-stuffed poblano peppers are one of the more unusual dishes.

At the Westin Los Cabos, **Arrecifes** (Carr. Transpeninsular km 22.5, tel. 624/142-9000, dinner daily, mains US$15-25) is the more formal of the two main restaurants; jazz music plays over the sound of waves crashing on the beach below, and the menu emphasizes seafood dishes with a continental twist. The other restaurant, **La Cascada** (Carr. Transpeninsular km 22.5, tel. 624/142-9000, breakfast and dinner daily, mains US$15 and up), underwent a US$900,000 renovation in 2006. It features illuminated onyx cube tables, a fire-pit lounge, and a menu of creative *tapas del mundo,* or small plates from around the world paired with wines that match the flavors of the food.

And at the One&Only Palmilla, guests can dine at *palapa*-style **Agua Restaurant** (Carr. Transpeninsular km 7.5, Palmilla, tel. 624/146-7000, breakfast, lunch, and dinner daily), featuring Mediterranean cuisine and a view of the sea.

Pecan-encrusted sea bass, mesquite-grilled prawns, and live lobster anchor the menu at **Pitahayas** (Carr. Transpeninsular km 10, Cabo del Sol, tel. 624/145-8010, www.pitahayas.com, 5:30pm-10:30pm daily, mains US$15-40), at the Sheraton Hacienda del Mar. An underground wine cellar complements the menu of fresh seafood and mesquite-grilled entrées. You'll need to wear formal resort attire if you plan to dine here.

ITALIAN AND CONTINENTAL

In the Misiones del Cabo complex, **Sunset da Mona Lisa** (formerly Da Giorgio, Carr. Transpeninsular km 5.5, tel. 624/145-8160, www.sunsetmonalisa.com, 8:30am-11pm daily, mains US$15-35) draws a crowd for sunset views and Italian fare. A multilevel patio overlooks the bay and Cabo San Lucas.

MEXICAN

Puerta Vieja (Carr. Transpeninsular km 6.3, tel. 624/104-3252, www.puertavieja.com, mains US$10-25) prepares Mexican dishes at reasonable prices, but the real reason to come is for the ocean views. The menu is available in Spanish or English. Guacamole was surprisingly bland on one visit.

One more kilometer east, the same owners run the simple **Villa Serena Restaurant** (Carr. Transpeninsular km 7.5, tel. 624/145-8244, www.villaserenarestaurant.com, 7am-11pm daily, mains US$5-30), next to the Villa Serena RV Park. Tables are arranged under a *palapa* roof and beside a small swimming pool, in true Baja style. This is a wonderful

the open-air dining room at Puerta Vieja

stop for a breakfast of *chilaquiles* (salsa or mole over crisp tortilla triangles), served with poblano chiles and shredded chicken (US$7). Non-coffee drinkers can order Mighty Leaf teas. *Huachinango* (red snapper), barbecue chicken, and *tampiqueña* beef are recommended for lunch or dinner. Lobster *machaca* (dried) is a house specialty, for US$20, and on Sundays, the kitchen serves up Spanish paella. A small play structure entertains little ones, but there is no beach access from the restaurant.

BREAKFAST

For an easy breakfast or lunch near the Cabo San Lucas Country Club, **Vips** (pronounced BEEPS, Carr. Transpeninsular km 2, tel. 624/144-7140, www.vips.com.mx, daily 7am-10pm, mains US$5-15) is a Denny's-like chain located in the Walmart shopping center, in a separate building closer to the highway. Order a cheese omelet for US$8 or the crepes with ham and spinach for US$10. Kids will love this place (parents not so much) because their pancakes come (without warning) with a scoop of vanilla ice cream and an assortment of sweet toppings including sprinkles, jam, M&Ms, and chocolate sauce. Children also get special Transformers and My Little Pony menus and napkins and hidden picture placemats. A small McDonald's-like play structure offers a few extra minutes of entertainment while you finish your coffee. This restaurant is exceptionally clean and servers are very friendly. A little Spanish helps with the ordering, but there is an English menu as well.

GROCERIES

The **Mega supermarket** (at the intersection of Paseo Los Cabos and Carr. Transpeninsular, tel. 624/142-4524) in San José is the best place to find staples and specialty foods.

There are no grocery stores in the Cabo Real or Cabo del Sol developments. Plan on driving toward Cabo San Lucas or San José del Cabo to stock up on supplies.

If you want to stock up on fine wines, spirits, and gourmet foods, **La Europea** (Carr.

© NIKKI GOTH ITOI

chilaquiles for breakfast at Villa Serena Restaurant

Transpeninsular km 6.7, tel. 624/145-8755, 9am-8pm Mon.-Fri., 9am-9pm Sat.) is the place to shop. Look for the main store at the first stoplight as you enter Cabo San Lucas from the east. Credit cards are accepted. Near Costco, **Vinoteca** (Camino del Cerro 225 Int. Local 2, Col. Pedregal, Cabo San Lucas, tel. 624/143-7795, www.vinoteca.com) is a Mexican-owned chain selling wine from around the world and liquor, including tequila.

Costco (Carr. Transpeninsular km 4.5, tel. 624/146-7180, 9am-9pm daily) and **Home Depot** (Carr. Transpeninsular km 6.5, tel. 624/105-8600) have stores close to Cabo San Lucas. Other big-box stores in the vicinity include Office Max, Office Depot, Walmart, and Sam's Club.

A real find for natural and organic foods near Punta Ballena and Esperanza Resort is the **Santa Carmela Super Market & Deli** (Carr. Transpeninsular km 6, tel. 624/104-3478, www.mercadostacarmela.com). From the outside, the store looks like any other mini-super. Inside, the aisles are stocked with local fruits and veggies, baked goods, whole-wheat pastas, organic dairy, baby essentials, and multiple shelves of gluten-free foods. Top off your cart with a bottle of Baja California or imported wine. You can also get bottled water in a variety of sizes.

Information and Services

VISITORS CENTER

The concierge at your hotel is the best place to get visitor information along the Corridor. Further information may be available through the **Los Cabos Convention & Visitors Bureau** (tel. 624/143-4777, www.visitloscabos.travel). Alternatively, you can stop in at the visitors center in San José del Cabo or Cabo San Lucas.

POST OFFICES

The nearest postal services are in San José del Cabo (Plaza Ley, Paseo de los Misiones, 8am-5pm Mon.-Fri.) and Cabo San Lucas (Lázaro Cárdenas at 16 de Septiembre, 8am-4:30pm Mon.-Fri. and 9am-1pm Sat.).

INTERNET ACCESS

All of the resorts along the Corridor offer high-speed Internet services. Some only do so in public areas, while others offer in-room access. A few of these hotels still charge additional fees for using the Internet, but many others include it for the cost of your stay. Numerous cafés in Cabo San Lucas and San José del Cabo offer Wi-Fi for patrons.

EMERGENCY SERVICES

For emergencies, dial 066. The nearest facilities are in San José del Cabo and Cabo San Lucas. If you are located near San José, the main *centro de salud* (hospital, tel. 624/142-2770) is located on Calle Doblado between Colegio Militar and Márquez de León. An **AmeriMed hospital** has opened in Plaza Cabo

Ley (Paseo de los Misiones s/n, tel. 624/105-8550, 24 hours). For medical assistance, visit the **Walk-in MediClinic** (Carr. Transpeninsular km 28, tel. 624/130-7011) in the El Zalate Plaza. The facility has an emergency room, lab, pharmacy, and ambulance. Two other options are **BlueMedicalNet** (tel. 624/104-3911), which operates a clinic in the Plaza Misión, next to HSBC Bank, and **Médica Los Cabos** (Zaragoza 128, tel. 624/142-2770), near the Pemex station. All will respond to emergencies 24/7.

Near Cabo San Lucas, head to **AmeriMed** (Pioneros Building Loc. 1, Blvd. Lázaro Cárdenas, tel. 624/143-9670), which has a bilingual staff trained to handle emergencies, along with OB/GYN care and a family practice. The clinic is open 24/7 and accepts most insurance policies. **BlueMedicalNet** (tel. 624/104-3911, 24/7 daily) operates a clinic in the Plaza del Rey, across from Home Depot.

BANKS

There are no banking services in the Corridor region, however most resorts can exchange currency at inflated rates. Numerous ATMs are available in Cabo San Lucas and San José del Cabo.

FUEL

Pemex stations are located at kilometer 5, just outside Cabo San Lucas, and near the Westin, between kilometer 24 and kilometer 25.

THE CORRIDOR

Getting There and Around

The majority of Los Cabos visitors arrive by air, but you'll meet many who have traveled by car, boat, or bicycle, or even on foot. Public transportation by bus is also a possibility. Once you've arrived, you can do without a car if you plan to stay at an all-inclusive resort. Resorts along the Corridor are a 30- to 60-minute drive from the airport.

GETTING THERE
By Air
Los Cabos International Airport (SJD, Carr. Transpeninsular km 44, tel. 624/146-5111, http://aeropuertosgap.com.mx/english/airports/loscabos-airport) serves San José del Cabo, the Corridor, and Cabo San Lucas. Additional airport information is available at www.sjdloscabosairport.com, but this is not the official airport website.

The process of going through passport control and customs can take as little as 15 minutes or more than an hour, depending on how many people are working and if other flights have arrived at the same time. After you go through passport control, you'll proceed to the baggage claim area. Claim your bags and have your paperwork ready to show the customs official. You'll be asked to run your bags through a scanner and to press a button that determines whether your bags will be randomly searched. Sometimes, you'll cruise through immigration only to find yourself in a much longer customs line with one X-ray machine scanning luggage from multiple flights. Relax and enjoy the people-watching. The wait is all part of the experience.

Several international rental car agencies have desks in the terminals. For most brands, you'll need to ride a shuttle to off-airport pickup locations, all of which are very close to the terminal. These days, you'll almost always get a better deal if you reserve ahead of time. During busy holiday periods, most agencies will sell out of cars entirely. They tend to give cars on a first-come, first-served basis, regardless of whether you have a reservation or not.

By Car
Most of the big auto rental agencies have desks at Los Cabos International Airport as well as offices in or near San José and San Lucas. Rates are similar across most companies, and since car rentals don't require a deposit up front, it doesn't hurt to make a reservation in advance. You can always cancel if you change your mind. When you reserve or prepay for a car online, the price typically will not include Mexican liability insurance. Be sure to factor this cost (around US$25 per day for the minimum required coverage of US$50,000) into your

SAMPLE TAXI FARES FROM CABO REAL

Taxis are a convenient, though somewhat expensive, way to get around the Los Cabos Corridor. Here are some examples of the going rates to key destinations in the region. The starting point for these fares would be the Cabo Real development, which includes the Hilton, Meliá, Las Ventanas, and Zoëtry Casa del Mar resorts, as well as the Cabo Real golf course. The prices are for up to four passengers. Additional charges of US$2-8 per additional passenger may apply.

• Los Cabos International Airport	US$40
• Costa Azul	US$20
• San José del Cabo	US$22
• La Playita	US$27
• Puerto Los Cabos	US$35
• Cabo San Lucas	US$25
• Pacific Beaches	US$28

travel planning. Vehicles range from standard transmission subcompact sedans to SUVs, wagons, Jeeps, pickup trucks, and vans. Independent agencies sometimes include insurance in the rates.

If you're driving yourself, there are two ways to reach the towns along the Los Cabos Corridor from the airport: Follow signs for the Carretera Transpeninsular (Highway 1) south through town, passing through several stoplights before you reach the town of San José. Continue on the Carretera Transpeninsular another 10-20 minutes for destinations along the Corridor or about 30 minutes to Cabo San Lucas. Alternatively, if you don't mind paying a toll of about US$2.25 (MEX$28), you can exit the airport onto the *quota,* a fast four-lane road with no exits until you enter San José at the junction of Paseo Los Cabos and the Mega grocery store plaza. If you pick up a rental car off-site, you'll have to return to the terminal to get to the toll road. The roundabout at the intersection with the Carretera Transpeninsular can be an intimidating entry into town, especially if you are trying to go left into downtown San José. Wait for a break in the traffic or turn right and go about 1.6 kilometers to the *Retorno* sign. Exit right and then turn left under the highway and left again to reenter the highway heading back toward San José.

By Bus

A steady stream of **Aguila buses** (tel. 624/143-5020, www.autotransportesaguila.com) provide transportation between Los Cabos and La Paz and on to other points north. Schedules and fares are posted online, and you can purchase tickets in advance online.

By Sea

The nearest ferry service to the mainland operates between La Paz and Mazatlán. You can book tickets in La Paz or online through **Baja Ferries** (tel. 612/123-0208, 612/123-6600, or 800/122-1414, www.en.bajaferries.com).

There are now two full-service marinas in the Los Cabos area. **Marina Cabo San Lucas** (Lote A-18 De la Dársena, tel. 624/173-9140, www.igy-cabosanlucas.com) is still the main docking facility for those arriving by sea. But the new **Marina at Puerto Los Cabos** (Paseo de los Pescadores, Col. La Playa, tel. 624/105-6028, www.marinapuertoloscabos.com) is open and designed to hold up to 500 boats, including the largest luxury yachts.

GETTING AROUND

Many resorts offer **shuttles** to San José del Cabo and Cabo San Lucas for guests who want to see a little more than their hotel grounds. **Car rental agencies** have offices at many of the larger resorts.

CABO SAN LUCAS

Baja travelers tend to love or hate Cabo San Lucas (pop. 56,800) with great passion. Some relish the crowded beach clubs, two-for-one happy hours, all-you-can-drink sunset cruises, and late-night dance clubs. The scene is anything but Mexican, but the energy and pure silliness are infectious, and with all this partying going on, it would seem impossible not to have a good time.

© LAUREN SWIFT

HIGHLIGHTS

LOOK FOR 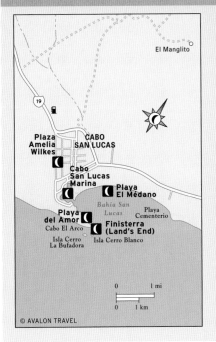 TO FIND RECOMMENDED SIGHTS, ACTIVITIES, DINING, AND LODGING.

Playa El Médano: A visit to Cabo San Lucas would not be complete without a stroll along this busy tourist beach, located within walking distance of the marina and downtown (page 80).

Playa del Amor: This two-sided beach just outside the Cabo San Lucas harbor faces calm waters on its eastern Bahía San Lucas side and pounding surf on the western Pacific side (page 81).

Cabo San Lucas Marina: The daily and nightly action in Cabo takes place in and around this busy marina (page 90).

Plaza Amelia Wilkes: Head to Cabo's original town plaza for a quiet place to relax (page 90).

Finisterra (Land's End): Every tour boat in Cabo visits Finisterra and its 62-meter-high arch, El Arco. This granite rock formation marks the end of the Baja Peninsula and the point where the Sea of Cortez merges with the Pacific Ocean (page 91).

CABO SAN LUCAS

For other travelers, the intensity is too much, the timeshare sales pitches too aggressive, and the overall experience far too Americanized.

Whether you love it or hate it, there's no denying that Cabo San Lucas is one of a kind. Its natural beauty surprises most first-time visitors: The dramatic arch stands at Land's End; Playa del Amor connects the Pacific Ocean to the Sea of Cortez; and the peaks of the Sierra de la Laguna rise in the distance.

The town attracts a surprising variety of visitors, from partying singles to thirtysomethings with kids, and from cruise-ship passengers to scuba divers and sportfishing enthusiasts. Food and accommodations are correspondingly diverse. Cabo has luxury resorts and vacation rental villas as well as modest condos, budget motels, and trailer parks. You can eat world-class sushi, shrimp by the kilo, or simple Mexican *antojitos*. The downtown shopping plazas sell everything from Sergio Bustamante sculptures to hand-embroidered dresses. Venture away from the immediate tourist area and you'll find a grid of dirt roads lined with ordinary Mexican homes and small businesses.

As the second-largest municipality in Baja California Sur after La Paz, Cabo San Lucas has struggled to cope with fast-paced growth over the past two decades. Most of the development has centered around the hillside Pedregal neighborhood, along Playa El Médano, and most recently on the Pacific coast north of Playa Solmar.

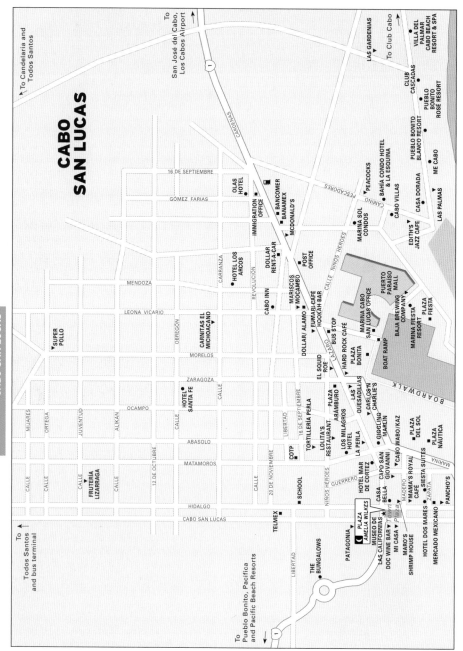

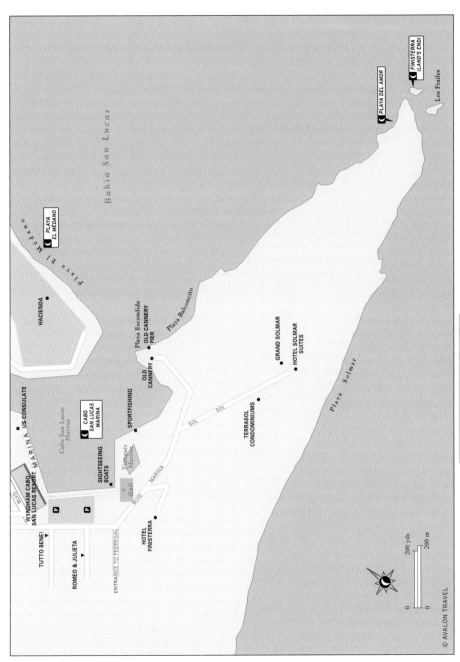

© AVALON TRAVEL

THE BEST DAY IN CABO SAN LUCAS

The best day in Cabo San Lucas starts early and ends late. Fill your morning with outdoor adventure, then rest and restore your energy for a night on the town.

Stay in a downtown or beach hotel, and fuel up for the day at **Mama's Royal Café,** near Plaza Amelia Wilkes. Head to **Playa El Médano** to rent a kayak or hire a water taxi for a ride over to **Playa del Amor (Lover's Beach).** Bring snorkeling gear and snacks, and spend the morning exploring a beach that touches two major bodies of water at the same time: the Bahía San Lucas on one side and the Pacific Ocean on the other. Paddle back before the wind kicks up, or flag down a water taxi for the ride back to shore.

For a late lunch, order **Baja-style fish tacos** from one of the beach clubs along Playa El Médano. Depending on the season, the partying should be in full swing by now. Hang around if you care to join in the silliness, or else head back to your hotel for a midday siesta. If it's a hot day, head to the **Puerto Paraíso** shopping mall to cool off indoors.

Start the evening with a round of margaritas at one of the **open-air bars** along the marina. Dinner will involve fresh-catch and ocean views at **Hacienda Cocina Y Cantina,** located between the marina and Playa El Médano. For a more casual option downtown, try **Maro's Shrimp House.**

After dinner, head to **Cabo Wabo** for live music and late-night frivolity, or the trendsetting **Passion Club and Lounge** at the ME Cabo resort for international DJ music. Most of Cabo's dance clubs will stay open till dawn.

In 2010 the town completed a series of infrastructure improvements that resulted in new road surfaces, sidewalks, traffic lights with pedestrian signals, and spiffy new signage. Services related to tourism and the construction business drive the local economy today.

ORIENTATION

Cabo San Lucas is a compact town with most sights and attractions located in one of three areas: **Playa El Médano** has many of the larger resorts and trendy beach clubs, while resorts along the **Pacific Beach zone** tend to offer a quieter environment for guests. Most of the town's popular bars and restaurants are clustered in the **downtown** and **marina** area. You can easily walk from downtown or the marina to Playa El Médano and back again. It's best to drive or take a cab or shuttle to the Pacific Beach locations.

Beaches

◖ PLAYA EL MÉDANO

Cabo San Lucas offers the rare combination of a large tourist destination with a well-developed beach area within walking distance of the town, plus several pristine beaches just minutes away by boat. And when you've exhausted all these possibilities, the beaches along the Corridor and closer to San José are only a short drive away.

The partying crowd congregates at beach clubs along Playa El Médano (Dune Beach) beginning in the late morning. This long, sandy beach starts at the entrance to the inner harbor and parallels the old road to San José (Camino Viejo a San José) for several kilometers heading northeast. A wide range of travelers cross paths on this beach each day: Families mingle with college kids who swim with their bottles of beer; fortysomethings stroll by in string bikinis, dogs chase Frisbees in the surf, and a constant parade of vendors sells silver and beaded jewelry, sombreros, embroidered bracelets, ceramics, beach wraps, hammocks, and, best of all, fresh fruit. You can swim here any time of year, though the water is warmest July-October. On busy days, keep an eye out for boats landing on the beach. Inexperienced Jet Ski drivers routinely cruise into the roped-off swimming areas. You can book just about any water activity from the beach, including rental of personal watercraft, kayaks, stand-up paddle boards, boogie boards, catamarans, and snorkeling gear. Options for food and facilities at the beach include *palapa* bars, beach clubs, and resort restaurants.

PACIFIC BEACHES
◖ Playa del Amor
At the southernmost tip of the cape, Playa del Amor (Love Beach), also known as Playa del Amante (Lover's Beach), offers a rare opportunity to dip a toe in two different bodies of water from the same beach. This two-sided beach touches both the Sea of Cortez in Bahía San Lucas and the Pacific Ocean (where the beach is called Playa Divorceado). The beach is narrow on the bay side and opens into a wide, sandy expanse on the ocean side. You can swim and snorkel on the bay side, but heavy surf pounds the exposed western shoreline, creating a dangerous undertow.

Water taxis and glass-bottom boats from the Cabo San Lucas marina shuttle passengers to and from the beach for US$8-12 round-trip. (Ask to see the boat before you pay, as some are in much better shape than others. Should the engine fail and cut your trip short, the person you paid will likely be nowhere in sight.)

There are no docking facilities at the drop-off point, which is on the narrow bay side of the beach. *Panga* drivers drift as close as possible to shore, but passengers inevitably get wet on the way in and out. Wear water shoes and protect any electronic gear. Shade is limited to a few rocky overhangs (get there early to claim a spot, or bring your own umbrella), and there are no commercial services at the beach, except for an occasional vendor selling cold drinks. Bring a cooler and pack your own lunch.

Another option for getting to Playa del Amor is to rent a kayak (US$10 pp/hour) on Playa El Médano and paddle across the bay. It's best to go in the morning, when the water is calm; the paddle takes about 40 minutes one-way.

Playa Solmar
To escape the crowds or cool off in an ocean breeze, head to Playa Solmar on the Pacific coast. This exposed beach has a steep slope and strong undertow, making it unsafe for swimming. But for sunbathing and whale-watching, it's a find. Though the beach is public, access is available only through one of the three resorts on the beach, or by making the strenuous climb over the rocks from Lover's Beach. Follow Boulevard Marina to the sign for the Hotel Solmar on the right, and park at the resort.

Water Sports

SNORKELING AND SCUBA DIVING
Cabo San Lucas offers a variety of unique opportunities for underwater exploration. A strategic location between tropical and temperate zones and the presence of a vast submarine canyon bring large pelagics such as giant mantas, hammerhead sharks, and amberjacks very close to shore, along with a colorful mix of tropical species. Boat rides are relatively short (as little as five minutes to the closest sites), and the terrain is dramatic. There are wall dives, submerged boulder fields, drift dives, and a one-of-a-kind dive that begins in the Sea of Cortez, rounds the point at Land's End, and ends in the Pacific Ocean.

Pacific Beaches
Playa del Amor is a great place to snorkel on your own or with a guide. Just offshore from

SAND FALLS

Many scuba divers come to Cabo San Lucas hoping to see the unusual sand falls—rivers of sand flowing between rocks and over the edge of a canyon wall beginning 30 meters below the surface. The sand falls lie within the national marine preserve, close to Playa del Amor.

The Scripps Institute of Oceanography first discovered the phenomenon in 1960, and Jacques Cousteau later made the sand falls famous in his television series.

Divers should note that the sand rivers typically run in stormy weather; during extended periods of calm seas, when diving conditions are otherwise best, you may not be able to see the falls in action. But there is plenty to see at the site, whether or not the sand is flowing. The canyon walls support marine life big and small. Graceful eagle rays, good-sized grouper, and tiny zebra eels are just a few of the sightings divers may experience on these dives.

this beach, **Pelican Rock** is another good snorkeling site, though given its proximity to the harbor, it can get crowded during the high season. Boats out of San Lucas make the trip to Bahías Chileno and Santa María on the Corridor for snorkeling and shallow diving, but you can also reach these sites yourself by car.

Guided scuba dives tour many of the same sites as snorkelers, making it convenient to accommodate mixed groups (but also making it more crowded, both above and below the surface). Also, given the proximity of these dive sites to the harbor, the loud and constant rumble of boat traffic overhead makes for an annoying distraction.

The most popular dive sites in the **Cabo San Lucas Marine Preserve** include Pelican Rock, Neptune's Finger, and the point at Land's End. Pelican Rock and Neptune's Finger begin at shallow depth (6-8 meters) and then descend over boulders or along a wall into a vast submarine canyon, as diver skill, air consumption, and visibility allow. All these dives take place in a protected marine preserve, an unusual feature to have so close to a town the size of Cabo San Lucas.

The **Land's End** dive begins in the surge under a sea lion colony on the bay side of the point and ends with an underwater swim around to the Pacific side, covering varied underwater topography along the way. Guitarfish, schooling amberjack, green sea turtles, and countless other species are likely to make an appearance on this dive.

Cabo San Lucas dive shops can also arrange trips to Cabo Pulmo on the East Cape for reef dives in a protected marine park and the Gordo Banks, where advanced divers with experience in deep dives and strong currents have the opportunity to view hammerheads, whale sharks, and giant mantas, among other pelagics. The dive usually circumnavigates the top of a seamount at a depth of about 41 meters.

Dive Guides and Outfitters

Just about any local resort or hotel can arrange guided dive trips and equipment rentals for their guests. Some have their own shops on-site, while others book through one of the many independent shops in town. Dive operators typically organize two outings per day, weather permitting. Morning boats leave the harbor around 9am, and the afternoon shift departs around 1pm. Mornings tend to be less crowded above and below the surface. In the afternoon, the wind kicks up and boat traffic increases, making water entries and exits a little trickier.

Manta (Blvd. Marina #7D Local 37 Int. Plaza Gali, tel. 624/144-3871, www.caboscuba.com) is a professionally run PADI shop conveniently located at Playa El Médano. Its custom-designed 35-foot boat holds 15 divers comfortably; additional 28-foot and 26-foot boats accommodate up to 10 divers each. All

© NIKKI GOTH ITOI

A diver is done for the day.

three boats are equipped with radios, first-aid kits, and oxygen. For local dives in the Cabo San Lucas Marine Preserve, advanced and novice divers often share the same boat but have separate dive guides, since easy and advanced dives start at the same points. (Experienced divers go deeper and stay under longer than beginner groups.) Knowledgeable boat captains and a friendly international guide staff make for a safe and enjoyable dive experience. An earlier morning start at 8:30am helps avoid the crowds. Rental gear is in good shape, with Sherwood regulators; Aqualung and Genesis BCDs; and Akona, Body Glove, and Scuba Pro wetsuits. In addition to standard 80-cft tanks, smaller (63 cft) and larger (100 cft) sizes are available. A two-tank dive costs US$90. The office has moved from Camino de los Pescadores to Boulevard Marina.

Sunshine Dive & Charter (tel. 624/105-1793, U.S. tel. 949/226-8987, www.divecabo.com) is another reputable shop in the Plaza Marina.

Local dive instructors prefer PADI-certified **Eagle Divers** (Plaza Embarcadero Local 3, tel. 624/125-0008, www.eagledivers.com) for advanced diving. A trip to Gordo Banks runs US$165. This shop also offers scuba courses for kids aged eight and older.

Live-Aboards

Amigos del Mar (tel. 624/143-0505, fax 624/143-0887, toll-free U.S. tel. 800/344-3349), next to Solmar Fleet on the west side of the harbor, arranges luxury live-aboard dive trips to the Socorro Islands, Guadalupe Island, Gordo Banks, Los Frailes, El Bajo, Cabo Pulmo, and other more remote sites aboard the 112-foot *Solmar V* (www.solmarv.com, US$1,795/eight days). The boat holds a maximum of 22 divers and 10 staff members.

Snorkel Tours
DOWNTOWN AND THE MARINA

Pez Gato (Camino del Cerro 215, El Pedregal, tel. 624/143-3797, www.pezgatocabo.com, tours 10am-2pm daily, US$49) organizes four-hour sail and snorkeling tours to Bahía Santa María, along the Corridor, aboard one of three catamarans. The tour includes two hours of water exploration at Santa María, plus lunch and cold drinks. Kids under 12 are free.

SunRider Adventure (tel. 624/143-2252, U.S. tel. 619/240-8669, www.sunridertours.com, US$60, kids under 10 free) has three boats and prepares Mexican buffet meals onboard. A snorkeling lunch tour to Playa Santa María for US$55 per person includes the buffet and an open bar. Cash only.

Equipment

Most dive shops rent snorkel and dive equipment in packages or à la carte, so if you forget your fins or your mask strap breaks, you'll be able to borrow a replacement for the day. Repairs are a different story, however. If you're bringing your own gear, have it serviced before you leave home; check your computer batteries and bring spare parts. Despite the number of dive shops, replacement parts are difficult, if not impossible, to come by in Baja.

Recompression

Clínica de Especialidades (López Mateos btwn. Morelos and Vicario, tel. 624/143-3914 or 624/143-2919) has a hyperbaric recompression chamber that is available to recreational divers for emergencies.

SURFING AND STAND-UP PADDLING (SUP)

Cabo San Lucas proper is not a surf destination, though the action isn't far away by car. In summer there is surf along the Corridor, and in winter the closest waves are north along the Pacific near Todos Santos.

Playa El Médano

Stand-up paddling rentals and instruction are available from several stands along Playa El Médano.

KAYAKING
Playa El Médano

Playa El Médano is calm enough most of the time for launching kayaks easily, and you can rent from vendors along the beach for US$10 per person per hour or US$50 for a half day.

The water is calmest in the morning, and it takes about 40 minutes to get to Playa del Amor, so it's best to get an early start. Beware of larger watercraft on the bay, and if you are a beginning paddler, stick close to the beach, regardless of the conditions.

BOATING
Downtown and the Marina

The **Cabo San Lucas Marina** (Lote A-18 de la Dársena, tel. 624/173-9140, www.igy-cabo-sanlucas.com) is now owned by Island Global Yachting, a company that develops and manages luxury marinas around the world. Its 380 slips line the inner harbor and can accommodate yachts up to 200 feet in length. Services include 24-hour security, wireless Internet, and a desalination plant for water. There is a swimming pool, laundry facilities, hot showers, storage, a two-lane boat ramp, and a state-of-the-art fuel dock with both diesel and gasoline. The on-site boatyard and 75-ton lift can handle just about any standard repair. Rates are US$340 per week or US$1,250 per month for a 20-foot boat, and up to US$2,814 per week or US$10,325 per month for a 79-foot boat. Reservations are accepted online. Office hours are 9am-5pm Monday-Saturday, 10am-3pm Sunday.

Cabo San Lucas offers a greater variety of shops, restaurants, and services within walking distance of the marina than the new Puerto Los Cabos marina at La Playita near San José. As an official port of entry into Mexico, Cabo San Lucas has a **port captain's office** (Calle Matamoros at 16 de Septiembre).

Cape Marine (Plaza Marina, Local J2-3, tel. 624/143-4970, www.capemarinecabo.com, 8am-6pm Mon.-Sat.) carries hardware, apparel, yachting supplies and tools, and fishing equipment. Credit cards are accepted.

CRUISES
Playa El Médano

An abundance of glass-bottomed tour boats depart frequently from the marina and from Playa El Médano 9am-4pm each day. The standard 45-minute tour costs US$8-12 per person and covers Pelican Rock, the famous Land's End arch, and the sea lion colony. For no extra charge, the crew will let passengers off at Playa del Amor near the arch; you can flag down any passing boat from the same fleet and catch a ride back to the marina later in the day. Be sure to see the boat you will board before you pay, as engines can be old and unreliable, and you may not get your money back if the trip is aborted due to engine failure. **Dos Mares** (tel. 624/143-4339) is one of the oldest fleet operators; **Esperanza's Fleet** (tel. 624/144-4666, US$12 or US$22 with snorkeling gear rental) is another option, with four large glass-bottomed *panga* boats.

Downtown and the Marina

A handful of larger boats head out of the harbor in the late afternoon to catch the sunset over the Pacific Ocean. The usual route is to head out to the arch and around the point, up as far as the Solmar and Pueblo Bonito hotels. These sunset cruises usually include all the beer and margaritas you can drink, which can make for an entertaining boat ride. You can make reservations directly through the cruise companies or at any hotel in town (for no extra charge).

The all-the-margaritas-you-can-drink sunset cruise aboard one of the **Pez Gato** catamarans (Camino Del Cerro 215, El Pedregal, tel. 624/143-3797, www.pezgatocabo.com, Mon.-Sat.) is a memorable experience. The tunes are all from the 1980s—from Toto and Abba to Bon Jovi—and the crowd is a mix of older couples and families. A hardworking staff from the mainland sees that drinks are replenished and no one falls overboard. **Jungle Cruise Tours** (tel. 624/143-7530, US$45 pp) does a similar cruise, except it's adults-only. Boats leave from the marina at 6pm in spring and summer and 5pm in fall and winter.

A larger cruise ship, **Caborey** (Blvd. Marina, inside the Wyndham Cabo San Lucas Resort, tel. 624/143-8269, toll-free U.S. and Canada tel. 866/460-4105, www.caborey.com) runs a dinner cruise for US$92 per person and a margarita cruise with appetizers for US$55. Kids under 10 are half price.

Two modern-day pirate ships take passengers back to the days when the English stalked the Spanish Manila galleons from hiding spots behind the rocks at Land's End. The 29-meter **Buccaneer Queen** (Dock 1, Cabo San Lucas Marina, near the Hacienda Beach Club, tel. 624/144-4217, www.buccaneerloscabos.com, US$45-69 pp) races around the bay and heels like it's racing in the America's Cup (passengers must wear life preservers). Choose among the whale-watching, snorkeling, and sunset tours. The **Sunderland** (tel. 624/105-0177, www.the-cabopirateship.com) is a historic tall ship built in 1885. Tours are family friendly, except for the loud noise from the cannon.

WHALE-WATCHING
Downtown and the Marina
During the winter months, adult and juvenile gray whales entertain resort-goers all along the Los Cabos coast with their spouting and breaching. Many of the glass-bottom boat operators also offer whale-watching cruises to get you a little closer to the action; however, note that these are not the close encounters that you can have in the breeding grounds farther north. If you are determined to touch a whale, you'll need to head to Bahía Magdalena, Laguna San Ignacio, or Laguna Ojo de Liebre near Guerrero Negro.

In business for more than a decade, **Cabo Expeditions** (Blvd. Marina, Wyndham Cabo San Lucas Resort, tel. 624/143-2700, www.caboexpeditions.com.mx, US$85 pp) does a better job than most at training its staff in safety procedures and knowledge of marine life. Guides must be PADI-certified rescue divers with emergency response training. The organization is active in whale rescue, beach cleanup, and other local conservation programs. Tours on inflatable Zodiac boats depart at 8am, 10:30am, 1pm, and 3:30pm mid-December-mid-April. In addition to whale-watching, Cabo Expeditions offers snorkeling, parasailing, and some underwater experiences for non-certified divers: "snuba" (underwater helmet diving) and rides aboard a semisubmersible vessel, Cabo Submarine (painted bright yellow, of course). Look for the Cabo Expeditions office inside the Wyndham Cabo San Lucas Resort on the marina.

PERSONAL WATERCRAFT
Playa El Médano
On a calm day, a WaveRunner or Jet Ski can be a fast and fun way to explore the bay and Playa del Amor, and you don't have to be a speed demon to enjoy the ride. Vendors along Playa El Médano offer rentals for around US$40 per half hour.

FISHING
Downtown and the Marina
Fish counts may not be what they used to be a few decades ago, but recreational fishing remains a popular activity throughout the Los Cabos area, and Cabo San Lucas has the widest variety of charters and related services. The legendary Bisbee Tournament takes place each October, with thousands of boats on the bay. In

the peak season, hundreds of boats depart the Cabo San Lucas marina each morning in search of prized billfish (blue, black, and striped marlin and sailfish), plus tuna, wahoo, and dorado. It's not uncommon for boats to hook 1,000-pound marlin and multiple billfish in one outing. Depending on the season, you might also catch red snapper, yellowtail, sierra, jack crevalle, roosterfish, and grouper.

Cabo San Lucas boats report an average of almost one billfish per departure, and multiple catches are not unusual. Fortunately, the boats also report a high release rate (95 percent or better), meaning they return the fish to the water to fight another day. A universal system of flags reveals the action that took place on any given boat that day: A red flag with a T means the boat caught and released a billfish, while a blue triangular flag means the crew caught and killed a billfish. Boats may legally keep one billfish per boat, but most charter operations strongly discourage the practice.

For marlin fishing, captains generally head to San Jaime Banks, 29 kilometers southwest of Cabo Falso, or Golden Gate Banks, 31 kilometers west of Cabo Falso. Anglers frequently catch dorado and wahoo as well in these areas.

There are three ways to fish the waters near Cabo San Lucas: by cruiser (motorboat equipped with fish-finders, tackle, captain's chairs, and wells for live bait), in a *panga* (simple aluminum skiff), or from shore (surf casting).

SPORTFISHING CRUISERS

Numerous outfitters arrange sportfishing trips aboard cruisers (US$350/day on a 28-foot boat with up to four anglers; US$550/day on a 36-foot boat with up to six anglers). A few outfits charge extra for the license, gear, tax, and ice, but most include these items in the daily fee. Bait, however, always costs extra. **Pisces Fleet** (Blvd. Marina at Madero, tel. 624/143-1288, U.S. tel. 619/819-7983, www.piscessportfishing.com) is one of the oldest and most conservation-minded fishing operations in Cabo. It offers two different rates: Bareboat prices,

in which customers bring their own lunch and handle their own catch when they return, are US$445 for a 28-foot cruiser for up to four people, US$580 for a 31-foot Bertram for up to six people, and US$900 for a 31-foot Cabo Express (up to six people). The bareboat rate includes crew, ice, tackle, coffee, and sweet rolls before departure. All-inclusive packages add drinks, box lunches, fishing licenses, and live bait, plus filleting and freezing services for your catch. The fleet includes yachts of every size, all the way up to the 111-foot *Crystal* (US$9,500 for up to 12 anglers). Half-day rates are available for many boats.

After many years of fishing the Baja Peninsula from a home base in the United States, "Renegade" Mike moved to Cabo San Lucas, bought a 31-foot Bertram, and set it up the way he wanted to fish. He has earned a reputation for top-notch service and high-quality gear, including two-speed reels and bamboo gaffs, which he makes himself. Within his first few months of operation, Mike had completed several days of two-digit marlin releases. Contact him at **Renegademike Sportfishing Charters** (tel. 624/129-9581, U.S. tel. 619/591-8969, www.renegademikesportfishing.com, US$550/day).

Dream Maker Sportfishing (Locale 20, Wyndham Cabo San Lucas Resort, tel. 624/143-7266, www.dreammakercharter.com) leads five-hour and eight-hour trips with a fleet of nine boats that includes everything from a 22-foot *panga* (US$175/5 hours) to a 42-foot sportfisher (US$1,250 all-inclusive or US$1,050 boat only).

Located at the Bahía Hotel, **Gaviota Sportfishing** (toll-free U.S. tel. 800/932-5599, www.gaviotasportfishing.com) has experienced captains and 11 boats ranging from 26- to 36-foot cruisers. All-inclusive packages for four (US$755, including tax, or US$595 boat charter only) come with tackle, bait, lunch, and a case of beer, soda, or bottled water. The same package for two aboard a 26-foot cruiser is US$440 (US$360 boat charter only). Boats leave at 7am and return at 3pm.

If you don't want to contact an outfitter

directly, you can arrange guided fishing trips through any major hotel. A few, including the Solmar and Finisterra, run their own fleets.

First-timers are sometimes surprised and frustrated by the amount of time it takes before they actually have lines in the water. Getting bait, cruising out to the banks, and returning to the harbor are all part of the time that will be spent on a day of fishing. You can save time by buying bait in advance and requesting to fish destinations closer to shore.

PANGA FISHING

The most economical—and exhilarating—way to plan a Baja fishing adventure is to hire a local *panguero* for a few hours; however, options for these simple skiffs are limited in Cabo San Lucas, where most visitors prefer the luxury cruiser experience. The best bet is to head to La Playita near San José del Cabo. If you can find one, a day of *panga* fishing will cost around US$175 for five hours in a three-person, 22-foot boat. **Dream Maker Sportfishing** (Locale 20, Wyndham Cabo San Lucas Resort, tel. 624/143-7266, www.dreammakercharter. com) is one of a few outfitters that have a *panga* in their fleet. Typical catches include cabrilla, grouper, and sierra, but even marlin are possible with the right captain in the right place at the right time. Prices won't include rental gear or fishing licenses. Some will fillet the fish you catch for no additional cost. Be forewarned; if you happen to go out on a *panga* when the fish are on, you may well tire of the action long before your captain is ready to return to shore.

As one *panguero* told us in the midst of a prolonged fishing frenzy, "When the fish are here, you fish!"

BAIT, TACKLE, AND FISH PROCESSING

Minerva's Baja Tackle (Blvd. Marina at Madero, tel. 624/143-1282, www.minervas.com, 9am-7pm Mon.-Sat.), next door to Pisces Fleet, carries a wide selection of gear and tackle for your fishing adventure. It is also the designated Los Cabos representative to the International Game Fish Association (IGFA).

You can buy fresh bait at the docks along the marina for a few dollars and hire local pros to clean and fillet your catch. Another option for cleaning, processing, vacuum-packing, and freezing is **Gricelda's Smokehouse** (Loc. 19 and 20 in the Tesoro Hotel complex, tel. 624/143-7266, www.dreammakercharter.com) on the marina.

Pacific Beaches
SURF CASTING

If you want to fish without parting with the cash for a full day aboard a cruiser, you might try casting into the surf from shore. You don't need a license, and your catch might include sea bass, sierra, and red snapper. Playa Solmar offers the best conditions, but it is a dangerous location because of the strong undertow. Sleeper waves often strike here, catching even the most experienced anglers off guard. A safer place to try is the old pier at the entrance to the harbor. Fishing is permitted at the northeast end of Playa El Médano.

Adventure Sports and Tours

PLAYA EL MÉDANO
Horseback Riding

Several stables offer horseback tours along Playa El Médano and into the mountains nearby. The going rate is about US$30 per hour. **Red Rose (La Rosa) Riding Stables** (Carr. Transpeninsular km 4, across from Cabo San Lucas Country Club, tel. 624/143-4826) offers custom trips and lessons. **Rancho Collins** (Camino Viejo a San José, tel. 624/143-3652, 8am-noon and 2pm-6pm daily), across from Club Cascadas, has 45 horses that are healthy and in good shape. Look for a pretty palomino near the road or book through your hotel.

Skydiving and Parasailing

Look for **Skydive El Sol** (tel. 624/129-7173, www.skydiveelsol.com, daily year-round), a relative newcomer to Cabo San Lucas, near Club Cascadas on Playa El Médano. The going rate is US$250 for a tandem jump that includes one minute of free-fall time. Plan on a two-hour outing from start to finish. For an additional US$130, you can return home with a video and photographs of the entire experience. Skydive El Sol needs at least two jumpers to book a trip.

The **Caborey** luxury cruise ship (tel. 624/143-8260, www.caborey.com) offers parasailing trips at a rate of US$35 for an 8- to 10-minute ride.

Organized Tours

Most of the outfitters in Los Cabos service the entire region (Cabo San Lucas, the Corridor, and San José del Cabo) and specialize in more than one activity. For example, **High Tide Los Cabos** (Arambura s/n Zazata, San José del Cabo, tel. 624/142-0424, www.hightideloscabos.com) offers a three-hour kayak tour of El Arco (US$70), a guided snorkel tour around the bays of Los Cabos (US$70), a day of surf lessons at Cerritos (US$120), and a day-long Jeep tour of Todos Santos (US$415 for three people). **Cabo Adventures** (U.S. tel. 888/526-2238, www.cabo-adventures.com) also organizes a long list of activities and tours, including desert mountain biking rides. **Rancho Tours** (tel. 624/143-5464, www.ranchotours.com) leads walking tours of La Paz and Todo Santos for US$69 per person, as well as glass-bottom boat tours and ATV rides near Cabo San Lucas.

PACIFIC BEACHES
ATVs

When you've had enough of the water, you might begin to explore the area's kilometers of open beaches and inland attractions via ATV (not permitted near swimming or turtle-nesting areas). A number of outfitters offer these tours, and any hotel or activity stand along the marina can make a reservation. Current prices are around US$60 per person single or US$80 double. **Camino Aventura** (tel. 624/143-2050, www.caminoaventura.mx) has locations at the Hilton, Tesoro, and Villas de Palmar hotels, plus an outpost on Highway 19 on the way to Playa Migriño. It allows two riders per ATV at a discounted rate. **Amigos Moto Rental** (tel. 624/144-4161) rents ATVs for US$25 per hour or US$120 per day. Guided tours of Migriño Beach and/or Candelaria cost US$70-90 for a single rider.

Golf

PLAYA EL MÉDANO

Just beyond the Cabo San Lucas city limits (although not on the beach), the 300-hectare **Cabo San Lucas Country Club** (Carr. Transpeninsular km 3.7, tel. 624/143-4653 or 624/4653-4654, toll-free U.S. tel. 888/298-1132, www.golfincabo.com, US$79-200) is one of the more reasonably priced courses in Los Cabos. There are many other more exclusive and more expensive options along the Corridor.

PACIFIC BEACHES

Private courses have also drawn attention from world-class golfers. Ranked 58th in *Golf Magazine's* Top 100 Courses in the World and #1 course in Mexico by *Golf Digest,* **Diamante** (beachfront, tel. 624/172-5811, www.diamantecabosanlucas.com, US$305 for 18 holes) is home to The Dunes Course, an 18-hole, par-72 course that combines desert, dunes, and ocean with a challenging course and a steep price tag. Diamante also broke ground in 2012 on a brand-new course designed by Tiger Woods, to be named El Cardonal.

Spas and Yoga

DOWNTOWN AND THE MARINA

The **Marina Fiesta Spa** (Blvd. La Marina, Lotes 37 y 38, tel. 624/145-6020, www.marinafiestaresort.com/spa_reservation.php) at the Marina Fiesta Resort & Hotel offers a full-service spa menu, featuring massages (US$90-175 for 50 minutes), body treatments (US$60-120), facial treatments (US$60-100), beauty salon services (US$10-60), and waxing (US$20-60).

Aura Spa at the Wyndham Cabo San Lucas Resort (Blvd. Marina s/n, tel. 624/173-9300 or 800/716-8770, toll-free U.S. tel. 800/543-7556, www.wyndham.com) is a basic but full-service spa offering massages, aromatic facials, body wraps, and beauty salon services.

PLAYA EL MÉDANO

The ME Cabo resort's **YHI Spa** (Playa El Médano, tel. 624/145-7800, toll-free U.S. tel. 800/336-3542, www.me-cabo.com, 9am-9pm) offers *temazcal* (sweat lodge), massage, yoga, and hydrotherapy services.

Casa Dorada's **Saltwater Spa** (Pescador s/n, tel. 624/163-5757, www.casadorada.com, toll-free U.S. tel. 866/448-0151) offers a full menu of massage and body treatments with products from Pevonia Botanica.

At Villa del Arco you can find the **Desert Spa** (Camino Viejo a San Jose km 0.5), which features a traditional Mexican hacienda-style design. Massages here cost US$103 for 50 minutes and US$136 for 80 minutes. Eye treatments and facials range US$66-146, while body scrubs and treatments price at US$66-136. Waxing and beauty services are also available, as well as services tailored specifically to men.

Cabo Mind Body Fitness (www.cabovillas. com) offers Pilates and Bikram yoga sessions in the privacy of your own villa, but prices are correspondingly steep: Pilates sessions run US$125-225 per person per hour (or US$45 pp per hour for groups of seven or more). Yoga classes cost US$110-160 per person per hour (or US$30 pp for groups of 10 or more). Discounts apply for pairs and triples, too, so it pays to buddy up.

PACIFIC BEACHES

The **Armonia Spa** (Cabo Pacifica, tel. 624/142-9696, toll-free U.S. tel. 800/990-8250, www.pueblobonitopacifica.com) at the

Pueblo Bonito Pacifica resort offers 50-minute massage treatments for US$110. Choices include hot stone, Shiatsu, four-hands, deep-tissue, Swedish, and pregnancy massage. Located in the basement of the hotel, the spa setting is a bit cave-like but quiet and peaceful, with a friendly and professional staff. To find the resort and spa, follow the main street through Cabo San Lucas (Lázaro Cárdenas), past the plaza and up the hill. The road will curve to the right and back to the left, and the name will change to Boulevard Herrera. Keep going up the hill about a kilometer and a half until you reach a stop sign with the Pueblo Bonito entrance and sign on the left. Currently, the sign says Pueblo Bonito Sunset Beach, but this is also the entrance for the Pueblo Bonito Pacifica.

Auriga Spa at Capella Pedregal (Camino del Mar 1, tel. 624/163-4300, www.capella-hotels.com/cabosanlucas) is a state-of-the-art 10,000-square-meter facility with ocean views and four signature treatments that correspond to the lunar phases. Other services include a range of massage styles, body therapies, facial treatments, and manicures/pedicures. A 90-minute treatment here averages US$280.

The Sea Spa at the Grand Solmar Land's End Resort & Spa (Av. Solmar 1-A, tel. 624/145-7575, spagrandsolmar@solmar.com) is another option for relaxation and premium ocean views.

Sights

DOWNTOWN AND THE MARINA
◖ Cabo San Lucas Marina

Much of the Los Cabos tourist activity takes place at or near the Cabo San Lucas Marina and along a wide boulevard that wraps around the harbor. The most popular bars and restaurants are clustered here along the waterfront. You can hire water taxis and book all kinds of recreational tours from the many vendors who compete aggressively for your business. Many snorkeling tours and sunset cruises depart from the main dock, located on the southwest side of the marina, near the mouth of the inner harbor.

Several plazas along the marina contain cafés, shops, and service businesses. At the north end of the harbor, the **Puerto Paraíso** is a three-level shopping center with a cinema, bowling alley, art galleries, boutiques, and American food chains such as Häagen-Dazs and Johnny Rockets. Plaza Bonita has an outdoor coffee stand and Internet café.

The Wyndham Cabo San Lucas Resort, with its labyrinth of hallways and passages, occupies a long stretch of the marina on the southwest side of harbor. Nearby, the US$40 million **Pabellón Cultural de la República,** or Cultural Pavilion, opened in 2011 with great fanfare. To date, the center has hosted musical performances, theater productions, and a few movie screenings during the Baja International Film Festival. A museum and parking structure are in the future plans.

A gray five-story cinderblock building remains an unfortunate eyesore on Boulevard Marina. It was abandoned in the late 1980s and has been in an ownership dispute ever since.

On busy days, multiple cruise ships shuttle thousands of passengers into this downtown area. They wander the streets looking for souvenirs and familiar shops like Diamonds International. But at day's end, they return to their cabins, leaving the nightlife to those who've arrived by air and car.

◖ Plaza Amelia Wilkes

Set back a few blocks from the tourist corridor, the original town plaza (btwn. Hidalgo and Av. Cabo San Lucas, cross streets Madero and Lázaro Cárdenas) has a pretty gazebo and several benches where you can enjoy a break from the frenzy at the marina. The plaza hosts various festivals, often with live music and dancing.

It is also home to a small natural history museum, **Museo de Historia Natural Cabo San**

the new Pabellón Cultural de la República

Lucas (tel. 624/105-0661, mcsl@loscabos.gob. mx, 10am-2pm Mon., 10am-7pm Tues.-Fri., 10am-2pm and 4pm-8pm Sat., 10am-8pm Sun.), that has been open since 2006. Exhibits in seven different rooms cover the astronomy, geology, paleontology, archaeology, biodiversity, and history of the region. In one quick visit, you'll learn about plate tectonics, the Pericú, the Jesuit missions, and the flood of 1939. Admission is by donation.

Across from the plaza on Avenida Cabo San Lucas is the unassuming Iglesia de San Lucas, which dates back to the 18th century and holds regular worship services today.

One boutique hotel (Casa Bella), a popular coffee shop, and several trendy restaurants line the streets surrounding the plaza.

PACIFIC BEACHES
◖ Finisterra (Land's End)
You know you've reached the end of the road in Baja when the towering granite rock formations and signature arch at Finisterra, or Land's End, come into view. Just about every tour boat that departs the Cabo San Lucas Marina heads to the 62-meter El Arco to stage a postcard-perfect photo op. In most conditions, the boat captain can pull right up to the arch. On rare, exceptionally low tides, sand appears under the arch and you can walk through the passage. Nearby rocks host a colony of sea lions, while pelicans congregate at the Roca Pelicano, a popular snorkeling and scuba diving site.

If you're the sort of traveler who avoids the well-beaten tourist path, consider making an exception for this sight. It's generally not as crowded as you might expect, and the dramatic effect of sunlight dancing on the cliffs and wildlife playing in the sea spray is truly spectacular.

view from Plaza Amelia Wilkes

© NIKKI GOTH ITOI

Shopping

The streets of Cabo are chockablock with places to buy souvenirs, apparel, fine art, tequila, cigars, and more. Upscale shops line the Plaza Fiesta, near the Marina Fiesta hotel, and most of the luxury stores inside the Puerto Paraíso mall are open for business.

DOWNTOWN AND THE MARINA
Arts, Crafts, and Souvenirs

Across from the main dock, the **Marina Mercado** (Cabo San Lucas Marina, Lot 4, 9am-5pm daily) is an arts and crafts market with dozens of vendors selling embroidered dresses, carved ironwood figures, ceramics, and jewelry. Sellers expect to bargain. Inquire about prices at several places before you decide to buy.

Taxco (Guerrero and Blvd. Marina, tel. 624/143-0551, 9am-6pm daily) has a good selection of silver jewelry. **Joyería Alberto** (Matamoros btwn. Niños Héroes and Lázaro Cárdenas, no tel., 9am-6pm daily) is a satellite of a well-regarded Puerto Vallarta jeweler.

Dos Lunas (Plaza Bonita and Puerto Paraíso locations, tel. 624/143-1969, 9am-6pm daily) has pretty sundresses, handbags, and the like, and **Cartes** (Plaza Bonita, tel. 624/143-1770, 9am-9pm Mon.-Sat., 9am-4pm Sun.) carries rustic furniture, Talavera pottery, and classy accents for the home.

Across from Mi Mariscos restaurant at the corner of Paseo a la Marina and Camino Viejo a San José, **Chile & Anis** (tel. 624/143-7454, 9am-8pm Mon.-Sat.) is a Baja arts and crafts store with silver jewelry, wood crafts, mirrors, and ceramics for sale. Upscale crafts line the shelves of **Mi Mexico Magico** (Loc. 52, tel. 624/143-5153, 8am-9pm daily) in the Marina Fiesta plaza.

Just across the street from Maro's Shrimp

THE PERICÚ

The Pericú were the first inhabitants of the Los Cabos area. They were a nomadic people whose territory extended from Cabo San Lucas to San José and up to Cabo Pulmo on the East Cape. Early Spanish explorers took interest in the vicinity of San José del Cabo when they discovered freshwater in the Río San José. While the Spanish set up camp near San José, favoring its protected estuary and abundant freshwater, English pirates, including Francis Drake and Thomas Cavendish, dominated the cape and bay at San Lucas. In a major blow to the Spanish, Cavendish captured, looted, and sank the 600-ton Manila galleon *Santa Ana* in 1578, in the same waters where modern cruisers troll for game fish.

The Pericú proved to be less tolerant of the Spanish than neighboring tribes to the north had been. Following a series of uprisings in the 1720s, Jesuit priest Nicolas Tamarál came from La Purísima in 1930 to establish a permanent mission and military outpost that would guard the estuary from further attacks by pirates and indigenous people. He planted orchards and moved the mission site around a few times before settling on the current town center, which afforded views of the harbor without all the bugs.

Padre Tamarál baptized more than 1,000 Pericú in the first year of the mission, but peace lasted only until 1734, when the Pericú rebelled once again, this time to protest a Spanish decree against polygamy. They burned four missions in Southern Baja and killed Tamarál in the battle.

Few of the Pericú remained by 1767, when the Jesuits were expelled from Baja California. But the mission persevered under the Dominicans. In the following decades, the Spanish built a garrison at San José, turning the mission into a military outpost that resupplied the Manila galleons on their way to and from the Philippines. To learn more about the earliest settlers of the area, visit the Museo de Historia Natural Cabo San Lucas.

House on Hidalgo is **Casanova** (tel. 624/144-4534 or 624/172-0498), offering a large selection of jewelry, including diamonds, tanzanite, rubies, and emeralds set in a variety of metals, from 14-carat gold to platinum.

Fine-Art Galleries

In the lobby of the Wyndham Cabo San Lucas Resort, a **photography gallery** (U.S. tel. 831/480-4411) displays prints by Tomas Spangler (www.fotomas.com), whose work depicts images and scenes unique to the Baja Peninsula. A representative is available 10am-2pm Monday-Saturday.

Golden Cactus Gallery (Guerrero and Madero, tel. 624/147-5287, www.goldencactus-gallery.com) features the works of artist Chris MacClure in a second-story studio. MacClure's work captures local Baja imagery, and he has created commissioned paintings of yachts, airplanes, and the like for celebrity clients, including John Travolta.

Cigars

Many stores sell Cuban cigars in Los Cabos, but fakes are rampant. Buy from a reputable merchant if you want the real thing. And remember; Cubans never go on sale. **La Casa del Habano** (formerly J&J Habanos, Blvd. Marina near Madero, tel. 624/143-6160 or 877/305-6242, www.jnjcabo.com) has a walk-in humidor and a few tables inside. Prices are steep, but you can be confident that you're getting what you pay for.

Wine and Liquor

La Europea (tel. 624/145-8755, 9am-8pm Mon.-Fri., 9am-9pm Sat.) has opened a small street-level store in the Puerto Paraíso complex. This satellite of the larger main store on the Corridor has the best selection and competitive prices on wines from around the world, plus a fairly complete list of liquors and gourmet foods. It's also a great place to grab a sandwich for lunch.

Sporting Goods

Head to **Cabo Sports Center** (Plaza Náutica, tel. 624/143-4272, 9am-7pm daily) for beach gear, water shoes, and basic supplies for golf, swimming, surfing, snorkeling, boogie-boarding, and mountain biking. **Minerva's Baja Tackle** (Blvd. Marina at Madero, tel. 624/143-1282, 9am-7pm Mon.-Sat.), next door to Pisces Fleet, is the one-stop shop for lures and tackle.

Books and Magazines

Cabo San Lucas does not have a dedicated English-language bookstore; however, several shops in town stock a few titles. They include **Minerva's Baja Tackle** (Blvd. Marina at Madero, tel. 624/143-1282, www.minervas.com) for fishing books and **Bahías Jiromar** (Puerto Paraíso Local 284, tel. 624/144-3250) for newspapers, magazines, and some books. In addition, most of the larger resorts carry at least a few pocket fiction titles in their gift shops.

Shopping Mall

Upscale **Puerto Paraíso** (tel. 624/144-3000, www.puertoparaiso.com, 9am-10pm), a shopping mall on the east side of the marina, is the first of its kind in Southern Baja. Most stores are now open, and the mall contains a mix of luxury boutiques, international chains, and entertainment venues. You'll find everything from Sergio Bustamante artwork to Diamonds International and many familiar brands, such as Tumi, Kenneth Cole, and Nautica. There is even a Curves exercise center. Food options include Ruth's Chris Steak House, Häagen-Dazs, Houlihan's, and Johnny Rockets. There is also a bowling alley on the third level. Clean public restrooms and inexpensive underground parking are added conveniences.

Nightlife and Entertainment

With an emphasis on booze and music, Cabo nightlife begins early and ends late. On any given night, there are dozens of options for entertainment. The drinking begins at the bars along the marina and moves to the dance clubs around midnight. The clubs stay open until 3 or 4am, at which point the party moves to any hotel that will tolerate the noise.

DOWNTOWN AND THE MARINA
Bars

One of the most famous bars in Cabo is the **Giggling Marlin** (Matamoros at Blvd. Marina, tel. 624/143-0606, www.gigglingmarlin.com), with a nightly dance show and signature block-and-tackle hoist from which well-imbibed patrons hang upside down like hooked marlins.

Among the row of bars and restaurants along the marina in Plaza Bonita, **The Nowhere Bar** (tel. 624/143-4493, www.nowherebar.com, 11am-1am daily, margaritas US$5) is a popular stop, especially during March Madness NCAA basketball championships. At happy hour (5pm-9pm), you'll get two drinks (served in glasses, not plastic) for the price of one, whether you need them or not.

Rips Bar & Grill, located in front of Cabo Wabo (Plaza del los Mariachis, ripsbar@gmail.com) is famous for its line of rainbow shots. **Cabo Lounge** on Boulevard Marina (tel. 624/116-2238) is popular with locals and known for its flaming Cabo Fire Shot.

Friday is tango night at super-chic **Barometro** (tel. 624/143-1466, 10pm-2am daily) on the Plaza Marina.

At two-story **Desperados Restaurant and Cantina** (Morelos at Niños Heroes, tel. 624/143-4331, 1pm-midnight Mon.-Thurs., 1pm-3am Fri., 1pm-4am Sat., 1pm-11pm Sun., mains US$10-30) you can watch whatever sports event happens to draw the biggest crowd that day. On Saturday nights a Latin rock band called La Flaca plays 10:30pm-2:30am. Pay a US$12 cover and your cervezas cost just 1 peso each the rest of the night.

Dance Clubs

Cabo's discos are empty before 11pm and packed from midnight on. Among them all, none embodies the party-till-you-drop Cabo spirit better than **El Squid Roe** (Lázaro Cárdenas at Zaragoza, tel. 624/143-0655, noon-3am daily). Giant margaritas and piña coladas appear two at a time to set the mood. Balloons and confetti fall from the sky, while staff and patrons climb on tables, form 50-person centipedes, and whoop it up on the dance floor.

Rock-and-roll music artist Sammy Hagar often celebrates his birthday by performing at the club he owns, **Cabo Wabo** (Guerrero btwn. Madero and Lázaro Cárdenas, tel. 624/143-1188, www.cabowabo.com, 7pm-2am daily). Open since 1992, the club plays recorded and live music. Hagar often makes a New Year's Eve appearance as well.

The space that was once Zoo Bar and Club is now the ultra-trendy and very sexy **Pink Kitty Nightclub** (Blvd. Marina and Cárdenas, 624/182-4914, www.thepinkkittycabo.com). Its modern baroque boudoir setting involves Italian blown glass chandeliers, moray eelskin leather seating, and an all-female staff. The club draws a crowd and tends to alternate between Top 40 and electronic music. This is one of the more upscale nightclubs in Cabo, so don't expect to get in wearing jeans and a T-shirt. Thursday is locals' night, featuring two-for-one drinks and bottles 9pm-midnight.

Mandala Nightclub (Cárdenas between Morelos and Zaragoza, tel. 624/158-8233) thinks of itself as "Las Vegas in Cabo." With its light-up dance floors, flashing LED lights, and heavily techno/electronic music, Mandala ensures a sensory overload. Drinks here are among the most expensive of the Cabo clubs.

At **Mambo Café** (Blvd. Marina, tel. 624/143-1484), the Caribbean-style decor and music were imagined from a fusion of classical tropical melodies and newer Latin pop. Tiered seating gives way to an enormous dance floor. This place is high energy, and serious dancers make their way here to put on as much of a show as the live music. Thursday night is ladies' nights, and women drink free 9pm-11pm.

Cabo's first alternative club, **The Rainbow Bar** (Marina Cabo Plaza, tel. 624/143-1455, daily 4pm till late, closed July-Sept.), has catered to a primarily gay crowd for more than a decade but welcomes all. Known for techno/disco music, Magic Mango Margaritas, and scantily-clad staff, the club is a fun place to experience a diverse crowd.

Cinema

On the second floor of the Puerto Paraíso mall, **Cinema Paraíso** (Cabo Bello at Gómez Farais, tel. 624/143-1515), with 10 theaters, shows a mix of blockbusters and independent films from Mexico, the United States, and elsewhere around the world. The VIP area has comfortable reclining leather seats.

Festivals and Events

Bike races, fishing tournaments, golf tournaments, music festivals, and national holidays are just a few of the gatherings that take place in Cabo San Lucas each year. Baja.com (www.

WABORITA, THE SIGNATURE CABO WABO DRINK

The signature Cabo Wabo drink looks like a tropical fish—blue on the bottom and green on top. Here's how to make one when you get home:

- 1 oz. tequila
- ½ oz. Damiana liqueur
- ½ oz. orange liqueur
- ½ oz. lime juice

Shake and serve straight up with a dash of blue curaçao.

© LAUREN SWIFT

Playa El Médano

baja.com) has the most up-to-date listing of events online.

The annual **Stars and Stripes Fishing & Golf Tournament** (www.starsandstripestournament.com) takes place in June and raises money for children in Mexico and the United States. This is a family-friendly event, and the fun continues well into the night. Performers such as Super Diamond provide the Friday night entertainment. The largest of the fishing tournaments is **Bisbee's Black and Blue Marlin Jackpot Tournament** (tel. 624/143-1622, www.bisbees.com), held for three days each October.

The **San Lucas Fiesta** takes place on October 18 and includes a traditional mix of music, dancing, crafts, and foods.

PLAYA EL MÉDANO
Bars and Dance Clubs
Several beachfront clubs play DJ tunes and lead willing participants in silly drinking games most of the day and night. The scene can get quite ridiculous at times. You'll find this crowd congregating at places like **The Office** (Playa El Médano at Camino Pescadores, tel. 624/143-3464, lunch and dinner daily) and **Medano Beach Club** (Playa Médano, next to ME Cabo, tel. 624/143-6554, www.themedanobeachclub-cabo.com, US$20-35).

The ME Cabo is home to the popular **Passion Club and Lounge** (Playa Médano, 624/145-7800, 10pm-4am Thurs.-Sat.), featuring international DJ music. The club is right on Playa El Médano, underneath the resort, so when the time comes to move the party inside, this is often the first choice. Music features house and dance mixes to complement the vibrant color scheme and sultry decorations. Note that resort guests get in for free, but for non-guests the cover can climb up to US$20, one of the most expensive in town. Ladies drink free on Thursday night.

For sunset views, head to the newest outpost of the **Baja Brewing Co.** (tel. 624/143-9199, noon-11pm daily), atop the Cabo Villas resort, on Camino de los Pescadores, a short walk up from Playa El Médano. Artisanal beers on tap

© NIKKI GOTH ITOI

Baja Brewing Co. at Puerto Paraíso

are made of water, barley, yeast, and hops—about as simple as it gets, and a most unusual find in Southern Baja. There is live music on Monday, Thursday, and Saturday. Order from a menu of pub fare. The hamburger buns are made fresh daily on-site.

The beachfront *palapa* bar at **Hacienda Cocina Y Cantina** (Calle Gomez Farias s/n, tel. 624/163-3144, www.haciendacocina.com, Mon.-Sat. 7:30am-10pm, Sun. 7:30am-1pm, drinks US$4-11) serves *micheladas* (a beer drink), mojitos, and margaritas. There are also a few wines by the glass and a couple of *agua frescas* for a non-alcoholic option.

For nightly jazz music, try **Edith's** (tel. 624/143-0801, www.edithscabo.com, 6pm-1am daily), a block from Playa El Médano, on the west side of Camino de los Pescadores.

PACIFIC BEACHES
Bars
Each of the resorts on the Pacific side has a bar or lounge where you can relax with a cocktail and enjoy the ocean views. Bartenders at **Capella Pedregal** (Camino del Mar, tel. 624/163-4300) mix creative tropical drinks. Try the signature Capella Sling.

Food

Cabo San Lucas offers a wide range of culinary delights, including some world-class dining; however, many of its restaurants are expensive tourist-oriented establishments, rather than authentic local eateries. You'll have to venture away from the marina district to find enjoy real Mexican food at uninflated prices.

DOWNTOWN AND THE MARINA
Mexican
Platters heaped with Mexican delights arrive family style at **(Hacienda Cocina Y Cantina** (Calle Gomez Farias s/n, tel. 624/163-3144, www.haciendacocina.com, Mon.-Sat. 7:30am-10pm, Sun. 7:30am-1pm, mains US$13-27). Starters include a tuna *aguachile* (ceviche in a watery, chile-based broth), green ceviche, and crab flautas (fried, stuffed, and rolled tortillas) with mango Baja slaw and hibiscus sauce. Main dishes range from lobster enchiladas to *arrachera* and *molcajete* (stone bowl) of skirt steak and grilled chicken. This is beachfront dining at its best—excellent food and ocean views too.

Located in one of the oldest adobe buildings in town, **Mi Casa** (Av. Cabo San Lucas, opposite the plaza, tel. 624/143-1933, www.micasarestaurant.com, dinner 5:30pm-10:30pm daily, lunch noon-3pm Mon.-Sat., mains US$15-30) prepares authentic Mexican specialties, including *chile en nogada* (stuffed poblano chiles; a traditional Independence Day dish) and *cochinita pibil* (pork marinated in a strongly acidic citrus juice and roasted while wrapped in banana leaves) from the Yucatán.

The restaurant has its own tortilla station and makes its own *mole poblano* (a complex Mexican sauce made of more than 20 ingredients, featuring a combination of *ancho, pasilla, mulato,* or chipotle peppers) from scratch, and it takes a staff of 15 cooks to keep up with the demand. The ambience is festive, with hand-painted murals on the walls of an indoor/outdoor dining area, primary colors for chairs and tables, and mariachi groups passing through all evening long. The service and food quality seem to have improved of late.

The more contemporary **O Mole Mío** (Plaza del Sol, Blvd. Marina, tel. 624/143-7577, 11:30am-11pm daily, mains US$10-20) specializes in various kinds of chicken mole. An artist from Guadalajara designed the unique interior of the restaurant with glass and metal accents.

Join the locals at **La Perla** (Lázaro Cárdenas at Guerrero, no tel., 9am-4:30pm Mon.-Sat., mains US$4-5) for inexpensive and tasty burritos, enchiladas, *chilaquiles* (salsa or mole over crisp tortilla triangles), tacos, *licuados* (fruit smoothies), and *comida corrida* (fixed-price lunch; 1pm-4pm, US$5). Another option for real Mexican food is **Lonchería Lolita's** (Niños Héroes at Matamoros, tel. 624/143-6586, 7am-7:30pm Mon.-Sat., mains US$7-13), where you can order *huachinango* (red snapper) and *champurrado* (hot chocolate made with cornstarch).

Family-run **Las Gardenias** (Camino al Hacienda at Niños Heroes, no tel., 8am-5pm Tues.-Sun., tacos US$2, mains US$10-25) is a mainstay that attracts a loyal following of visitors and locals. Plastic tables and chairs and minimal decor put the emphasis on the food: tacos of nearly every kind, including *barbacoa* (lamb), *nopales* (cactus), *cochinita pibil* (slow-roasted pork) and the house specialty, shrimp *molcajete* served in a stone mortar.

Portions are large at **Pancho's Restaurant and Tequila Bar** (Hidalgo, off Blvd. Marina, tel. 624/143-0973, www.panchos.com, 7am-11pm daily, dinner mains US$18-40), but prices still seem high. Breakfast is a slightly better deal, and the bar pours hundreds of different kinds of tequila. English is spoken.

Tequila shrimp, made with the restaurant's own label, and lobster burritos are standout entrées at Sammy Hagar's **Cabo Wabo Restaurant** (Guerrero btwn. Madero and Lázaro Cárdenas, tel. 624/143-1188, www. cabowabo.com, 11am-11pm daily, mains

© NIKKI GOTH ITOI

Pancho's Restaurant and Tequila Bar, near Plaza Amelia Wilkes

US$17-28). Try the Waborita cocktail to start the meal off right. Downstairs, the Cabo Wabo Cantina serves a more casual menu.

Known for its signature salsa bar, which has some 20 different variations on the theme, **Felix** (Zapata and Hidalgo, tel. 624/143-4290, 4pm-10pm daily, mains US$15-20) began serving tacos and has expanded to a full menu of shrimp and traditional Mexican dishes, such as *posole* (hominy stew), over the years. The restaurant shares its indoor and outdoor space with Mama's Royal Café during the day.

Desperados Restaurant and Cantina (Morelos at Niños Heroes, tel. 624/143-4331, 1pm-midnight Mon.-Thurs., 1pm-3am Fri., 1pm-4am Sat., 1pm-11pm Sun., mains US$10-30) serves hearty fare with a Mexican/Tex-Mex theme. Free Wi-Fi makes this a good place to stop in for just a drink and some *botanas* (snacks). You can also watch whatever sports event happens to draw the biggest crowds that day.

Happily removed from the bustle of downtown, **❰ La Fonda** (Hidalgo btwn. Obregón and 12 de Octubre, tel. 624/143-6926, 1pm-10pm daily, mains US$10-30) serves some of the best traditional Mexican dishes in town. The menu features empanadas, *sopes* (traditional fried corn and meat dish), ceviche, chicken mole, *cochinita pibil* (slow-roasted pork), and, for adventurous eaters, some more exotic delights.

Seafood

Casual **❰ Mocambo de Los Cabos** (Vicario and 20 de Noviembre, tel. 624/143-6070, noon-10pm daily, mains US$10-20) has an extensive menu of seafood cocktails, plus fish and shellfish entrées, like a fish fillet gratin and a grilled *pargo* (snapper) fillet.

Try the *pescado zarandeado* (red snapper served whole in a tomato-based broth) or grilled fish *meniore* style (in a sauce of garlic, butter, white wine, and capers) at **Mariscos Mazatlán** (Mendoza and 16 de Septiembre, tel. 624/143-8565, 11am-10pm daily, mains US$10-15). The menu also includes 12 different preparations of shrimp. This restaurant has a second, less touristy location in San José del Cabo, on the west side of the Carretera Transpeninsular on the way to the airport.

Near the Ace Hardware store at the corner of Camino Real and Paseo de la Marina, **Mi Casa de Mariscos** (tel. 624/143-6898, salesmicasa@gmail.com, 1pm-10:30pm daily, mains US$13-29) has a raw bar with shrimp, scallops, and oysters; "barely touched" dishes like ceviche and seared fresh catch; and fully cooked entrées like *huachinango frito a la talla* (fried whole red snapper). The restaurant is located in a striking hacienda-style building, and it's owned by the same folks who operate Mi Casa.

Japanese and Mexican flavors meet at **Nick-San Restaurant** (Lte. 10, Blvd. Marina, tel. 624/143-4484, www.nicksan.com, 11:30am-10:30pm Tues.-Sun., mains US$20 and up), and sushi connoisseurs cannot rave enough about the results: tuna tostada, *pulpo* (octopus) carpacchio, cabrilla (sea bass) *misoyaki*, *hamachi* (yellowtail) curry, and

© NIKKI GOTH ITOI

seafood platter at Maro's Shrimp House

sashimi *serranito* are just a few examples. The restaurant ranks among the world's best in its class. Plan to spend about US$50-100 per person.

On the marina near the Marina Fiesta hotel, **Baja Lobster Co. Seafood Grill** (formerly El Shrimp Bucket, Blvd. Marina Locals 37-38, tel. 624/145-6011, 6am-11pm daily, mains US$10-20 and up) specializes in all things lobster: tacos, curry, pasta, salad, bisque, and more. At **The Shrimp Factory** (Blvd. Marina at Guerrero, tel. 624/143-5066, noon-11pm daily, mains US$10-20), you can order shrimp or lobster by the kilo (US$20-30 per half kilo)—served with bread, salad, and crackers—and go to town.

The shrimp and lobster combo (US$17) is the way to go at **Maro's Shrimp House** (Hidalgo btwn. Madero and Zapata, tel. 624/355-8060, mains US$14-20), where owner Maro and his high-energy staff greet a loyal clientele by name. Start with a bowl of tortilla soup; then order the fresh shellfish by the kilo and the house-special Bulldog, if you dare. The best dish for landlubbers is the sizzling *molcajete* (stone bowl) with slices of skirt steak or chicken (also available with excellent prawns). An excellent recent visit satisfied with buttery, tender lobster, delicious grilled shrimp, and sizable margaritas. For dessert, Maro's wife makes homemade coconut and chocolate ice cream as well as chocolate cake. This small open-air restaurant is easy to find across the street from La Dolce and Mama's Royal Café. A half kilo of medium-size shrimp costs US$14, and a half kilo of lobster is US$20.

On the marina next to Pisces Fleet and near the Tesoro Resort, **Captain Tony's** (tel. 624/143-6797, 6am-9:30pm daily, mains US$11-30) will cook your fresh catch. A bucket of five beers goes for US$10.

Owner Salvador Vidal opened the nautical themed **Lorenzillo's** (Marina Cabo San Lucas, tel. 624/105-0214, www.lorenzillos.com.mx, US$17-35) in 2003. Lobster arrives fresh daily from Lorenzillo's Lobster Farm, and the menu also includes fish, pasta, and steak options. Try the signature Xtabentun Flaming Coffee

Cocktail, made from a Yucatán liqueur of rum, anise, and fermented honey.

On the marina, family-oriented **Solomon's Landing** (tel. 624/143-3050, www.solomonslandingcabo.com, 7am-11pm daily, mains US$10-30), behind the Tesoro Hotel, prepares tasty shellfish entrées.

Argentinian

These days, the best steaks in town are grilled to order at the understated **◖ Patagonia** (5 de Mayo, tel. 624/143-3874, www.patagonia.freevar.com, 5pm-10:30pm Mon.-Sat., mains US$15-30), an Argentinian steakhouse located just a few blocks away from the main restaurant zone. The setting is no frills, and the food is top-notch—as in grass-fed beef and sweetbreads that rank among the best anywhere. Order a bottle of red wine or an ice-cold beer to wash it down.

Italian

On Plaza Amelia Wilkes, next to Mi Casa, **DOC Wine Bar** (Av. Cabo San Lucas btwn. Lázaro Cárdenas and Madero, tel. 624/143-8500, www.docwinebarcabo.com, 1pm-11pm Mon.-Sat., mains US$8-15) draws a crowd for wines by the glass and Italian fare.

Southern Italian defines the hearty cuisine at **Capo San Giovanni** (Guerrero at Madero, tel. 624/143-0593, www.caposangiovanni.com, 5pm-11pm Tues.-Sun., mains US$13-32). The restaurant is located roughly across from Cabo Wabo.

Salvatore's Italian Restaurant (Zapata btwn. Guerrero and Hidalgo, tel. 624/105-1044) serves up hearty lasagna, chicken parmesan, and osso buco in a courtyard setting. Large portions of American-style lasagna, reasonably priced, are a hit.

Spanish

Olé Olé (Plaza Bonita Loc. 3A, tel. 624/143-0633, 7am-11pm daily, mains US$15-40) faces the marina at Plaza Bonita. The large outdoor tapas bar features Spanish cuisine and dinner combos. Paella (US$22) is served from 1pm on Sunday (and sometimes on Friday).

Taquerías and Quick Bites

To find the local fast-food options, you need to venture away from the marina. Calles Morelos and Ocampo are good bets for tacos, *tortas* (Mexican sandwiches), seafood cocktails, and the like. The **Carnitas Los Michoacanos** chain has two locations in town (Vicario btwn. Carranza and Obregón, tel. 624/105-0713, and on Hwy. 19 across from Soriana, tel. 624/146-3565, www.losmichoacanos.com). For *tacos al pastor* (shepherd's style, served from a rotisserie grill), try **El Palacio del Taco** (16 de Septiembre btwn. Morelos and Vicario, cell 624/147-6894, 8:30am-3am daily).

Las Quesadillas (Blvd. Marina at Lázaro Cárdenas, tel. 624/143-1373, 7am-2am daily, mains US$6-13), opposite Arámburo Plaza, is a good bet for late-night dining.

In the plaza below Cabo Wabo, **Taco Loco** (Guerrero btwn. Madero and Lázaro Cárdenas, no tel.) serves bean, chicken, pork, and shrimp tacos for US$1 each. **La Luna** (Camino Real, tel. 624/105-0132, noon-10pm Tues.-Sat., noon-6pm Sun.), behind the Pueblo Bonito Rosé resort, serves wraps, burgers, and tacos.

Gordo Lele's (tel. 624/109-1778), on Calle Matamoros, does tacos with a twist: carne asada with tomatoes and corn mixed in, and a Beatles performance while you dine. Authentic it is not, but for most travelers, a meal here turns into a memorable experience.

Delis

You can order sandwiches at **La Europea** (no tel., 9am-8pm daily, mains US$5-12), just outside the Puerto Paraíso mall. There are a few tables out front, overlooking the marina. Air-conditioned booths are a comfortable place to grab a sandwich (and check your email with free Wi-Fi) at **Señor Greenberg's Mexicatessen** (tel. 624/143-5630, www.senorgreenbergs.com, 24 hours daily, mains US$5-12), which has several locations, including a new deli next to Johnny Rockets in the Puerto Paraíso mall.

Breakfast and Cafés

One of the best places to get breakfast in Cabo

San Lucas these days is **❮ Mama's Royal Café** (Hidalgo btwn. Zapata and Madero, tel. 624/143-4290, 7:30am-2pm daily, mains US$7-15). Brightly colored woven linens serve as tablecloths in this small indoor/outdoor café. Start with the signature mango mimosa, served in a giant sundae glass. Then move on to the traditional breakfast burrito or the chef's creative interpretation of *chilaquiles*, in which the tortillas are cut in strips instead of wedges and served with a medley of seasoned vegetables (avocado, mushrooms, spinach, and tomato) instead of smothered in sauce. The menu features exceptionally fresh ingredients. The only downside: no espresso drinks.

The English-speaking staff at the **Stop Light Bar and Grill** (Lázaro Cárdenas and Morelos, tel. 624/143-4740, breakfast, lunch, and dinner daily, mains US$6-19) serves a decent breakfast of eggs, pancakes, and *chilaquiles.* Portions are large, and cocktails are served in glasses, not plastic. Dinner fare includes ceviche, snails, sandwiches, salads, and enchiladas as well as lobster, steak, and pasta.

Starbucks has finally made an appearance in Cabo (Plaza Bonita), but so far, the cafés are holding their own. **Theory Café** (tel. 624/143-5518, from 10am daily, mains US$8-12), in the center of Plaza Bonita, serves lattes, mochas, and frappes, and plays music like the Red Hot Chili Peppers. Use your laptop or theirs for wireless Internet.

Cabo Coffee Company (Hidalgo and Madero, tel. 624/105-1130, www.cabocoffee.com, 6am-10pm daily) has expanded to a new Internet café with high-speed wireless connections, across from its original roasting facility. This is your stop for 100 percent organic brews. The Wi-Fi is free and the shop offers a wide range of reasonable beverages, pastries, and sandwiches. A satellite location is also available outside the **Giggling Marlin** (Matamoros at Blvd. Marina).

Among the many dockside restaurants by the marina, **Baja Cantina** (Dock L-M, tel. 624/143-1591, www.bajacantina.com.mx, mains US$7-15) serves tasty jalapeno poppers, artichoke and spinach dip, and other starters for US$5-8, as well as fish, burgers, and Mexican plates for dinner. Wireless Internet is a plus. Look for a second location at Playa El Médano near where Camino Pescadores ends at the beach (tel. 624/143-9773).

Café Cabo (Cardenas s/n Colonia Centro 6, tel. 624/144-4777, www.cafecabo.com.mx, 6:30am-10pm Thurs.-Tues.) has affordable beverages and breakfast and lunch items, English and Spanish newspapers, and reliable free Wi-Fi.

Groceries

Most visitors buy supplies for their Cabo San Lucas stay at **Soriana** (Mex. 19/Carr. Todos Santos and Calle Guajitos, tel. 624/105-1290, www.soriana.com), a Walmart-esque superstore, or at Costco on the Corridor. But there are some smaller options right in town that carry brands from Mexico and the United States. They include **Almacenes Grupo Castro** (southwest corner of Morelos and Revolución, tel. 624/143-0566), **Supermercado Sánliz** (three locations: Blvd. Marina at Madero, Ocampo at Matamoros, and Vicario at López Mateos), and **Supermercado Arámburo** (Arámburo Plaza, Lázaro Cárdenas at Zaragoza, tel. 624/143-1450). There is also a **Chedraui** (tel. 624/146-7200) on the east side of Highway 19, just north of the junction with the Carretera Transpeninsular and before the Soriana. On the east side of town, warehouse-style **City Club** (Blvd. Lázaro Cárdenas at Paseo del Pescador, tel. 624/143-9492, www.soriana.com) has groceries, produce, and baked goods.

Pescadería El Dorado (5 de Febrero btwn. Abasolo and Ocampo, tel. 624/143-2820) is a good bet for fresh fish and shellfish. You can buy fresh tortillas at **Tortillería Perla** (Morelos btwn. Hidalgo and Matamoros, tel. 624/143-1381).

Next to the entrance to the Pedregal community, **La Baguette** (Blvd. Lázaro Cárdenas, tel. 624/142-1125, 8:30am-7:30pm Mon.-Sat.) specializes in pastries, bagels, and breads from Europe and the United States. For a sweet tooth, the **Swiss Pastry** (Hidalgo at Lázaro

Cárdenas, across from the plaza, tel. 624/143-3494, 7am-4pm Mon.-Sat.) has homemade chocolates and candies as well as a variety of pastries.

For fresh fruits and vegetables, head over to **Frutería Lizarraga** (Matamoros at Av. de la Juventud, tel. 624/143-1215). And for organic produce and imported wines, try **Tutto Bene!** (Blvd. Marina, opposite the Wyndham Cabo San Lucas Resort, tel. 624/144-3300, 9:30am-9pm daily).

PLAYA EL MÉDANO
International

At **Edith's** (tel. 624/143-0801, www.edithscabo.com, 6pm-1am daily, mains US$30-50), near Playa El Médano on the west side of the Camino de los Pescadores, you can enjoy views of Bahía Cabo San Lucas and Land's End as long as the sun's up and a hearty dinner of prime rib, rack of lamb, or any number of regional specialties through the evening hours. Prices here seem unreasonably high.

At **Nikki Beach,** the trendy beach club of the ME Cabo resort, a lounge music beat keeps people moving all day long and well into the night. Nonguests pay a day-use fee for access to the pool, towels, and lounge beds. Sunbathers eat from a menu of pricey sushi rolls (US$10-15), Kobe beef sliders (US$20), and fish tacos (US$15). Choose a shaded table on the deck, enjoy full sun at a table on the sand, or retreat to the poolside terrace restaurant. Drinks tend to be watered down, but the service is prompt and friendly. **Medano Beach Club** (Playa Médano, next to ME Cabo, tel. 624/143-6554, www.themedanobeachclubcabo.com, US$20-35) has a restaurant, full bar, nightly live entertainment, and beach amenities including showers and lounge chairs.

Las Palmas (tel. 624/143-0447, lunch and dinner daily) offers a somewhat classier dining experience and a menu of burgers, seafood, and Mexican plates (lunch mains US$8-15; dinner menus are more expensive).

In the same vicinity, **Billygan's Island** (tel. 624/143-0402, lunch and dinner daily) and the Mango Deck are similar.

Seafood

For upscale dining on the beach, you can't beat **Las Palmas** (Playa el Médano, a few buildings northeast of Camino de los Pescadores, tel. 624/143-0447, laspalmascabo@hotmail.com, 10am-11pm daily, mains US$10-15). Choose a table on the raised patio or on the sand below, order the signature shrimp carousel dish, and enjoy the views.

The appetizer list at **Peacocks Restaurant and Bar** (Camino de los Pescadores at Vicario, tel. 624/143-1858, 6pm-10pm daily, mains US$20-30) demonstrates the creative powers of its chef: salmon tartar tower, calamari fusilli in a cilantro pesto, and sautéed lobster dumplings. Combined with the garden setting, the menu makes for an enchanting evening.

A string of dance club bar/restaurants lines the beach at Playa El Médano in front of Casa Dorada: One of the best known among these is **The Office** (Playa El Médano at Camino Pescadores, tel. 624/143-3464, lunch and dinner daily), but travelers often cite inflated prices here.

PACIFIC BEACHES
Seafood

Dinner at ◖ **El Farallón** at the Capella Pedregal resort (Camino del Mar 1, tel. 624/163-4300, www.capellahotels.com/cabosanlucas) begins with selecting your own fresh catch of the day—it then gets weighed and bagged, in a sort of staged fish market experience, then handed off to the chef to prepare for your meal. Fish fillets run US$70-80 per pound. A soup and trio of appetizers are included with the meal: seabean salad, crispy calamari, and sea bass ceviche. Desserts such as mixed berry crepes, rice pudding, and poached pears cost US$10 additional.

Mediterranean

Near the Solmar and Finisterra hotels, **Romeo y Julieta** (Camino al Pedregal, tel. 624/143-0225, www.restaurantromeoyjulieta.com, 4pm-11pm daily, mains US$10-20) aims to create a Spanish/Mediterranean feel with a menu

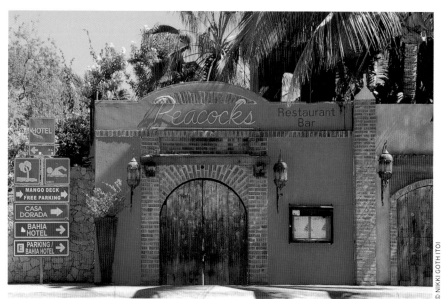

For a fine dining experience, try Peacocks Restaurant and Bar.

of mesquite wood-fired pizza and homemade pasta dishes.

Italian

Also downtown, **La Dolce Italian Restaurant & Pizzeria** (Hidalgo and Zapata, tel. 624/143-4122, www.ladolcerestaurant.com, 5pm-midnight daily, mains US$10-20) serves a full menu of pastas and pizzas, plus Italian starters and desserts. The restaurant has another location in San José del Cabo.

Information and Services

TOURIST ASSISTANCE

The **Los Cabos Tourism Trust** (Fideicomiso de Turismo de Los Cabos) has an office on Lázaro Cárdenas Edificio Posada (tel. 624/143-4777, toll-free U.S. tel. 866/567-2226).

COMMUNICATIONS
Postal Services

The local **post office** (Lázaro Cárdenas at 16 de Septiembre) is open 8am-4:30pm Monday-Friday and 9am-1pm Saturday. It's next to McDonald's and across from the Mini Market, in a yellow building with a clock on top.

Mail Boxes Etc. (Blvd. Marina 39-F, Plaza Fiesta, tel. 624/143-3033, fax 624/143-3031) carries mailing supplies, postage stamps, and magazines.

Internet Access and Telephone Services

Cabo San Lucas has experienced a proliferation of Internet cafés, although they seem to come, change hands, and go faster than the taco stands. Coffee shops and real estate offices are good places to check. Prices have come down quite a bit in recent years, settling at about US$2-6 per hour. If you travel with your own computer, wireless Internet access is also widely available in Los Cabos hotels and campgrounds—and many also have public computers available for guest use.

The lobby of the **Siesta Suites Hotel** (Zapata btwn. Guerrero and Hidalgo, tel. 624/143-2773) has three fast PCs (with USB ports) for US$3 per hour.

There are several places in town where you can enjoy a latte or cappuccino while you check your email: **Theory Café** (tel. 624/143-5518), in the center of Plaza Bonita, opens at 10am daily. **Cabo Coffee Company** (Hidalgo and Madero, tel. 624/105-1130, U.S. tel. 619/819-7953, www.cabocoffee. com) has expanded to an Internet café with high-speed wireless connections. A satellite location is also available outside the Giggling Marlin.

Public telephone booths are scattered around town, and long-distance services are often found inside Internet cafés.

EMERGENCY SERVICES

Dial 066 for emergency situations. Check the *Los Cabos Gringo Pages,* available in many hotels, for English-speaking doctors and clinics. **AmeriMed** (Pioneros Building Loc. 1, Blvd. Lázaro Cárdenas, tel. 624/143-9670) has a bilingual staff trained to handle emergencies, along with OB/GYN care and a family practice. The clinic is open 24/7 and accepts most insurance policies. **BlueMedicalNet** (tel. 624/104-3911, 24/7 daily) operates a clinic in the Plaza del Rey, across from Home Depot.

BANKS

There is no shortage of ATMs in Cabo San Lucas, and U.S. currency is accepted just about anywhere; however, in most cases, you'll get a better deal if you pay in pesos. All of the banks and ATMs are located in the downtown area. You can exchange money 8:30am-noon Monday-Saturday at **Bancomer** (Lázaro Cárdenas btwn. Hidalgo and Guerrero, tel. 624/143-2992), **Banamex** (Hidalgo at Lázaro Cárdenas, tel. 624/143-0767), and **Santander Serfín** (in Arámburo Plaza, tel. 624/144-4730). Avoid exchanging money at the airport or other money-change stands in town, as they will always charge you more.

LANGUAGE COURSES

California Conexion (locations vary, tel. 624/108-2095, thecaliforniaconexion@hotmail.com) holds Spanish classes for beginners and intermediate students.

Expat and longtime San Lucas resident Jill Holmdohl offers **private language instruction** (tel. 624/143-6973, bichomeisha@yahoo.com).

IMMIGRATION

Cabo's **migración office** is on the north side of Boulevard Lázaro Cárdenas between Gómez Farías and 16 de Septiembre, across from the Banamex.

U.S. CONSULATE

The **U.S. consular agency** (C-4, Blvd. Marina, tel. 624/143-3566, usconsulcabo@hotmail. com, 10am-1pm Mon.-Fri.) in Cabo San Lucas is at Plaza Náutica. This is the place to go if you lose your passport or for other emergencies.

CABO SAN LUCAS

Getting There and Around

BY AIR

Los Cabos International Airport (SJD, Carr. Transpeninsular km 44, tel. 624/146-5111, http://aeropuertosgap.com.mx/english/airports/loscabos-airport) serves San José del Cabo and Cabo San Lucas. Additional airport information is available at www.sjdloscabosairport.com, but this is not the official airport website.

Several international rental car agencies have desks in the terminals. For most brands, you'll need to ride a shuttle to off-airport pickup locations, all of which are very close to the terminal. These days, you'll almost always get a better deal if you reserve ahead of time. During busy holiday periods, most agencies will sell out of cars entirely. They tend to give cars on a first-come, first-served basis, regardless of whether you have a reservation or not.

A shuttle (*colectivo*) into the Cabo San Lucas area runs US$15 per person. A private taxi from the airport to Cabo San Lucas costs US$75 for up to four passengers.

BY CAR

If you're driving yourself, there are two ways to reach Cabo San Lucas from the airport: Follow signs for the Carretera Transpeninsular south through town, passing through several stoplights before you reach the town of San José. Continue on the Carretera Transpeninsular another 10-20 minutes for destinations along the Corridor or about 30 minutes to Cabo San Lucas. Alternatively, if you don't mind paying a toll of about US$2.25 (MEX$28), you can exit the airport onto the *quota,* a fast four-lane road with no exits until you enter San José at the junction of Paseo Los Cabos and the Mega grocery store plaza. If you pick up a rental car off-site, you'll have to return to the terminal to get to the toll road.

For trips from Cabo San Lucas to the Corridor and beyond, a rental car comes in handy. Rates are lower from the airport, but if you only want the car for a day or two of a longer trip, then renting in town makes sense. Options include **Budget/Fox** (Wyndham Cabo San Lucas Resort, Lázaro Cárdenas, www.budgetbaja.com), **Dollar** (Lázaro Cárdenas s/n btwn. Vicario and Mendoza, tel. 800/801-0365, U.S. tel. 800/002-8343, www.dollarloscabos.com, 7am-8pm daily), **Avis** (Hotel Pueblo Bonito Rosé, Playa El Médano, tel. 624/143-2422, ext. 2847, and Pueblo Bonito Sunset Beach, Predio Paraíso Escondido s/n, tel. 624/143-4607, 8am-10pm daily, both locations), and **Thrifty** (ME Cabo, Playa El Médano s/n, tel. 624/144-0406).

Other ways to get around include mopeds and ATVs. Look for vendors advertising these services along Boulevard Marina.

BY TAXI

The majority of Cabo San Lucas visitors get around by foot and by cab. A taxi ride around town should cost around US$6, but it's always a good idea to ask for a quote before you hop in.

You can hire water taxis from the marina in front of the Tesoro Hotel to Playa El Médano (US$3) and Playa del Amor (US$8-12, round-trip only).

BY BUS

A steady stream of **Aguila buses** (tel. 624/143-5020, www.autotransportesaguila.com) provide transportation between Los Cabos and La Paz and on to other points north. Schedules and fares are posted online, and you can purchase tickets in advance online. Current fares are about US$15 from Cabo San Lucas to La Paz and US$20 from San José to La Paz.

BY SEA

The nearest ferry service to the mainland operates between La Paz and Mazatlán. You can book tickets in La Paz or online through **Baja Ferries** (tel. 612/123-0208, 612/123-6600, or 800/122-1414, www.en.bajaferries.com).

There are now two full-service marinas in the Los Cabos area. **Marina Cabo San Lucas** (Lote A-18 De la Dársena, tel. 624/173-9140, www.igy-cabosanlucas.com) is still the main docking facility for those arriving by sea. But the new **Marina at Puerto Los Cabos** (Paseo de los Pescadores, Col. La Playa, tel. 624/105-6028, www.marinapuertoloscabos.com) is open and designed to hold up to 500 boats, including the largest luxury yachts.

TODOS SANTOS AND THE WEST CAPE

A few hundred meters past the modern Soriana shopping com-plex in Cabo San Lucas, the urban sprawl abruptly ends, cows reclaim the road, and the Pacific Ocean eventually pops into view. A lone trailer or two have set up camp along the shore, but you can't quite tell which dirt road they drove to get there. If it's late fall or early winter, wildflowers may still dot the landscape

© NIKKI GOTH ITOI

HIGHLIGHTS

LOOK FOR **C** TO FIND RECOMMENDED SIGHTS, ACTIVITIES, DINING, AND LODGING.

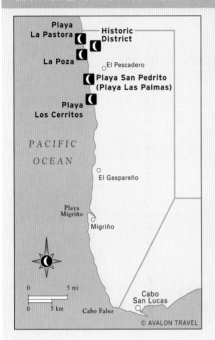

C Playa Los Cerritos: This is the best beach for learning to surf in the greater Los Cabos area (page 112).

C Playa San Pedrito (Playa Las Palmas): Rimmed with a row of palms, this beach can be swimmable on the calmest of days, and it's a scenic place for a picnic on just about any day (page 113).

C La Poza: Birds and other marine creatures congregate at the freshwater lagoon in Todos Santos. Walk the perimeter at sunset, starting at the road near Posada La Poza and Los Colibris Casitas (page 113).

C Playa La Pastora: Surfers head to this long, exposed beach north of town when winter swells roll in (page 115).

C Historic District: Appreciate the colonial roots of Todos Santos by strolling the narrow streets and wandering in and out of the galleries, shops, and cafés (page 120).

with a splash of color.

Welcome to the West Cape, the least developed stretch of coastline on the lower part of the Baja Peninsula. Now paved and expanded to four lanes almost start to finish, Highway 19 connects Cabo San Lucas to Todos Santos and meets the Carretera Transpeninsular just south of La Paz. Housing developments are still few and far between. Several large real estate projects are in the early stages near the farming community of El Pescadero and close to Cabo San Lucas, leaving the middle stretch to the pelicans, rancheros, fishers, and the occasional ATV tour.

Once considered a stopover on the drive from La Paz to Cabo San Lucas, bohemian

Todos Santos has become a destination in its own right. Surfers, artists, retirees, exotic bird rescuers, and yoga students all cross paths here, and at least several hundred of them are permanent expat residents. Over the last few years, Todos Santos has basked in the attention of its designation as a Pueblo Mágico—one of only 23 small towns in Mexico given government funding to make their culture and history more accessible to tourists and travelers. Foreign and Mexican locals alike remain optimistic that the town will be able to preserve its artsy character even as the number of visitors increases.

A few development efforts have persevered through the global economic recession, notably at Playa Los Cerritos, in El Pescadero,

TODOS SANTOS

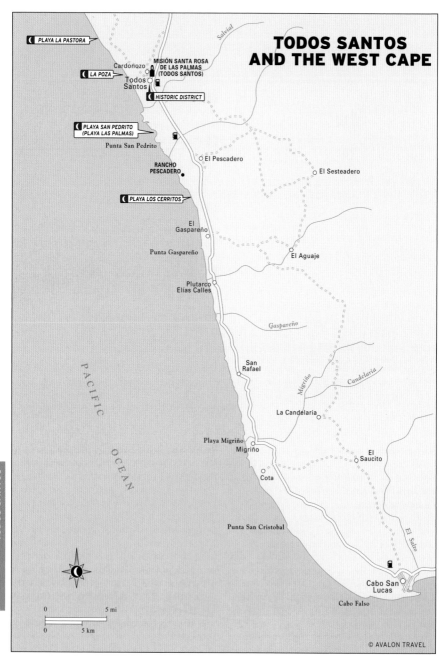

THE BEST DAY IN TODOS SANTOS AND THE WEST CAPE

Art, culture, and adventure anchor any perfect day in Todos Santos. Start your morning with a surf check or a walk around **La Poza.** After, join the locals at **La Esquina** café for coffee from Chiapas and healthy eats.

Pick up any gear you need in town, pack a picnic lunch, and drive to **Playa Los Cerritos** to spend the middle of the day on the beach. Take a surf lesson, go for a swim, build a sand castle, get a massage, or read a book.

When you've had enough of the sun and sand, head back toward town, stopping at **Baja Beans Roasting Co.** in El Pescadero if you need an afternoon caffeine fix, or **Rancho Pescadero** for a round of drinks on the terrace.

If you are planning to cook your own meal for dinner, turn off the highway at Punta Lobos and meet the local *panga* fishers when they return around 3pm. You can purchase the day's fresh catch minutes after it has arrived on shore and prepare it any way you like.

Back in Todos Santos, browse the shops and galleries in the historic district, wander through the **Centro Cultural,** and then return to your hotel or vacation rental before dinner.

When you are ready to venture out again, the evening's plan begins with a drink at the **Todos Santos Inn,** followed by dinner in the historic district. Try **Desertu Cocina** for Basque-inspired cuisine, **El Pastorcito** for *tacos al pastor* (marinated pork tacos), or **Tre Galline** for Italian fare. Linger as long as you like, as the options for nightlife are few. Todos Santos all but shuts down at Baja midnight, or 10pm.

and along the beaches north of Todos Santos. Longtime residents lament the addition of new hotels and homes, while business owners welcome potential new customers.

Beaches

WEST CAPE

Just about every dirt road heading west from Todos Santos ends at the beach. But few of them are paved or signed, which means you may be in for an adventure when you try to find a particular spot along the coast. Ask for directions before you set out, and remember that routes often shift a little with each successive season of rain—and with ongoing road construction. With the exception of Los Cerritos near El Pescadero and sometimes Playa Las Palmas/San Pedrito, beaches near Todos Santos are not swimmable because of strong currents, heavy surf, and rocky bottoms. (The exception may be in summer, when the swell subsides for long periods of time.) Plan to sunbathe, fish, stroll the beach, or surf, but save the splashing around for the pool.

Playa Migriño

Early explorers once believed that a cape three kilometers west of Cabo San Lucas marked the southern tip of the peninsula. Later cartographers discovered the mistake and named the cape Cabo Falso. Today the wide, sandy beach is protected so that sea turtles can lay their eggs undisturbed; once a popular destination for ATV tours from Cabo San Lucas, the dunes are now off limits as well, due to pending development. An abandoned lighthouse, **El Faro Viejo,** was in operation from 1895 to 1961; some years back, the original lens was moved to a modern lighthouse located higher on the beach.

Inland from Cabo Falso, Highway 19 enters the foothills of the Sierra de la Laguna and reaches the village of Migriño. The coast here

TODOS SANTOS

© LAUREN SWIFT

sunset over the Pacific

consists of a long, sandy beach dotted with rocks and a small estuary at the mouth of Río Candelaria.

In winter surfers can find a right point break at the north end of the beach, but the camping is no more. Rancho Migriño has moved in, with new home sites for sale.

Playa Migriño is easily accessible from Cabo San Lucas (about 15 minutes by car), with access roads at kilometer 94 and kilometer 97. The beach is about 2.5 kilometers west of the highway on either road.

◖ Playa Los Cerritos

The West Cape's most popular beach awaits at kilometer 64 (12.8 km south of Todos Santos). A handful of new businesses now provide food and accommodations, and some camping options are once again available.

Road construction obscured the sign to Playa Los Cerritos at last check, but the dirt road to the beach is well traveled, and signs to Hacienda Cerritos point the way. From the turn, drive 2.7 kilometers southwest until you

reach the sandy parking area. Sheltered by Punta Pescadero at its north end, the beach is usually safe for swimming, though you should ask at the surf shops about currents and riptides before getting in the water. Also keep a lookout for flying surfboards on busy days. Throw on a pair of goggles and you may even catch a glimpse of a spotted eagle ray gliding by just offshore. Boogie boarding is another popular activity.

This is generally a good beginner surf spot, but it can get big in the right conditions. Several surf shops rent boards and offer lessons.

The only food right on the beach comes from **Los Cerritos Beach Club** (tel. 624/143-4850, www.cerritosbcs.com, breakfast, lunch, and dinner daily, mains US$7-20), which offers a menu of ceviche, pasta, sandwiches, and the like. It has a full bar as well as restrooms for paying customers.

About five kilometers south, near kilometer 75, a new real estate development, **Tortuga del Sol,** is making slow progress on its proposed 123 home sites.

Beaches near El Pescadero

As you approach El Pescadero from the south (km 62), hilly terrain gives way on the west side of Highway 19 to a series of flat, cultivated fields fed by underground springs, most of which are bordered by a single row of tall corn stalks to break the wind. Between fields of cherry tomatoes and basil, a number of palm-lined dirt roads meander to the water's edge. Though still much smaller and more spread out than its neighbor to the north, El Pescadero has evolved in recent years from a cluster of simple *tiendas* and *loncherías* (food stands) into a more developed business center with its own Pemex and Oxxo convenience store. The first major real estate development underway in the area is the 20-hectare gated community of **Playa Agave Azul,** but progress is very slow. More development is under way at nearby Playa Los Cerritos.

Local expat residents here are involved with **turtle conservation efforts,** through egg collection and baby turtle release programs as well as the building of an educational amphitheater, designed in the shape of a turtle, to promote ecological awareness. Visit www.bajaturtle.com for more information.

Dirt roads heading to the beach can be a bit tricky to navigate. There are few street names or signs, and many roads dead-end at someone's driveway. The easiest way to find most of El Pescadero's waterfront attractions is to follow a wide dirt road with a row of palms in the median that meets Highway 19 just across from the Sandbar restaurant. If you've rented a place along this stretch of coast, be sure to get specific directions to find it.

Playa San Pedro

Playa San Pedro extends north from El Pescadero to Punta San Pedro. It is filled with cobblestones near the point but is sandy the rest of the way south. Surfable waves break along the north end of the beach. The access road may be difficult to find at kilometer 59 due to road construction. Once off the pavement, follow the dirt road 3.1 kilometers west to the beach.

TODOS SANTOS
◖ Playa San Pedrito (Playa Las Palmas)

Hard to find Little San Pedro Beach (km 56-57) also goes by the name of Palm Beach. With its fan palms and salt marsh, you might forget you're in the desert here. Enclosed by rocky points at either end, the beach can offer good swimming, shore fishing, and surfing, depending on the swell. Watch for riptides near the points. Beach camping is permitted on the sand. The access road to San Pedrito is across from the Campo Experimental buildings on Highway 19. Stay left when you reach the ruined mansion and you'll arrive at the south end of the palm orchard. From here, it's a short walk to the water's edge.

Punta Lobos and Puerto Algodones

Starting south of town, local fishing boats launch out of Punta Lobos, marked by a rocky point and sea lion colony on the south side of a sandy cove. The *pangas* return to shore around 3pm; watch the captains time the waves so that they can safely run the boats onto the beach. You can often buy fresh catch directly from the *pangueros*. If you walk north along the beach, past the lighthouse, you'll reach **Playa Las Pocitas** and **Playa La Cachora.**

The signed access road to Punta Lobos leaves Highway 19 about two kilometers south of Todos Santos at kilometer 54. As you near the beach, you'll see the ruins of an old turtle cannery. To walk to Punta Lobos from town (20-30 minutes each way), follow Calle Pedrajo southwest one long block to a wide dirt road. Turn left and follow this road until you can see the lighthouse on your right; take the next dirt road west to Punta Lobos.

Between Punta Lobos and Playa San Pedrito, an old port bound by cliffs was used in the early 20th century to ship fresh produce, sugarcane, and canned fish. Climb (carefully) out to the old pier or to the summit above it for some of the most memorable views. Strong swimmers may be comfortable getting in the water here, but pay attention to currents and tides.

The access road to this secluded bay is rough and steep in parts. Turn off Highway 19 toward Punta Lobos and turn left when you pass the cannery ruins (before the beach). You probably won't be able to make it all the way to the port. Alternatively, leave your car at Punta Lobos; it will take about an hour to get there by foot.

Local outfitters, such as Todos Santos Eco Adventures, lead cliff walks here if you prefer to have a guide.

◖ La Poza

Bird-watchers rejoice in this freshwater lagoon located west of the *huerta* and south of La Cachora road—and just beyond the tide line. With dunes in front and palms behind, La Poza provides ideal habitat for a long list of birds, including pelicans, herons, egrets, gulls, frigate birds, ibis, ducks, cormorants, sandpipers, and stilts. The beach in front of the lagoon is called Playa Las Pocitas, and it meets Playa La

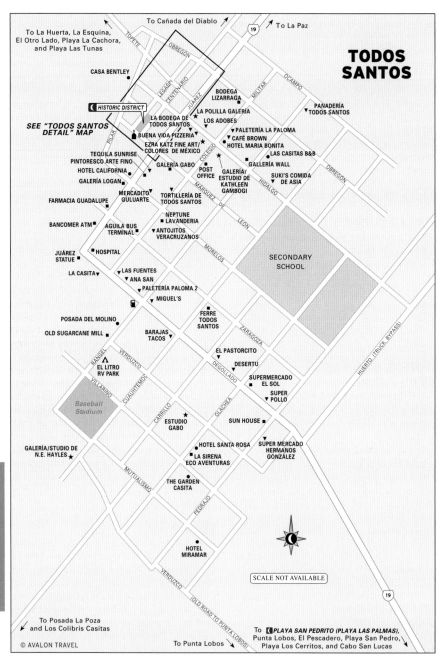

To Cañada del Diablo

19 To La Paz

To La Huerta, La Esquina,
El Otro Lado, Playa La Cachora,
and Playa Las Tunas

TODOS SANTOS

CASA BENTLEY

HISTORIC DISTRICT

*SEE "TODOS SANTOS
DETAIL" MAP*

BODEGA
LIZARRAGA

LA POLILLA GALERÍA

PANADERÍA
TODOS SANTOS

LA BODEGA DE
TODOS SANTOS

LOS ADOBES

BUENA VIDA PIZZERIA

PALETERÍA LA PALOMA

CAFÉ BROWN

EZRA KATZ FINE ART/
COLORES DE MÉXICO

HOTEL MARIA BONITA

LAS CASITAS B&B

TEQUILA SUNRISE
PINTORESCO ARTE FINO

GALERÍA GABO

GALLERÍA WALL

HOTEL CALIFORNIA

POST
OFFICE

GALERIA/
ESTUDIO DE
KATHLEEN
GAMBOGI

SUKI'S COMIDA
DE ASIA

GALERÍA LOGAN

MERCADITO
GULUARTE

TORTILLERÍA DE
TODOS SANTOS

FARMACIA GUADALUPE

NEPTUNE
LAVANDERIA

BANCOMER ATM

AGUILA BUS
TERMINAL

ANTOJITOS
VERACRUZANOS

JUÁREZ
STATUE

HOSPITAL

LA CASITA

LAS FUENTES

ANA SAN

SECONDARY
SCHOOL

PALETERÍA PALOMA 2

MIGUEL'S

FERRE
TODOS
SANTOS

POSADA DEL MOLINO

BARAJAS
TACOS

OLD SUGARCANE MILL

EL PASTORCITO

EL LITRO
RV PARK

DESERTÚ

SUPERMERCADO
EL SOL

SUPER
POLLO

Baseball
Stadium

ESTUDIO
GABO

SUN HOUSE

GALERÍA/STUDIO DE
N.E. HAYLES

HOTEL SANTA ROSA

LA SIRENA
ECO AVENTURAS

SUPER MERCADO
HERMANOS
GONZÁLEZ

THE GARDEN
CASITA

HOTEL
MIRAMAR

SCALE NOT AVAILABLE

To Posada La Poza
and Los Colibris Casitas

© AVALON TRAVEL

To Punta Lobos

To PLAYA SAN PEDRITO (PLAYA LAS PALMAS),
Punta Lobos, El Pescadero, Playa San Pedro,
Playa Los Cerritos, and Cabo San Lucas

19

TODOS SANTOS

Cachora to the north, where La Cachora road meets the coast.

A word of warning: The lagoon appears to be shallow but is in fact very deep. Most of the time it is separated from the ocean by a high sand dune; however, the dune occasionally breaks in large swells, and when this happens, a trickle of water out of the lagoon can turn into a towering wall of water almost instantly. Unsuspecting visitors have drowned in these situations. Stay back from the water's edge and monitor the wave patterns at all times.

To reach the beaches and the lagoon from downtown, start on Calle Topete near the Galería de Todos Santos and follow it north, down a small hill and around to the west, across the orchard. Turn left at the first sand road, which comes immediately before a low rock wall. If you start going uphill and pass La Esquina restaurant on your left, you've gone too far. La Cachora road heads west to the beach, passing a few homes and an inn or two along the way.

A steep and rocky path also skirts to La Poza to the south. Turn southwest off Degollado (Highway 19) onto Calle Olachea or Calle Carrillo and follow the blue and white signs to Posada La Poza. Park along the road (not in the spots that are reserved for guests of the inn) and walk to the end of the road, where the short trail begins.

◖ Playa La Pastora

If you skip the turnoff to La Cachora and drive past the rock wall up the small hill, you'll find yourself in the *otro lado* (other side) of Todos Santos, with yet more beaches at the end of unnamed dirt roads and a few housing developments in various states of completion. Follow this coastal road about 5.6 kilometers farther northwest to a wide arroyo that leads to a sandy beach. Resist the urge to drive all the way up onto the sand to check the surf from your car. Chances are you will get stuck. The break is a right point in a northwest swell and occasionally also a beach break in a south swell.

North to Punta Márquez and Punta Conejo

If you're up for some serious off-road exploration, continue north along the coastal road. After Playa La Pastora, the road veers east and reaches a T, from which you can turn right to get back to Highway 19 or turn left to continue northwest more or less parallel to the coast. At Rancho los Inocentes (57 km from La Pastora), you can once again head inland (straight) to rejoin the Carretera Transpeninsular north of La Paz (29 km from Rancho los Inocentes) or turn left to stay on the coast. This road eventually reaches Punta Márquez (24 km north of Rancho el Tomate) and Punta Conejo (18 km north of Punta Márquez), two well-known points for surfing. This entire stretch of the Pacific coast is lined with sandy beaches and, in winter, surfable breaks on a succession of reefs and points. You can camp anywhere along the shore—just be sure to bring all your supplies, as the nearest commercial outposts are a long drive away.

Water Sports

WEST CAPE
Surfing

Surfable waves pound the West Cape in winter, from Playa Migriño all the way to Punta Márquez, north of Todos Santos. Beginning in the south, Migriño has an exposed right point and hollow beach break. Punta Gaspareño, a rock-bottomed right point break at kilometer 73, breaks best in large west or northwest swells. Playa San Pedro (km 59, site of the former San Pedrito RV park) offers fairly consistent right reef and beach breaks; paddle out from the beach to avoid urchins on the reef. A little farther north, Playa San Pedrito has another beach break, best enjoyed during a west or north swell.

Popular with novice surfers, Playa Los Cerritos has several left and right beach breaks. Ask the local shops about currents and riptides before you hop in for the first time. Experienced surfers will enjoy the right break off the point on larger northwest and south swells. Vacation rentals in the Pescadero area are popular with some surfers, while others prefer to camp north of Todos Santos.

The **Pescadero Surf Camp** (Hwy. 19 km 64, www.pescaderosurf.com, tel. 612/134-0480) offers cabanas, campsites, board rentals, and instruction. The Costa Azul Surf Shop and El Diablo Blanco rent boards at Los Cerritos from dawn till dusk. **Mario Surf School** (Cerritos Beach, tel. 612/142-6156, www.mariosurfschool.com) also rents boards (US$20/day) and offers lessons (US$60/hour), ding repair, and accessories you may have forgotten at home. Two blue beach umbrellas near the lifeguard tower serve as Mario's office, or look him up through **Todos Santos Eco Adventures** (www.tosea.net).

Swimming

Most of the beaches along the West Cape are exposed to heavy surf; however, on calm days Playa Los Cerritos and Playa Las Palmas offer sheltered conditions for an ocean swim. At Las Palmas, the middle section of the cove is usually the safest. Toward the north and south ends, the water looks shallow and inviting, but riptides pose a danger.

TODOS SANTOS
Surfing and Kayaking

Winter months are best for surfing the Todos Santos area, as well, when the local breaks catch the strong northwest swell. In summer the action moves south to the Los Cabos Corridor between Cabo San Lucas and San José del Cabo or to lesser-known spots around the lower East Cape.

Contact Mario Becerril, owner of **Mario Surf School** (tel. 612/142-6156, www.mariosurfshop.com) for lessons, rentals, and ding repair. He is a highly reputable instructor, with several other instructors on staff, all of whom have experience with the local breaks.

La Sirena Eco-Adventures (Olachea btwn. Villarino and Verduzco, tel. 612/145-0353, U.S. tel. 213/265-9943, www.lasirenakayaksurf.com) rents surfing equipment and supplies, offers surfing instruction (US$55/hour), and leads kayak tours (US$60) to the old port. **Iguana de los Mangos** (tel. 624/114-1351, www.bajasurtodossantos.com, US$150 per day) also leads kayak trips.

Fishing

Since it lacks a marina or protected harbor (other than the abandoned pier at Puerto Algondones), Todos Santos does not have much of a charter fishing business. However, if you speak Spanish, you can talk to the *pangueros* (fishers) to arrange a day of sportfishing. Prices average about US$30 per hour, usually with a three-hour minimum. Alternatively, contact **Todos Santos Eco Adventures** (Cerro La Poza, Guaycura, tel. 612/145-0189, www.tosea.net, US$175 for 2 nights, US$275 per boat per day) or **La Sirena Eco-Adventures** (Olachea off Degollado, tel. 612/145-0353, www.lasirenakayaksurf.com, US$275 for five hours) to arrange guided trips. With accommodations and sportfishing services in Todos Santos and La Paz, **Iguana de los Mangos** (tel. 624/114-1351, www.bajasurtodossantos.com, US$250 per day) launches a *panga* from Punta Lobos.

Playas San Pedrito (Palm Beach), San Pedro, and Los Cerritos are among the easiest (and safest) places for surf-casting from shore. Experienced locals also head to La Pastora and points north. The catch from shore includes sierra (mackerel), cabrilla (sea bass), *pargo* (snapper), and robalo (snook). **Ferretería Oasis de Todos Santos** (Rangel at Zaragoza, tel. 612/145-0754, 8am-3pm and 4pm-7pm Mon.-Fri., 8am-4pm Sat.) carries some fishing supplies. You can buy live bait from the local fishers at Punta Lobos.

Whale-Watching

Whale-watching from Todos Santos is from a distance, compared to the up-close encounters you can have in the birthing lagoons farther north. But an afternoon spent watching juvenile gray whales breach and slap their tails offshore while you sip margaritas on a rooftop deck makes for great entertainment nonetheless. December-April are the best months for catching the whales on their journey up the coast.

Pangueros at Punta Lobos may be willing to take passengers out to see the whales for about US$30 an hour; book at the beach or through any of the hotels in town.

La Sirena Eco-Adventures (Olachea off Degollado, tel. 612/145-0353, www.lasirena-kayaksurf.com) leads whale-watching trips (US$55 pp for three hours). **Todos Santos Eco Adventures** (Cerro La Poza, Guaycura, tel. 612/145-0189, www.tosea.net) also includes whale-watching with local fishing cooperatives out of Punta Lobos in Todos Santos as part of its multiday trips. **Iguana de los Mangos** (tel. 624/114-1351, www.bajasurtodossantos.com, US$150 per day) is another option.

Hiking, Biking, and Adventure Sports

WEST CAPE
Rancho Pilar
Originally from La Paz, **Cuco Moyron** (Hwy. 19 km 73, ranchopilar@hotmail.com) is an artist, craftsman, and naturalist who uses recycled tire-rubber soles to make custom-fit sandals (US$35 a pair). He and his wife, Pilar, also make pottery, jewelry, and hats of woven grass. They have campsites available on their property. Cuco leads informative trips through the Sierra de la Laguna. Allow a week to make arrangements. At kilometer 73, take the dirt road toward the beach until you see the Rancho Pilar sign on the left.

TODOS SANTOS
Todos Santos Eco Adventures (Cerro La Poza, Guaycura, tel. 612/145-0780, www.tosea.net) leads half-day outings to nearby rock art, waterfalls, cliff walks, and to observe mountain potters at work in nearby San Vicente and La Candelaria for US$55 as well as overnight trips to the Sierra de la Laguna, fishing trips (US$275 per boat for up to six hours), and horseback riding (US$100 per trip).

A 90-minute walking tour of historic sites in Todos Santos is US$15 per person. They are also now offering a "sea-to-sea" hike, from the Pacific Ocean to the Sea of Cortez.

La Sirena Eco-Adventures (Olachea btwn. Verduzco and Villarino, tel. 612/145-0353, www.lasirenakayaksurf.com) leads similar trips, including whale-watching (US$55 pp for three hours), fishing (US$275 for five hours on the water with tackle and lunch for four people), and waterfall hikes (US$50 pp).

Todos Santos Eco Adventures (Cerro La Poza, Calle Guaycura, tel. 612/145-0189, www.tosea.net) arranges one-day and multiday hikes, including a trip to visit a celebrated local mountain potter named Doña Ramona, who welcomes guests to experience her family's working ranch for a day. A variation of this day trip involves a back-roads jaunt over to La Candelaria to meet yet more potters. The rugged, and often impassable, Naranjos road heads southeast from a point near Playa Los Cerritos and crosses the Sierra de la Laguna to join the Carretera Transpeninsular between Santa Anita and Caduaño.

Spas and Yoga

WEST CAPE

Yandara Yoga Institute (Hwy. 19 km 73, www.yandara.com) offers yoga instructor courses several times a year. Students prepare most of their meals from the house *huerta* (garden). At kilometer 73, take the dirt road toward the beach until it ends and then turn left. Another studio at the Mini Super Los Arcos, across from the Pemex, offers **Hatha yoga** classes taught in Spanish (tel. 612/130-3006, 9am-10:30am Mon., Wed., Fri., US$5/class).

Rancho Pescadero (www.ranchopescadero. com) offers morning yoga classes beginning at 9am daily, plus advanced classes at 4pm on Sunday, Tuesday, and Friday (US$4 per class). Several massage therapists have set up tables on the beach at Playa Los Cerritos. Call Minerva (tel. 624/164-6766) to inquire or book on the spot (US$20 for 30 minutes or US$35 for a full hour).

In a brick building three rows in from the beach, **Los Bules Day Spa** (Playa Congrejos, El Pescadero, tel. 612/118-1062, www.pescadise.com) offers deep-tissue, hot-stone, or Swedish massage (US$50), body wraps (US$45), and facials (US$40-70)—plus a Native American *temazcal,* or sweat lodge (US$20). The proprietor, Maria, is also a gourd artist. Her gallery on the property contains pitchers, bowls, animals, candles, and teacups—all crafted from hard-shelled bottle gourds.

TODOS SANTOS

Hatha and Ashtanga yoga classes meet several times a week at La Arca building on Topete (Hatha at 8am Mon., Wed., Fri., Ashtanga at 9am Tues., Thurs, Sat., US$6 per class) and at the Hotelito (road to Playa La Cachora, tel. 612/145-0099, www.thehotelito.com) at 9am Tuesday and Thursday mornings. In the same location, **El Dharma de Todos Santos** (tel. 612/145-0676, www.eldharma.com) holds dharma talks and *vipassana* meditation classes 10am-11:30am Sunday.

Tai chi chuan classes take place at the Centro Cultural 4pm-5:30pm on Wednesdays October-June for around US$6.

Casa Bentley offers massage treatments (US$50 for 30 minutes) and yoga instructions for groups of three or more. Book ahead at the Casa Bentley website (www.casabentley-baja.com). The **Guaycura Aena Spa** (Lesaspi at Topete, tel. 612/175-0800, www.guaycura. com) offers massage and body treatments (US$90-100) and a steam room.

Aloha Massage owner Diane Moore (tel. 612/119-7045) will come to your Todos Santos *casita* to provide massage, Reiki, and reflexology services as well as yoga instruction and spa treatments.

Sights

WEST CAPE
La Candelaria

A small ranching settlement in the sierra foothills, La Candelaria is worth a side trip if you want to get away from the crowded beaches and have an off-road adventure. Known for its pottery and *curanderos* (healers who specialize in herbal treatments), the town is most often visited by guided ATV tours, which stop to buy the inexpensive ceramics and swim in the palm oasis. Fewer than 100 people live here year-round, raising livestock and tending to crops of citrus, avocado, and mango. The village itself consists of simple homes with *palapa* roofs, a church, and a school.

There are two ways to reach La Candelaria

if you want to drive yourself. The most direct, via Migriño, requires four-wheel drive. The longer route from Cabo San Lucas has more turns and forks, but you can make it in most regular vehicles.

FROM PLAYA MIGRIÑO

The route follows the Río Candelaria 9.1 kilometers southwest from Highway 19 near Playa Migriño. The turnoff is not signed. Look for a dirt road three kilometers south of kilometer 94, or about a half kilometer north of the main Playa Migriño turnoff (km 97). The road is sandy and narrow in places. Do not attempt the drive in the rainy season.

FROM CABO SAN LUCAS

From downtown Cabo San Lucas, drive along Boulevard Lázaro Cárdenas east toward San José and turn left at Boulevard Constituyentes (also labeled Av. Reforma on some maps) and the sign for La Paz Via Corta. Follow this street northwest toward Todos Santos and La Paz, past a soccer field on the left. At the power plant on the right side, turn onto a wide dirt road (1.7 km from the intersection of Blvd. Lázaro Cárdenas and Blvd. Constituyentes).

From here, La Candelaria is 22 kilometers away, assuming you manage to find all the correct turns on the first try. Turn right 4.3 kilometers from the highway at the sign for La Candelaria and Los Pozos. Pass through the fence and cattle guard—an attendant may be on guard to prevent livestock theft. Watch for cattle in the road from here on.

Twelve kilometers from the highway, the road forks. Stay left, ignoring the right branch, which goes to San Felipe and El Sauzal. Next come the ranches and adobe ruins of Los Pozos. There is a small chapel 14 kilometers into the drive (measuring from the highway). Keep following signs for La Candelaria and La Trinidad, ignoring any smaller branches off the main road.

Soon the Pacific Ocean comes into view. About 21 kilometers from the highway is a turnoff for Rancho San Ramón, after which is another fork. Both branches will get you to

La Candelaria, but the right fork is quicker. It crosses an arroyo, passes a turn to La Trinidad, and then arrives in La Candelaria.

BY ATV

An easier way to visit La Candelaria is by guided ATV tour. Several companies have rental stands along Highway 19, near Playa Migriño. Contact **Camino Aventura** (Hwy. 19 km 104-105, tel. 624/105-8413, www.caminoaventura.mx), **Motosol** (Hwy. 19 km 99.5, Migriño, tel. 624/143-9393, www.atvsmotosol.com; 8am-7pm daily; US$70-95), or **Amigos** (tel. 624/144-4161, www.amigosactivities.com.mx) to make a reservation. Tours run US$65-90 for single riders, US$85-120 for doubles, and usually include helmets, goggles, bandanas, training, bottled water, and a bilingual guide.

TODOS SANTOS
((Historic District

A stroll along streets near the historic town plaza reveals hundred-year-old homes made of brick and some adobe, many of them now owned by outsiders and carefully restored in an array of pastel colors. Oversized windows and doors framed by decorative pilasters (rectangular supports that look like flat columns) are a signature design, borrowed from the Classic Revival style of architecture. The present-day Café Santa Fé on Calle Centenario, facing the plaza, is one of the largest adobe structures left standing in town. The facades on the surrounding streets are likely to look more homogenous in coming years, as a uniform appearance is one of the contingencies of funding made available through the Pueblo Mágico program. Check Baja.com for the timing of the annual historic home tour, when owners open their doors to visitors.

Centro Cultural Profesor Nestor Agúndez Martínez

To immerse yourself in Todos Santos's past, visit the **Centro Cultural Nestor Agúndez Martínez** (Juárez at Obregón, tel. 612/145-0041, 8am-5pm Mon.-Fri., 9am-1pm Sat.-Sun., free admission), which occupies a large brick building on Calle Juárez that once served as the town's schoolhouse. It was named for a local high school teacher who passed away in 2009. Several exhibits inside cover the anthropology, ethnography, and history of the area, including a few examples of modern art and handicrafts. Murals in the lobby depict scenes from Baja's history. They were painted in 1933 as a public works project during the administration of President Álvaro Obregón. Among the highlights are arrowheads, pottery, and other artifacts as well as photos of important figures in the town's history, local sugar mills, and silver mines at El Triunfo.

Los Pinos Park

This small park on Colegio Militar between Zaragoza and Degollado across from the Aguila Bus Terminal has become a pleasant gathering place since the addition of a large, modern play structure for kids. Buy a treat from the snack bar or a *paleta* (popsicle) from up the street and relax while the little ones climb to their heart's content.

Shopping

WEST CAPE
Arts and Crafts

A string of *artesanías* selling colorful Mexican blankets, hammocks, and pottery lines the highway south of El Pescadero. **Imelda's Curiosidades** (Hwy. 19 km 66, no tel.) carries all kinds of Mexican trinkets, from hand-painted figurines to blankets and clothes.

A handful of Candelaria artisans make pottery, baskets, and rustic furniture. At kilometer 69, **The Blanket Factory** (no tel.) is a popular stop for organized tours. Shop here for handmade rugs, blankets, clothing, and hammocks (US$60-80), or request a custom design.

TODOS SANTOS

Todos Santos has a growing collection of boutiques that are fun to browse if you want to return home with gifts or something special for yourself. The quality is generally high, but note that most of the inventory in these stores comes from the mainland, not from Baja. Most of the shopping centers around the historic district near the plaza. Upscale shops and galleries line the narrow side streets off Calle Topete, near the Todos Santos Inn. More affordable souvenir shops can be found along Calles Hidalgo and Márquez de León.

Home Furnishings, Gifts, and Jewelry

Emporio Hotel California (Juárez btwn. Morelos and Márquez de León, tel. 612/145-0217, 10am-7pm daily) has apparel, jewelry, ceramics, coffee-table books, posters, and other gifts on display in a large storefront adjoining the hotel.

Mangos Folk Art (Centenario btwn. Topete and Obregón, tel. 612/145-0451, 10am-5pm Tues.-Sat.) specializes in folk art from mainland Mexico, woodcarvings, and Guatemalan textiles.

Also on Centenario at Topete, **Manos Mexicanas** (tel. 612/145-0538, 10am-5pm Mon.-Sat.) has arts and crafts from Guadalajara and Michoacán on the mainland, plus ceramics created by local artist Rubén Gutiérrez and other locally made goods, such as Desert Soaps (www.desertsoaps.com) from the East Cape.

Joyería Brilanti (Centenario 24 btwn. Topete and Obregón, tel./fax 612/145-0799, www.brilanti.com, 10am-5pm Mon.-Sat.) has a distinctive history as one of the earliest silver designers from Taxco on the mainland. Today the business is run by the son of the original founder, Ana Brilanti, who counted First Lady Eleanor Roosevelt among her distinguished customers. In addition to a beautiful selection of silver pieces, the gallery has sculptures and paintings for sale.

The smell of lavender wafts out of **Heartsease,** where Canadian Gwenn McDonald (Juárez at Hidalgo, tel. 612/132-0095, heartsease@mts.net, 10am-5pm Mon.-Sat.) makes natural soap and skincare products. This is the place to get moisturizer for your face when the desert climate starts to take its toll. Gwen also makes a natural bug repellent that's safe for kids. Call in advance to book a Swedish or Shiatsu massage or Reiki and foot reflexology (US$60 for one hour).

New in 2010, **GotBaja** (Juárez at Hidalgo, www.gotbajamaps.com, 9am-8pm daily) publishes handy, free tourist maps for Todos Santos, La Paz, and the East Cape. The store sells souvenir T-shirts (including kids' sizes), mugs, stickers, magnets, key chains, and the like.

Clothing

Boutique Santa Maria (tel. 612/145-0009, 9am-6:30pm daily), located across from the Centro Cultural on Juárez, carries casual cotton apparel made on the mainland in Guadalajara. There are styles for men, women, and kids.

Books

El Tecolote Books/Libros (Juárez and Hidalgo, tel. 612/145-0295, katemlewis@yahoo.com, mid-Oct. through May, 10am-5pm Mon.-Sat., 11am-3pm Sun., reduced hours in summer) is a book lover's shop—the kind of place that makes you want to run an independent bookstore in your retirement. The owner stocks the shelves with a mix of foreign and Mexican periodicals, new and used paperback fiction, and hardcover design and coffee-table books, plus maps and a good section of Baja-related titles. It's no Borders or Barnes & Noble, but whether you want to read Tom Clancy or Graham Greene, chances are you'll find something you like at this shop. Bilingual children's books make a nice gift for kids. You can also buy books on tape and rent or buy movies. Besides the books, the store carries some art supplies. Note: The store stays open seven days a week from mid-October until the crowds dwindle in May. After that, the hours are five days a week for the duration of the low season.

Arts and Crafts

For less expensive souvenirs, several vendors usually are set up near the plaza, though their names change frequently. **Bazar Agua y Sol** (tel. 612/145-0537, 10am-5pm Mon.-Sat.) has jewelry, sculptures, pottery, and paintings. Credit cards are accepted here.

Pintoresco (Colegio Militar at Zaragoza, tel. 612/145-0222, cell tel. 612/158-8457, 10am-7pm Mon.-Sat.) is divided into two locales in the same shopping gallery: The first features more tourist-oriented crafts from various parts of Mexico, including textiles, jewelry, and decorations; the second is next door and features fine art, all of Mexican origin. The gallery is at Local #5 in the shopping gallery on Colegio Militar at the corner of Zaragoza.

Artist Studios and Galleries

The art scene in Todos Santos has come of age, with more than a dozen galleries representing internationally known artists from the United States and Mexico. Although the founder of the town's artist colony, Charles Stewart, passed away in 2011, he is remembered fondly and the community continues to grow.

In a new location next to the Centro Cultural, **Galería de Todos Santos** (Juárez, tel. 612/145-0500, www.galeriadetodossantos.com, 10am-5pm Mon.-Sat.), established in 1994, is one of the few in town representing both local and foreign artists and, accordingly, diverse styles. Among those represented here are owner Michael Cope himself, celebrated local artist Erick Ochoa, and the whimsical stylings of Jennifer Power.

Jill Logan creates the original oils and mixed media works featured in the **Galería Logan** (tel. 612/145-0151, www.jilllogan.com, 10am-5pm Mon.-Sat., by appointment Sun.). Logan has an extensive education in fine art, and her work

has been exhibited across the United States as well as in Mexico.

La Paz native Ezra Katz, known for murals and etchings featured in a number of Cabo San Lucas restaurants and hotels, has opened **Galería Indigo** (Juárez at Hidalgo, tel. 612/137-3473, 10am-5pm Mon.-Sat. or by appt.), featuring John Comer, Lindy Duncan, Lesley Rich, and others in addition to his own artwork. **Galería/Studio de N. E. Hayles** (Cuauhtémoc, tel./fax 612/145-0183, www.nehayles.com, 11am-4:30pm Mon.-Sat.) displays unique paper-tile mosaics, multimedia art, and tables fashioned by artist-owner Nanette E. Hayles. **Galería Wall** (Hidalgo and Colegio Militar, a few feet away from Café Brown, tel. 612/145-0527, www.catherinewallart.com, 11am-4pm Mon.-Sat.) shows Mexican-themed original oils by artist Catherine Wall.

Gabo Galería (Márquez de León, btwn. Juárez and Colegio Militar, tel. 612/145-0514, gaboartist@hotmail.com, 10am-4pm Mon.-Sat.) features paintings by Gabo, who was born in Mexico, studied in Europe, and settled in La Paz in 1978. In the years since, he has played a major role in the art scene in La Paz and Todos Santos. His works are known for their bright colors and humorous style. Tours of his studio are by appointment only, while the gallery keeps regular hours.

Nightlife and Entertainment

WEST CAPE
Bars

When Todos Santos residents want to go out for a night on the town, they head to El Pescadero. Todos Santos may have more shops and restaurants, but El Pescadero has the **Sandbar** (Hwy. 19 km 63, tel. 612/130-3209, 3pm till late Wed.-Sat. and Mon., 9am-10pm Sun.), with a pool table, live music, and daily happy-hour specials as well as occasional cook-your-own kebab dinners. Wednesday is all-you-can-eat pizza, and on Sunday, the restaurant shows NFL games all day and serves breakfast, lunch, and dinner.

Grab a cold, hand-crafted ale at the **Cerritos Brewing Company** (Central El Pescadero, tel. 612/130-3246, www.cerritosbeachbrewing.wordpress.com, 2pm-10pm Tues.-Sat. and 1pm-8pm Sun.). Spirits, cocktails, and non-alcoholic beverages are also available. The Brews and Blues House Band plays every Sunday at 4pm, and Wednesdays and Saturdays bring in locals and gringos alike for open mic nights.

TODOS SANTOS
Bars

Todos Santos itself has a number of options for

grabbing a few drinks and enjoying the company of your hosts or fellow travelers, but places shut down around "Baja midnight," or 10pm, so if you want to carry on later than that, you'll need to move the party back to your own place.

In the historic Todos Santos Inn, **La Copa Bar** (Legaspi 33, tel. 612/145-0040, 5pm-9:30pm Wed.-Fri., wine bar 5pm-9:30pm daily) is a classy venue with romantic appeal. The entrance is on Calle Topete.

The bar in the Hotel California's uniquely decorated **La Coronela** (Juárez btwn. Morelos and Márquez de León, tel. 612/145-0525), frequented by local expats as well as the hotel's guests, is a fun place to have a few drinks. Stop in for live music on Saturday evenings.

On Thursday, Friday, or Saturday night, head over to **Mario's Bar** (Calle La Cachora, tel. 612/145-0099, 5pm-10pm Thurs.-Sat.) at the Hotelito for cocktails, wine, sushi, *satay,* and Indian curry, served by the town's best-known surf instructor.

Performing Arts

The restored **Teatro Márquez de León** (Legaspi at Márquez de León, no tel.) hosts music and dance performances, often during the annual October town fiesta. Before the La Paz city theater was built, Todos Santos had the only true theater in the state.

Festivals and Events

Fiesta Todos Santos takes place in October each year, around the feast day of the Virgen del Pilar (October 12). This four-day extravaganza begins on the second Saturday of the month and involves dances, sports competitions, horse races, theater performances, and amusement-park rides. Most of these events center around the town plaza.

The Christmas holidays are especially festive in Todos Santos, where for 12 days beginning on the **Día de Guadalupe** (December 12), local residents hold nightly candlelight processions to the Iglesia Nuestra Señora del Pilar. The season culminates in a midnight Mass worship service on **Christmas Eve.**

Created by musician Peter Buck of REM, the **Todos Santos Music Festival** has become an annual event to benefit the Palapa Society of Todos Santos. The the festival grows larger each year as more musicians and fans flock to town throughout January to participate.

In late January or early February, the government-funded **Todos Santos Art Festival** takes place with sculptures, paintings, ceramics, and other visual works by local artists. Performing arts groups also arrive from out of town to participate in the event. In late February, the **Todos Santos Film Festival** brings national and international actors, writers, and filmmakers to town to celebrate cinema. Then in early March, the **Todos Santos Latin Film Festival** comes to town.

Also once a year, usually in February or March, historic homes in Todos Santos open to the public. Check Baja.com for more information.

In mid-May, the **Gastrovino Food and Wine Festival** in Todos Santos celebrates the food and wines of Baja, paired with live music and art.

Food

WEST CAPE

Restaurant Migriño (Hwy. 19 km 102, no tel., hours vary, mains US$5), on the west side of the highway, serves basic *antojitos* and refreshingly cold beer. Another road stop is the dirt-floored **Los Idolos de Mexico** (Hwy. 19 km 79, no tel., hours vary, mains US$5). They keep it simple but tasty with *carnitas* (braised pork) and tacos *de pescado* and *de camarón*.

Lonchería Rosita (tel. 612/130-3094, 8am-8pm daily, mains US$5), on the east side of Highway 19, near the Pemex, is small with a *palapa* roof. Try its pork tamales or *machaca* (dried beef) burritos.

At the entrance to Pescadero is **Carnitas Michoacán** (no tel.), the most talked about taco stand in town.

The friendly **Marina's** (Hwy. 19 km 62, no tel., mains US$3-7) offers a nice variety of fish and shrimp tacos, plus quesadillas, a soup of the day, and the huge cheese/carne asada *mixto* (US$3).

Popular with locals and expats alike for its casual fare, **❮ Felipe's Restaurant** (Hwy. 19 km 61, no tel., hours vary Wed.-Mon., mains around US$8) makes delicious Mexican and seafood dishes at nongringo prices for breakfast, lunch, and dinner. This place serves an excellent shrimp chile relleno and even better *arrachera* (skirt steak).

Grill your own kebabs at the **Sandbar** (Hwy. 19 km 63, tel. 612/130-3209, 3pm till late Wed.-Sat. and Mon., 9am-10pm Sun.) or just pop in for daily happy-hour specials as well as weekly all-you-can-eat pizza. Show up for all-you-can-eat spaghetti on Thursday, reggae night with live music on Friday (for which there is a US$2-3 cover charge), and disco night on Saturday. On the highway near The Sandbar is **Napoli Pizzeria** (Carr. 19, El Pescadero, no tel.), a popular option for wood-fired pizzas fresh out of the open ovens.

The **Los Cerritos Club** (Hwy. 19 km 66.5, Playa Los Cerritos, tel. 624/143-4850, cell 624/129-6315, 7am-8pm daily, mains US$5-20) is a great place for a beer and a burger after a good surfing session; stay long enough to enjoy the sunset. Live music plays Friday and Saturday nights.

Art & Beer (Hwy. 19 km 69, no tel., hours vary) serves large signature cocktails—creative variations on the Bloody Mary—which come generously garnished with all manner of shellfish. You must agree to buy a drink or a meal in order to view the art on display. Fish dishes cost US$20.

❮ Baja Beans Roasting Co. (Hwy. 19 km 63, Pescadero, tel. 612/130-3391, www.bajabeans.com, 7am-3pm Tues.-Sat.) is the local hangout for caffeine and Internet access. The owner (a former professional hockey player from Vancouver) and his wife roast coffee beans from Puebla in an antique roaster on-site. They also squeeze fresh juice from fruit growing on their own trees, including guava and guayabana. Order your espresso, pourover, or chai latte and add a scone or baked treat of the day, then settle in at a shaded patio table to get some work done. The Sunday brunch and market have become a popular weekend ritual for many community members. If you are driving from Cabo San Lucas, turn left after the Pescadero Pemex.

For a gourmet meal in a resort setting, **❮ Rancho Pescadero** (tel. 612/135-5849, www.ranchopescadero.com, 7am-9pm daily, mains US$20-30) serves breakfast, lunch, and dinner during the high season, November-May. With previous experience at the Market Restaurant at the One&Only Palmilla in Los Cabos, executive chef Rodrigo Bueno has created a menu that blends local ingredients with international accents. His favorite dish on the menu of late is the grilled Nagano pork chop served with organic roasted vetegables grown in the resort's own garden. Special ingredients such as local cheese, Yurimon beans from the hills nearby, and housemade Cornish

artisanal mocha at Baja Beans Roasting Co.

sardines appear elsewhere on the menu. The new Garden Restaurant, open Friday and Saturday, is a new addition to the dining options; guests can still eat on the patio or in the open-air dining area upstairs. Seafood dishes include ceviche, fish tacos, chile ancho, and honey-glazed fresh catch. There is also a rib eye steak for heartier fare. Cooking classes and culinary events are now a regular occurrence at the resort, including a Gastrovino Festival in May, Culinary weekend in November, cooking classes every Monday and Wednesday, and Friday ceviche classes on the beach for guests. The culinarily inclined should be sure to talk to chef Bueno, and he will personally cook something special for the meal. The bar closes at 9pm. Reservations are required.

Groceries
Sundays bring a **Farmers Market** (Hwy. 19 km 63, Pescadero, tel. 612/130-3391, www. bajabeans.com, 8am-1pm Sun.) to Pescadero,

held at Baja Beans Roasting Company. **Mini Super Los Arcos** (no tel.) on Highway 19 near the Pemex stocks basic groceries, and the owners welcome special orders. **Mini Super Los Cerritos** (Hwy. 19 km 63, no tel.) sells cold beer and ice as well as some arts and crafts. At kilometer 61 you can buy strawberries direct from the farmers at US$1-2 per basket.

TODOS SANTOS
Contemporary and Traditional Mexican
On the back patio of a beautifully restored adobe house, **Los Adobes** (Hidalgo btwn. Juárez and Colegio Militar, tel. 612/145-0203, www.losadobesdetodossantos.com, 9am-9pm Mon.-Sat., 9am-5pm Sun., mains US$15-22) prepares gourmet Mexican cuisine with prices to match. The menu includes grilled fish entrées, chicken mole, and steak fajitas.

El Gusto! at Posada la Poza on Playa La Cachora (tel. 612/145-0400, 11:30am-3:30pm and 5:30pm-9pm Fri.-Wed.) is the only beach-front restaurant in Todos Santos. A tapas menu is available on the Whale Terrace. The menu changes based on what organic produce is available, but there is usually a wide variety of seafood and meat choices. El Gusto! is a popular spot for sunset margaritas.

The latest incarnation of the BajaMed trend has popped up at █**Desertu Cocina** (formerly Il Giardino, Degollado btwn. Raul Carrillo and Olachea, tel. 612/145-0199, Mon., Tues., and Thurs.-Sun. 1pm-10pm, mains US$20). The restaurant is a creative endeavor that brings the flavors of the Basque region to Baja California Sur. A native of Spain, chef/owner Jose Uribe worked for the top restaurant in San Sebastian prior to moving to Mexico City and then Todos Santos. The restaurant offers brick oven pizzas as a holdover from the previous owners, but the seafood is the reason to come—in particular the cabrilla if it's in season. And if you can't decide among the evening's specials, Jose will be happy to choose for you.

The Distillery (Hidalgo, tel. 612/145-0098, www.thedistillery.mx, 8am-9pm Tues.-Sun.) was brand-new to Todos Santos in December of 2012. Here, agave and other hard liquors are distilled. They feature a wine room and have a menu of dishes including traditional Mexican, seafood, salads, and tapas.

Inside the Todos Santos Inn, **Landi's** (tel. 612/145-0020, 9am-9pm Mon.-Sat., dinner mains US$8-15) offers traditional Mexican and some fusion dishes, such as fettuccine *al tequila*, to please the gringo palate. Live music plays on Thursday. Known for lightly battered chiles rellenos smothered in sautéed tomatoes and onions, **Miguel's** (Degollado and Rangel, tel. 612/145-0733, 8am-9pm daily, mains US$6-10) also serves enchiladas, burritos, and cheeseburgers. A dozen tables are arranged on a sand floor under a *palapa* roof. The owner has opened a second restaurant at Playa Los Cerritos.

You'll be hard-pressed to find anything on the menu over US$7 at **Restaurant la Ramada** (Militar and Obregón, no tel., 9am-9pm Mon.-Sat., mains US$3-8). This local spot serves tacos, tostadas, and the like in a clean kitchen with friendly service; it's open for breakfast, lunch, and dinner.

For casual dining (plastic tables under a *palapa* roof), █**Ataxcon** (Militar at Hidalgo, tel. 612/176-1275, 8am-7pm Mon.-Sat.) serves traditional Mexican dishes of the state of Guerrero on the mainland at reasonable prices.

Seafood

Located a few doors down from El Tecolote Books/Libros, █ **Fonda El Zaguán** (Juárez btwn. Topete and Hidalgo, tel. 612/131-6769, noon-9pm Mon.-Sat., US$6-15) is an open-air restaurant that does seafood right. Fish takes the center stage in its ceviche dish, unlike at many other places that serve it. Choose basil, poblano, or peanut sauce for your fish fillet. If *robalo* (snook) is available, get the fish tacos or order it as a fillet. The margaritas are strong, and the sangria is refreshing on a hot afternoon. Specials are usually written on a chalkboard out front.

Restaurant las Fuentes (Degollado and Colegio Militar, tel. 612/145-0257, 7:30am-9:30pm Tues.-Sun., mains from US$6) is a large open-air restaurant that has benefited from the rerouting of truck traffic away from the downtown area. The house special, *pescado empapelado,* is fish baked in paper with tomatoes and mild chilies.

At a busy intersection near the Pemex, **La Casita** (Degollado at Militar, tel. 612/145-0192, http://lacasitatapasandwinebar.com/default.aspx, tapas for US$8-13) emphasizes organic produce and fresh seafood, served as small plates. Coconut shrimp and tequila jalapeno sea bass are among the most memorable dishes. Its wine bar is stocked with some of the best Baja labels at reasonable prices as well as others from around the world. Red table linens and candlelight create an intimate atmosphere, but the persistent din of traffic right outside makes it a safe place to bring the kids, too.

Asian and International

Hotel California on Calle Juárez boasts the atmospheric **La Coronela** restaurant/bar (Juárez btwn. Morelos and Márquez de León, tel. 612/145-0525, 7am-11pm daily, dinner mains US$8-20). Prepared by a Belgian chef, the international menu has some creative dishes, such as almond-crusted Pacific oyster tacos and yellowtail in an opal basil/ginger/coconut sauce. Visa and MasterCard are accepted.

Across from the Pemex, **Ana San Sushi Bar** (Degollado at Militar, tel. 612/137-9856, 1pm-9pm Mon.-Sat.) prepares sushi, sashimi, soups, and salads.

Suki's (Hidalgo btwn. Rangel and Cuauhtémoc, 612/145-0847, 5pm-9pm Tues.-Sat.) offers a moderately priced menu of pan-Asian cuisine, with pad Thai, teriyaki, and Korean specialties.

These days, when resident expats want to dine out on the town, they head to **Michael's at the Gallery** (Juárez at Topete, tel. 612/145-0500, 5pm-9pm Thurs.-Sat., reservations recommended) to enjoy creative Asian cuisine in an open-air sculpture garden.

Italian

With a 20-year track record for excellence, **Café Santa Fé** (Centenario 4, tel./fax 612/145-0340, noon-9pm Wed.-Mon., mains US$20 and up) is this town's best-known and highest-ranked restaurant. It offers a broad menu of high-end Italian fare, including wood-fired pizzas, ravioli, fish *crudo,* and fresh pasta. Given its international acclaim, you will pay U.S. prices here.

At ❏ **Tre Galline** (Topete and Juárez, tel. 612/145-0274, 2pm-10pm Mon.-Sat., mains US$15-20), Angelo and Magda Dal Bon serve delicious northern Italian fare in a less formal atmosphere at more reasonable prices. Starters may include homemade rolls, eggplant Parmesan, and a celery soup with smoked trout. Main dishes range from homemade pasta to a daily fresh catch and organic roasted chicken. Magda's cakes and imported espresso complete the meal. This is where local Italian families come to celebrate special occasions. In the morning hours, Angelo and Magda also run Caffé Todos Santos.

Buena Vida (Hidalgo at Militar, cell tel. 612/348-8178, noon-3pm and dinner from 5pm Mon.-Fri., dinner from 5pm Sat.-Sun.) offers a dinner menu of pizzas (US$10), salads, and wines.

Antojitos and Fast Food

❏ **Tres Hermanos** on Márquez de León between Juárez and Militar (8am-2pm daily) is among the best taco stands in town. Try the clam tacos for something different. Local Mexican residents praise **Barajas Tacos** (8am-11pm daily on Degollado (Hwy. 19) toward the south edge of town, for serving authentic *carnitas* (braised pork) and *tacos de pescado y camarones* during the day and *tacos de carne asada* and *papas rellenas* (stuffed potatoes) at night.

Next to Cafélix, **Boyitacos** (Juárez at Hidalgo, tacos US$1-2, mains US$5-8) prepares tasty *papas rellenas*—baked potatoes layered with butter, cream, mushrooms, corn, and choice of meat or *mixtos* with cheese. Plastic tables are arranged under a *palapa* roof with a ceiling fan. Order drinks from the fully stocked bar and watch the traffic roll by on Calle Juárez.

❏ **El Pastorcito** (Degollado at Carrillo, mains US$3-7) wins hands-down for the best *pastor* around, served traditional-style with raw onions and cilantro. This is where the mariachi bands from Los Cabos stop to eat their lunch. Meals begin with a tray of four fresh salsas. If pork isn't your thing, try the tacos *de pollo,* carne, or chorizo. Look for an outdoor grill and patio with red and blue plastic tables on the east side of Degollado, at the speed bumps and across from the turn to La Poza.

Cafés

Attention to detail and a love of improvisation set ❏ **Café Brown** (Hidalgo and Colegio Militar, tel. 612/145-0813, 8am-8pm Wed.-Sun., mains US$4-9) apart from your average small-town café. Enjoy a limited menu of home-style cooking made from quality ingredients (Sonora beef, breads from a bakery in La Paz) while you check your email on the fastest wireless connection in town (US$2/hour). Friendly and attentive service sets the tone; good music completes the experience. Art that doesn't have permanent gallery space often finds a home here. And from informal cooking classes and independent films to percussion instruction and salsa dancing, owners Iker and his wife love to throw a good party. Iker also offers cooking classes around town. Look for Café Brown in the back of the Maria Bonita Hotel (formerly Hotel Misión del Pilar) complex.

Next to Boyitacos, **Cafélix** (Juárez near Hidalgo, tel. 612/145-0568, 7am-10pm Mon.-Sat., 9am-10pm Sun., mains US$4-6) makes good coffee, bagels, hot breakfasts, smoothies, and more. The Wi-Fi is free and reliable.

The smell of homemade bread and mini donuts wafts out of ◖ **Caffé Todos Santos** (Centenario 33, tel. 612/145-0300, 7am-2pm Mon., 7am-9pm Tues.-Sun., mains US$6-12) in the morning. This is the place to get your espresso fix, with fresh pastries, waffles, and omelets to boot.

Five minutes north of town on the way to La Pastora, ◖ **La Esquina** (Topete at Horizonte, tel. 612/145-0851, www.laesquinats.com, 7am-7pm Mon.-Sat., mains US$3-6) offers strong coffee, build-your-own sandwiches with three different kinds of homemade bread, excellent soup of the day, and a huge variety of fresh fruit juices and smoothies as well as a great selection of loose leaf and bagged teas. There's free wireless—and they do occasional movie screenings in the evenings as well as hosting eco-café nights, featuring discussions on local ecological issues. Pick up your own bag of organic coffee beans from Chiapas. Drop by on Wednesday mornings for a farmers market 9am-noon.

If all you need is a cup of coffee, look for **Café Combate** (Juárez, Hwy. 19, no tel., hours vary) on the way to La Paz.

Next to Buena Vida Pizza, **Pastelería La Espiguita** (Hidalgo at Militar, tel. 612/145-0878, laespiguita@yahoo.com, hours vary) makes a long list of *licuados* (smoothies) and pastries to go with the drinks.

Groceries
Basic food supplies line the shelves of several markets in town, including **Mercadito**

Guluarte (next to Hotel Guluarte), **Tienda Disconsa** (Colegio Militar), **Super Mercado Hermanos González** (Pedrajo), and **Supermercado El Sol** (Degollado, open till 10pm nightly). A second El Sol is on the road to Playa La Pastora one block west of Hacienda Inn Todos Santos.

La Siempre Viva (Juárez and Márquez de León, open from 7am) sells meats, cheeses, produce, and honey from local farms and ranches. It usually opens an hour or two earlier than the competition, and it carries some household goods and ranch supplies in addition to groceries.

Panadería Todos Santos (Rangel and Ocampo, 2pm-8pm or until sold out Mon.-Sat.) sells a full lineup of Mexican breads, including *bolillos* and *pan dulce*—all baked in a wood-fired oven. The bakery occupies an unsigned two-story brick building at the north end of Calle Rangel near Ocampo. Bread lovers enjoy it, as there aren't many places like this one around.

You can buy fresh *tortillas de maíz* for about US$1 per kilo at the **Super Tortillería de Todos Santos** (Colegio Militar btwn. Morelos and Márquez de León). Head to Punta Lobos to buy fresh seafood directly from the *pangueros*. Closer to town, **Pescadería Todos Santos** (Degollado btwn. Cuauhtémoc and Carrillo, hours vary) carries a sampling of the local catch. **Bodega Lizarraga** (Colegio Militar and Obregón, www.bodegalizarraga.com.mx) has the biggest selection of fruits and vegetables in town, and it's without question the cleanest.

Homemade ice cream awaits at **Paletería la Paloma** (8am-9pm daily), on Colegio Militar next to Maria Bonita Hotel, along with icy fresh fruit *paletas* (popsicles). Pushcart vendors sometimes sell *paletas* around town. **Nevería Rocco** (Hidalgo btwn. Centenario and Juárez, 11am-9:30pm Mon.-Sat., 10am-2pm Sun.), a small shop in a pink house, sells Carnation ice cream and *paletas*.

When the tacos and beer catch up with you, head to ◖ **Pura Vida** (tel. 612/169-2095, www.posadadelmolinots.com, 8am-5pm Mon.-Sat., mains US$4-8) for healthier fare. Located inside the Hotel Posada del Molino, this tiny store stocks local organic eggs, soy milk, Sprouted brand breads and tortillas, Brown Cow yogurt, desert honey, herbal teas, and a limited selection of Asian foods. Order a smoothie or panini and enjoy the patio setting.

La Esquina Farmers Market takes place 9am-noon Wednesday morning. Vendors sell organic produce, artisan cheeses, tamales, handicrafts, and more. On Saturday a similar market tales place at La Cañada del Diablo.

For a bottle of top-quality, made-in-Baja wine, browse the shelves at **La Bodega de Todos Santos** (Hidalgo btwn. Juárez and Militar, tel. 612/152-0181, 11am-7pm Tues.-Sat.), where Mac and Alexandra, distributors of boutique Baja California (Norte) wines to local restaurants, now sell directly to the public as well. The shop carries wines from Bodega Barón Balch'é, Mogor Badan, Viñas Pijoan, Vinisterra, Victor Torres Alegre y Familia, and others. Inside the shop, you can view a map and photos of the wine country and ask the owners about this relatively undiscovered grape-growing region. Prices are reasonable, starting at about US$15 per bottle. On Monday 5pm-8pm, Mac and Alexandra pour tastings and wines by the glass, with local cheeses and tapas from local restaurants. Pick up a bottle of olive oil cultivated in the Valle de Guadalupe while you're there.

Information and Services

TOURIST ASSISTANCE

Todos Santos does not have an official tourist office, but most businesses in town are usually able to answer visitors' questions. **El Tecolote Books/Libros** (Juárez and Hidalgo, tel. 612/145-0295, katemlewis@ yahoo.com) is usually a good place to start. If you speak Spanish and want information on the sierra backcountry, go to La Siempre Viva, which is where the ranchers often go to stock up on supplies. You can also visit Baja.com for up-to-date information on the Todos Santos area.

POSTAL AND TELEPHONE SERVICES

The post office in Todos Santos has moved to the outskirts of town at Villarino between Olochea and Piacentini. It's supposed to be open 8am-1pm and 3pm-5pm, but the hours tend to be erratic, since the manager is often out delivering mail.

Long-distance phone calls can be made from several Ladatel phones around town, including one on Hidalgo, near El Tecolote Books/ Libros. **El Centro de Mensajes Todos Santos (The Message Center),** in the lobby of Hotel California (Juárez btwn. Morelos and Márquez de León, tel. 612/145-0525, fax 612/145-0288, messagecenter1@yahoo.com, 8am-3pm Mon.-Fri., 8am-2pm Sat.) offers long-distance service at reasonable rates. The office also provides fax, DHL, mail forwarding, travel, and answering services.

For mobile phone needs, there are Telcel stores on Militar at Zaragoza, on Militar at Hidalgo, and on Degollado next to the Pemex.

INTERNET ACCESS

Many Todos Santos guesthouses and hotels now have wireless Internet service. In addition, **Café Brown** (Hidalgo and Colegio Militar, tel. 612/145-0813, 8am-8pm Wed.-Sun.), in the Hotel Maria Bonita complex, has high-speed access on its own PC or via a wireless connection. Cafélix and La Esquina are also good options for free Wi-Fi on the go.

Many places in the Pescadero area now have wireless Internet; locals congregate at Baja Beans Roasting Company. **Gonver's Coffee Shop** (located exactly across from the Pemex, no tel.) charges US$2 per hour for the use of one its computers, and the service is free if you buy a coffee or a muffin. This place makes great smoothies.

EMERGENCY SERVICES

For **police, fire,** and **Red Cross** services, call 612/145-0445. The **Centro de Salud** (tel. 612/145-0095, open 24/7 for emergencies) is at the corner of Calle Juárez and Degollado. **Farmacia Guadalupe** (Juárez, tel. 612/145-0300) fills prescriptions 24/7. Another option is **Farmacia Genericos y Similares** (Hidalgo at Militar), in the Maria Bonita Hotel complex.

BANKS

You can withdraw dollars or pesos from the ATMs in town. **Banorte** (Juárez at Obregón, no tel., 9am-4pm Mon.-Fri.) will cash travelers checks or exchange dollars (passport required). **Bancomer** (no tel.), at Juárez and Zaragoza, is another option.

GAS

There is a **Pemex** station in town at the intersection of Militar and Degollado (Highway 19) and one at kilometer 50-51 on the way north to La Paz. Count your change carefully at either one.

El Pescadero has the only Pemex between Cabo San Lucas and Todos Santos, as well as an Oxxo convenience store. For emergencies, call 612/145-0445 or head to Todos Santos or the Los Cabos area for medical services. Buses en route to La Paz and Cabo San Lucas stop across from the Pemex.

HARDWARE AND AUTO PARTS

Ferre Todos Santos (Zaragoza at Rangel, tel. 612/145-0565, 8am-2pm and 3pm-6:30pm Mon.-Sat.) has employees who speak English and stocks a decent selection of hardware goods. **Ferretería Oasis de Todos Santos** (Rangel at Zaragoza, tel. 612/145-0754, 8am-3pm and 4pm-7pm Mon.-Fri., 8am-4pm Sat.) has fishing supplies as well as plumbing and electrical parts.

Across from Neptune's laundry, well-stocked **Autopartes de la Rosa** (Militar btwn. Morelos and Zaragoza), 10am-6pm Mon-Sat.) can help with a variety of automotive needs.

CLASSES

Guillermo Bueron (cell 612/161-4165, g_bueron@yahoo.com) teaches Spanish-, English-, and French-language classes at the Centro Cultural (Juárez at Topete) using the Berlitz approach. He offers group and individual classes at all levels. Classes take place at 9am Monday-Friday. Check the **Todos Santos Inn** website (www.todossantosinn.com) for weeklong packages that include two hours of language instruction per day, plus accommodations. **Casa Bentley** (www.casabentley.com) also arranges on-site classes with Guillermo for its guests.

VOLUNTEER OPPORTUNITIES

Todos Santos has a few well-organized non-profit organizations working toward the betterment of the community that accept temporary volunteers—as well as a wide variety of donations, from sheets and pillows to toys and books for children. Those traveling with some extra time and/or the desire to integrate themselves into the community might like to hook up with some of those organizations and leave the place a little better than they found it.

The Palapa Society of Todos Santos, A.C. (Obregón 15, tel. 612/145-0299, www.palapasociety.org), founded in 2003, is a multicultural nonprofit Mexican Civil Association that provides programs, events, and activities for children in the area—as well as medical services, educational scholarships, English-language instruction, and environmental education. Visitors can get involved by mentoring a child in English for a day, assisting local artists in mural-painting workshops, or visiting the Todos Santos bilingual library. Proceeds from some of the town's events, such as the February Historic Home Tour, benefit this organization and its programs.

For the environmentally inclined, **Tortugueros Las Playitas A.C.** (www.todostorutgueros.org) seeks volunteers for its sea turtle conservation work November through April. This is a great way for kids and adults to get involved in an initiative that affects visitors and residents alike.

For an organized trip that includes some volunteering, check the **Todos Santos Eco** Adventures site (www.tosea.net). For more ideas, stop by the **Centro Cultural** (tel. 612/145-0041) on Calle Juárez at Topete.

Getting There and Around

The drive from Cabo San Lucas to Todos Santos via Highway 19 and the West Cape takes approximately one hour—making it an easy day trip for visitors who are staying in the Los Cabos area—or a slightly longer drive (90 minutes) directly from the airport.

You can take in most of what Todos Santos has to offer in a full day of sightseeing, covering the historic buildings and galleries in town and a beach or two along the coast. But as with most other towns in Baja, you'll enjoy the West Cape infinitely more if you stay long enough to wander kilometers of virgin, as-yet-undeveloped beaches stretching north and south from Todos Santos along the Pacific, explore the steep western escarpment of the Sierra de la Laguna, or simply hang out and soak up the small-town ambience.

Backpackers often plan multiday trips into the sierra from the West Cape. If that sounds too challenging, guides also run half-day hikes as well as trail rides on ATVs. A day of fishing or surfing could also lengthen your stay. Of course, if you're into these activities, a day probably isn't enough. Surfers can easily spend a week or a month trying to master the winter breaks here. And the fishing—whether by boat, surf rod, or hand line—is just as addictive.

BY AIR

Todos Santos is more or less equidistant from the Los Cabos and La Paz airports. A shuttle from Los Cabos costs approximately US$150, while a shuttle from La Paz runs US$200-300.

BY CAR

Though not essential, most travelers will want to have a car while staying in the West Cape and Todos Santos, as the beaches and sights are spread out from the two small towns. If you don't rent a car at the airport or drive your own from the United States, you can rent one in Todos Santos. Mexican-owned **Fox Rent a Car** (formerly a Budget affiliate, Márquez de León 4, tel. 612/145-0087, toll-free U.S. tel. 855/225-2411, www.foxrentacar.com, 8am-6pm Mon.-Sat.) offers a small fleet of cars from economy to SUV.

Highway 19 connects Todos Santos to Cabo San Lucas to the south and La Paz to the north. From the Los Cabos airport, follow the Transpeninsular Highway (Highway 1) toward Cabo San Lucas and take the turnoff for Todos Santos/Highway 19. From La Paz, follow the Carretera Transpeninsular south to the turnoff for Highway 19, which is now four lanes the entire way to Todos Santos. There are numerous Pemex stations in La Paz, Todos Santos, Pescadero, and Cabo San Lucas. If you need a mechanic during your visit, there are a couple of options in Todos Santos, but you may have to head south to Cabo San Lucas for complicated transmission work.

BY TAXI

A small fleet of blue vans parked next to the park in Todos Santos can provide taxi service around town for US$5 a trip. Taxi service to El Pescadero is about US$20. A van all the way to Los Cabos International Airport will cost around US$200; vans can hold 8-15 people with luggage. Call 612/145-0063 for more information.

BY BUS

Nine Aguila buses a day connect Todos Santos to La Paz and Cabo San Lucas. The La Paz and Cabo San Lucas bus trips take about two

TODOS SANTOS

hours and cost about US$8 per person; a bus all the way around to San José del Cabo costs US$12; to Tijuana, US$130. Tickets are sold on the buses, which arrive at and depart from Colegio Militar and Zaragoza (for San José del Cabo and Cabo San Lucas) or in front of Karla's Lonchería (for La Paz). In El Pescadero, buses stop across the street from the Pemex.

ACCOMMODATIONS

Whether you are a first-time or veteran Los Cabos visitor, finding a place to stay involves an overwhelming variety of choices. There are all-inclusive resorts, boutique hotels, basic motels, bed-and-breakfasts, condominiums, timeshares, and villas of all sizes. (And some resorts mix and match, to give even more choice.) You can be at the beach, on a golf course, or in town.

COURTESY OF PUEBLO BONITO LOS CABOS

HIGHLIGHTS

LOOK FOR (TO FIND RECOMMENDED LODGING.

COURTESY OF ME CABO

the spa at ME Cabo

(**Posada Yuca Inn:** This inn, just off the plaza in the heart of San José del Cabo, offers simple accommodations for budget travelers in a prime location (page 135).

(**Casa Natalia:** This boutique-style accommodation with a European flair is ideal for travelers looking for a sophisticated place to stay (page 137).

(**Hilton Los Cabos Beach & Golf Resort:** This is the best resort for families traveling with young children (page 146).

(**Dreams Los Cabos Suites Golf Resort & Spa:** This perennial favorite for a high-end all-inclusive stay is popular with travelers celebrating major events or anniversaries (page 149).

(**The Bungalows:** This welcome oasis from the bustle of downtown Cabo San Lucas has

a warm and friendly staff and delicious daily breakfast options (page 153).

(**ME Cabo:** A trendy crowd frequents this see-and-be-seen adults-only hotel. This is where the party crowd enjoys rooms with ocean views, reasonable prices, and good service (page 159).

(**Rancho Pescadero:** For romance and contemporary style just steps from the surf, lock in your spot at this couples getaway in El Pescadero (page 165).

(**Todos Santos Inn:** History buffs will appreciate the colonial charm at this inn in the heart of bohemian Todos Santos (page 170).

(**Los Colibris Casitas:** These hilltop vacation rental homes offer unobstructed ocean views and eco-tours of the area (page 172).

You can book directly with a resort or private owner or use a booking service or property management company. And you can spend US$50-950 a night, depending on your budget and the level of comfort you seek.

If you'd like a quieter location where you can look at the beach but swim in a pool, the Corridor or hotel zone of San José would be a good choice. If you want to surf, consider Playa Costa Azul, just outside San José, or one of the Cabo Real resorts on the Corridor. For swimming and nightlife within walking distance of your hotel, head to Cabo San Lucas.

High-end resorts feature a full list of amenities, usually including air-conditioning, direct-dial phones, satellite TV, multiple swimming pools, swim-up bars, tennis courts, hot tubs, fitness centers, kids' club, and beach *palapas,* plus on-site restaurants and bars. Some resorts also have their own dive centers, spa services, horseback riding, and ATV rental services. High-speed wireless Internet, VoIP phones (free long distance), and flat-screen TVs are often included as well.

Vacation rental condos or villas, or condo-style hotels, afford the most flexibility, as you can cook some of your own meals and venture out for others. Many of the newest condo complexes are concentrated near Playa Costa Azul, between San José and the Corridor. Most are on or near the beach, and many have tennis courts, swimming pools, and laundry facilities; however, the persistent sound of traffic on the Carretera Transpeninsular is a drawback to this location. You can rent units directly from private owners by searching for listings online (on www.craigslist.com and www.vrbo.com, for example) or by contacting a property management service. (Many of these services also advertise on the private-owner sites.)

If you are thinking about a year-end holiday vacation, book as far in advance as possible. Repeat visitors reserve many of the most popular rooms and rentals as much as a year in advance for the weeks around Christmas and New Year's Day. February and March are popular, too, and despite the number of choices for accommodations, there are a handful of resorts—including the One&Only Palmilla, Dreams, and Riu Palace—that seem to be full almost all the time. Flexible travelers need not plan so far ahead, and they are often rewarded with better deals.

San José del Cabo

Besides the major hotels and "condotels" in the Zona Hotelera along the beach, San José offers some smaller, reasonably priced inns in the town itself. A downtown location puts you close to shops and restaurants, with a short drive or long walk to the beach. Condos and hotels along Playa Azul are about a 5- to 10-minute drive from town, depending on traffic. Rates are given for double occupancy in the high season (holiday rates may be higher) and do not include 12 percent tax and 10 percent service charge, unless otherwise noted. Discounts may be available for stays of a week or longer.

CENTRO HISTORICO
Under US$100
◖ POSADA YUCA INN
A few steps from Plaza Mijares, on the same block as the Casa de la Cultura, the charming **Posada Yuca Inn** (Obregón 1A, tel. 624/142-0462, www.yucainn.com.mx, US$40-50) is something of a mix of a hostel, bed-and-breakfast, and motel. It has three simple hotel-style rooms, each with its own refrigerator, remote-control air-conditioning, and private bath. Additional bunk rooms offer even less-expensive hostel-style accommodations for US$16 per

person and US$25 for two. The inn has its own water purification system, so you don't need to buy drinking water. Walk to the San José del Cabo Mercado Organico on Saturday mornings and return to the inn to prepare your meal in the shared *cocina* (kitchen). The owner, Rogelio Lopez, whose nickname is Yuca, grows Mexican oregano, *epazote* (used in enchilada sauce), and other herbs, as well as vegetables, in several raised beds in the courtyard of the inn; plus there are numerous fruit trees on the property—grapefruit, oranges, *guanábanas* (soursop), and lemons. Guests are welcome to pick whatever is ripe. Amenities include a swimming pool, Wi-Fi, and parking at the backside of the building. The inn does not typically offer daily maid service but will change your towels as needed.

HOTEL POSADA SEÑOR MAÑANA
Hotel Posada Señor Mañana (Obregón 1B, tel./fax 624/142-1372, US$40-70) has several rooms connected by a labyrinth of ramps and ladders. Each room has a ceiling fan and private bath with hot water. A community kitchen encourages guests to get to know each other. Hammocks look up into mango and coconut trees. Transportation to and from the airport is available for just US$20.

HOTEL COLLI
One of the oldest hotels in town, **Hotel Colli** (Hidalgo btwn. Zaragoza and Doblado, tel. 624/142-0725, www.hotelcolli.com, US$55-70) has a dozen small and clean rooms with simple furnishings, newly tiled baths, and hot water in a building just off the plaza. Its rooms come with ceiling fans, air-conditioning, and private baths. Bottled water is a plus, and the friendly service makes for a comfortable stay. As with any of the downtown hotels, noise is likely to be a minor nuisance at night, but all is usually quiet by about 11pm. There is secure parking under the hotel.

BEST WESTERN HOTEL & SUITES LAS PALMAS
The **Best Western Hotel & Suites Las Palmas** (Carr. Transpeninsular km 31, tel. 624/142-2341, www.suiteslaspalmas.com, US$85) is not in the downtown area, but it makes a satisfactory stop for a night on your way in or out of the area. The pros: a friendly staff, reasonable rates, and the possibility of substantial discounts during peak travel times. Easy access to the more local eateries is another plus, and small kitchenettes mean you can stock up on groceries at the Mega the night before a drive to the East Cape. The cons: A front-row seat next to the highway means the sound of traffic will lull you to sleep. Decor is about as basic as it gets. On one visit, the room and bath were clean enough, but they didn't exactly sparkle. Dishes in the cabinet were sticky, and the dish sponge had been recycled.

CIELITO LINDO BED AND BREAKFAST
Within easy walking distance to the San José del Cabo art district, **Cielito Lindo Bed and Breakfast** (Obregón and Guerrero, tel. 624/130-6338, www.hotelcielitolindo.com, US$37-60) offers clean and basic accommodations. Amenities include a continental breakfast, cable TV, and free Wi-Fi. Hotel staff willingly helps organize visits to and guided tours of local galleries and wineries.

US$100-200
EL ENCANTO INN
In the heart of San José's growing art district, **El Encanto Inn** (Morelos 133, tel. 624/142-0388, U.S. tel. 210/858-6649, www.elencantosuites.com, US$100-190) encompasses two buildings on Calle Morelos. Fluffy towels, king-size beds, and remote-control air-conditioning are a few of the special touches at the newer property, El Encanto Suites. The two-story hacienda surrounds a small swimming pool and courtyard. More economical standard and garden suites are in the original inn. Rooms here are popular with travelers who plan a one-night stopover before heading to or from the East Cape; over the years, some guests have complained about duplicate charges and other complications with advance reservation payments. A café near the pool serves breakfast and drinks, and you can park for free in a gated, but not guarded, lot

across the street. The on-site El Encantado Day Spa offers manicures, pedicures, and massage treatments.

TROPICANA INN

Behind the Tropicana Bar and Grill and set back from busy Boulevard Mijares, the **Tropicana Inn** (Mijares 30, tel. 624/142-1580, www.tropicanainn.com.mx, US$130-200) has 37 rooms and several suites set around a pleasant courtyard, with a fountain, heated swimming pool (a nice feature for winter stays), and several cages of tropical birds to greet you each day. Rooms and baths are on the small side and should be up for renovation soon, but all the standard amenities are there: phones, air-conditioning, Wi-Fi, small fridge, coffeemaker, and satellite TV. Rooms on the ground level tend to be noisy as other guests pass by or linger by the pool. Inquire whether the multicourse continental breakfast is included with your rate—it's a pretty good deal. The inn has a spa with a full menu of treatments.

Over US$200

C CASA NATALIA

Internationally acclaimed **Casa Natalia** (Mijares 4, tel. 624/142-5100 or 888/277-3814, www.casanatalia.com, US$165-375) sets the standard for luxury boutique hotel accommodations in Los Cabos. It has become a favorite venue for small weddings and other formal celebrations. Its 14 rooms and two suites are designed with a contemporary, European flair, including original artwork. Private (though extremely small) terraces with hammocks face a heated swimming pool. And the attached Mi Cocina restaurant (6:30pm-10pm daily, mains US$18-32), run by owner Natalie Tenoux's husband, Loïc Tenoux, is just steps away. This is not the place for children under the age of 13.

ZONA HOTELERA

Occupancy rates for the hotels along Playa California have been climbing in recent years to match those of their busier Cabo San Lucas peers, though you may still be able to negotiate

a deal during off-peak seasons. Whether you choose a hotel or condo, beware that demolitions, renovations, and new construction are in progress all over this area, even during the peak travel season. There's a good chance you'll end up next to, above, or below a noisy construction zone. The hammering, sawing, and drilling typically begins at 8:30am and lasts till 5:30pm. Do your homework before you book. Most of the resorts in this area are all-inclusive only. For more flexible meal plans, consider expanding your search to the Los Cabos Corridor.

Under US$100

MARISOL BOUTIQUE HOTEL

A friendly staff, excellent location, and clean and affordable rooms make the **Marisol Boutique Hotel** (Plaza Garuffi, off Paseo del Malecón, tel. 624/142-4040 or 624/145-2244, www.marisol.com.mx, US$45-60) ideal for travelers on a budget or those who just don't need the resort experience. The hotel is located in Plaza Garuffi, between the Barceló resort and Las Mañanitas condos, one block from the beach and a short stroll to the Mega supermarket and a few restaurants. Rooms come with TVs, refrigerators, and free Wi-Fi. A complimentary continental breakfast is served Monday-Saturday. Because there are only eight rooms, reservations are essential.

US$100-200

HOLIDAY INN RESORT LOS CABOS ALL INCLUSIVE

At the far northeastern end of the Zona Hotelera, next to the Estero San José, the 400-room **Holiday Inn Resort Los Cabos All Inclusive** (formerly the Presidente InterContinental, Paseo del Malecón, tel. 624/142-9229, toll-free U.S. tel. 877/859-5095, www.ichotelsgroup.com, US$180-270) is an older property with a convenient location to downtown San José. Rooms are a bit outdated, meals are reportedly decent, and the resort has separate activities areas for adults and families. Timeshare sales can be a nuisance here.

SAN JOSÉ DEL CABO ACCOMMODATIONS

	Type	Location	Rates
Barceló Los Cabos	All-inclusive	San José del Cabo	US$250 and up
Bel Aire Collection Resort & Spa Los Cabos	Resort	San José del Cabo	US$120 and up
Best Western Aeropuerto	Hotel	San José del Cabo	US$90
Best Western Hotel & Suites Las Palmas	Hotel	San José del Cabo	US$85
Cabo Azul Resort	Resort	San José del Cabo	US$300-800
Cabo Surf Hotel	Resort	San José del Cabo	US$300-625
Casa Natalia	Boutique hotel	San José del Cabo	US$165-375
Cielito Lindo Bed and Breakfast	B&B	San José del Cabo	US$37-60
Desire Resort & Spa Los Cabos	All-inclusive	San José del Cabo	US$170 pp and up
El Delfin Blanco	B&B	San José del Cabo	US$57-99
El Encanto Inn	Hotel	San José del Cabo	US$100-190
The Grand Mayan Los Cabos	All-inclusive	San José del Cabo	US$155 and up
Hola Grand Faro Los Cabos	All-inclusive	San José del Cabo	US$220 pp and up
Holiday Inn Resort Los Cabos All Inclusive	All-inclusive	San José del Cabo	US$180-270
Hotel Colli	Hotel	San José del Cabo	US$55-70
Hotel El Ganzo	Resort	San José del Cabo	US$250
Hotel Posada Señor Mañana	Hotel	San José del Cabo	US$40-70
La Fonda del Mar Bed and Breakfast	B&B	San José del Cabo	US$75-95
La Marina Inn	B&B	San José del Cabo	US$80-165
Las Mañanitas	Condo	San José del Cabo	US$225-475
Marisol Boutique Hotel	Boutique hotel	San José del Cabo	US$45-60
Mykonos Bay Resort	Condo	San José del Cabo	US$130-290
Posada Chabela Bed and Breakfast	B&B	San José del Cabo	US$79-110
Posada Real Los Cabos	Resort	San José del Cabo	US$120-210 pp
Posada Yuca Inn	Hotel	San José del Cabo	US$40-50
Royal Solaris Los Cabos Hotel	All-inclusive	San José del Cabo	US$145-175 pp
Sampaguita Luxury Townhouse/Condominiums	Condo	San José del Cabo	US$200-300
Tropicana Inn	Hotel	San José del Cabo	US$130-200

Best Feature(s)	Why Stay Here	Best Fit For
Sophisticated atmosphere	Spa and large events	Luxury lovers
Champagne at sunset and beachside spa services	Sunbathing and attentive service	Couples or small groups
Airport-adjacent	Convenience	Budget travelers
Reasonable rates and friendly staff	A place to crash on your way in or out of the area	Budget travelers
Spa and nightly poolside performances	Luxury and entertainment	Adult travelers
Surf school	Learn to surf	Adventure seekers
Charming decor and no children under 13	Quiet retreat, weddings, and other adult celebrations	Couples or small groups
Location	Steps from the art district	Budget travelers
Clothing optional	Free yourself	Alternative lifestyle
Authentic Mexican experience	Steps from the marina	Solo, budget, or travelers looking to fish
Location	In the heart of the art district	One-night stopovers
Nightly shows and entertainment	Location	Couples or small groups
Location	Proximity to downtown San José del Cabo	Business travelers
Location	Walking distance to the Estero San José and downtown entertainment	Budget travelers
Clean and affordable	Friendly service right downtown	Budget travelers
Brand new at Puerto Los Cabos	Access to the Puerto Los Cabos marina	Yachters
Central location	Affordability	Budget travelers
Value	Modest accommodations at a good value	Budget travelers
Steps from the marina	Sportfishing	Anglers
Convenient to town	Beach vacation with condo amenities	Families
Friendly staff and great location	Great value	Retirees
Beachfront location	Beach vacation with condo amenities	Budget travelers
Welcoming proprietor	Great value and service	Families, couples, LGBT travelers
Location	Modest accommodations at a good value	Budget travelers
Shared kitchen and gardens, steps from the plaza	Community feel for a good value	Budget travelers
Latin show	Convenience	Families
High-end lodging close to town	Beach vacation with condo amenities	Families
Spa and heated pool	Modest accommodations at a good value	Budget travelers

view of Playa California from Posada Real Los Cabos

THE GRAND MAYAN LOS CABOS

The Grand Mayan Los Cabos (Paseo del Malecón, toll-free U.S. tel. 866/802-0674, www.thegrandmayan.com, US$155 and up), which opened in 2007, has a stunning reception area and offers a Wednesday-evening Mayan dinner theater performance and a weekly Fiesta Mexicana. Guests can choose from four restaurants to dine and from a full menu of treatments at the Brio Spa.

ROYAL SOLARIS LOS CABOS HOTEL

On the northeast side of the Crowne Plaza, the **Royal Solaris Los Cabos Hotel** (Paseo del Malecón Lte. 10, Zona Hotelera, tel. 624/145-6800, toll-free U.S. tel. 866/289-8466, www.clubsolaris.com, US$145-175 pp) is one of Los Cabos' most family-friendly, all-inclusive resorts. A water park and club for kids will keep the little ones busy, and there is also a teen club for the 12-17 crowd. Most of its 389 rooms have ocean views, and guests can dine at five restaurants and three bars. Entertainment options include a Tehuacan dinner theater show and karaoke night. A free snorkeling tour comes with a stay of four nights or more.

POSADA REAL LOS CABOS

The 148 rooms at the **Posada Real Los Cabos** (Paseo del Malecón, tel. 624/142-0155, toll-free U.S. tel. 800/448-8355, www.posadareal.com. mx, US$120-210 pp) are a great value, whether you choose an all-inclusive or European meal plan. Last renovated in 2000, this is a Best Western property and one of the oldest hotels in the region. Clean rooms and friendly staff balance out the somewhat dated decor. Ocean- and garden-view rooms come with two double beds or one king-size bed (mattresses can be hard), air-conditioning (recently upgraded), phone, safe, and TV. Wi-Fi is free. The property has a pool with two hot tubs and swim-up bar, plus its own restaurant. Guests also get discounted rates on car rentals, massage services, fishing trips, and rounds of golf. Rates cover meals, drinks, tips, and tax. Guests enjoy handmade quesadillas on Friday nights and a Mexican buffet for brunch on Saturdays and Sundays. Other nights of the week, the buffet rotates among Italian, seafood, prime rib, international, and other themes.

BEL AIRE COLLECTION RESORT & SPA LOS CABOS

At the **Bel Aire Collection Resort & Spa Los Cabos** (Carr. Transpeninsular km 29, tel. 624/163-4750, www.belaircabos.com, from US$120), guests can dine at one of three restaurants and walk the long stretch of beach adjoining the resort, though it is not safe for swimming. The Collection Spa offers a range of services, including massages, facial treatments, and yoga, as well as specialty packages for couples. Enjoy a complimentary glass of champagne every night at sunset. Guests note the excellent staff service but recommend requesting a room in the resort's newer building.

Over US$200

CABO AZUL RESORT

The **Cabo Azul Resort** (Paseo Malecón, tel. 877/216-2226, www.caboazulresort.com, US$300-800) offers private villas on the beach, close to the intersection of Boulevard Mijares and Paseo Malecón. This is a luxury property with the requisite list of amenities, including a full-service spa called Paz, where a 50-minute massage runs US$120, manicures and pedicures start at US$45, and body treatments like "Draining Onyx" cost US$170-215. The resort's three-level infinity-edge swimming pool features fire-dancing platforms for nightly poolside performances. Dining options include three restaurants and a swim-up pool bar. This place is best for adult travelers. Child care can be arranged through an outside service, but the resort does not have a kids' club or babysitting on-site.

HOLA GRAND FARO LOS CABOS

Hola Grand Faro Los Cabos (formerly Crowne Plaza Los Cabos, Paseo del Malecón,

tel. 624/142-9292, toll-free U.S. tel. 866/365-6932, www.cploscabos.com, US$220 pp and up) hosted the 2013 Ironman Expo. Its large guest room terraces and a saltwater infinity pool are distinguishing features. Children aged four and up can play in the kids' club while adults relax by the pool. Meals are standard resort buffets, served in several on-site restaurants. High-speed Internet access costs US$16 per day. The on-site Natura Room offers a full menu of massage, body, and facial treatments (US$90-110 for 50 minutes). The resort offers free and secure parking underground.

BARCELÓ LOS CABOS

Situated between the Desire and Posada Real resorts along the Zona Hotelera, **Barceló Los Cabos** (formerly The Grand Baja, Paseo del Malecón 5D, tel. 624/146-7500, toll-free U.S. tel. 800/227-2356, www.barcelo.com, US$250 and up), fully renovated in 2009, is now a suites-only all-inclusive resort. Amenities include an American sports bar, smoking lounge, six themed restaurants, U-Spa, gym, and convention center.

DESIRE RESORT & SPA LOS CABOS

Clothing is optional at **Desire Resort & Spa Los Cabos** (formerly the Fiesta Inn, Paseo del Malecón, tel. 624/142-9300, toll-free U.S. tel. 888/201-7551, toll-free Can. tel. 800/655-9311, www.desireresorts.com, US$170 pp and up). Reactions ranged from shock to awe when this couples-only establishment opened in 2006, catering to upscale, "liberated" adults. A red and dark brown color scheme with hand-painted murals of scenes from the *Book of Kama Sutra* set the mood. A clothing-optional pool and whirlpool tub, L'Alternative Disco, and Sensuous Playroom take it over the top. The resort's 150 rooms and suites have king-size beds and flat-screen TVs, among a complete list of standard amenities. From the beach, curious onlookers can recognize the resort by shoulder-height bamboo screens on the terraces that allow for private sunbathing.

PLAYA COSTA AZUL
Under US$100
POSADA CHABELA BED AND BREAKFAST

Just outside of San José del Cabo is the **Posada Chabela Bed and Breakfast** (Tropical 11, tel. 624/172-6490, www.posadochabelacabo.net, US$79-110), offering four casitas for two-night-minimum stays. The casitas overlook Playa Costa Azul, and amenities include continental breakfast, pool, and bar. Owner Rose Ann is known for her friendly, attentive service, and she warmly welcomes guests of all lifestyles, including LGBT travelers.

Over US$200
CABO SURF HOTEL

When the waves are rolling in at Playa Acapulquito, surfers and surfing spectators fill the 22 rooms, suites, and villas of the **Cabo Surf Hotel** (Carr. Transpeninsular km 28, tel. 624/142-2676, U.S. tel. 858/964-5117, www.cabosurfhotel.com, US$300-625). The hotel is part of a Mexican-owned hotel company. Highlights here include marble floors, satellite TV, and in-room Wi-Fi. The largest villas accommodate up to eight guests. You can book a lesson through the Mike Doyle surf school, and when you've had enough of the action in the water, retreat to the on-site spa to recuperate. Then you can dine under an open-air *palapa* at the **7 Seas**, where choices include blue crab tostadas, fresh Baja clams au gratin, and a sea bass and spinach-stuffed chile pepper. The Cabo Surf Hotel hosted the first Ironman Los Cabos triathlon competition in March 2013.

PUERTO LOS CABOS
Under US$100
EL DELFIN BLANCO

At **El Delfin Blanco** (Pueblo La Playa, tel. 624/142-1212, tel./fax 624/142-1199, www.eldelfinblanco.net, US$57-99), Osa Franzen maintains several clean cabanas that are situated about 300 meters from the beach with views of the water. The place attracts independent travelers who seek an authentic Mexican experience as well as a good value in accommodations. You may hear the wind rustling through palm-thatched roofs and dogs barking at night, but you'll also be steps away from the new marina and park at La Playita. Walk to several restaurants or shop in town and cook your own meals in the shared outdoor kitchen.

LA FONDA DEL MAR BED AND BREAKFAST

About 6.5 kilometers past La Playita and Puerto Los Cabos, on the coastal road that hugs the East Cape, **La Fonda del Mar Bed and Breakfast** (Laguna Hills, tel. 624/113-6368, www.buzzardsbar.com, US$75-95) has three rooms with *palapa* roofs, American-style beds, and tile floors. Each has its own half bath but shares a shower. For families, there is a larger suite with a pullout couch and private bath. Guests may order anything off the Buzzard's menu for breakfast, including the famed eggs Benedict on Sunday. The inn is situated almost on the beach, and it's a very short walk along an arroyo to the water's edge. To find La Fonda del Mar, follow the road to La Playita, turn left at the first traffic circle, and go about 6.5 kilometers, following signs for Laguna Hills and El Encanto. The inn changed hands in 2010 and is now under Canadian ownership.

US$100-200
LA MARINA INN

Just steps from the new *panga* marina, **La Marina Inn** (formerly La Playita Inn, Pueblo La Playa, tel./fax 624/142-4166, www.lamarinainn.com, US$80-165) has managed to stay its course through all the development and change around it. This three-story Mexican-style inn is a good choice if you are planning to fish or simply want to stay away from the hustle and bustle of downtown San José. Its air-conditioned rooms each have a large shower and two queen beds. Amenities include a small pool and an authentic Mexican seafood restaurant, La Marina.

© PAUL ITOI

Hotel El Ganzo

Over US$200
HOTEL EL GANZO

The upscale **Hotel El Ganzo** (Blvd. Tiburon s/n, Col. La Playita, Puerto Los Cabos Marina, tel. 624/105-6600, www.elganzo.com, US$250) opened in December 2012. This stylish hotel features a rooftop sushi bar, infinity pool, and even an on-site recording studio. The 72 guest rooms are both chic and comfortable with luxurious amenities.

AIRPORT
Under US$100
BEST WESTERN AEROPUERTO

A new **Best Western Aeropuerto** hotel (Acceso al Aeropuerto M-14C L-05, US$90) opened at the Los Cabos International Airport in late 2012. There is nothing charming about it, but it is sparkling new, and if you were to land after dark and need a place to crash before driving the next day, it's a better option than none at all.

CONDOMINIUMS AND CONDO HOTELS

Condominium complexes are sprouting up on the outskirts of San José as fast as all-inclusive resorts. Las Olas (closest to the lookout point at Zippers surf break), El Zalate (next to the Coral Baja timeshare resort), and Sampaguita (closer to the hotel zone) are just a few of the more recent properties to open. Owners rent vacant units to visitors for anywhere from US$120 a night for a studio or one-bedroom to around US$450 or more for a deluxe two- or three-bedroom unit. Rates can vary quite a bit even within the same complex, depending on location and views and how the unit is furnished. Be sure to inquire how close the unit is to the highway and whether there is construction underway inside the building. At Mykonos and other complexes nearby, the persistent sound of heavy traffic on the Carretera Transpeninsular can drown out the sound of waves crashing onto the beach. Discounted weekly and monthly rates are sometimes available.

The payment process for a condo is different from reserving a hotel room: Property managers typically require a deposit of 50 percent of the rental fee by check or direct deposit to a U.S. bank account and the remaining amount by cash upon arrival. Cleaning fees are often added to the rental fee. Sometimes full payment is required before arrival—all the more reason to get the information you need before committing to a particular unit.

MYKONOS BAY RESORT
Mediterranean-inspired **Mykonos Bay Resort** (Carr. Transpeninsular km 29, tel. 624/142-3789, one-bedroom US$130-290) rents one- and two-bedroom condos in three buildings, each with air-conditioning, satellite TV, kitchen, and washer/dryer. Amenities include a basic gym and lighted tennis court. Buildings B and C have larger units and are closest to the beach and quieter than Building A, which has smaller units and picks up more noise from the highway.

LAS MAÑANITAS AND SAMPAGUITA LUXURY TOWNHOUSE/CONDOMINIUMS
Within walking distance of the Mega shopping plaza as well as the beach, the sprawling **Las Mañanitas** complex has some of the nicest condos around for US$225-475 per night. Next door, **Sampaguita Luxury Townhouse/Condominiums** is newer and smaller, with only 14 units in a quiet, gated complex that has a pool, hot tub, and tennis court. Two-bedroom units run about US$200-300 per night. To inquire about these properties you need to contact the individual owners through www.vrbo.com, www.craigslist.org, a booking service, or property management company.

Booking Services and Property Management Companies
BAJA PROPERTIES
Baja Properties (Doblado and Morelos, tel. 624/142-0988, toll-free U.S. tel. 877/464-2252, www.bajaproperties.com) manages one-, two-, and three-bedroom rentals in Las Mañanitas for US$250-525 per night as well as a few less expensive locations.

NASH GROUP PROPERTIES
Nash Group Properties (Paseo Finisterra #107, www.bajaholidays.com), run by the owners of the Casa del Jardín B&B, manages several rental properties in Mykonos, Las Olas, and a few other complexes.

SEASIDE VACATIONS
SeaSide Vacations (tel. 250/999-1095, www.sea-side.com) has a variety of units in several buildings in the area.

The Corridor

The most upscale and well known resorts in Los Cabos are clustered along a stretch of coastline between San José del Cabo and Cabo San Lucas, known as the Tourist Corridor. These are purpose-built mega resorts, designed to cater to your every need—including food/drink, recreation, exercise, romance, entertainment, child care, and, of course, relaxation. Prices for accommodations begin around US$250-400 for the Sheraton and Hilton, climb to US$500 for the Westin and Marquis, and top out at US$700-1,000 per night or more for the One&Only Palmilla, Esperanza, and Las Ventanas. The lowest rates at each resort typically require full payment at the time of booking, and cancellation fees apply. All-inclusive packages are attractive to many value-conscious travelers. Travel club memberships such as AAA can yield a discount of US$100 or more per night. The standard rates do not include 12 percent tax and 15 percent service, unless otherwise noted. Resorts are listed geographically, from east (near San José del Cabo) to west (near Cabo

San Lucas). All properties in this area are over US$200.

NEAR SAN JOSÉ
Over US$200
ONE&ONLY PALMILLA

The oldest resort in Los Cabos is also one of the destination's most expensive—and most popular—places to stay. Originally built in 1956 by "Rod" Rodríguez, son of former Mexican president Abelardo Luis Rodríguez, the **One&Only Palmilla** (Carr. Transpeninsular km 27, tel. 624/146-7000, toll-free U.S. tel. 866/829-2977, www.oneandonlyresorts.com, US$600 and up) has a prime location against a cliff on Punta Palmilla near San José. Over the years, it has grown from one hotel to encompass an entire resort community. Like Esperanza, this is a place for travelers who want to be pampered and are willing to pay for the personal service—which includes everything from loaner iPods and sunglasses cleaning at the pool to golf cart shuttles to get you to and from your room. The result is a private and relaxing five-star vacation. Activities include yoga, spa treatments, and golf. You can watch cooking demonstrations and dine at **Herb Garden** or the Mediterranean **Agua Restaurant.**

WESTIN RESORT & SPA LOS CABOS

A dramatic architectural interpretation of the arch at Land's End stands at the center of the **Westin Resort & Spa Los Cabos** (Carr. Transpeninsular km 22.5, tel. 624/142-9000, toll-free U.S. tel. 800/598-1864, www.westin-loscabos.com, US$350-700). Mexican architect Javier Sordo Magdaleno designed the hillside resort with bright colors and views from every vantage point.

The chain's signature Heavenly Beds are reason enough to stay here. Separate tubs and showers in large marble bathrooms add even more of a distinctive touch.

Several restaurants on-site provide a variety of dining experiences; they include eclectic **Arrecifes** and **La Cascada,** which serves tapas from around the world.

A European-style spa offers body wraps, mud baths, and massage treatments inside or on the beach. Guests have golf privileges at the Cabo Real Golf Course, about 2.5 kilometers southwest.

SECRETS MARQUIS LOS CABOS

From the inlaid turquoise stones that accent resort corridors to perfectly filtered light in the spa rooms, meticulous attention to detail and contemporary Mexican decor set the tone for a stay at the **Secrets Marquis Los Cabos** (Carr. Transpeninsular km 21.5, tel. 624/144-2000, toll-free U.S. tel. 877/238-9399, www.secretsresorts.com/marquis, US$450-700). Opened in 2003, the resort was designed to reveal ocean views from every angle. Guests can move from their room to a restaurant, the spa, or the gym without losing sight of the sea.

Originally Mexican-owned, the resort became a Secrets all-inclusive property in 2012. The Marquis's 237 rooms have soaking tubs and showers, Bulgary bath fixtures, mahogany woodwork, flat-screen TVs, and exquisite linens. Each morning, hotel staff delivers breakfast to guests through a private pass-through alcove. In addition, rooms and common areas showcase contemporary Mexican paintings and sculpture. And if you fall in love with the eclectic furnishings, as many guests apparently have, you can buy your own from a furniture store on the premises. Twenty-eight *casitas* have their own swimming pools. A 929-square-meter spa sets the hotel apart. Proximity to the highway and small balconies are the only obvious disadvantages at this resort. Adults only.

CABO REAL
US$100-200
MARBELLA SUITES EN LA PLAYA

Marbella Suites en la Playa (Carr. Transpeninsular km 17, tel. 624/144-1060, www.marbellasuites.com, US$83-319) offers a selection of 41 affordable rooms. This "hidden gem" sits among a string of larger, pricier resorts and provides many of the same amenities. A secluded beach, El Tule, is ideal for fishing or simply relaxing and taking in the sun, and the hotel has an observation deck

THE CORRIDOR ACCOMMODATIONS

	Type	Location	Rates
Dreams Los Cabos Suites Golf Resort & Spa	All-inclusive	Corridor	From US$400
Esperanza Resort	Resort	Corridor	US$600-850
Fiesta Americana Grand Los Cabos	Resort	Corridor	US$450-600
Hacienda Encantada Resort & Spa	Resort	Corridor	US$225-800
Hilton Los Cabos Beach & Golf Resort	Resort	Corridor	From US$250
Las Ventanas al Paraíso	Resort	Corridor	From US$750
Marbella Suites en La Playa	Resort	Corridor	US$83-319
Meliá Cabo Real All Inclusive Beach & Golf Resort	All-inclusive	Corridor	From US$250
One&Only Palmilla	Resort	Corridor	US$600 and up
Secrets Marquis Los Cabos	All-inclusive	Corridor	US$450-700
Sheraton Hacienda del Mar	Resort	Corridor	From US$400
Westin Resort & Spa Los Cabos	Resort	Corridor	US$350-700
Zoëtry Casa del Mar Los Cabos	Resort	Corridor	From US$500

for whale-watching and sunsets. La Terraza restaurant is open for breakfast, lunch, and dinner and includes a full bar. Free Wi-Fi, an oceanfront pool, two hot tubs, billiards, table tennis, and a new sports bar complete the services Marbella provides its guests. Limited elevator service and numerous stairs could make accommodations difficult for guests with disabilities.

Over US$200
◖ HILTON LOS CABOS BEACH & GOLF RESORT

Next to the Secrets Marquis Los Cabos and Meliá Cabo Real resorts, the **Hilton Los Cabos Beach & Golf Resort** (Carr. Transpeninsular km 19.5, Cabo Real, tel. 624/145-6500, wwww.hiltonloscabos.com, from US$250) is our favorite pick for families with children young and old. The resort features Mediterranean architecture, a beautiful infinity pool, and a complete list of luxury-style amenities, plus a most favorable location on Playa Bledito. This is one of the few swimmable beaches along the Corridor, and it's ideal for kids and grown-ups who want to splash around in the sea. Snorkeling, body surfing, and swimming are all possible a short walk across the sand from your room. You can rent kayaks and WaveRunners at the beach as well.

All 375 rooms have an ocean view and private balcony in this W-shaped property. Rooms were renovated in 2005 by designer Paul Duesing and have large baths with soaking tubs, separate showers, and L'Occitane products. Premier rooms work well for families because they have an extra sitting room and two full baths.

Best Feature(s)	Why Stay Here	Best Fit For
Location	Convenience of an all-inclusive plan with decent food	Single adults or couples
Trainer in residence fitness program	Pamper yourself	Wellness retreat
Golf	Proximity to Cabo del Sol golf course	Golfers
Spa	Low-key luxury	Couples seeking a slower pace
Swimmable beach, kids' club, and spa	Friendly staff, great location	Families
Spa, restaurants, infinity pool	Luxury and romance	Honeymooners and foodies
Location	Smaller than other resorts with same great amenities	Single adults, fishers, couples
Swimmable beach	Location	Golfers
Golf	Five-star experience	Golfers
Spa	Romance	Couples
Pools and golf	Golf in Cabo del Sol	Families
Architecture and kids' club	Ocean views	Families
Romance	Romantic old-world setting	Couples, honeymooners

On the pool deck, guests can order swim-up tacos and sushi, as well as the usual assortment of beverages. And the staff here seemed to know most of their guests by name. The Hilton is not all-inclusive, so you can choose to dine at one of several restaurants on-site or drive 15 minutes to either San José del Cabo or Cabo San Lucas for more options.

An award-winning child-care center, the Vacation Station, is run by a staff member of more than 10 years named Imelda Munoz Padilla. She is a big part of the reason families return over and over to vacation here. Kids ages 4-12 can drop in for any part of the day, 9am-5pm, to make whales, postcards, and scrapbooks; sing karaoke; or watch movies and play Xbox Kinect. On-site babysitters are available for US$20/hour for up to two children ages two or older, when parents want to enjoy an evening out on the town. (For babysitting past 11pm, you must pay an additional US$30 for the sitter to get a cab home. And children under two must have a dedicated sitter.) Special teen spa nights in the Cabo Kids Oasis include non-alcoholic tropical drinks, massage, reflexology, hair/makeup, and mani-pedi services. A variety of kids-only and parent/child spa packages are available as well.

Special activities include yoga and bonfires twice a week. You might even get lucky enough to see a sea turtle egg hatching during your visit.

During the Christmas holiday season, 60 percent of the guests are repeat visitors. Best of all, there are no timeshare sales at this resort, so you won't be approached by salespeople who try to convince you to consider an unplanned real estate purchase.

© NIKKI GOTH ITOI

side view of Las Ventanas al Paraíso

MELIÁ CABO REAL ALL INCLUSIVE BEACH & GOLF RESORT

Owned and operated by Spain-based Meliá Hotels International, the **Meliá Cabo Real** (Carr. Transpeninsular km 19.5, Cabo Real, tel. 624/142-2222, toll-free U.S. tel. 888/956-3542, www.melia.com/home.htm, from US$250) is an all-inclusive resort with more than 300 rooms and suites. It is located between the Hilton and Las Ventanas resorts, across the highway from the Cabo Real Golf Course. Most rooms have marble baths, balconies, and ocean views—although some rooms do face the garden or golf course instead. This is one of few resorts along the Corridor (besides the Hilton) that's located on a swimmable beach, Playa Bledito, thanks to a man-made jetty.

LAS VENTANAS AL PARAÍSO

Romance defines the experience at **Las Ventanas al Paraíso** (Carr. Transpeninsular km 20, tel. 624/144-2800, toll-free U.S. tel. 888/767-3966, www.rosewoodhotels.com/en/ lasventanas, junior suites US$750 and up), which celebrated its 15th anniversary in 2012. Accordingly, one of your first choices upon arrival here will be selecting bed linens from the sheet menu. Known for its underground service tunnels, designed to hide some of the infrastructure and busy staff that keeps the place running, the property is run by Rosewood Hotels and Resorts. Colors are earthy and warm for an intimate ambience.

Large guest suites feature inlaid stone-and-tile floors and adobe fireplaces. Computerized telescopes help guests find whales offshore. Three spa suites have space for in-room treatments, as well as rooftop terraces with outdoor hot tubs. Everyone else can book treatments at the on-site spa. A large infinity pool has "high-tech" pebbles that change color according to the color of the sky and sea.

Memorable culinary experiences add a unique twist to the usual resort stay. This may be the only resort in the region with its own tequila sommelier. Signature dishes of The Restaurant include Ensenada mussels in *molcajete* (a stone bowl) cooked in dark beer, chipotle, tomatillo, and *acuyo* (an herb); grilled local ling cod fish fillet with cantina-style lentils in a green tomatillo and cilantro sauce; and braised beef ribs in *pascalito sauce* (mole made from roasted pumpkin seeds and serrano chiles), pico de gallo, and with homemade tortillas. The chefs source ingredients up and down the Baja Peninsula. Some of the produce even comes from their own organic garden on-site. Guests can join Saturday morning cooking classes, or sign up for a multi-course tasting menu of regional specialties on Thursday Guaycura Nights. In an Iron Chef-type program, guests can challenge executive chef Fabrice Guisset by preparing a dish of their own in the Herb Garden demo kitchen. If the meal earns top marks, the dish gets added to the menu for one week. Anyone who participates gets a free shot of tequila.

Private movie nights on the beach, complete with wine and gourmet Mexican *botanas* (snacks), are another signature Las Ventanas diversion. Multiday spa and meal packages are

© NIKKI GOTH ITOI

condos at Zoëtry Casa del Mar Los Cabos

available. For guests who want to venture away from the resort, Mini Cooper S convertibles, BMW motorcycles, and off-road Hummers are available for rent.

ZOËTRY CASA DEL MAR LOS CABOS

On a smaller scale, the hacienda-style **Zoëtry Casa del Mar Los Cabos** (Carr. Transpeninsular km 19.5, tel. 624/145-7700, toll-free U.S. tel. 800/227-9621, www.zoetryresorts.com/casadelmar, US$500 and up) appeals to honeymooners, couples, and other adults traveling without children. This is another all-inclusive AM Resorts property, run by Zoëtry Resorts and located between the Las Ventanas and Dreams resorts. Its 63 ocean-view suites feature private balconies, luxury bed linens, teak furniture, marble baths, and Mexican artwork. This is an intimate boutique property with six swimming pools, tennis courts, and a small spa, Sueños del Mar. Other special touches include a welcome bottle of tequila, sparkling wine and fresh fruit delivered daily, afternoon tea service, and one complimentary 20-minute spa treatment per stay. Guests may also use the facilities at the neighboring Dreams resort, as the two properties are owned by the same parent company. A handful of Hollywood stars stayed here for the first Baja Film Festival in the fall of 2012.

The hotel shares its site with a condo complex of the same name, Casa del Mar. Condo owners/renters may use the pools, tennis courts (somewhat dated), and designated restaurants; they are also welcome to book spa appointments, but the small fitness center is off limits.

Avoid the over-priced Tapanco Restaurant. Both food quality and service would have been an absolute disappointment at any price. The beachfront Mezquite grill, however, makes a decent burger.

◖ DREAMS LOS CABOS SUITES GOLF RESORT & SPA

A favorite for all-inclusive accommodations among wedding parties, honeymooners, and anniversary celebrants, **Dreams Los Cabos Suites Golf Resort & Spa** (Carr.

Transpeninsular km 18.5, Cabo Real, tel. 624/145-7600, toll-free U.S. tel. 866/237-3267, www.dreamsresorts.com, from US$400) is an AM Resorts property with 308 suites and all the amenities of a full-service resort. Guests can choose to dine at any of four restaurants serving seafood, Asian cuisine, steaks, and Mexican dishes. For a little extra romance, book a private candlelight dinner by the water's edge. Twenty-four-hour room service also is available.

There are five bars, three pools, and a long list of recreational activities, including yoga, archery, bocce ball, horseshoes, and Euro bungee. An added bonus: No wristbands are required. Evening entertainment consists of live performance, big-screen movies, and rotating theme nights. Honeymoon packages include a champagne breakfast in bed. The Dreams Spa by Pevonia offers a relaxing aromatherapy salt glow treatment. And the Explorers' Club has supervised science- and nature-themed activities for children ages 3-12. Activities include sandcastle competitions and campouts on the beach.

Book ahead if you have your heart set on a stay at Dreams; this popular resort has one of the highest occupancy rates in Los Cabos.

CABO DEL SOL
Over US$200
SHERATON HACIENDA DEL MAR
You won't have to get up at the crack of dawn to reserve a chaise lounge at the **Sheraton Hacienda del Mar** (Carr. Transpeninsular km 10.5, Cabo del Sol, tel. 624/145-8000, toll-free Mex. tel. 800/903-2500, toll-free U.S. tel. 888/625-5144, www.sheratonhaciendadelmar. com, from US$400); an abundance of patio furniture was part of the resort design. Even better, a poolside concierge helps guests plan the day's activities without having to leave the pool.

Mediterranean defines the look and feel of this sprawling resort, which has 270 rooms and 31 suites. The hotel has several options for dining and entertainment. Best known among these is **Pitahayas** (tel. 624/145-8010, 5pm-11pm daily, mains US$15-40), which prepares

variations on a Pacific Rim theme. You can also dine inside or out at the more casual **Tomates** (tel. 624/145-8000, breakfast, lunch, and dinner daily, mains US$10-15), serving a fusion of Mexican and international dishes. Guest rooms were freshened up in 2012. At the same time, the resort built a new Adventure Kids Club featuring flatscreen TVs and a new pool. Look for the beautifully landscaped Cabo del Sol exit ramp near kilometer 10.

FIESTA AMERICANA GRAND LOS CABOS
Adjacent to the Cabo del Sol golf course is the family-oriented **Fiesta Americana Grand Los Cabos** (Carr. Transpeninsular km 10.3, Cabo del Sol, tel. 624/145-6200, toll-free U.S. tel. 800/343-7821, www.fiestaamericanagrand. com, US$450-600), with 250 ocean-view guest rooms and suites and a secluded beach. Rooms are spread across six floors and feature private balconies. The resort's restaurant, **Rosato** (tel. 624/145-6200, dinner daily, mains US$15-20), serves northern Italian cuisine.

NEAR CABO SAN LUCAS
Over US$200
HACIENDA ENCANTADA RESORT & SPA
Located just outside Cabo San Lucas, **Hacienda Encantada Resort & Spa** (Carr. Transpeninsular km 7.3, tel. 624/163-5555, www.haciendaencantada.com, US$225-800) has 150 rooms decorated in desert colors. Amenities include a restaurant and spa. This place has a reputation for aggressive timeshare sales tactics. The resort's restaurants and bars close at 10pm, so be prepared to travel outside the resort for late-night entertainment.

ESPERANZA RESORT
By many accounts, the **Esperanza Resort** (Carr. Transpeninsular km 7, Punta Ballena, tel. 624/145-6400, toll-free U.S. tel. 866/311-2226, www.esperanzaresort.com, US$600-850) leads the pack for outstanding guest service among the luxury resorts in Los Cabos. Open since 2002 and located at Punta Ballena, close to Cabo San Lucas, its 57 units (one to four bedrooms) feature original

COURTESY OF ESPERANZA RESORT

Esperanza Resort at Punta Ballena

Mexican artwork and handcrafted furnishings. Amenities include flatscreen TVs, iPod docking stations, and yoga mats. Enjoy complimentary popsicles, fruit skewers, and hand/foot massages poolside. Loaner iPods are also available, pre-loaded with music. Yoga classes are offered daily for no additional charge. The signature spa has indoor steam caves and waterfalls, with treatments that incorporate local fruits and vegetation. The oceanfront Mediterranean restaurant, the **Signature Restaurant at Esperanza,** open for breakfast, lunch, and dinner, completes the picture. Pets live well here too, with custom beds, fancy linens, and their own room-service menu. Esperanza has its own art gallery with works by contemporary Mexican painters and sculptors for sale. A new Trainer in Residence program brings renowned wellness instructors on-site to help guests meet their fitness goals. Language instruction, salsa dancing, and guided tours are also offered.

A four-night minimum stay is required for all weekend bookings January-April except February and March, when a seven-night stay is required. The nearby **Santa Carmela Super Market & Deli** (Carr. Transpeninsular km 6, Local B, tel. 624/104-3478, www.mercadostacarmela.com) is a convenient stop for organic groceries and snacks, including gluten-free products.

Cabo San Lucas

You can find just about any type of accommodations in Cabo San Lucas, from simple and reasonably priced motels to boutique inns and luxury resorts. There are condos and villas for rent as well. Most visitors prefer to stay at the beach, but the better values are downtown or on the outskirts of town, away from the water.

DOWNTOWN AND THE MARINA
Under US$100
CABO INN HOTEL

You can easily walk to the marina and the Puerto Paraíso mall from the two-story **Cabo Inn Hotel** (20 de Noviembre btwn. Vicario and Mendoza, tel. 624/143-0819, U.S. tel. 619/819-2727, www.caboinnhotel.com, US$50-70), but with the central location comes a whole lot of noise, and readers have shared disappointing experiences in staying here. Here are some factors to consider before you book: Its 22 rooms are mostly small and dark, especially the ones without windows. Beds have foam mattresses and baths have curtains instead of doors. Air-conditioners are old and often loud. Some rooms have refrigerators. Two rooftop *palapa* rooms give travelers a sense of the real Baja; one has its own whirlpool tub and both come with bug nets over the beds. There is a full kitchen and shared TV in the common area, as well as a very tiny "social" pool. The managers do ask guests to adhere to a number of house rules, which are reasonable, but the tone in which they are presented may not sit well with some travelers. The owner has installed wireless Internet throughout the property. Credit cards are accepted for advanced reservations only; you'll need cash if you show up unannounced.

SIESTA SUITES HOTEL

The **Siesta Suites Hotel** (Zapata btwn. Guerrero and Hidalgo, tel. 624/143-2773, toll-free U.S. tel. 866/271-0952, www.cabosiestasuites.com, US$60-80) completed a top-to-bottom remodel in 2007. Highlights include granite counters, new bath fixtures, and new queen beds. In business since 1992, it is owned by a couple originally from Southern California who converted an old apartment building into the hotel. Several of Cabo's best restaurants are steps away. The hotel has 15 suites with kitchenettes (including microwaves and toaster ovens) and separate bedrooms and five hotel-style rooms. All are air-conditioned and come with satellite TV. Repeat guests enjoy the sundeck, barbecue, and "social" pool; secured parking is another plus.

HOTEL LOS ARCOS

The **Hotel Los Arcos** (Vicario and Revolución, tel. 624/143-2477, hotelplazalosarcos@hotmail.com, US$55) opened in December 2005 with 32 clean rooms in a two-story building with cable TV, air-conditioning, and wireless Internet.

HOTEL MAR DE CORTEZ

The centrally located and well-worn **Hotel Mar de Cortez** (Blvd. Lázaro Cárdenas at Guerrero, tel. 624/143-0032, toll-free U.S. tel. 800/347-8821, www.mardecortez.com, US$57-74) has seen better days, but it is much loved by its loyal patrons, many of whom return for the same week year after year, and still manages to stay full in the high season. Its *muy tranquilo* setting provides a welcome respite from the noisy, crowded streets of downtown Cabo San Lucas—yet puts guests conveniently close to all the action (except the beach, which is a 20-minute walk). Clean, air-conditioned rooms each have one queen and one twin bed, some with a bit of a slope, and dimly lit baths. There are no TVs and no phones, but there is free Wi-Fi. Guests can rent a small refrigerator for US$10 per day. Enjoy the small pool and patio area, which are shaded by date palms, or dine in the on-site restaurant and outdoor bar.

honeymoon suite at The Bungalows

LOS MILAGROS HOTEL

Friendly and attentive service makes for a memorable stay at **Los Milagros Hotel** (Matamoros 116, tel. 624/143-4566, U.S. tel. 718/928-6647, www.losmilagros.com.mx, US$85), which has a dozen large rooms with air-conditioning and private baths; a few rooms include kitchenettes as well. It has a cactus garden on the roof, a tiny pool in the courtyard, and free Wi-Fi.

HOTEL SANTA FE

Now owned by **The Villa Group** (www.villagroupresorts.com), **Hotel Santa Fe** (southwest corner of Zaragoza and Obregón, tel. 624/143-4403, toll-free U.S. tel. 877/845-5247, www.hotelsantafeloscabos.com, US$40-80) is a well-maintained property with 46 studios surrounding a pool. Each studio has a sliding glass door, tile floor, renovated bath, kitchenette, and relatively new furnishings as well as air-conditioning, satellite TV, and phone. Amenities include wireless Internet, off-street parking, 24-hour security, a small counter restaurant with outdoor seating (7am-7pm daily), laundry, and a mini-super (7am-7pm daily). A free beach shuttle service is provided.

CASA PABLITO BED AND BREAKFAST HOTEL

A few blocks from the town center, **Casa Pablito Bed and Breakfast Hotel** (Hidalgo and Ortega, tel. 624/143-1971, toll-free U.S. tel. 866/444-1139, US$90) was originally built to house employees of the Club Cascadas resort. A few years back, the building was converted into a traditional Mexican hacienda-style inn with 14 suites set around a pool and *palapa*-shaded breakfast area. Rooms have either one queen or two twin beds, plus kitchenettes, air-conditioning, and cable TV. This location will work for you if you don't mind a fairly long walk to most of the shops and restaurants downtown.

US$100-200
◖ THE BUNGALOWS

An authentic Baja-style inn that's removed from most of the action downtown, **The Bungalows** (Dorado and Lienzo Charro, tel. 624/143-5035, toll-free U.S. tel. 888/424-2226, www.thebungalowshotel.com, US$95-210) is a good option for small groups or any travelers who like to stay off the beaten path. A stay here begins with a welcome *licuado* drink made of honeydew melon or whatever fresh fruit is ripe. Breakfast rotates among pancakes, waffles, eggs, and the like. Fresh fruit smoothies are another morning treat, and the coffee flows all day.

Eight suites have separate sleeping areas, air-conditioning, kitchenettes, and TVs. Bottled water is provided in the suites. The honeymoon suite has its own terrace with city views. Six two-bedroom bungalows can accommodate 4-6 guests each. There's no smoking, inside or out. The small but nicely designed grounds hold a swimming pool and barbecue.

Guests here unanimously praise co-owner Eric and his mom for their personal service and attention to detail. You can walk down the hill to Plaza Amelia Wilkes in about 10 minutes.

CABO SAN LUCAS ACCOMMODATIONS

	Type	Location	Rates
Bahía Hotel	Hotel	Cabo San Lucas	US$130-180
The Bungalows	B&B	Cabo San Lucas	US$95-210
Cabo Inn Hotel	Hotel	Cabo San Lucas	US$50-70
Cabo Villas	Hotel	Cabo San Lucas	US$180-500
Capella Pedregal	Resort	Cabo San Lucas	US$575
Casa Bella	B&B	Cabo San Lucas	US$160-190
Casa Contenta	B&B	Cabo San Lucas	US$160-195
Casa Dorada	Resort	Cabo San Lucas	From US$200
Casa Pablito Bed and Breakfast Hotel	B&B	Cabo San Lucas	US$90
Club Cabo Hotel and Campground Resort	Hotel	Cabo San Lucas	US$55-85
Club Cascadas de Baja	Hotel	Cabo San Lucas	US$200
Grand Solmar Land's End Resort & Spa	Resort	Cabo San Lucas	US$400-750
Hacienda Beach Club and Residences	Hotel	Cabo San Lucas	From US$695
Hotel Finisterra	Resort	Cabo San Lucas	US$115-180
Hotel Los Arcos	Hotel	Cabo San Lucas	US$55
Hotel Mar de Cortez	Hotel	Cabo San Lucas	US$57-74
Hotel Riu Palace Cabo San Lucas	All-inclusive	Cabo San Lucas	US$300-450
Hotel Santa Fe	Hotel	Cabo San Lucas	US$40-80
Hotel Solmar Suites	Hotel	Cabo San Lucas	US$140-280
Los Milagros Hotel	Hotel	Cabo San Lucas	US$85
Marina Cabo Plaza	Hotel	Cabo San Lucas	US$100
Marina Fiesta Resort & Hotel	Resort	Cabo San Lucas	US$240-380
Marina Sol Resort	Hotel	Cabo San Lucas	US$110-140
ME Cabo	Resort	Cabo San Lucas	US$220 and up
Pueblo Bonito Los Cabos	Resort	Cabo San Lucas	US$400 and up
Pueblo Bonito Pacifica	Resort	Cabo San Lucas	US$400-500
Pueblo Bonito Rosé	All-inclusive	Cabo San Lucas	US$400 and up
Pueblo Bonito at Sunset Beach	Resort	Cabo San Lucas	US$190-330
Siesta Suites Hotel	Hotel	Cabo San Lucas	US$60-80
Villa del Arco	Resort	Cabo San Lucas	US$295-340
Villa del Palmar Cabo Beach Resort & Spa	Resort	Cabo San Lucas	US$200-400
Villa La Estancia	Resort	Cabo San Lucas	US$215-300
Welk Resort Sirena del Mar	Resort	Cabo San Lucas	US$350
Wyndham Cabo San Lucas Resort	Resort	Cabo San Lucas	US$65-194

Best Feature(s)	Why Stay Here	Best Fit For
Bar Esquina	Basic and affordable accommodations	Budget travelers
Divine breakfasts and hospitality	Attentive and personal service	Couples, honeymooners, or small groups
Central location	Affordability	Budget travelers
Short walk to Playa El Médano	Beach scene and fine dining	Beachgoers and foodies
Ocean views	Ultra-luxury lodging	Those for whom money is no object
Restored colonial-style rooms	San José del Cabo feel in Cabo San Lucas	Couples, small groups
Rooftop terrace with view of Land's End	Intimate, homey feel	Couples, small groups
Playa El Médano access	Beach scene and nightlife	Partying on the beach
Close to the town center	Modest accommodations for a good value	Budget travelers and those less keen on the party scene
Neighboring forest and bird sanctuary	Affordability	Budget travelers
Private villas	Quiet	Families and small groups
Arhcitecture and Pacific Ocean views	Golf	Retirees
Vacation rentals up to four bedrooms	Location, close to downtown and the beach	Families
Location, beachfront swim-up bar	Access to Pacific beaches	Retirees
Central Location	Affordability	Budget travelers
Location	Right downtown but still quiet	Budget travelers
Largest all-inclusive	Vacation in a box	Travelers who prefer not to leave the resort
Newly renovated kitchens	Affordable rates	Families and budget travelers
Private fishing fleet and live-aboard boat	Activities from tennis to water sports	Fishers and divers
Rooftop cactus garden	Friendly service at affordable rates	Families and budget travelers
Marina views	Easy access to downtown and Playa El Médano	Families or small groups
Location	Central to downtown Cabo San Lucas	Partiers
Location	Easy walk to either downtown or Playa El Médano	Looking for a balance of beach and city
Trendy	Nightlife	Trend-setters
Central to Playa El Médano	Convenience	Families
Pacific beach location	Privacy and seclusion	Couples
Central to Playa El Médano	Convenience	Couples
Pacific beach location	Privacy and seclusion	Couples
Location and affordability	Steps to the best restaurants in Cabo	Foodies looking to dine in Cabo
The Buccaneer (pirate-themed bar)	Location	Couples or small groups
Desert Spa at Villa del Arco	Beachfront location	Families
Location	Location	Couples or small groups
Private beach	Peaceful setting close to Cabo San Lucas	Families
Location	Central to downtown Cabo San Lucas entertainment	Partiers

LOS CABOS TIMESHARES

Few visitors board their flight to Los Cabos intending to buy a timeshare. Yet the timeshare market is booming as the destination evolves. Timeshares now command higher prices and higher occupancy rates than hotels. Nearly six million people now participate in fractional ownership vacation models (also called vacation clubs), and they spend US$1 billion a year on their condos and villas. How do so many travelers come to change their minds between arrival and departure?

LOS CABOS IS A BEAUTIFUL PLACE

It's a lot easier to pack up and head home when you know you can return again and again.

THE PITCH IS ALL AROUND

Timeshare salespeople disguise themselves as activities coordinators, concierges, restaurant hosts, rental car agency staff, and even grocery store clerks. Their goal is to draw unsuspecting visitors into a friendly conversation—*Is this your first time in Los Cabos? Where are you staying? Would you like to go whale-watching today? Can I help you find the sugar?*—and then invite them to a 90-minute presentation over breakfast in

exchange for any number of giveaways. With prices ranging US$15,000-25,000, "owning" a timeshare in a world-class destination can be an attractive proposition. Why not hear what they have to say?

THE FREEBIES ARE ENTICING

Salespeople may offer US$200 in cash, free whale-watching or snorkeling tours, sunset horseback rides, restaurant coupons, and more. The deal gets better the longer you resist. Not a bad way to finance part of your trip if you don't mind giving up part of a day.

Everyone thinks they can work the system, and many who participate in a presentation do resist the temptation to buy. Some even sign up for a second pitch on their next visit. But here's the catch. . . .

TIMESHARES ARE NOT REAL ESTATE

They are vacations. When you buy a timeshare, you prepay for vacations at a discounted rate. If you like the idea of returning to a familiar place in Los Cabos for one or two weeks each year, this model can make a lot of sense.

On hot days or late nights, you might want to take a cab back to the inn.

MARINA SOL RESORT

Close to downtown but also within easy walking distance of Playa El Médano, **Marina Sol Resort** (tel. 624/143-3231, toll-free U.S. tel. 877/255-1721, www.marinasolresort.com, US$110-140) has basic one- and two-bedroom condos arranged around a pretty courtyard and swimming pool. A wheelchair-accessible room is available. The lobby has several independently operated businesses, including a convenience store, day spa, and laundry service.

MARINA CABO PLAZA

On the east side of the marina, next to the Marina Fiesta Hotel, between downtown and

the beach, the **Marina Cabo Plaza** condominium hotel (Blvd. Marina 39, tel. 624/143-1833, www.marinacaboplaza.com, US$100/day or US$700/week) has 63 rooms with tiled floors and balconies with impressive views of the marina below. Guests share a swimming pool.

CASA BELLA

Casa Bella (Hidalgo 10, tel. 624/143-6400, U.S. tel. 626/209-0215, www.casabellahotel. com, Oct.-July, US$160-190) brings a San José del Cabo feel to downtown Cabo San Lucas. Its 11 rooms are set in a restored colonial-style home across from the town square and Mi Casa restaurant. Rooms have ornate wooden doors, antique-style furnishings, oversized tiled showers, and remote-control air-conditioning. An enclosed patio has a small pool with several

IT'S HARD TO SAY NO

Sales reps choreograph every aspect of the pitch, from the upbeat music to the champagne and cheers of congratulations echoing around the room. They face intense pressure to sell, so if the first approach doesn't win you over, there will be one or two more pitches as you attempt to leave the room. (Biannual weeks? Off-season weeks? Trial membership? Free Jet Ski tour? Take our survey before you go?) As prices come down, the deal gets sweeter, and suddenly you either begin to feel guilty for accepting all the freebies or you think you're crazy for not taking advantage now that you've negotiated the terms so low. Bottom line: That 90-minute breakfast presentation could result in a US$10,000 charge on your credit card.

YOU MAY NOT GET WHAT YOU PAID FOR

Timeshare developments typically begin selling when construction has just begun—sometimes they don't get finished, or when they do, they don't always shape up as promised. Stories abound of frustrated timeshare purchasers who don't get the weeks they originally bought or whose reservations seem to get lost every time they book. Services may not be available as promised, and the quality of the accommodations may change as the years go by.

Also, because timeshare owners aren't year-round residents, they usually lack both a sense of community and a sense of responsibility toward the local environment. For the developer, timeshares mean huge profits, as the same space is sold repeatedly in one-week segments. Because land in Baja is relatively inexpensive, considering the charming scenery and climate, it seems to attract get-rich-quick developers who show a decided lack of respect for the fragile Baja environment.

PROCEED WITH CAUTION

Timeshares are not all bad, and attending a presentation may be a worthwhile experience for a variety of reasons. Just be sure you know what's coming before you give away any of your precious vacation time. And don't buy without considering all the options.

---

chaise lounges. The family that owns this inn lives on the premises and opens their living room as a common area to guests.

WYNDHAM CABO SAN LUCAS RESORT

It's impossible to miss the sprawling **Wyndham Cabo San Lucas Resort** (formerly Tesoro Los Cabos Hotel, Blvd. Marina s/n, tel. 624/173-9300 or 800/716-8770, toll-free U.S. tel. 800/543-7556, www.wyndham.com, US$65-130 European plan or US$183-194 American plan) on the west side of the marina. This property has changed hands several times in the last decade, and its latest owner is taking steps to update the infrastructure and improve the guest experience. The pool has been recently renovated, but guests say that noise is remains an issue.

Over US$200
MARINA FIESTA RESORT & HOTEL

Not quite as large as the Wyndham, but still an imposing presence on the marina, is the **Marina Fiesta Resort & Hotel** (Blvd. La Marina, Lotes 37 y 38, tel. 624/145-6020, toll-free U.S. tel. 877/243-4880, www.marinafiestaresort.com, US$240-380). This property gets high marks for a central location, but the noise coming from nearby bars and round-the-clock construction has bothered guests. The resort has recently added an all-inclusive option for guests. Amenities include a swimming pool and views of the marina, but guest rooms could use a cosmetic overhaul. The timeshare pitch comes on strong from the moment you walk in the door. The resort still seems overpriced.

PLAYA EL MÉDANO
US$100-200
CLUB CABO HOTEL AND CAMPGROUND RESORT

East along Playa El Médano, and set back a ways from the beach, clean and cozy **Club Cabo Hotel and Campground Resort** (tel./fax 624/143-3348, www.clubcaboinn.com, US$55-85) is also dog friendly. It has a handful of suites and bungalows, some with *palapa* roofs, all with air-conditioning and king-size beds. Owners Irene and Martin Rozendaal, a Mexican and Dutch husband-and-wife team, have been in business since 1992. Their property borders the only remaining expanse of mesquite forest in the area, which is also a bird sanctuary. On the grounds are laundry machines, a large fridge for storing freshly caught fish, and a swimming pool with an attached whirlpool tub. The hotel provides wireless Internet and a shuttle to town (a 15- to 20-minute walk).

BAHÍA HOTEL

Bahía Hotel (Pescador s/n, tel. 624/143-1890, U.S. tel. 914/432-3307, www.bahiacabo.com, US$130-180), just off Camino de los Pescadores above Playa El Médano, has lost most of its ocean views due to construction of the Casa Dorada complex right in front. Its studios have minimally equipped kitchenettes, air-conditioning, satellite TV, and direct-dial phones. Giant sculpted concrete shells frame the beds as headboards, and bamboo doors enclose the bathroom and closet. Faucets and tiling have aged a bit. The property includes laundry facilities, a decent restaurant, pool with hot tub and swim-up *palapa* bar, and free parking in a gated lot. Rates here include tax. Like most affordable Cabo San Lucas locations, the place is overrun with college students on spring break during the month of March. The outdoor **Bar Esquina** (lunch mains US$6-12, dinner mains US$15-25) is a nice addition to the casual dining options in the neighborhood.

CLUB CASCADAS DE BAJA

Part of the Trading Places International network of timeshares, **Club Cascadas de Baja** (Camino Viejo a San José, tel. 624/143-1882, toll-free U.S. tel. 800/365-9190, ext. 400, www.clubcascadasdebaja.com, one-bedroom US$200), at the east end of El Médano, has 110 thatched-roof villas, plus two swimming pools and tennis courts. You can make reservations online.

CASA CONTENTA

About 1.5 kilometers east of Cabo San Lucas and 800 meters above the Carretera Transpeninsular, **Casa Contenta** (tel. 624/143-6038, www.cabocasacontenta.com, US$160-195/day or US$1,050-1,300/week) has five air-conditioned rooms with private baths in a three-story home with a swimming pool and wireless Internet throughout. Take a yoga class, book a spa treatment, or simply enjoy the view of Land's End on the rooftop terrace. There's a three-night minimum.

Over US$200
VILLA DEL PALMAR CABO BEACH RESORT & SPA

Families particularly like **Villa del Palmar Cabo Beach Resort & Spa** (Camino Viejo a San José km 0.5, tel. 624/145-7000, toll-free U.S. tel. 877/845-5247, www.villadelpalmar-cabo.com, junior suites US$200-400, including tax, three-night minimum), with 458 junior suites and one- to three-bedroom ocean-view deluxe suites. Each unit has a kitchenette, marble bath, and balcony. There are two pools (one with a bar), two lighted tennis courts, a fitness center, and restaurants. Some units are available only by the week. Guests have access to the Desert Spa at Villa del Arco.

CABO VILLAS

Near Edith's on Camino de los Pescadores and a short walk up from Playa El Médano, **Cabo Villas** (tel. 624/143-9166, fax 624/143-2558, www.cabovillasbeachresort.com, US$180-500) has pricy one-bedroom, one-bath units and two-bedroom, two-bath units in a couple of white towers. This is a great location for access to the beach scene as well as fine dining options.

COURTESY OF ME CABO

sunbathing in style at ME Cabo

VILLA LA ESTANCIA

Next door to the Villa del Palmar, **Villa La Estancia** (Camino Viejo a San José km 0.5, tel. 624/143-8121, U.S. tel. 619/683-7883, www. villalaestancia.com, US$215-300) has 156 units ranging in size from one bedroom to three bedrooms, as well as standard guest rooms and junior suites. Prices include tax, and there is a three-night minimum.

VILLA DEL ARCO

Villa del Arco (Camino Viejo a San Jose km 0.5, tel. 624/145-7200, toll-free U.S. tel. 888/880-8512, www.villadelarcocabo. com, US$295-340) has three buildings with junior suites as well as one- and two-bedroom units. Prices include tax, and there is a three-night minimum. The hotel's Desert Spa offers individual and package treatments in a European-style spa. Order drinks, burgers, tacos, and ice cream in the pirate-themed bar called The Buccaneer, which is anchored in one of the swimming pool areas.

◖ ME CABO

The **ME Cabo** (Playa El Médano, tel. 624/145-7800, toll-free U.S. tel. 800/336-3542, www. me-cabo.com, US$220 and up) is a Spanish-owned Sol Meliá property with 151 remodeled rooms and suites built in a horseshoe shape around a large pool and patio area with great views of El Arco and San Lucas Bay. Reasonable prices, a convenient location, trendy beach club, and inviting spa make this a popular spot for hipster travelers, many of them European. This is a good choice for an adults-only experience. On the plus side, most rooms have ocean views, towels are large and fluffy, baths feature Aveda products, and hotel service is prompt. As for the minuses, rooms on the fifth floor, three levels above the club (and presumably other floors as well), echo sound from the lobby and disco/bar below. As with most places this close to the El Médano beach scene, the resort attracts a fun-loving crowd that's here to party hard, especially on weekends. The resort's new YHI Spa (9am-9pm) offers *temazcal,* massage, yoga, and hydrotherapy services. Its **Tequila Fusion Mexican**

Enjoy breakfast by the sea at the Pueblo Bonito Rosé.

Restaurant (daily 6pm-11pm) serves *tapas,* taquitos, and specialty margaritas as well as a full menu of premium tequilas. Wi-Fi is free.

PUEBLO BONITO RESORTS

The Pueblo Bonito group has four well run properties in Cabo San Lucas. The original **Pueblo Bonito Los Cabos** (Playa El Médano s/n, tel. 624/142-9797, toll-free U.S. tel. 800/990-8250, www.pueblobonito-loscabos.com, US$400 and up) is a white adobe five-story building designed in a Mediterranean theme. From the tiles on the roof to the chaise lounges, blue and white form the dominant color scheme. Its 147 junior and luxury suites surround an attractive free-form swimming pool. Room features include kitchenettes and views of the bay. Cilantro's beachfront restaurant serves a menu of tasty seafood dishes (daily 11am-11pm). The resort is all-inclusive. Its kids' club is open to children ages 4-11. Wi-Fi is included.

Farther away from downtown along the beach, the all-inclusive **Pueblo Bonito Rosé** (tel. 624/142-9898, toll-free U.S. tel. 800/990-8250, www.pueblobonito-rose.com, US$400 and up) has a striking Baroquethemed lobby. Its 260 suites have private balconies, kitchenettes, and hand-painted terra-cotta floors. There are four on-site restaurants and a full-service spa.

HOTEL RIU PALACE CABO SAN LUCAS

About five kilometers east of Cabo San Lucas, beachfront **Hotel Riu Palace Cabo San Lucas** (Camino Viejo a San José km 5.5, tel. 624/146-7160, toll-free U.S. tel. 888/666-8816, www.riu.com, US$300-450) comprises a town unto itself, with 642 guest rooms—booked almost all the time, according to travel agents—and all-inclusive (only) meal plans. Part of a large international hotel chain, the lively Riu has so many dining and entertainment options that most guests never leave the resort during their visit. Rates include taxes.

WELK RESORT SIRENA DEL MAR

The **Welk Resort Sirena del Mar** (Carr. Transpeninsular km 4.5, Cabo Bello, tel.

624/163-4600, U.S. tel. 800/932-9355, www. cabosirenadelmar.com, US$350) is a time-share resort just outside of Cabo San Lucas that opened in 2010. It offers very clean rooms with ocean views, a friendly staff, two pools, and a full-service spa. There are 64 villas in all, in one- and two-bedroom sizes. Guests have access to a small private beach. The entrance to the hotel is hard to find: Look for a small blue sign across from the Vinoteca store, and use the *Retorno* exit ramps to turn around if needed.

CASA DORADA

One of the newest luxury properties to open along Playa El Médano is **Casa Dorada** (Pescador s/n, tel. 624/163-5757, www.casa-dorada.com, toll-free U.S. tel. 866/448-0151, US$200 and up), where guests enjoy mango margaritas upon arrival. Modern kitchens, large baths, contemporary design, and a stellar location are some of the pros. Suites range in size from studio to two-bedroom. There have been some maintenance issues, and rooms above the Mango Deck are reportedly noisy. Its Saltwater Spa offers a full menu of massage and body treatments with products from Pevonia Botanica.

HACIENDA BEACH CLUB AND RESIDENCES

After several years of demolition and construction, the **Hacienda Beach Club and Residences** (tel. 866/300-0084, www.haci-endacabosanlucas.com) opened in 2010 on 22 acres in a prime location on Playa El Médano yet also close to downtown and the marina. Luxury vacation rentals range from one to four bedrooms in size. Prices start at US$695 per night.

PACIFIC BEACH

Hotels in this area are wonderfully remote—an ideal setting if you are looking for peace and quiet. If you plan to enjoy the downtown scene, you will need to drive, shuttle, or taxi there and back.

To get to any of the Cabo Pacifica resorts,

follow Lázaro Cárdenas, the main boulevard through town, west past Plaza Amelia Wilkes, until it curves to the right and becomes Herrera. Go through a traffic circle and continue following this street around a few S-turns and up the hill toward the Pacific Ocean. Along the way, two blue and white signs indicate the way to Cabo Pacifica. At the stop sign, turn left into the driveway that says Pueblo Bonito Sunset Beach. This is the entrance for all the Cabo Pacifica resorts. Tell the attendant at the gate which resort you want to visit, and then proceed along a long landscaped boulevard that descends down the ridge to the resorts and beach below.

US$100-200
HOTEL FINISTERRA

One of the oldest hotels in Cabo, the **Hotel Finisterra** (tel. 624/143-3333, toll-free U.S. tel. 855/224-5144, www.finisterra.com, US$115-180) stands on a ridge overlooking the Pacific Ocean. There are two parts to this resort: an original building built into the hillside but set back from the beach, and two newer towers collectively called the Palapa Beach Club, which are on the beach and overlook the pool. A well-equipped business center makes for a comfortable office away from home. It has leather chairs, five flat-screen TVs, and several Dell computer stations. Wireless Internet costs US$10 a day. A 1,040-square-meter swimming pool with whirlpools and a swim-up bar sits on the beach at the foot of the Palapa Beach Club. Beds are on the firm side, and there are a variety of views on the older Finisterra side of the resort. Be sure to request city, marina, garden, or ocean views when you book. Guests can use lighted tennis courts, a sauna, and swimming pool. A spa and wedding chapel are on-site. Access to this hotel is via Marina Boulevard.

HOTEL SOLMAR SUITES

Another historic property close to Land's End is the **Hotel Solmar Suites** (tel. 624/145-7575, U.S. tel. 310/459-9861 or 800/344-3349, www.solmar.com, US$140-280), which features 180

infinity pool at the Grand Solmar Land's End Resort & Spa

rooms and suites on the beach with separate timeshare/condo units overlooking the beach. An older section of units directly on the beach has lower ceilings and less natural light; newer units are set back from the sand but have high ceilings, better lighting, and newer furnishings. Amenities include tennis courts, an aquatic center, and two heated pools with swim-up bars and hot tubs. The hotel's **La Roca** restaurant (6am-10pm daily, mains US$6-15) cooks your fish any way you like it. The Solmar is well known among anglers for its fishing fleet and among divers for its luxury live-aboard boat, the *Solmar V* (www.solmarv.com). Access to this hotel is via Marina Boulevard.

Over US$200
GRAND SOLMAR LAND'S END RESORT & SPA

Wedged between sheer cliffs and the sands of Playa Solmar, a few boulders away from Land's End, the new **Grand Solmar Land's End Resort & Spa** (Av. Solmar 1-A, tel. 800/344-3349, www.grandsolmarresort.com,

US$400-750) is an architectural wonder. Popular with the Baby Boomer generation, the resort opened its doors in 2011, and two out of three planned phases were complete as of late 2012. Sparkling infinity pools with expansive Pacific Ocean views invite relaxation. Murphy beds in every room are a space-saving way to accommodate families or additional travelers. There were about 160 rooms and suites available at press time, with more to come in the next phase of development. Given all the ongoing development, the timeshare sales pitch comes on strong here. The chef in the Grand Solmar's **La Roca** restaurant came from the Las Ventanas resort on the Corridor. The resort's Sea Spa is open 9am-5pm.

An added bonus for anglers: Guests here have access to the largest sportfishing fleet in Cabo San Lucas. Boats range from a single-engine rental for four that runs about US$430 to a 36-foot Chriscraft twin-engine boat, available for US$725. If fishing isn't for you, the marina is just a short walk from the resort and provides plenty of shopping, food, and nightlife.

CAPELLA PEDREGAL

Cliffside **Capella Pedregal** (Camino del Mar 1, tel. 624/163-4300, www.capellahotels.com/cabosanlucas, US$575) has 66 ocean-view rooms in a five-story building, plus villas and *casitas* for rent. This property has become the most favored Cabo San Lucas luxury resort among discerning travelers. Beds are king-size, and rooms come with a long list of luxury amenities, including a spa, private plunge pool, and twice-a-day maid service. Pets are even allowed. There are three restaurants on-site: **Don Manuel** serves traditional Mexican dishes in an elegant setting. **El Farallón** is modeled after a seafood market. And the **Beach Club** serves more casual fare. Learn to make ceviche, tamales, or salsa and moles in one of the resort's one-day cooking classes (US$70 pp). To find the hotel, turn right off Marina Boulevard onto Camino del Mar, then take the immediate left turn into Capella Pedregal.

PUEBLO BONITO AT SUNSET BEACH

Open since 2002, the **Pueblo Bonito at Sunset Beach** (Cabo Pacifica, tel. 624/142-9999, toll-free U.S. tel. 800/990-8250, www.pueblobonitosunsetbeach.com, US$190-330) has 324 suites on a 20-hectare hillside overlooking the Pacific, behind the Pedregal development. Amenities include a hilltop "sky pool," a main pool that overlooks the beach, tennis courts, and a free shuttle into town (drop-off at the Pueblo Bonito Blanco on Playa Médano). Fitness facilities cost extra (US$15/day), and massages run a steep US$130 at the Spa at Sunset Beach (8am-7pm daily). Two-for-one happy hour lasts exactly one hour, so it's best to load up on beverages during that time. Eat tacos and chicken sandwiches and the like poolside, or enjoy sushi in the bistro.

PUEBLO BONITO PACIFICA

The newest Pueblo Bonito property, **Pueblo Bonito Pacifica** (Cabo Pacifica, tel. 624/142-9696, toll-free U.S. tel. 800/990-8250, www.pueblobonitopacifica.com, US$400-500), opened in 2005. Couples in search of a romantic getaway like the no-kids factor at this boutique-style resort. Its 154 rooms, including 14 suites, are appointed in minimalist fashion, with a sand and ivory color scheme. Those who want nightlife find the location a bit too remote. Strolling along the beach is discouraged due to heavy surf; you can, however, rent a bed on the beach for US$20 an hour. There is a free shuttle to town or cabs for US$10 one-way. The on-site **Armonia Spa** offers a variety of massage treatments, including hot stone, Shiatsu, four hands, deep-tissue, Swedish, and pregnancy massage (US$100 for 50 minutes).

Booking Services and Property Management Companies

Delfin Hotels & Resorts (toll-free U.S. tel. 800/524-5104) has condos in the Terrasol complex. It also books for Casa Contenta B&B and most of the all-inclusive resorts. **Cabo Villa Rentals** (toll-free U.S. tel. 877/473-1946, www.cabovillarentals.com, 8:30am-5pm daily) manages condos in the Terrasol and Villa La Estancia complexes and three- to five-bedroom villas in the Pedregal development. **Earth, Sea & Sky Vacations** (toll-free U.S. tel. 800/745-2226, www.cabovillas.com) represents 90 luxury villa rentals, ranging from two- to nine-bedroom units, with a starting price of US$1,500 per night, as well as 30 resorts. **Pedregal Escapes** (Camino de La Plaza 145, Fraccionamiento Pedregal, tel. 624/144-3222, www.pedregalescapes.com) is the vacation rental division of the company that developed the Pedregal gated community on the west side of Cabo San Lucas. It manages two- to five-bedroom villas, plus even a few larger homes. Prices start at about US$450 per night, and some properties require a security deposit.

Camping and RV Parks

Three kilometers northeast of Cabo San Lucas off the Carretera Transpeninsular, the Mexican-owned **Vagabundos del Mar RV Park** (Carr. Transpeninsular km 3, tel. 624/143-0290, www.vagabundosrv.com) has 52 slots with full hookups but no dump station. Rates are US$24 per day or US$140 per week, with a 10 percent discount for members of the

Vagabundos del Mar travel club. The park is not on the beach; however, campers return year after year to enjoy the peaceful surroundings, comfortably away from the frenzy of activity in downtown Cabo San Lucas. There are four double-size pull-through spaces, and more than half of the spaces are designated annual rentals with *palapas.* Book early if you want to get a spot at this popular park. No caravans. Facilities include a restaurant, bar, flush toilets, *palapas,* showers, a pool, and new laundry machines.

On Playa El Médano, the campground part of **Club Cabo Hotel and Campground Resort** (tel. 624/143-3348, www.clubcaboinn.com, US$16-19) has 10 sites for tent camping and another 10 for small RVs. Guests may use clean restrooms, hot showers, and a hot tub. There is a lounge area with hammocks, table tennis, a swimming pool, wireless Internet, and secure parking.

Villa Serena RV Park (Carr. Transpeninsular km 7.5, toll-free U.S. tel. 888/522-2442, US$21/day, US$112/week, US$391/month) has 54 spaces with full hookups but no shade, as well as laundry, restrooms, and hot showers. In the adjacent **palapa restaurant** (tel. 624/145-8244, 7am-10pm daily, mains US$12-25), a La Paz native serves delicious food (coconut shrimp, whole red snapper) at reasonable prices. Visit www.gaviotasportfishing.com to make a reservation online.

For primitive camping on the beach, you need to head out of town to the Pacific beaches along Highway 19 or the Gulf coast along the East Cape.

Todos Santos and the West Cape

Overnight guests in Todos Santos can choose from a variety of luxury and modest hotels, bed-and-breakfasts, and private vacation rentals. As more visitors arrive each year, new properties are opening, old ones are renovating, and others are just raising prices without making significant improvements. Many properties are now up for sale, and if water and sewer rights are worked out, several large resorts may be coming to the area in the not-too-distant future.

The principal complaint that many first-time visitors express is frustration with the noise that comes with staying in a non-resort town. From the rumble of 18-wheelers to the persistent dog-barking and chicken-clucking, Todos Santos can feel like a town that doesn't sleep. In general, places closer to the beach are quieter (though not silent, and farther from town). Before you book, ask your host what to expect at night. Locations near La Poza and El Otro Lado (north side of town) mean a longish walk to town but more convenient beach access.

To avoid confusion, be aware there are three accommodations in town with "Todos Santos" in their name: The Hacienda Todos Los Santos is in the palm grove at the end of Avenida Juárez; the Todos Santos Inn is on Calle Topete, with its own wine bar; and the Hacienda Inn Todos Santos is north of town. Details for each are given in this section.

WEST CAPE
Several longtime El Pescadero inns change hands each year, and new places are opening each season. The most celebrated opening of late is Rancho Pescadero. A number of private homes have opened up as vacation rental properties.

Under US$100
SAN PEDRITO SURF HOTEL
On the beach in Pescadero, 3.5 kilometers from the wide dirt road that leaves Highway 19 across from the Sandbar, the **San Pedrito Surf Hotel** (www.sanpedritosurf.com, US$70-105) is a remodel of the former Casa Cyrene. Now owned by two families from

Hawaii, the property has five *casitas*. The surf bunkhouse has been converted into a two-bedroom family *casita*. All have full kitchens and king-size beds. Other amenities include bottled water, basic cooking utensils and spices, and linens. There is a washer/dryer on the property.

CASA SIMPATICA

Also in a beachfront location and a little south of the San Pedrito Surf Hotel, **Casa Simpatica** (http://todossantos.cc/casasimpatica.html, US$65, three-night minimum) features four clean, open air *casitas,* each with a queen-size bed and private bath; guests share an outdoor kitchen. Owner Gary Faulk provides Internet access.

LAS PALMAS TROPICALES

At the San Pedrito surf break, **Las Palmas Tropicales** (www.tropicalcasitas.com, US$50-120) has five *palapa*-roof *casitas* (four with kitchens) with tiled baths and wireless Internet.

SIERRA DE LA COSTA

Friendly Rob and Lorinda Costa from Santa Cruz, California, own **Sierra de la Costa** (www.sierradelacosta.com, US$75, three-night minimum), close to the San Pedrito surf break. Super-clean beach bungalow rentals have queen-size beds, tiled baths, private patios, and gas barbecues.

HOTELITO LOS CARDONES

Set back from the water's edge at Playa Los Cerritos, behind Miguel's restaurant, **Hotelito Los Cardones** (Playa Los Cerritos, www.loscardonesbaja.com) has one ocean-view suite (US$85) and a camping *palapa* area (US$10).

VILLAS DE CERRITOS

With ocean views, Wi-Fi, and a small swimming pool, **Villas de Cerritos** (Playa Los Cerritos, tel. 612/151-3728, www.villasdecerritosbeach.com, US$60) has six two-bedroom villa rentals (US$120-160) and several studio bungalows for US$60 per night.

US$100-200
EL POZO HONDO

Near the San Pedrito Surf Hotel, **El Pozo Hondo** (pozohondobcs@yahoo.com, US$100-110) is a bed-and-breakfast with two *palapa*-roof bungalows surrounded by mango, avocado, and citrus trees. Guellermo prepares excellent coffee for guests every morning.

Over US$200
LA ALIANZA

Marble floors, robes, Egyptian cotton sheets, and fluffy towels are among the luxury amenities at **La Alianza** (tel. 612/118-3423, www.bajaturtle.com, US$110-195), a five-room property located between Cerritos and San Pedrito point. Guests share a third-floor *palapa*-roof deck and common kitchen. A separate two-bedroom *casita* has one bath and a kitchen for US$150. All units have access to Wi-Fi. Commissioned works from local artisan Cuco Moyron add an authentic Baja twist to the grounds and home. This is the place to stay if you want privacy and that extra-special touch. Owner Debora McIntire is involved with local sea turtle conservation activities to protect the leatherbacks and olive ridleys that nest on the beach in Pescadero. Inquire about participating in a baby turtle release August-December and the large leatherbacks January-March.

◀ RANCHO PESCADERO

Sunflowers bordering an organic vegetable garden lean in the breeze along the driveway that leads to **Rancho Pescadero** (tel. 612/135-5849, www.ranchopescadero.com, US$185-425). Its 27 guest rooms include continental breakfast delivered to your door, daily yoga classes, and the use of two swimming pools, fishing poles, and surfboards. Lounge in daybeds on the beach or book an oceanside massage. A beer lounge on the terrace and lower-level restaurant are open to the public (7am-9pm daily). No pets or kids under 12. Rancho Pescadero does not have a street address. To find the hotel, turn west on the first main dirt road south of the Pescadero Pemex. Follow this road for 1.6

roof deck at Rancho Pescadero

kilometers toward the ocean and turn right at the T, and signs will point the way from there.

Vacation Rentals
OSPREY SAN PEDRITO
Osprey San Pedrito (Playa San Pedrito, www.bajaosprey.com, US$110-180) is a home divided into three suites, each with its own bedroom, bath, and kitchen. One of the suites on the main level has two bedrooms. The units may be rented separately or together. Cook your own meals in the fully equipped kitchen or walk along the beach to the bar/restaurant at Rancho Pescadero.

DR. ROBERTS OCEANFRONT OASIS
Featuring new construction and a location right on the beach, **Dr. Roberts Oceanfront Oasis** (no tel., www.bajaroberts.com, US$70-120) has a main house that sleeps seven and rents for US$350/night, plus a smaller apartment, surf

room, and bungalows for smaller groups. Visit the website to make reservations.

VILLA DEL FARO
For kids (and the young at heart), the highlight of a stay at **Villa del Faro** (tel. 612/145-0087, www.todosantosguide.com/villadelfaro, US$4,000/week) is the curved waterslide that deposits swimmers into a 12-meter saltwater pool rimmed with fiber-optic lights that glow after dark. Located at the south end of Pescadero Beach, the villa was built to handle a crowd, with three kitchens, five bedrooms, and a hot tub, plus massage and maid services and catering available by request. For more entertainment, there is a Ping-Pong table, volleyball court, and 52-inch television.

ALHAJA DE BAJA
Between the Los Cerritos and San Pedrito surf breaks, **Alhaja de Baja** (no tel., www.alhaja

debaja.com, US$990/week) is a recently remodeled two-bedroom house with king-size beds.

Surf Camp
PESCADERO SURF CAMP

On the east side of Highway 19 at kilometer 64, **Pescadero Surf Camp** (tel. 612/134-0480, www.pescaderosurf.com, US$30-60) is a good place for die-hard surfers to meet kindred spirits. Options for lodging include a cabana for six with its own kitchen and bath or camping under a *palapa* (US$10 pp/night). Guests may use the swimming pool, hot showers, and shared outdoor kitchen.

TODOS SANTOS
Under US$100
MARIA BONITA HOTEL

The **Maria Bonita Hotel** (Militar at Hidalgo, tel. 612/145-0850, mariabonitahotel@prodigy. net.mx, US$40-55) has an office and 12 guest rooms on the second floor, above the popular Café Brown. Though rooms are plain, the clean off-white walls, updated curtains and bedspreads, and comfortable mattresses make for a pleasant stay. Small but clean bathrooms have shower stalls with glass doors and hot water aplenty. A great value, this hotel is a wise choice for budget travelers who need a place to crash for the night. Rates include tax.

BED AND BREAKFAST LAS CASITAS

At **Bed and Breakfast Las Casitas** (Rangel btwn. Obregón and Hidalgo, tel./fax 612/145-0255, US$60-100), Canadian artist Wendy Faith has lovingly restored four *chiname* adobe cottages and one four-person suite over the last decade. Set among lush landscaping, rooms are small, with low ceilings, one bed, and brightly colored walls and ceilings. Accommodations here are basic but artsy, with hand-painted murals in some rooms and the artist's own glasswork in others. Breakfast includes the bed-and-breakfast's own blend of coffee. An authentic *palo de arco casita* (covered patio) houses the owner's studio.

HOTEL SANTA ROSA

To get to the **Hotel Santa Rosa** (Olochea btwn. Verduzco and Villarino, tel. 612/145-0394, www.hotelsantarosa.com.mx, US$70), go three blocks south of the Pemex station on Calle Degollado, turn right on Calle Olachea, and go two blocks. There are eight rooms with kitchenettes and queen beds, plus a well-maintained pool, hot tub, and enclosed parking. The hotel offers a 5 percent discount for weeklong stays, 10 percent off for two weeks, and 33 percent off for a monthlong reservation. Wi-Fi available.

IGUANA DE LOS MANGOS

In the Las Tunas area two kilometers north of town, **Iguana de los Mangos** (cell 612/119-7880, www.bajasurtodossantos.com, US$90) is a newer studio *casita* that sleeps two adults and up to two children. Special touches include fluffy towels and luxury bed linens, plus a rooftop terrace, hammock, barbecue, and daily breakfast. It's about a 10-minute walk to the water's edge.

US$100-200
JARDÍN DE PILAR

Set among towering palm, mango, and banana trees, **Jardín de Pilar** (Pilar btwn. Topete and Hidalgo, tel. 612/145-0386, US$130-150) has two beautifully appointed *casitas* for rent. Details include colorful high-end linens and bamboo accents, as well as wireless Internet and swimming pool.

HOTELITO

On the road to Playa La Cachora, the **Hotelito** (tel. 612/145-0099, www.thehotelito.com, US$125-135) is a boutique-style inn with four cottages that blend a modern Mexican and European style. For recreation, the inn has a small swimming pool and morning yoga classes twice a week. Rates include breakfast. On all but the hottest days you can comfortably walk about a kilometer to the beach or into town.

TODOS SANTOS ACCOMMODATIONS

	Type	Location	Rates
Alhaja de Baja	Rental	West Cape	US$990/week
Arriba de la Roca	Boutique hotel	Todos Santos	US$275-295
The B&B at Flora del Mar	B&B	Todos Santos	US$115-125
Bed and Breakfast Las Casitas	B&B	Todos Santos	US$60-100
Casa Bentley	B&B	Todos Santos	US$110-190
Casa Simpatica	B&B	El Pescadero	US$65
Casablanca B&B	B&B	Todos Santos	US$90-150
Casa Colina	Rental	Todos Santos	US$195
Dr. Roberts Oceanfront Oasis	Rental	West Cape	US$70-120
El Pozo Hondo	B&B	El Pescadero	US$100-110
Garden Casita	Rental	Todos Santos	US$300/week
Guaycura Hotel	Hotel	Todos Santos	US$175-350
Hacienda Inn Todos Santos	Hotel	Todos Santos	US$110-140
Hacienda Todos Los Santos	B&B	Todos Santos	US$125-225
Hotel California	Hotel	Todos Santos	US$110-190
Hotelito	B&B	Todos Santos	US$125-135
Hotelito Los Cardones	B&B	Los Cerritos	US$85
Hotel Posada del Molino	Rental	Todos Santos	US$90-110
Hotel Santa Rosa	Hotel	Todos Santos	US$70
Iguana de los Mangos	B&B	Todos Santos	US$90
Jardín de Pilar	B&B	Todos Santos	US$130-150
La Alianza	B&B	Los Cerritos	US$110-195
Las Casitas Cal y Canto	Rental	Todos Santos	US$150-200
Las Flores Posada	Rental	Todos Santos	US$65-95
La Sirena Eco-Adventures	Rental	Todos Santos	US$700/week
Las Palmas Tropicales	B&B	El Pescadero	US$50-120
Las Puertas	Rental	Todos Santos	US$135-175
La Supercionfola	Rental	Todos Santos	US$55-100
Los Colibris Casitas	Rental	Todos Santos	US$115-195
Maria Bonita Hotel	Hotel	Todos Santos	US$40-55
Osprey San Pedrito	Rental	West Cape	US$110-180
Pescadero Surf Camp	Camping	Pescadero	US$30-60
Posada La Poza	Boutique hotel	Todos Santos	US$140-425
Rancho Pescadero	Resort	El Pescadero	US$185-425
San Pedrito Surf Hotel	Hotel	El Pescadero	US$70-105
Sierra de la Costa	Hotel	West Cape	US$75
Todos Santos Inn	Hotel	Todos Santos	US$125-225
Villa del Faro	Rental	West Cape	US$4,000/week
Villas de Cerritos	Rental	West Cape	US$60
Villas La Mar	Rental	Todos Santos	US$185

Best Feature(s)	Why Stay Here	Best Fit For
Recently remodeled	Private	Couples and small families
Views, gourmet breakfast	Luxurious amenities and solar-powered living	Couples, honeymooners, solo travelers looking for relaxation
Pet-friendly, beach path, and dance floors	No-frills but comfortable with delicious breakfasts	Couples and sporty types
Charming, artsy decor	Good value and good breakfast	Couples and solo travelers
Heated pool and outdoor kitchen	Contemporary luxury	Families, couples, and solo travelers
Private open-air casitas on the beach	Modest accommodations for a good value	Beachgoers and budget travelers
Full gourmet breakfast daily	Prime hospitality	Couples and solo travelers
Large, airy home	Private	Couples and small families
Beachfront location	Affordability	Families and small groups
Fresh fruit and great coffee	Intimate setting, close to the beach	Families and beachgoers
Unique redbrick design	Affordability	Couples and independent travelers
Rooftop pool and spa	Location	Couples
Comfy bathrobes and good bar	Great value	Families and small groups
Location	Walk to town or to the beach	Families or couples
La Coronela restaurant	Unique, individually decorated rooms	Small groups or solo travelers
A blend of Mexican and European style	Great value	Couples and solo travelers
Ocean views	Great value	Families and budget travelers
Breakfast on-site	Studio-style	Couples and small families
Discounts for longer stays	Modest accommodations for a good value	Budget travelers
Fluffy towels and luxury linens	Comfortable with a 10-minute walk to the beach	Families
Colorful and luxurious linens	Lovely casitas set amongst the trees	Couples and families
Luxury amenities, seasonal sea turtle releases	Comfort and unique art from Baja artists	Couples
Proximity to surfing	Location	Families and small or large groups
Private and cozy	Affordability	Families, couples, and independent travelers
Short walk to the beach	Variety of sizes and styles	Families and groups
On the surf break	Affordable accommodations on the break	Surfers
Baja-style furnishings	Great views	Couples and families
Secluded, intimate feeling	Location, midway between beach and town	Independent travelers
Stunning views and creative decorative touches	Authentic feel	Couples and families
Clean rooms and comfortable mattresses	Modest accommodations for a good value	Budget travelers
Beachfront location	Intimate setting	Couples
Access to prime waves	Affordability	Die-hard surfers
Ocean views, Swiss bed linens, on-site sweat lodge	Swiss quality and efficiency at a relaxed Baja pace	Families, couples, solo travelers
Luxury resort amenities	Everything you need in one spot	Couples, small groups
Full kitchens and king-size beds	On the beach	Surfers and families
Super clean	Basic and affordable accommodations	Budget travelers
Private terraces, La Copa Bar	Elegant accommodations	Couples and solo travelers
Water slide and saltwater swimming pool	Built to handle a crowd	Families and groups
Large, private villas and bungalows	Water sports	Active families and water sport enthusiasts
New	Hillside villas	Families and groups

HACIENDA TODOS LOS SANTOS

Much loved for its location, sparkling pool, and friendly service, **Hacienda Todos Los Santos** (Juárez, tel. 612/145-0547, www.tshacienda.com) has three *casitas* and four suites, each with its own personality. All have air-conditioning, private terraces, and spacious bathrooms. Casa Santa Luz (US$190) has a queen-size bed, TV/VCR, and fireplace. Casa del Palmar (US$165) is a studio suite with multiple terraces, king-size bed, and TV/VCR. Casita del Encanto (US$125) is a studio suite complete with two patios, queen-size bed, and seating area. Casa de los Santos has one room (US$125) and three suites (US$185-225), and the whole house rents for US$850 a night. The upstairs suites have great views of the surrounding farmland. Amenities on the property include Wi-Fi, swimming pool, and gardens for strolling. Walk to town or the beach.

CASA BENTLEY

Centrally located in the historic district, **Casa Bentley** (Calle Pilar 99 at Hidalgo, tel. 612/145 0276, www.casabentley.com, US$110-190) offers five contemporary guest suites in three houses—one is a restored adobe structure and the other two are modern stone construction. Guests enjoy air-conditioning, luxury linens, and use of a heated swimming pool. Access to an outdoor kitchen is provided with some units and available by special arrangement for the others.

CASABLANCA B&B

Owners and hosts Isabel and Gabriel give a warm welcome to guests at their **Casablanca B&B** (La Poza, Todos Santos, tel. 612/145-0832, www.casablancabb.com, US$90-150). Isabel's full gourmet breakfast each morning comes with rave reviews, and guests can stay in one of two rooms. The first suite offers a king-size bed and the other holds two full beds. The suites have their own private entrances and guests are welcome to spend time in the main house as well. A private terrace with a hammock and free Wi-Fi complete a stay here.

THE B&B AT FLORA DEL MAR

Four suites and a second-floor studio apartment make up the layout of the **B&B at Flora del Mar** (San Sebastian, Todos Santos, 612/153-5354, www.floradelmar.net, US$115-125). Guests are treated to a pet friendly B&B setting about 2.5 kilometers from the heart of Todos Santos. Rooms are clean and comfortable, but no-frills. Amenities include a pool, two dance floors, an easy path to the beach, and a tennis court. Guests praise owner Marilyn's hospitality and fantastic breakfasts.

HACIENDA INN TODOS SANTOS

On the road to La Pastora, the **Hacienda Inn Todos Santos** (tel./fax 612/145-0193, US$110-140 with continental breakfast) is about two kilometers from the center of town. The inn has a swimming pool and restaurant with a bar. All 14 rooms and suites have air-conditioning, cable TV, and comfy bathrobes. Turn right at the El Sol II grocery store to find the inn.

◖ TODOS SANTOS INN

A stay at the elegant **Todos Santos Inn** (Legaspi 33 at Topete, tel./fax 612/145-0040, www.todossantosinn.com, US$125-225) takes visitors back to the town's sugarcane era in the 19th century. Housed in a restored brick building, the inn is beautifully designed and appointed with high ceilings, antique furnishings, and tile floors. Amenities include private terraces, ceiling fans, and air-conditioning. Guests enjoy use of a small pool and the on-site La Copa Bar. Spanish-language instruction is available, either separately or as a package with accommodations (10 hours for US$200).

HOTEL CALIFORNIA

Last renovated in 2003, two-story **Hotel California** (Juárez btwn. Morelos and Márquez de León, tel. 612/145-0525, www.hotelcaliforniabaja.com, US$110-190) has 11 rooms and suites, a small swimming pool, and courtyard garden. It also has its own restaurant, **La Coronela,** and a gift shop called **Emporio Hotel California.**

© NIKKI GOTH ITOI

view of boutique hotel Posada La Poza, Todos Santos

Over US$200
POSADA LA POZA
Posada La Poza (tel. 612/145-0400, www.lapoza.com, US$140-425) blends the relaxed pace of life in Baja with a Swiss sensibility for quality and efficiency. Hosts Jörg and Libusche Wiesendanger opened the hotel in 2002. Guests stay in one of four garden suites, two junior suites with private hot tubs, or the master suite. Suites here come with views of the lagoon and ocean beyond, plus air-conditioning, a CD player, and Swiss bed linens. Guest rooms and common areas also feature Libusche's oil and acrylic paintings. You can splash around in a large saltwater swimming pool, soak in the saltwater 10-person whirlpool tub, enjoy the small beach area right in front of the inn, watch for whales from the deck, or borrow a bicycle for a ride into town. And when you've had your fill of the great outdoors, you might give yourself an aromatherapy treatment in the on-site sweat lodge, which is filled with heated lava rocks topped with eucalyptus leaves, rosemary, or other herbs. Internet access is available. Rates include continental breakfast, and **El Gusto!** restaurant serves hearty Mexican and international dishes like pork loin, rib eye, and lobster. The road to La Poza is well marked: Turn southwest off Degollado (Highway 19) onto Calle Olachea or Calle Carrillo and follow the blue and white signs.

GUAYCURA HOTEL
In a restored two-story dormitory on Calle Topete, **Guaycura Hotel** (Lesagpi at Topete, tel. 612/175-0800, www.guaycura.com.mx, US$175-350) offers 14 luxury guest rooms, three of which have ocean views. Guests can lounge by the small rooftop pool in the morning, take a stroll around town or head to the beach midday, and return for spa treatments in the afternoon.

ARRIBA DE LA ROCA
Guests at **Arriba de la Roca** (Hwy. 19 km 74.3, Todos Santos, tel. 612/149-2639, www.arribadelaroca.com, US$275-295) refer to it as "Heaven on a rock." Owners and hosts

Maurice and Shelby have margaritas and appetizers waiting for guests at sunset and provide a full gourmet breakfast each morning. Other amenities include a pool and 800-thread count sheets. The hotel is solar powered and does not have phones or televisions in the casitas, though Wi-Fi is available for free. Guests can choose from three casitas or rent the entire hotel for up to 10 people (US$9,975/week).

GUESTHOUSES AND VACATION RENTALS
Under US$100
LA SUPERCIONFOLA

Over the last decade, a fun-loving retired couple from Italy has built six guest *casitas* on their Las Brisas area property, collectively known as La Supercionfola and located on the west side of Camino a Las Tunas. Each *casita* has a clear view of the ocean and dunes before it, and the sand is a five-minute walk from your door. Simple yet elegant designs are beautifully constructed with separate private kitchens and sculpted concrete counters. Two units have two bedrooms each, two are one-bedroom *casitas*, and one is a studio. All but the studio have private kitchens. Though in a somewhat developed area, the landscaping makes the setting feel secluded and completely private. The location is about 10 minutes from town—ideal for independent travelers.

Contact manager Emy Festa, who also manages the **Gemma Inn** (tel. 612/123-5508, cell 612/168-7937, info@gemmagroup.it) in La Paz for details. Longer-term stays are preferred, and the rates are US$55/night or US$300/week for the studio (two-night min.), US$500/week for the one-bedroom *casitas,* and US$700/week for the two bedroom *casitas.* Inquire about discounted monthly and half-year rates.

GARDEN CASITA

The **Garden Casita** (Olachea and Mutualismo, tel./fax 612/145-0129, www.todossantos-baja.com/gardencasita.htm, US$300 week) is a unique redbrick guesthouse with a *palapa* roof. The *casita* has a living area, separate bedroom, and patio with enclosed courtyard. Wireless

high-speed Internet is included, and the long-term rates include weekly maid service.

LAS FLORES POSADA

Las Flores Posada (formerly Jane's Place, Pedrajo and Villarino, tel. 612/145-0216, www.todossantosguide.com/vacationrentals/lasfloresposada.htm, US$65-95) has four cozy but well-worn *casitas* on an acre of property centered around a courtyard with a fountain. There are three studio bungalows, each with private bath and kitchen, and a main bungalow with two bedrooms, kitchen, and living room.

HOTEL POSADA DEL MOLINO

Named for the sugarcane mill ruins that adjoin the property, **Hotel Posada del Molino** (Rangel and Progreso, tel. 612/145-0233, www.posadadelmolinots.com, US$90-110) has four air-conditioned studios next to a swimming pool. Each studio has a queen-size bed, wireless Internet, satellite TV, and kitchenette. Breakfast at the on-site Pura Vida café makes a nice way to start the day.

LA SIRENA ECO-ADVENTURES

Situated in a residential neighborhood off Calle Degollado, midway between downtown and the beach and next to the Hotel Santa Rosa, **La Sirena Eco-Adventures** (Calle Olachea btwn. Villarino and Verduzco, tel. 612/145-0353, U.S. tel. 213/265-9943, www.lasirenakayaksurf.com) rents a few different vacation rentals, including the three-bedroom, three-bath Casa Los Amigos (US$700/week), which can fit up to eight people comfortably and is a short walk to the beach.

US$100-200
⟨ LOS COLIBRIS CASITAS

At **Los Colibris Casitas** (Cerro La Poza, Calle Guaycura, tel. 612/145-0189, www.loscolibris.com, US$115-195/night, US$800-1,200/week), the friendly proprietors of Todos Santos Eco Adventures, Sergio and Bryan Jáuregui, offer two rental homes and two *casitas* on their hillside property, with stunning ocean views overlooking the freshwater estuary and beach beyond.

© NIKKI GOTH ITOI

Casa Colina

Tiled baths have rain showers and sculpted concrete countertops. Lampposts made of decorative tree trunks, colorful linens, and hummingbird feeders are few of the special touches. Units have ceiling fans, some with air-conditioning, well-equipped kitchens, bottled water, and iPod docking stations for music. Outdoor space is limited, given the steep incline of the property, but a small infinity pool and hot tub on a stone terrace give the illusion of more space.

LAS PUERTAS

On the road leading to Playa la Cachora, **Las Puertas** (tel. 612/145-0373, www.alaspuertas. com, US$135-175) offers a large two-bedroom guesthouse, a one-bedroom guesthouse, and a suite with ocean views. All the structures are nicely furnished, private, and built in classic Baja style with *palapa* roofs and adobe walls. The ocean-view suite is the newest addition and has the nicest furnishings, a fireplace, and exceptional views. Daily maid service is included.

CASA COLINA

Managed by the owners of Los Colibris, **Casa Colina** (tel. 612/145-0780, www.casacolina-ts. com, US$195/night, US$1,200/week) is a two-story, two-bedroom home with a little more space inside and out, and a private—though very steep—driveway. Large picture windows in the bedrooms and kitchen open to spectacular ocean views, while balconies on both bedrooms face the mountains. Each bedroom has a king-size bed with luxury linens, ceiling fan, and its own bath. The casa also has a fully equipped kitchen. The trail around La Poza is a short walk downhill from the house.

VILLAS LA MAR

Villas La Mar (Cerrada Guaycura 26, tel. 612/145-0116, www.hotelvillaslamar.com, US$185) rents several newly constructed villas built against a hillside on the south side of La Poza. From Degollado, follow the signs toward Posada La Poza and Los Colibris.

LAS CASITAS CAL Y CANTO

About four kilometers north of town in the La Tunas area, **Las Casitas Cal y Canto** (www.calycanto.com, US$150-200) consists of three newly constructed two-story homes on a five-acre property on the east side of the road. Design accents include Saltillo floors, Talavera tiles, outdoor showers, and mesquite furniture. Swing in a hammock on the patio or walk 10 minutes to the beach. In winter, proximity to the break at La Pastora, three kilometers away, is a plus for surfers. Together, the *casitas* can accommodate a group of 18 people.

EXCURSIONS

The promise of calm seas, steady winds, and abundant game fish lures many adventure-seekers away from the resorts of Los Cabos to the remote beaches and rocky points of the East Cape—and increasingly also to the silver mining ghost towns, traditional ranchos, and freshwater springs hidden deep in the mountainous interior.

© NIKKI GOTH ITOI

HIGHLIGHTS

LOOK FOR  TO FIND RECOMMENDED SIGHTS, ACTIVITIES, DINING, AND LODGING.

❰ Cabo Pulmo: Reef-building corals, crystal waters, and white-sand beaches attract divers, snorkelers, and kayakers to Bahía Pulmo and Playa La Sirenita (page 189).

❰ Santiago Town Plaza: Shaded by mature trees and lined with a row of colonial buildings, this plaza is a perfect place to relax after a trip to the nearby hot springs or waterfall (page 198).

❰ El Triunfo: This ghost town in the mountains along the Carretera Transpeninsular was once a silver-mining boomtown and the largest community in Southern Baja (page 198).

❰ Cañon de la Zorra: At the edge of the Sierra de la Laguna, near Santiago, a 10-meter waterfall plunges over smooth granite rock into a swimmable lagoon (page 201).

❰ Isla Espíritu Santo: The best-known of the islands off La Paz entertains paddlers, divers, and boaters with white-sand beaches and rock reefs. You can camp in several places on the island (page 207).

❰ Malecón Álvaro Obregón: You haven't experienced La Paz until you've strolled the waterfront promenade at sunset. Visitors and residents alike pause to watch the dramatic display of color. Take a break for a cocktail or an ice cream and enjoy the afternoon breeze (page 215).

Some of Baja's prettiest and most secluded beaches line the Gulf coast between Bahía de las Palmas and San José del Cabo, at the southern tip of the peninsula. And along this stretch, the opportunities for deep-sea fishing, windsurfing, kiteboarding, kayaking, stand-up paddling, snorkeling, and scuba diving are among the best in the world. The region contains a few larger towns, such as Los Barriles, Santiago, and La Ribera, but for the most part, civilization consists of tiny fishing villages alternating with newer gringo enclaves. The vibe is low-key, and in many places, the lifestyle is still off the grid, with dirt

roads, *palapa*-roof bungalows, solar power, and satellite-only Internet and phone service.

Farther north, the state capital of La Paz offers the closest approximation you can find in Baja to a mainland Mexico city. A scenic *malecón* for strolling, opportunities for outdoor adventure, and creative culinary scene make La Paz worth the two-hour drive from Los Cabos. And the sunsets here are legendary. Allow a couple of days for this trip if you want to get out to the islands for a snorkeling, scuba diving, or kayaking experience. For the best kiteboarding in winter, consider a stay in La Ventana or El Sargente.

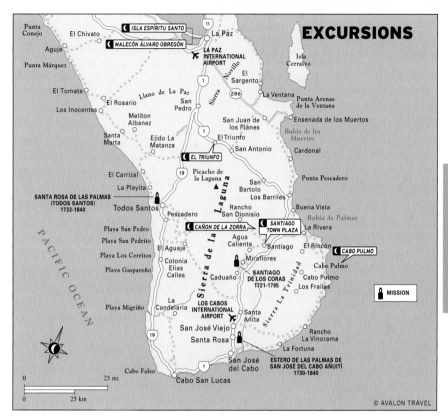

Los Barriles and Bahía de las Palmas

Wide and exposed Bahía de las Palmas is roughly 32 kilometers long, extending from Punta Pescadero in the north to Punta Arena at its southern end and including the sizable town of Los Barriles. The area experienced its first heyday in the 1960s as a fly-in resort for anglers. Fishing is still a draw in summer; however, two new sports have taken center stage in the winter months: Strong winds blowing out of the north combined with thermals generated by the inland peaks create ideal conditions for kiteboarding and windsurfing.

As with the rest of the Southern Baja coastline, land development is fast changing the profile of communities beside the bay. Second homes owned by retirees from the United States rim the shore, with a few resorts mixed in. In general, the bay gets less developed the farther north you go, but even the famed Hotel Punta Pescadero Paradise has expanded to become a full-service luxury resort.

The defining image of day-to-day life in Los Barriles these days is that of early retirees happily speeding along dirt roads on ATVs, which they ride to the supermarket, hardware store, beach, and everywhere in between. No longer the sole domain of sports fishers and windsurfers, the town has broadened its appeal with more guest accommodations, restaurants, and services—and a vibe that is friendly and relaxed.

A strip mall on the main access road from Highway 1 (Carretera Transpeninsular) is the de facto town center, with another row of commercial businesses along Calle 20 de Noviembre, heading north to Punta Pescadero. A row of gringo McMansions front the beach behind a stone retaining wall, and several developments are in varying stages of completion in the hills above and to the north of town. However, those in search of the "real" Baja should not despair; Los Barriles retains an authentic *tortillería,* plus roosters that roam the streets, a cement factory where blocks are still made by hand, numerous taco stands, and countless other family-owned businesses. Local Mexicans know each other by their *sobrenombres* (nicknames), and the untamed backcountry is just minutes away.

BEACHES
Punta Pescadero
The reef that extends out from the point at the north end of the bay is among the best places in the Sea of Cortez for snorkeling.

Los Barriles
This exposed beach is really about access to the water, for wind sports and/or sportfishing, depending on the season. Most of the town's services are a short walk from the sand.

WATER SPORTS
Kiteboarding and Windsurfing
The powerful side-shore winds at Los Barriles are best attempted by intermediate and advanced kiteboarders and windsurfers. In the peak season, November-April, wind speeds frequently exceed 20 knots and rarely drop below 18 knots. Beginners can usually get in the water during calmer early morning conditions. Instructors say windsurfers should know how to water-start or plan to take a lesson to learn how when they arrive. By 11am most days, the winds kick up a rolling swell (no breaking waves) that is fun for jumping. Frequent

"downwinders" to Buena Vista are a particularly fun way to enjoy the breeze. The trip begins at North Beach in Los Barriles and ends two hours later in Buena Vista, with a shuttle ride back to Los Barriles. Water temperatures average about 22-24°C in winter, with air temperatures around 26-27°C.

Fishing
Bahía de las Palmas is an exciting place to fish because the sea floor drops to great depths not far from the shoreline. The reef extending out from Punta Pescadero is great for triggerfish, barred pargo, and cabrilla. About a kilometer from land, you can find depths that exceed 100 fathoms. The popular Tuna Canyon, 6.5 kilometers south of Punta Pescadero, is the place to catch yellowfin tuna. Several charter services based along the bay offer trips on *pangas* (US$200-260/day) and cruisers (US$200-325/day). Bait costs around US$20-25 per day. A popular day trip when the conditions aren't too windy is to travel north by boat to Bahía de los Muertos, and fish on the way.

In Los Barriles, **Martin Verdugo's Beach Resort** (tel. 624/141-0054, www.verdugosbeachresort.com) and the **Hotel Palmas de Cortez** (tel. 624/141-0050, toll-free U.S. tel. 877/777-8862, www.vanwormerresorts.com) offer fishing packages; the concierge at the Hotel Palmas de Cortez can arrange fishing trips for guests and nonguests. In addition, **Baja's Awesome Sportfishing** (tel. 624/141-0231, U.S. tel. 208/788-2053, www.eastcaperv.com/awesome_sportfishing.html), headquartered at the East Cape RV Resort, operates two cruisers, a 30-foot island hopper, and a 32-foot Blackfin sportfisher. The most popular captains in Los Barriles and Buena Vista, including Julio Cota and Chuy Cota, book a year in advance for weekend visits, so plan your trip early.

Juan Carlos of **La Capilla Sportfishing and Eco Tours** (tel. 624/141-0611) runs charters on a diesel-powered *panga.*

Fish with Me (toll-free U.S. tel. 800/347-4963, www.fishwithme.com) owner Jerry Hall has been fishing the East Cape since 1973 and organizes group trips several times a year. Boat

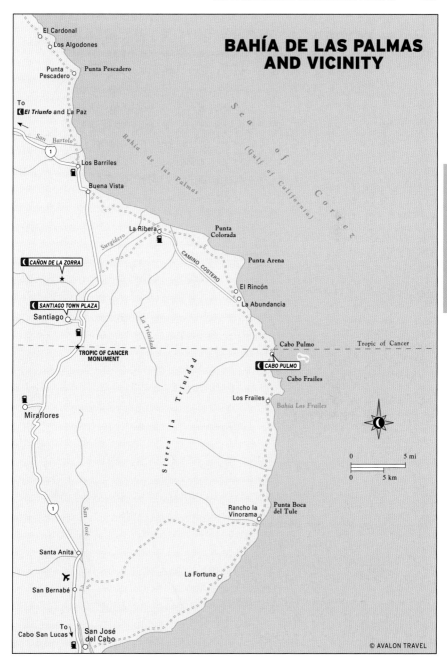

BAHÍA DE LAS PALMAS AND VICINITY

El Cardonal

Los Algodones

Punta Pescadero

Punta Pescadero

To El Triunfo and La Paz

San Bartolo

Los Barriles

Buena Vista

Bahía de las Palmas

Sea of Cortez (Gulf of California)

La Ribera

Punta Colorada

Surgidero

CAMINO COSTERO

Punta Arena

CAÑON DE LA ZORRA

El Rincón

SANTIAGO TOWN PLAZA

La Abundancia

Santiago

La Trinidad

Cabo Pulmo

Tropic of Cancer

TROPIC OF CANCER MONUMENT

CABO PULMO

Cabo Frailes

Miraflores

Los Frailes

Bahía Los Frailes

Sierra la Trinidad

0   5 mi

0   5 km

San José

Rancho la Vinorama

Punta Boca del Tule

Santa Anita

San Bernabé

La Fortuna

To Cabo San Lucas

San José del Cabo

© AVALON TRAVEL

EXCURSIONS

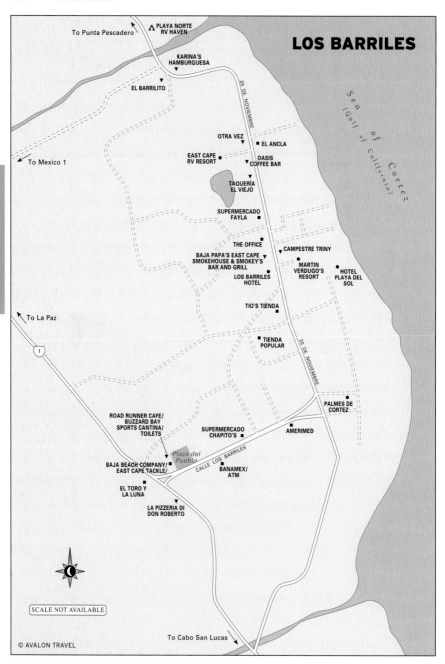

LOS BARRILES

To Punta Pescadero

PLAYA NORTE
RV HAVEN

KARINA'S
HAMBURGUESA

EL BARRILITO

20 DE NOVIEMBRE

To Mexico 1

OTRA VEZ
EL ANCLA

EAST CAPE
RV RESORT
OASIS
COFFEE BAR

TAQUERÍA
EL VIEJO

SUPERMERCADO
FAYLA

THE OFFICE

CAMPESTRE TRINY

BAJA PAPA'S EAST CAPE
SMOKEHOUSE & SMOKEY'S
BAR AND GRILL
MARTIN
VERDUGO'S
RESORT
HOTEL
PLAYA DEL
SOL
LOS BARRILES
HOTEL

To La Paz

TIO'S TIENDA

1

TIENDA
POPULAR

20 DE NOVIEMBRE

PALMES DE
CORTEZ

ROAD RUNNER CAFE/
BUZZARD BAY
SPORTS CANTINA/
TOILETS

SUPERMERCADO
CHAPITO'S
AMERIMED

Plaza del
Pueblo

CALLE LOS BARRILES

BAJA BEACH COMPANY/
EAST CAPE TACKLE/
BANAMEX/
ATM

EL TORO Y
LA LUNA

LA PIZZERIA DI
DON ROBERTO

Sea of Cortez
(Gulf of California)

SCALE NOT AVAILABLE

To Cabo San Lucas

© AVALON TRAVEL

© NIKKI GOTH ITOI

panga launch, Baja-style

EXCURSIONS

rentals are available, ranging from super-*pangas* (US$275/day) to super-cruisers (US$605-726/day). Tackle rental is US$10/day per person, and live bait runs US$20-30/day per boat. The biggest fish caught on a Fish with Me trip was a blue marlin that weighed in at 451 pounds.

Snorkeling and Scuba Diving
South of Los Barriles, Buena Vista has a reputable dive center located on the beach, next to the Vista del Mar trailer park. **Vista Sea Sport** (tel. 624/141-0031, Buena Vista, www.vistaseasport.com) is run by two PADI-certified dive instructors from Southern California who own three super-*pangas* and one cruiser. However, boat rides to the major sites—Cabo Pulmo, Los Frailes, Punta Pescadero, and Isla Cerralvo—are long and rates are higher (US$125-140 for a two-tank dive) than at shops based in La Paz or Cabo Pulmo. Scuba gear rental is US$30 with a tour. Airfills cost US$10; snorkeling gear US$10. Look for a giant earthmover that serves as the boat launch. To find the shop from the Carretera

Transpeninsular, take the turn across from the Calafia Hotel and then turn left at the T in the dirt road and follow the signs.

MOUNTAIN BIKING
Vela Windsurf Resort (Los Barriles, U.S./Canada tel. 541/387-0431 or 800/223-5443, www.velawindsurf.com) at the Hotel Playa del Sol rents Specialized brand mountain bikes for coastal and desert rides. Clip-less pedals are an option, so bring your shoes. They also have children's bikes, a trail-a-bike, and a kid's trailer.

ADVENTURE SPORTS AND TOURS
ATVs are a popular mode of transportation in Los Barriles. **Quadman** (tel. 624/168-6087, www.quadman.net), across from the Amerimed clinic on the north side of Calle Los Barriles near the T intersection at 20 de Noviembre, rents ATVs (US$99/day) and **Rhinos** (US$199/day). Rhinos seat four people, and you must be 35 or older to drive. ATVs have racks for fishing

save a day for snorkeling at Pulmo reef

poles, though riders must stay at least 20 meters from the high-tide line to protect turtle nests.

SPAS

Above the gym in the Hotel Palmas de Cortez, at the end of Calle Los Barriles, **Spa de Cortez** (tel. 624/141-0050, ext. 616, spadecortez@ yahoo.com) offers Swedish, therapeutic, and sports massage, plus aromatherapy, body scrubs, facials, and waxing services. A one-hour massage is US$80 and a 90-minute treatment is US$115. You can also contact **Claudia** (tel. 624/161-0325, claudiasaicam@hotmail.com) at the Spa de Cortez directly for appointments. **The While in Paradise Day Spa** (above Plum Loco Gift Shop in Los Barriles, tel. 624/150-5608, www.whileinparadisedayspa.com, appointment only) offers a range of skin, hair, and body treatments. A European facial runs US$55, a one-hour massage is US$50, and waxing services are US$12-65.

Ball Blast, Pilates, Zumba Gold, and TimeZone classes are all offered at the **Sukhasana Yoga and Pilates Studio** (Los Barriles, contact Sefi Held at sefiheld@sympatico.ca).

For foot reflexology, contact **Baja Foot Reflexology** (Los Barriles, tel. 624/141-0332, treaturfeet@yahoo.com).

SHOPPING

Los Barriles has the only real shopping in this part of Baja. Head to the small Plaza del Pueblo for essentials and gifts. **Baja Beach Company (**Plaza del Pueblo 8, Los Barriles, no tel., 9am-5pm Mon.-Fri., till 2pm Sat.), in the strip mall near Buzzard Bay, has ceramics, textiles, gifts, and a few books and maps. In the same plaza, **La Casa** (Plaza del Pueblo 10, Los Barriles, tel. 624/124-8057) sells kitchenware and other goods for the home. **Copper River Jewelry Designs** (Plaza Gaviota, Los Barriles, tel. 624/159-4780, Losbarriles4U@yahoo. com) sells jewelry designed and fabricated by Christine Rogers. **Big Tony** (Plaza Libertad, Los Barriles, no tel., 9am-7pm Mon.-Sat.) has good-quality beach clothing, shorts, bikinis, and accessories.

A small art shop run by local artist Sarah De La Vos is called **Galeria Los Angeles** (next to Caleb's Café, Los Barriles, tel. 624/141-0068). In addition to her own art, De La Vos sells paintings and carvings from artists throughout Mexico. Used clothing and goods can be picked up at **Suzie's Seconds Consignment Shop** (Plaza del Pueblo 12, Los Barriles, 624/141-0266, suzieseconds14@gmail.com).

On the highway, across from the main entrance to town, **El Toro y La Luna** (Carr. Transpeninsular, Entrada a Los Barriles, Los Barriles, tel. 624/141-0696, 8am-5pm daily) carries ceramic sinks, tiles, and other home furnishings.

FOOD

There are casual eateries along the shores of Bahía de las Palmas, with the greatest variety in Los Barriles. Seafood takes center stage on most menus. Los Barriles also has the only large-size grocery store in the area, **Supermercado Chapito's** (7:30am-10pm daily).

Punta Pescadero

The restaurant at **Hotel Punta Pescadero Paradise** (tel. 612/141-0101, toll-free U.S. tel. 800/332-4442, www.puntapescaderoparadise. com) is open to the public with theme dinners on different nights of the week. Turn off the Carretera Transpeninsular in Los Barriles and follow a dirt road 14 kilometers north until you reach the resort.

El Cardonal

El Cardonal's Hide-A-Way offers meals to guests and other visitors at **Loco Parrot Pub & Grill** (tel. 612/348-9793, hours vary, US$3-10) and serves a standard menu of Mexican fare. It offers a full breakfast menu that includes omelets and breakfast burritos. This is an out-of-the-way place, on a dirt road along the coast, and hours vary according to demand. Reservations are recommended. Expect to wait 35-45 minutes if you arrive unannounced.

Los Barriles

Restaurants in Los Barriles are multiplying in number and variety every season. Today's menus feature grilled fish and meats, traditional Mexican *platos,* pasta, sushi, pizza, sandwiches, soups, espresso, and, of course, mouthwatering tacos.

SEAFOOD

A favorite among locals for dinner, ◖ **El Barrilito** (20 de Noviembre, tel. 624/121-5856, elbarrilito@hotmail.com, lunch and dinner daily, mains US$6-15) serves large portions of fresh seafood under a large *palapa* at the bend in the road heading out toward Pescadero. Ceviche is a standout. Yako's Sushi-Bar (tel. 624/141-0050, noon-7pm daily, mains US$10-20) in the Hotel Palmas de Cortez, on the beach at the end of Calle Los Barriles, serves sashimi and rolls.

If you don't have your own fish to smoke, stop by **Smokey's Bar and Grill** (20 de Noviembre at Calle Don Pepe, tel. 624/141-0294, www.bajapapas.com, 9am-6pm daily) to enjoy someone else's fresh catch. The bar

has four flat-screen TVs and serves beer, sandwiches, and, of course, smoked fish.

MEXICAN

Run by the same owners as the once-famous Restaurant Balandra in Cabo San Lucas, which closed more than 30 years ago, ◖ **Campestre Triny** (20 de Noviembre at La Laguna, across from the East Cape Smokehouse, tel. 624/124-8067, campestre_triny@hotmail.com, 1pm-10pm daily, mains US$9-20) offers freshly prepared traditional Mexican fare, including specialties of *huachinango frito* (whole fried red snapper), paella, and imperial shrimp. High-quality ingredients and a somewhat upscale presentation are reflected in menu prices. This is also one of the few places in town that serves Negro Modelo beer. You can dine family style under a canopy of trees behind the main house or at your own table on the porch. Check out the collection of arrowheads hanging on the wall while you're there.

ITALIAN

Tío Pablo's (20 de Noviembre, Los Barriles, tel. 612/141-0330, www.tiopablos.com, 11am-10pm daily, mains US$7-20) is popular among gringos for pizzas and does orders to go. The restaurant was the first in town and serves American classics along with a full menu of Mexican fare. It has a separate bar area, outside seating, and karaoke night on Friday. The restaurant also serves as a popular local meeting place, and during the afternoon off-hours, tables of card games and Mah Jong are often going. Look for the restaurant on the west side of the main north-south street through town.

An Italian chef bakes pizzas in a wood-heated oven at ◖ **La Pizzeria di Don Roberto** (at the south-end entrance to town on Highway 1, tel. 624/141-0303, noon-9pm Tues.-Sun.), open since early 2008. Variations include the simple margarita pizza (US$10) and a calzone classico (US$17). Foodies rave about the quality of the food and level of service here. It's an unusual find in this part of the peninsula.

The **Bay View Bar & Grill** (tel. 624/141-0050, toll-free U.S. tel. 877/777-8862,

EXCURSIONS

www.vanwormerresorts.com, 11am-10pm daily, US$8-15) is open to the public for dinner. The restaurant has air-conditioning in the summer, which is a welcome amenity in the area. It offers a menu of pasta, fish, and seafood dishes prepared in an Italian style. The garlic shrimp comes highly recommended, and chefs will prepare your fresh catch for you.

For a diverse menu of Greek and Italian selections, **Apostoli** (Los Barriles, tel. 624/141-0303, noon-11pm Tues.-Sun.) will satisfy. The restaurant also has locations in San José del Cabo and Cabo San Lucas. The cuisine is primarily Greek but includes authentic Italian-style pizzas.

AMERICAN

Martin Verdugo's Restaurant (20 de Noviembre, approximately one block north of Calle Los Barriles, tel. 612/141-0054, 6am-noon daily, mains US$4-7) is a third-story restaurant that serves Americanized breakfast fare. *Chilaquiles* (salsa or mole over crisp tortilla triangles) arrive smothered in melted cheese but without the signature *queso fresco* on top. Omelets come with seasoned hash browns and a choice of toast or tortillas. Sea views and air-conditioning are the main draw. Service is friendly, though slow even by local standards.

Also on 20 de Noviembre, **Otra Vez** (tel. 612/141-0249, 5pm-10pm Mon.-Sat., mains US$8-20) is popular with local gringos, and the menu includes freshly prepared parrot fish, burgers, steaks, fresh salads, and pasta dishes. The former American owner passed away in 2012, and the restaurant is now operated by Italian owners. Pizzas are now available (try the *capricciosa* pizza for US$9), and there is more emphasis on pastas and other European fare. There is also a full bar, musical entertainment some evenings, and a salad bar.

ANTOJITOS AND FAST FOOD

During American football season, you're likely to find a number of tourists watching the game at ◖ **Taquería El Viejo (**20 de Noviembre, near El Oasis Coffee and Baja Land Deals, tel. 624/141-0826, breakfast and lunch daily). The restaurant has about a dozen shaded outdoor tables, where you can enjoy a breakfast of eggs, omelets, or *chilaquiles* for US$5-6, tacos for US$1-2, and burgers for US$5. Lunch specials vary daily (US$7-8).

Taquería Los Barriles (no tel., breakfast, lunch, and dinner daily), at the junction with the beach road, is packed all afternoon and evening for the great seafood and carne asada tacos; the breakfasts are cheap. The enormous super burros at La Palma Taquería (no tel., dinner daily) are a great value, too. Look for the sign on a surfboard just off 20 de Noviembre near Tío Pablo's.

Across the street from El Barrilito, on the inside of the bend that turns to Pescadero, **Karina's Hamburguesas** (no tel., dinner daily) serves carne asada (US$4), *papas rellenas* (stuffed potatoes, US$5), and other quick meals from a restaurant cart.

Back on the Carretera Transpeninsular, heading toward La Paz, Baja Cactus (north of the Pemex, no tel.) serves good Mexican food at reasonable prices.

CAFÉS

Oasis Coffee Bar (20 de Noviembre, past The Office, tel. 624/141-0711, daily) serves coffee for US$2 as well as hot and cold espresso drinks and smoothies for US$2-4. It shares the space with Baja Land Deals, so you can browse pictures of real estate for sale while you wait for your drink. High-speed wireless Internet service is free, and there are a few shaded tables outside.

Roadrunner Café (Plaza del Pueblo 5, tel. 624/124-8038, www.roadrunnercafe.com.mx, 7am-4:30pm Mon.-Fri., 7am-2pm Sat.-Sun.) has very good coffee and espresso (US$2), as well as eggs any style (US$3.50-6), served at tables inside or on the patio. Free wireless Internet is a plus.

For a quick bite of American-style food on the go, head near the banks and other new shops to **Deli's Café** (E. Highland in Plaza Gaviota, Los Barriles, tel. 909/882-3000, 7:30am-4pm Mon.-Fri., 8am-4pm Sat.). The deli offers baked goods, including baguettes, croissants, and other breads, along with a selection of salads, sandwiches, and desserts. Wi-Fi is available.

GROCERIES

On Calle Los Barriles, the main access road from the Carretera Transpeninsular, between Plaza del Pueblo and 20 de Noviembre, **Supermercado Chapito's** (7:30am-10pm daily) is the largest grocery store in town (or anywhere on the bay, for that matter), and it has a separate pharmacy inside. Newer **Tienda Popular** (7am-10pm daily), west of 20 de Noviembre, about one block north of the intersection with Calle Los Barriles, has opened just up the hill from Tío Pablo's. **Supermercado Fayla** (8am-6pm Mon.-Sat.), on 20 de Noviembre just past the Hotel Los Barriles, has basic food supplies as well as souvenirs, videos, and U.S. newspapers on Fridays. During the peak winter season, a bakery truck from La Paz visits town on Fridays, and a fresh produce vendor comes on Saturday mornings.

For a more natural variety of foods, try **Blue Wave Natural Foods** (North Los Barriles, tel. 624/132-6893, contact Tanya Higginson at bluewavenaturalfoods@gmail.com, 11am-3pm Tues.-Sat.), or head to the **Los Barriles Community Market** (tel. 624/141-0717, losbarrilescommunitymarket@gmail.com, Spanish speaking only).

Buy frozen or smoked fish or have yours prepared and vacuum-packed at the **Baja Papa's East Cape Smokehouse** (20 de Noviembre at Calle Don Pepe, tel. 624/141-0294, www.bajapapas.com, 9am-6pm daily). Allow 48 hours turnaround time.

For a sugar fix, head to **Charlie's Chocolates** (Calle Los Barriles, across from AmeriMed, 624/1552427, 10am-10pm Mon.-Sat., till 6pm Sun.) for a box of strawberries dipped in chocolate and topped with nuts.

ACCOMMODATIONS

Accommodations along Bahía de las Palmas range from all-inclusive hotels to modest hotels and RV parks to private vacation homes available for rent either by the owner or through a property manager. Los Barriles has the greatest concentration of options, but Punta Pescadero, Buena Vista, and La Ribera all have at least a couple of options.

Punta Pescadero
US$100-200

At the far north end of Bahía de las Palmas (13.6 km north of Los Barriles), the historic **Hotel Punta Pescadero** Paradise (tel. 624/141-0101, toll-free U.S. tel. 800/332-4442, www.puntapescaderoparadise.com, US$150-199; pets of any sort strictly prohibited) has 24 spacious rooms, each with a view of the bay, private terrace, air-conditioning, satellite TV, and refrigerator; some have cathedral ceilings and fireplaces for keeping warm on chilly winter nights. All rooms were renovated in 2005. King-size beds are made in crisp white linens with fluffy pillows and down comforters. During the windy season, ask for a room that faces southwest for a terrace that's sheltered from the El Norte gusts. A gracious staff speaks excellent English, and public areas include a restaurant with large picture windows, outdoor patio dining, small pool, lighted tennis court, and rental equipment for free diving (US$14/day), kayaking (US$10/hr), boating (US$15/hr), fishing (30-foot cruiser US$510/day, 28-foot cruiser US$400/day, super-*panga* US$300/day, *panga* US$250/day), and ATVs (US$20/hr).

The resort restaurant is open to the public with theme night menus—such as a traditional suckling pig roast on Saturday and romantic Italian nights beachside on Friday—and Sunday brunch. Guided trips include city tours of La Paz, a visit to the closely guarded local petroglyphs, and tours to the sites of former Spanish missions. Tour prices start at US$50, and tours range 2-8 hours in length.

El Cardonal
UNDER US$100

El Cardonal's **Hide-A-Way** (tel. 612/348-9793, www.elcardonal.net, US$79) offers six sparsely furnished suites. There are also spaces for RV (US$19/day for full hookups) and tent

(US$15/day) camping. Each of its large beach-front studios comes with two full-size beds, a sofa, kitchen, and ceiling fan. Amenities and services include a dump station, fishing boats, hot showers, 24-hour restaurant, laundry facilities, public telephone, horseshoe pit, volleyball net, picnic tables, ice, and rental shop with equipment for fishing, windsurfing, diving, kayaking (free with stay), and snorkeling. You can pick up the Wi-Fi signal from the restaurant/patio area. An all-inclusive fishing package runs US$599 for four days/three nights, two days of fishing, and all meals.

Los Barriles
UNDER US$100

Martin Verdugo's Beach Resort (20 de Noviembre, approximately two blocks north of Calle Los Barriles, Los Barriles, tel. 624/141-0054, www.verdugosbeachresort.com, US$75-85) has updated air-conditioning units in each of its 29 basic rooms, located in a two-story hotel next to the beach. Facilities include a small pool, boat launch, and restaurant. Kitchenettes are a plus here (though not in every room). When the wind is blowing hard, the pool at the Los Barriles Hotel offers more shelter. Service in the restaurant was a bit gruff on one visit, but guests praise the breakfast.

Off the beach but within walking distance to restaurants and shops, the exceptionally clean **◖ Los Barriles Hotel** (20 de Noviembre, approximately one block north of Calle Los Barriles, Los Barriles, tel. 624/141-0024, www.losbarrileshotel.com, US$73) looks unremarkable from the outside but feels something like a well-kept Swiss chalet inside. It has 20 spacious rooms set around a swimming pool with hot tub, each with high ceilings, two firm but comfortable queen-size beds, large tiled showers, and remote-controlled air-conditioning. Minimal but quality furnishings include rustic wooden dressers, tables, and headboards. There is no breakfast, but fresh coffee is always brewing. Popular with families, this hotel is a great value for the price.

Guests praise Patti, owner of **◖ Hotel Los Pescadores** (North Los Barriles between the two arroyos, tel. 624/121-8786, www.fisheastcape.com, pattimo@vom.com, US$60-72, pets welcome) for her gracious and welcoming nature, and many say they leave here feeling like part of the family. Each of eight rooms has two queen beds, free Wi-Fi, and a refrigerator. Other amenities include a pool and fully stocked cantina with outstanding margaritas. Fishing captains Lavo and Andres are well respected and have gained the loyalty of many clients. Fishing on one of the hotel's two well-maintained boats runs US$275/day including all rods, reels, and cooler with ice. Bait will cost about US$20. Half-day rates are also available for US$165.

US$100-200

The Van Wormer family runs two all-inclusive resorts in Los Barriles, including **Hotel Playa del Sol** (tel. 624/141-0050, toll-free U.S. tel. 877/777-8862, www.vanwormerresorts.com, US$120-145, closed Sept.), on the beach off 20 de Noviembre north of Calle Los Barriles. This property has 26 air-conditioned rooms that were remodeled in 2012, a pool that overlooks the beach, tennis and volleyball courts, a restaurant with outdoor seating, and bar with satellite TV. The resort rents windsurfing, kayaking, and fishing gear as well as mountain bikes. You can charter boats for a day of sportfishing (US$250-385 per day, not including fishing permits) or sign up for windsurfing lessons.

The second Van Wormer resort in Los Barriles is on the beach at the end of Calle Los Barriles, a little south of Hotel Playa del Sol; the **Hotel Palmas de Cortez** (Los Barriles, tel. 624/141-0050, toll-free U.S. tel. 877/777-8862, www.vanwormerresorts.com, US$130-160) offers 50 poolside, oceanfront, and garden-view rooms, plus several cabanas and condos that sleep up to six guests. Rates include three meals a day. Amenities include a driving range, infinity pool, and tennis and racquetball courts. You can rent windsurfing gear and fishing equipment and charter a fishing boat (US$275-500, not including fishing permits) through the resort. The Van Wormer family also runs the

Hotel Punta Colorada farther south along the East Cape.

Run by the owner/driver of a California-based motorsports team, the **C Agave Hotel & Cantina** (Carr. Transpeninsular km 108, U.S. tel. 760/275-0339, www.agavehote-landcantina.com, US$115-325, tax included) is a renovation of the former Casa Miramar Hotel. Its nine rooms enjoy a hillside location overlooking the beach, just off the Carretera Transpeninsular, across from the Pemex station. The property consists of a two-bedroom house and separate beachfront *casita*. It can accommodate up to 25 people. Owner Rick Johnson and Team Agave compete in the Baja 1000 each year. Although not on the premises, they can share a wealth of information about Baja via email or phone. They can also arrange cooking classes, massages, transportation, and other services for guests. This hotel operates somewhat like a vacation rental in the sense that the property managers do not stay on-site. They live nearby and stop in daily to attend to guests' needs. Additional highlights include a swimming pool, ocean views, and convenient beach access. The town center of Los Barriles is a short walk away.

OVER US$200

Among the newer accommodations in town are the suites at the **Villas de Cortez** (Los Barriles, tel. 624/141-0050, toll-free U.S. tel. 877/777-8862, www.vanwormerresorts.com, US$280-380), next door to the Hotel Palmas de Cortez, which is under the same ownership. Meal packages are available through the sister resort, or you can enjoy outstanding gourmet fare in the villas' new restaurant, La Taberna di Don Roberto, which impressed local foodies from the get-go with its authentic Italian cuisine (tel. 624/141-0050, 5pm-10pm Tues.-Sun.).

INFORMATION AND SERVICES
Tourist Assistance
Most travel-related services for towns along Bahía de las Palmas are located in Los Barriles. East Cape RV Resort owner Theresa Comber

in Los Barriles is the closest thing the area has to a chamber of commerce. Stop by to ask for advice on restaurants, day trips, and activities in the area. The larger resorts are also a good source of visitor information.

Emergency Services
Near the end of the main access road to Los Barriles, an **Amerimed Clinic** is open 8am-2pm and 4pm-6pm Monday-Saturday for medical needs. Call 624/141-0797 for emergencies.

La Ribera has a new health center as of 2010, thanks in part to funding from local developers. Find the **Centro de Salud La Ribera** (tel. 624/130-0067, 24 hours daily) next to the athletic fields on the way into town, on the south side of Avenida Santa María, past the turnoff to Cabo Pulmo.

Internet Access and Communications
East Cape RV Park, Sunset Rentals, and many cafés and private home-owners have wireless Internet. And some keep a computer set up for guest use.

The post office in Los Barriles closed a few years ago. **La Plaza del Pueblo shopping center** in Los Barriles, near the highway on the main access road, has clean public restrooms and public telephones.

Banking
Some businesses in these towns accept credit cards, but you'll still need cash (dollars or pesos) for tacos and the like. There is a **Banamex** (9am-4pm Mon.-Sat.) in Los Barriles at Plaza Libertad, which can exchange dollars to pesos and has the only ATM in the area.

Marine Services
For boating needs, the **Cabo Riviera Marina** (Calle Santa Maria de La Ribera, Plaza Montaño, tel. 624/130.0303, US tel. 619/819-9280, info@caboriviera.com.mx, www.caboriviera.com) has slips, water, and electrical and Wi-Fi services, as well as restrooms and showers, parking, a launch ramp, and 24-hour security.

Laundry

El Lavadero/The Washroom (20 de Noviembre, 624/132-4465, Mon.-Sat. 8am-3:30pm, closed mid-Aug. to mid-Oct.), near the Los Barriles Hotel, and **Lavamatica** (Plaza Libertad, no tel., 10am-6pm Mon.-Sat.) are the only places to have your clothes washed, unless you're staying at one of the full-service resorts or RV parks.

GETTING THERE AND AROUND

Towns along the East Cape are small and don't take much time to explore; you could easily take in a little of each in a four- to five-day excursion from Los Cabos. Day trips from Cabo San Lucas or San José del Cabo also are possible—either self-guided or with an organized tour group. Typical trips include a day of snorkeling at Cabo Pulmo or a scenic drive through the ghost towns of San Bartolo, El Triunfo, and San Antonio. It takes about one hour to drive from San José del Cabo to Los Barriles.

If you've come to Baja for a specific activity, such as fishing, diving, or kiteboarding, you'll likely want to stay in one place for a while. If fishing is your top priority, then it makes sense to stay in Los Barriles or Buena Vista and add a day of diving. But if diving is the draw, it's best to head north or south to be closer to the dive sites. And if you plan to drive along the Camino Rural Costero, as opposed to Highway 1, note that the unpaved 77-kilometer stretch between El Rincón and San José del Cabo can take up to four hours, depending on your vehicle and the condition of the road.

If you don't already have a car, **National Car Rental** (20 de Noviembre s/n, tel. 624/142-2424, 8am-4pm daily) maintains an outpost at the Hotel Palmas de Cortez in Los Barriles, but in most cases an ATV would be a better vehicle for getting around town. The closest Pemex is just south of Los Barriles on the Carretera Transpeninsular.

For airport transportation, contact **TurisPancho** (tel. 624/127-3122, www.turispancho.com).

Cabo Pulmo

The historic El Camino Rural Costero (Rural Coastal Road) begins south of La Ribera and follows the Gulf coast south to Pueblo La Playa, outside San José del Cabo.

Environmentalists celebrated a historic victory in this area in 2012 when then-president Felipe Calderón announced that the federal government would deny permits for the massive Cabo Cortés project near La Ribera. The landmark decision came amid concerns over the fragility of the coral reef system at nearby Cabo Pulmo. International and local conservation groups teamed up to raise awareness of the environmental issues at stake. Do your part to protect the wildlife here, and consider supporting the continued efforts of organizations such as San Diego-based Wildcoast.

The Camino Rural Costero is graded but not paved beyond the first few kilometers south of La Ribera. Most standard rental vehicles—and even small RVs—can negotiate the washboard and patches of soft sand, but the going will be slow, especially as you get farther south, where the road tends to be in pretty bad shape. High clearance is always helpful. During the rainy season, the road may be washed out in parts. Ask for updates before you plan your drive.

In spite of the difficult access (or perhaps because of it), a few enclaves along the way are growing into full-scale developments. You can still camp for free on the beach in places, but as is the case all along the coast, access is becoming increasingly limited as new developments lay cinder blocks and finish their first few homes.

In the midst of all the change, a few

EL CAMINO
RURAL COSTERO

It is paved for the first few kilometers and then becomes dirt the rest of the way south. It takes about 45 minutes to get to the turnoff from San José, and another 30 minutes from there to Cabo Pulmo.

BEACHES
❰ Cabo Pulmo

About 10 kilometers from where the pavement ends, the Camino Rural Costero climbs over a rise and presents a panoramic view of Bahía Pulmo—a shallow bay rimmed with a mix of coarse white sand and cobblestones—and the eight fingers of coral reef that are its main attraction. The road descends to parallel the beach along the bay and then passes through the center of a tiny fishing village-turned-vacation-and-retirement-community.

Modern-day Cabo Pulmo is a close-knit community made up mostly of older expats and several branches of a local Mexican family that has fished the area for generations. The oldest vacation homes were built right on the beach, but in recent years, construction has expanded west across the road and into the hills.

Most visitors these days come to explore the reef, from above and below, and to relax on the white-sand beaches that line the bay. The surface of the beach varies with the seasons: in winter, there are usually more stones and pebbles, particularly at the north end of the bay; in summer, the sand comes back and the rocks roll back into the sea.

The government has stepped up its conservation efforts in recent years, posting large signs, patrolling the park by boat, and collecting a US$4 park use fee from those who snorkel or dive in the bay. At last check, beachgoers did not have to pay the fee—only those who go into the water to view the coral.

There are several scuba diving operations in town, *panga* fishing charters, kayak rentals, and a long list of excursions up and down the coast and into the desert.

Given its small size, proximity to the beach, and comfortable accommodations, Cabo Pulmo is an excellent place for families with young kids (though the nearest medical clinic is

traditional ranchos continue to raise livestock—typically without fencing to keep the animals off the road.

To reach the Camino Rural Costero from Los Cabos, follow the Carretera Transpeninsular north out of San José through the towns of Miraflores and Santiago. Take the paved road signed La Ribera east at kilometer 93 off the Carretera Transpeninsular (at Las Cuevas) and go 20 kilometers to a Y intersection near the Lighthouse restaurant and town athletic fields. Bear right here, and you're on the beginning of the Camino Rural Costero.

© NIKKI GOTH ITOI

A *palapa* tips over in the wind at Cabo Pulmo.

in La Ribera, a 15-minute drive, and the closest hospital is in San José del Cabo).

Playa Los Arbolitos

A large marine park sign marks the way to this white-sand beach at the south end of Bahía Pulmo. Follow the Camino Rural Costero south about five kilometers from the village of Cabo Pulmo and look for the only dirt road on the left without a fence or gate. The turn is the last road you can take before passing Los Frailes Mountain. There are no services or facilities at this beach. Rent snorkeling gear and/or kayaks in Cabo Pulmo before you go.

Playa La Sirenita

The most attractive beach on Bahía Pulmo goes by many names: La Sirenita (The Mermaid) seems to be the most common one, but it is also known as Los Chopitos (The Squids) and Dinosaur Egg Beach. All the more enchanting for its difficult access, the beach is hidden at the base of a cliff that frames the southern end of the bay. You can only reach it by small boat

or kayak or by walking along a path from Playa Los Arbolitos to the north, which has a small parking lot. The beach is narrow but covered in white sand and dotted with rocks. The cove and beach are protected from winds coming out of the south, and you can snorkel around the rocks just offshore. A towering boulder pile marks the divider between Bahía Pulmo and Bahía de los Frailes; on its south-facing side lives a colony of sea lions.

Pulmo Reef System

The fragile hard-coral reef in Bahía Pulmo is one of only three coastal reefs in North America and the only living one in the Sea of Cortez. It plays a vital role in the health of the Sea of Cortez ecosystem and for this reason was designated a national marine park in 1995. Commercial fishing and sportfishing are banned within the park (this means no shore fishing, either), as is anchoring on the reef or anywhere in the bay. Both foreign and Mexican residents are committed to protecting the water and land from pollution, but they worry that

view of Bahía Pulmo

runoff from developments on land—especially from the mega-resorts that are just breaking ground—poses a serious threat to the reef.

The reef is made up of eight separate fingers, four of them close to shore and the other four farther out in the bay. Depths range 4.5-10.5 meters close to shore and as deep as 33 meters in the outer bay.

The abundance and variety of marine life here rivals anything you'll find in the Caribbean. The fact that the reef begins within a few meters from the shore makes it even more appealing. For divers, boat rides are a quick five-minute jaunt out into the bay; snorkelers can skip the boat ride altogether and hop right in from shore. You can find a wide variety of tropical fish, eels, and rays—as well as the occasional nurse shark—in waist-deep water.

Bahía de los Frailes

When winds out of the north whip Bahía Pulmo into a frothy mess, the next bay south, Bahía de los Frailes, is usually calm enough for snorkeling, diving, and fishing. The bay plunges to depths of 210 meters, which makes for slightly colder water temperatures than in Bahía Pulmo.

Following the Camino Rural Costero, it's about eight kilometers to the turnoff for this white-sand beach. Since Los Frailes lies just outside the national marine park, the fishing onshore and inshore tends to be especially good here. Anglers often catch roosterfish by casting into the surf; charters catch yellowfin tuna, grouper, dorado, and marlin within a few kilometers of the shoreline.

WATER SPORTS
Diving and Snorkeling

You can dive at Pulmo year-round, but the best conditions are in summer and early fall, when water temperatures exceed 26°C and visibility exceeds 30 meters. Guided drift diving is the norm here. Divers board a *panga* boat at the beach, zip over to the morning's dive site, and roll backward into the water to begin the dive. While divers drift with the current along the reef below, the boat captain follows the bubbles

Bahía de los Frailes

on the surface. The sides of the reef are jam-packed with colorful marine life. Green moray eels poke their heads out of rocky crevices, schools of tropical fish dart here and there, and the occasional sea turtle cruises by. It only takes a few dives to begin to recognize the tell-tale pile of shells in front of an octopus's den or the antennae of a spiny lobster hiding in a cave.

Besides the natural reefs, the wreck of a tuna boat called *El Vencedor* has evolved into an artificial reef. Dive boats also take groups to El Islote, a lone rock on the southern side of the bay, and to a sea lion colony near Bahía de los Frailes.

Several dive centers, located within 100 meters of each other, run guided tours from Cabo Pulmo. In the village center, the **Cabo Pulmo Beach Resort** (El Camino Rural Costero, tel. 624/141-0726, U.S. tel./fax 562/366-0398 or 562/366-0722, www.cabopulmo.com) operates a PADI-certified dive center with two boats, well-maintained gear, and experienced, professional dive guides. A two-tank boat dive costs US$75, and an equipment rental

package is US$20 with a boat dive. You do not need to be a guest of the resort to snorkel or dive with the shop. The dive center often hosts groups of day-trippers from resorts in the Cabo San Lucas area. These dives tend to be more crowded with novice divers. Call ahead to check the schedule if you want to do more advanced dives. Snorkeling tours are US$40 with gear, and single kayaks rent for US$35 a day.

Cabo Pulmo Divers (tel. 624/130-0235, cell 612/157-3381, www.cabopulmodivers.com) is another option, located in the Castro family complex, next to the Miscellanea Market. Rates are comparable to those at the Cabo Pulmo Beach Resort.

Next to La Palapa restaurant, in a blue building with a marine-life mural painted on its side, is **Cabo Pulmo Eco Adventures** (www.tourscabopulmo.com). Owner Juanito offers snorkel trips for US$40 and kayak rentals by the hour or day, and can arrange taxi service to La Sirenita beach. Juanito is very knowledgeable, bilingual, and the only person in town who can arrange trips to the nearby waterfall and hot springs. Call 624/166-4109 after 7pm.

The dive operators are also happy to arrange boat trips for non-divers interested in touring the bay, Playa La Sirenita, and the sea lion colony.

Newcomer **Cabo Pulmo Water Sports** (tel. 624/130-0367 www.cabopulmowatersports. com) offers dive trips and gear rental at competitive rates. It can also arrange fishing trips with local fishers.

Across the dirt road from Cabo Pulmo Divers, **East Cape Adventures** (tel. 624/130-0073 or 612/105-1671, www.eastcapeadventures.com) has a stand with snorkeling gear for rent and can arrange boat tours as well. Look for Manuel Castro next to the row of blue fins and wetsuits. If no one is there, wait a few minutes, as he is likely at the beach greeting or sending off boats.

Fishing

Commercial fishing and sportfishing are no longer permitted anywhere in Bahía Pulmo. *Panga* boats that launch from Pulmo have to go beyond the national marine park limit (8 km from shore) before putting in lines. On land, you have to travel about eight kilometers north or south of Pulmo proper to fish from shore. Kiki and Paco Castro offer half-day (US$180) and full-day (US$260) tours in their super-*pangas,* including gear and bait. Tuna and dorado are common offshore catches. Inquire at Cabo Pulmo Divers (www. cabopulmodivers.com) behind the La Palapa beachfront restaurant.

SHOPPING

A gift shop has opened in Cabo Pulmo on the main road across from El Caballero restaurant. **Nomade** (Mon.-Sat. 9am-6pm, Sun. 10am-4pm) is the place to pick up a giant manta T-shirt, watercolor painting, or set of postcards—all designed by local artists. Aromatic Desert Soaps make for great souvenirs as well. Farther south, the Crossroads Country Club at La Vinorama has similar gift items for sale.

FOOD

Cabo Pulmo's restaurants are notoriously understaffed, even during peak season. It can take up to 45 minutes or longer to be served, even at lunch. Like the other businesses in Cabo Pulmo, restaurants are clustered together along the Camino Rural Costero, so the best thing to do is find a point of reference, like the Cabo Pulmo Beach Resort, then ask around if you have questions about where a specific place is.

Adjacent to the Cabo Pulmo Beach Resort, **Nancy's Restaurant and Bar** (no tel., hours vary Thurs.-Tues., mains US$16-20) began as a trailer and two tables and has evolved into a full-scale restaurant with a rustic collection of tables beneath a *palapa* shelter. Fresh guacamole with homemade chips is a delightful way to begin the meal. Lobster enchiladas, crab cakes, and fresh catch (yours or Nancy's) are accompanied by crisp side salads.

The **Coral Reef Bar and Grill** (no tel., hours vary Wed.-Mon., mains US$10-20) is a cozy restaurant with a TV and bar located above the blue building that serves as the Cabo Pulmo Resort dive center.

 Restaurant El Caballero (no tel., 7am-10pm Fri.-Wed., mains US$6-14), on the opposite side of the road near Nancy's, has a varied menu of Mexican fare. It also has a bar and small assortment of groceries, drinks, and snacks for sale.

La Palapa (lunch and dinner Mon.-Sat., lunch plates US$4-10, dinner mains US$8-18), on the beach in front of the Cabo Pulmo Beach Resort, offers casual beachfront dining from a menu of fish tacos, carne asada, and other traditional fare. The great family-style, traditional Mexican seafood, always fresh and simple, is served by smiling Angeles—the sister of Juanito at Cabo Pulmo Eco Adventures.

In the Castro family complex, near Cabo Pulmo Water Sports, **Alicia's Restaurant** (mains US$4-15) is the best option for simple Mexican dishes served outside under a *palapa* roof. It can be chilly in the evening here when El Norte is blowing. Bring a sweater. The chiles rellenos are a top pick. Hours vary day to day and there is no phone, so it's best to stop by on your way to or from the beach. Bring your own wine or beer.

For groceries, several vendors make the rounds through town during the week. A bakery truck comes from La Paz on Wednesday; Ysidro delivers fish, scallops, and shrimp on Tuesday and brings similar seafood selections on Saturday morning. The **Miscellanea Market** (9am-7pm daily, limited summer hours), with colorful snails painted on the side of the building, is next to Cabo Pulmo Divers and stocks basic supplies, including dairy, juice, produce, bread, toiletries, candy, and canned goods. For a long stay, it's best to load up on groceries at Soriana or one of the other supermarkets in San José del Cabo or at Supermercado Chapitos in Los Barriles. Mexican food brands generally cost less than their U.S. counterparts. It's a good idea to buy ice, as the propane refrigerators in most Cabo Pulmo rentals cool very slowly, and a car full of groceries will take a long time to chill.

ACCOMMODATIONS

As new owners build and acquire properties in Cabo Pulmo, the number of rental options has increased—although the location remains off the grid, so don't expect air-conditioning, TV, Internet, and the works in the places you find here. Most high-season rates climb even higher during the peak season around Christmas and New Year.

You can camp for free on the beach at the south end of Bahía Pulmo or for US$5 per night at the north end.

UNDER US$100

For many years, **Cabo Pulmo Beach Resort** (El Camino Rural Costero, tel./fax 612/141-0244, 612/141-0884, or 612/141-0885, U.S. tel. 562/366-0398, U.S. tel./fax 208/726-1306, toll-free U.S. tel. 888/997-8566, www.cabo-pulmo.com, US$70-200) was the only option for short-term visitor accommodations in the area. The village has grown, bringing more properties and management services onto the market, but this beach resort is still a good option for beachside bungalows within steps of

the water. All of its *palapa*-roofed units feature kitchenettes or full kitchens, and some have barbecue grills. Many have second-story roof decks for catching a breeze in the afternoon or watching activity on the bay. Sheets and towels are provided. Like all accommodations in the village, power here is solar, with generators for backup only.

Marly Rickers also manages a handful of rentals in the same group of *casitas* for US$70-120 per night. Contact **Cabo Pulmo Casas** (tel. 877/754-5251, www.cabopulmocasas.com).

Across the dirt road from the Cabo Pulmo Beach Resort, Kent Ryan rents **Baja Bungalows** (www.bajabungalows.com, US$75-85), with a main house that has spectacular views from the upstairs master suite, plus a two-bedroom unit on the lower level and an additional bungalow and *palapa* suite with shared bath and full outdoor kitchen. The vibe here is always friendly and relaxed, with guests preparing meals and socializing in the common area kitchen. Kent also manages another house on an adjacent lot, with two separate units (upstairs and down). It has spectacular sea and mountain views from the upstairs unit. The house once belonged to musician (and former local character) Jimmy Ibbotsen of the Nitty Gritty Dirt Band. The house has been adapted to rental standards but holds many a good story from the musician's stay in Pulmo. The beach is a three-minute walk away.

Reinhard's Rentals (www.reinhardsrentals. com), across the street from Baja Bungalows at the metal palm-and-dolphin sculpted gate, offers two one-bedroom houses each for US$80 a night and one studio also for US$80. These rentals are popular with the fishing crowd and are owned and operated by one of the town's true characters, Reinhard and his dog, Max. Another plus for pet owners: These rentals are dog friendly.

US$100-200

El Encanto de Cabo Pulmo (U.S. tel. 619/618-1248, www.encantopulmo.com, US$105-195) brings a new standard of luxury to Cabo Pulmo. Think air-conditioning (extra cost), an espresso machine, and surround-sound entertainment with satellite TV. Designed by an artist and her husband, the home is indeed beautiful; the only caveat is that in Pulmo, there's always a chance that the power-intensive amenities won't be working when you visit. This town is an off-the-grid location that runs on solar and generator power, and when those sources of electricity run out, the air-conditioning unfortunately turns off. (Most guests find the ceiling fans adequate for cooling the home on all but the hottest of nights.) The house has three suites—two in a two-story main house and a third in a separate *casita*. Its garden setting is lovely (though not really private if both suites and the main house are in use). This property would work best for a group of six or more that rents out the whole property together. Wireless Internet is included. Individual suites rent for US$105-195 per night, and the whole house rents for US$365 per night.

Another vacation rental, **The Jewel of Cabo Pulmo** (Cabo Pulmo village, U.S. tel. 831/440-8811), has a master bedroom in the main house and a separate garden *casita* (US$160 for the for the house alone, and US$250 for both house and *casita*). This property is pet friendly. No smoking.

OVER US$200

For upscale accommodations, check out **Villa and Casa del Mar** (U.S. tel. 208/726-4455 or 888/225-2786, www.bajaparadise.com, US$210-450). This property includes a main house (US$450 per night for two guests) and attached studio (US$210 per night). Air-conditioning is available, although as with any Cabo Pulmo rental, it can only be used as long as there is enough power to run it. A few steps farther from the beach and centrally located in the village, the El Nido cottage (US$255 per night) has a full kitchen.

INFORMATION AND SERVICES
Emergency Services

Basic medical services are available in La Ribera

and Los Barriles, and the closest hospital is in San José.

Internet

Internet access via satellite is possible in Cabo Pulmo, but service is by no means reliable, and you cannot download large files, due to bandwidth restrictions from the service providers. A few private places throughout the village have Wi-Fi set up, and you may be able to get permission to use one of those networks. In an emergency, the owners of the different rentals can usually get a message out. For casual correspondence, plan to connect in San José or Los Barriles.

Banks

There are no banks or ATMs in Cabo Pulmo or Los Frailes, and few places except the largest resorts accept credit cards. U.S. or Mexican currency is accepted, and you can load up on cash at an ATM machine in San José, Los Barriles, or La Ribera. Be sure to get plenty of small bills, as many businesses cannot change larger bills. Some places accept travelers checks, but it would be best not to count on it.

GETTING THERE AND AROUND

Most visitors fly to Los Cabos, rent a car, and drive to Cabo Pulmo via the Carretera Transpeninsular (Highway 1) and then El Camino Rural Costero. From San José del Cabo, follow Highway 1 north 50.6 kilometers to an overpass at Las Cuevas and bear right (east) onto the single-lane road to La Ribera. From La Paz, pass Buena Vista heading south and take the exit for La Ribera. As you approach La Ribera (9.6 km), turn right before the soccer field. Follow the Camino Rural Costero 26 kilometers south to Cabo Pulmo. The drive should take about 40 minutes from the time you leave Highway 1.

If you are flying into San José and plan to drive the same day to Cabo Pulmo, aim to arrive no later than noon. By the time you get through passport control, retrieve your luggage, rent a car, and buy your groceries, several hours

ROUND-THE-CAPE ROAD TRIP

Travelers with a week or more can experience the many dimensions of the lower Baja Peninsula by making a circular route around the region via the Carretera Transpeninsular (Highway 1) and Highway 19, both paved. Extending a total distance of approximately 564 kilometers, this route takes visitors along the lower slopes of the Sierra de la Laguna, through the sierra's former mining towns, across the plains of La Paz, and along the coastlines of the East and West Capes as well as the Corridor between San José del Cabo and Cabo San Lucas.

It's possible to complete the loop by bus, but expect to do a fair amount of walking to get from the stops along the highway to the scenic coastal areas. A rental car affords more flexibility and convenience, and you can park easily in all the towns along the route.

This loop can be driven in two or three days, but since there are many towns worth exploring and activities to enjoy at each stop, most travelers prefer to allow a week or longer. For more of an adventure, consider widening the loop by taking the sandy Camino Rural Costero (Rural Coastal Road) from San José del Cabo to La Ribera.

DAY 1

Arrive at Los Cabos International Airport (SJD); transfer to a hotel in downtown San José del Cabo and spend the evening around town. Browse galleries in the historic **distrito del arte** (art district) and Mexican fire opal stores downtown before sitting down to a leisurely dinner of contemporary Mexican cuisine.

DAY 2

Drive to Cabo Pulmo via the Carretera Transpeninsular (1-1.5 hours), exiting at La Ribera and heading east to pick up the Camino Rural Costero. The last few kilometers will be on dirt road. Head straight for the beach and spend the rest of the day snorkeling the live coral reef that comes all the way into shore. Order fish tacos and an icy *michelada* (a beer drink) at one of several outdoor eateries. Book your activity of choice, such as fishing, kayaking, snorkeling, or diving, for the next morning.

Excursion

At Santiago, head west to reach the Cañon de la Zorra and a 10-meter waterfall, just a 10-minute walk from the parking lot.

Alternative Route

To avoid the off-road driving and relatively primitive accommodations, skip Cabo Pulmo and stay on the Carretera Transpeninsular until Los Barriles, popular with anglers, kiteboarders, and stand-up paddlers.

DAY 3

Spend the morning out at sea, and in the afternoon continue north along the Carretera Transpeninsular to La Paz (1.5-2 hours), stopping to explore the ghost towns of San Anto-

will have passed, and it is not advisable to drive the highway or Camino Rural Costero after dark. If you arrive in the afternoon, consider staying overnight in San José before departing for Cabo Pulmo the next day.

The closest gas to Cabo Pulmo is at La Ribera to the north. Be sure to fill up before heading south along the Camino Rural Costero.

Aguila bus service from San José will get you as far as Las Cuevas for about US$5 one-way, but from there you'll have to hitch a ride or arrange in advance for someone to pick you up. Another option for traveling sans auto is to contact one of the companies that transport divers from the Los Cabos area to Cabo Pulmo for the day. For example, Impala Transportation (tel. 624/141-0726 or cell 624/173-1476) has a van that holds 14 passengers. With notice, Cabo Pulmo Resort can arrange round-trip transportation from Los Cabos airport for a fee; a stop at a grocery store near the airport on the way up can be included.

Below Los Frailes, the road continues to hug

nio and El Triunfo along the way. Check in to a downtown hotel and walk the **malecón** at sunset. Enjoy *arrachera* (skirt steak) at Rancho Viejo, and then head out for drinks at Tailhunter Bar & FUBAR Cantina or Bar Salsipuedes on the *malecón*, or catch a music performance at one of many cultural venues around town.

DAY 4
Take a *panga* shuttle to Isla Espíritu Santo for a day of kayaking and snorkeling, or book a day of diving. Alternatively, paddle or drive to a few of the beaches along the Pichilingue Peninsula. Enjoy the views from one of the waterfront seafood restaurants at Playa El Tecolote. Spend the next morning exploring the Museo Regional de Antropología e Historia in downtown La Paz and shopping for pottery and other crafts.

Depart La Paz in the afternoon, heading south on the Carretera Transpeninsular to Highway 19, which leads to Todos Santos (45 min.). Check into a boutique hotel in town, such as the Todos Santos Inn or Casa Bentley, or choose a vacation rental near the beach. For dinner, savor *tacos al pastor* (marinated pork tacos) at Pastorcito, tapas and made-in-Baja wines at La Casita, or homemade Italian fare at Tre Galline.

Excursion
In winter, travelers with extra time can add a day for a gray-whale encounter in Bahía Magdalena, approximately 3.5 hours by car from La Paz.

DAY 5
Walk the historic district in Todos Santos, with brick buildings and colorful facades that date back to the late 19th century, when the town was Baja's sugarcane capital. Admire the artwork in a few of the town's dozen galleries. Drive north along the coast to Playa La Pastora or south along Highway 19 to Playa Los Cerritos, at kilometer 64, to stroll the beach in the afternoon. Continue south along Highway 19 to reach Cabo San Lucas before dark (one hour). Check into a hotel in downtown Cabo San Lucas or a resort along the Corridor, such as the new Welk Resort Sirena del Mar. For dinner, make a reservation at Hacienda Cocina y Cantina near Playa El Médano or try Patagonia for Argentinian steaks.

DAY 6
Hire a water taxi, paddle a kayak, or rent a WaveRunner to visit Playa del Amor, or plan a day of fishing or diving out of Cabo San Lucas. Wander the shops and enjoy afternoon cocktails at The Nowhere Bar or the Giggling Marlin along the marina. Take a nap so you can rally for the nightlife at Cabo Wabo or El Squid Roe after dark.

DAY 7
Schedule a massage for your last morning in paradise. Take a dip in the pool, hit the shops, and return to the airport with sand in your shoes.

the coast, climbing over hills and swerving inland here and there. The scenery alternates between traditional ranchos and new gringo developments, with beautiful desert flora in between. These days, the road is in pretty good shape between Los Frailes and Boca de la Vinorama and even on to Punta Gorda, but the last few kilometers before La Playita will test the sturdiness of the vehicle as well as the patience of the driver.

Sierra de la Laguna

When you've had your fill of white-sand beaches and salty air, the Sierra de la Laguna beckons, with 2,100-meter peaks and cascading waterfalls. No longer the sole domain of experienced backpackers, parts of the range are doable in a half-day excursion, with or without a guide, depending on your comfort level with navigating networks of dirt roads and missing a turn here or there. The reward is a rugged part of Baja that few travelers even know exists.

Most travelers who drive the Carretera Transpeninsular from La Paz to San José via Los Barriles and the East Cape blaze right by the historic mountain towns along the way. But a quick visit to any of these communities gives you a sense of what Baja California was like during the 19th-century silver-mining boom as well as a snapshot of present-day Mexican life in the peninsula's interior.

In the 19th century, two neighboring settlements in the Sierra de la Laguna formed the epicenter of Baja California's gold- and silver-mining boom; today El Triunfo and San Antonio are smaller, quieter communities sustained by agriculture and basket weaving, although there is talk and much controversy over proposed plans to begin mining operations again.

Miners first discovered silver in the area in the mid-18th century, near present-day San Antonio (then called Real de Minas de Santa Ana). The town became the first Baja municipality founded without a mission. In 1862 better mineral deposits were discovered near El Triunfo, and the Progreso Mining Company arrived in 1878, bringing with it thousands of workers from Europe and China. A thriving company town emerged with a population around 10,000 that was in many ways similar to the mining town that grew at the same time around Santa Rosalía, on the Gulf coast to the north. The miners built towering smokestacks, the largest of which, La Ramona, stands ten stories high. Historic photos of El Triunfo's mining towers are on display at the Centro Cultural in Todos Santos.

The two towns prospered until a hurricane flooded the mines in 1918. By 1926 the mines had closed and the towns were almost abandoned.

SIGHTS
◖ Santiago Town Plaza
The largest town along this stretch of the Carretera Transpeninsular, Santiago, was founded as a mission settlement and has evolved into a modern-day agricultural commerce center with a population of around 2,000. Located two kilometers west of the Carretera Transpeninsular, the town is overlooked by most Baja visitors, which allows it to retain an authentic Mexican feel despite its proximity to the Los Cabos tourist corridor.

On the north side of the town is a welcoming town plaza, with tall trees for shade and a handful of colonial buildings around its perimeter. The plaza makes a relaxing stop for a stroll or a place to enjoy a picnic lunch after a trip to the hot springs or waterfall nearby. Santiago hosts its town festival on July 25, the feast day of St. James. Services on the plaza include a post office, gas station, minimarket, produce market, and a few stores. The town has one well-known restaurant and hotel, plus a few *tiendas* and produce markets.

◖ El Triunfo
A short distance from the intersection of Highway 19 and the Carretera Transpeninsular, modern-day El Triunfo (pop. 350) makes an intriguing stop on the drive from Los Barriles to La Paz or Todos Santos. You'll know you've arrived at this ghost town when you reach the only bend in the road lined with aging brick structures and a few small businesses hoping to catch travelers passing through.

Begin with a walk around the mining ruins on the southwest side of the highway. These

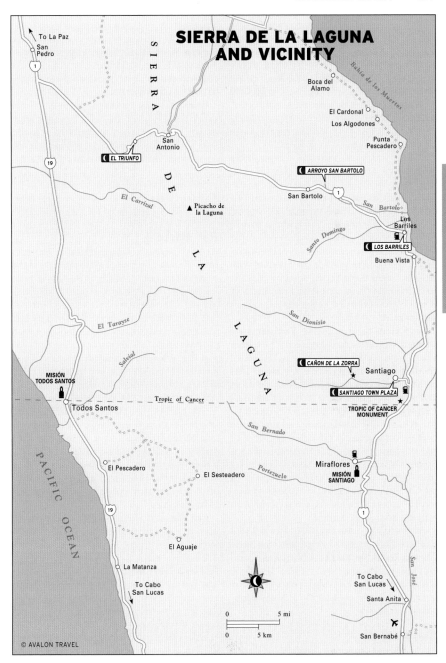

SIERRA DE LA LAGUNA AND VICINITY

To La Paz
San Pedro

SIERRA

DE

LA

LAGUNA

El Carrizal

▲ Picacho de la Laguna

El Tarayse

Salvial

MISIÓN TODOS SANTOS

Todos Santos

Tropic of Cancer

San Bernado

El Pescadero

El Sesteadero

Portezuelo

PACIFIC OCEAN

El Aguaje

La Matanza

To Cabo San Lucas

☾ EL TRIUNFO

San Antonio

Boca del Alamo

El Cardonal
Los Algodones

Punta Pescadero

☾ ARROYO SAN BARTOLO

San Bartolo

Bahía de los Muertos

San Bartolo

Los Barriles

☾ LOS BARRILES

Buena Vista

Santo Domingo

San Dionisio

☾ CAÑON DE LA ZORRA

★ Santiago

☾ SANTIAGO TOWN PLAZA

★ TROPIC OF CANCER MONUMENT

Miraflores

MISIÓN SANTIAGO

To Cabo San Lucas

Santa Anita

San José

To Cabo San Lucas

San Bernabé

0   5 mi

0   5 km

© AVALON TRAVEL

and a few restored colonial homes are the only signs of the town's glorious past. Browse the handicrafts, including handwoven baskets at El Mirador Artesanías (no tel.), which is two blocks west of the highway, at the south end of town. Then stop in for a bite to eat at ◖ **Café El Triunfo** (one block west of the main road, tel. 612/157-1625, 8am-6pm daily)—an unexpected find serving pizza, coffee drinks, and a tempting assortment of fresh breads.

Before you leave, visit the famed **Piano Museum** (Carr. Transpeninsular, no tel., 9am-6pm Mon.-Sat., US$2) to reflect on the town's glorious past. During its most prosperous years, classical music came into vogue, and pianos were shipped from Europe. Pianist Francisca Mendoza entertained the well-to-do with weekend concerts, and many of the instruments are on display inside the museum with bilingual signs. Look for an orange and white brick building on the east side of the highway. A small blue *Museo* sign points the way, but it's easy to miss.

Save time to explore the **Santuario de Cactus** (Cactus Sanctuary, Ejido El Rosario, Carr. Transpeninsular km 167, no tel., dawn till dusk daily, US$4) just outside town. This is the place to get acquainted with the flora of the desert. Bring along a copy of the *Baja California Plant Field Guide,* by Norman C. Roberts, for your stroll. About two hectares in size, the park has a short interpretive path with signs to identify the different species. If your Spanish is up to it, the enthusiastic caretaker likes to chat. The turnoff is on the west side of the Carretera Transpeninsular between kilometers 167 and 168. Follow the dirt road about 10 minutes to the park entrance.

A few of the tour operators based in La Paz and Todos Santos lead guided trips here. Contact **Todos Santos Eco Adventures** (Cerro La Poza, Calle Guaycura, tel. 612/145-0780, www.tosea.net) or Eduardo's Tours in La Paz (tel. 612/166-1657 or 612/152-1213, www.eduardostours.com).

San Antonio

At the junction of the paved road to Los Planes, a part-cobblestone, part-dirt road leads south into San Antonio, now a center of commerce for local ranchers with a few mini-supers. Drive about a kilometer and turn left at the T, and you will see an attractive town plaza on the left, followed by a large church. Tall palms and cobblestone streets border the plaza. Buy a cold drink at La Realeña (no tel.), a mini-market on the east side. There are public restrooms next to the school—oddly, three toilets in one open room. (Bring your own paper and hand sanitizer.)

San Antonio's town festival, the feast of St. Anthony, takes place on June 13, and residents from both towns show up for the celebration.

San Bartolo

As the Carretera Transpeninsular emerges from the sierra and prepares to descend to the coast once again, it passes through the farm settlement of San Bartolo (pop. 550) at kilometer 128. Attractive markets and eateries line both sides of the highway. You can buy mangoes, avocados, and other locally grown produce from markets along the road—or pick out a bag of homemade candies. Then grab a seat on a wrought-iron bench and enjoy the vista looking down on the palm-filled arroyo. **Restaurant El Paso** (no tel., hours vary, mains US$4-8) and **Dulcería Daniela's** (no tel., hours vary, mains US$4-8), on the east side of the highway, serve simple Mexican dishes as well as sweets. El Oasis (no tel., hours vary, mains US$4-8) sells fruit-filled *dulces* (sweets) and snacks and prepares simple meals. It's also a popular stop for guided tours from Los Cabos.

San Bartolo celebrates its patron saint day on June 19, just a week after San Antonio's town festival.

Arroyo San Bartolo

San Bartolo has one of the best water supplies anywhere in Southern Baja, and waterfalls along its arroyo are a popular way to cool off on balmy days. Organized tours from Los Barriles often travel here via ATV. But if you want to drive yourself to the falls, head to the village of San Bartolo and inquire at Rancho Verde for directions.

Hot Springs

Several waterfalls and hot springs are a short drive into the sierra from Santiago. Finding them involves navigating a series of turns along mostly unsigned dirt roads, although the state is beginning to make the area more visitor friendly with more pavement and signs at each of the ranchos to indicate what they grow or produce—and what they may have for sale.

The main hot springs are called **Agua Caliente, El Chorro,** and **Santa Rita**—and all three are just a few kilometers from town. Many residents and hotel managers along the East Cape can provide accurate turn-by-turn directions to these sites. The **Hotel Palomar** (tel. 624/130-2019) is a good place for information. A nominal admission fee (around US$3-5) may be required to enter the sites.

◖ Cañon de la Zorra

Freshwater is a sight to behold in the Baja desert landscape. For those travelers who would like to venture into the sierra but do not have time for a multiday hike, there is a 10-meter waterfall just 9.6 kilometers beyond Santiago that has a swimmable lagoon and is reachable by foot. At the far end of the divided avenue that leads into Santiago (as you approach the plaza), turn right and set your trip odometer to zero. At 0.48 kilometer, go straight through the dirt road intersection and head up the hill, past a sign for San Dionísio. At 1.29 kilometers and the crest of the hill, turn left. At 1.77 kilometers, turn right across a small arroyo and follow this road to 4.02 kilometers, where the road forks and there is a sign pointing to the right fork marked Cañon de la Zorra. Follow this fork to the end of the road at 9.66 kilometers and park at the trailhead. Small wooden outhouses are popping up in remote areas of the cape, and you'll find one of them here.

Go through the gate and follow the trail for 10 minutes down to the river bottom and the falls. The state has installed concrete steps to get to the waterfall now, instead of the rope, which used to scare off some potential visitors. And there is an entrance fee now of US$5. Note: As part of the Sierra de la Laguna Biosphere Reserve, this is a protected area, and pets are not allowed inside the park. The use of sunscreen is also prohibited if you are going to swim.

Rancho Ecológico Sol de Mayo (Calle Guadalupe Victoria 40-B, tel. 624/130-2055, www.ranchoecologicosoldemayo.com) offers rental cabanas and guided trips into the mountains. Stop by the office in town to make arrangements.

HORSEBACK RIDING

Rancho La Venta (Carr. Transpeninsular km 144.5, tel. 612/156-8947, www.rancholaventa. com) offers guided horseback rides (US$50 for up to 2 hours, US$70 for up to 3 hours, US$550 for overnight ride with meals and drinks) and trails for hiking and bird-watching.

FOOD

Decorated with local fossils, the **Palomar Restaurant-Bar** (tel. 624/130-2019, 10:30am-7pm Mon.-Sat., mains US$11-15), south of the plaza on the east side of Calzada Misioneros, serves seafood, enchiladas, steak, and burgers. Fresh guacamole is made from avocados grown in the courtyard. Homemade soups and *pescado al mojo de ajo* (fish cooked in garlic butter) are house specialties.

Past the Hotel Palomar on the north side of town, a road heads northwest to Rancho San Dionísio (23.5 km) and the Cañon San Dionísio approach into the Sierra de la Laguna. Owner Sergio Gomez (tel. 624/130-2019) can also contact guides from Rancho San Dionísio for hikers.

Tacos La Cascada (no tel., dinner daily), 200 meters from the plaza on the way to the waterfall, offers excellent carne asada, *mixto* (*carne* and cheese), and fish tacos for US$1.50 each.

ACCOMMODATIONS

Rancho Verde (Carr. Transpeninsular km 143/142, tel. 612/126-9103, U.S. tel. toll-free

888/516-9462, www.rancho-verde.com) advertises itself as a private RV community with lots for sale, but it does rent sites by the night as well (RVs US$12/day, US$72/week; tents US$8/day). Set on more than 1,200 hectares of sierra wilderness, this park offers a refreshing contrast to the increasing crowds and real estate development that are overtaking much of the Baja coast. Amenities include water, sewer, hot showers, and free Wi-Fi.

Just up the road, in a historic location on the mission trail, **Rancho La Venta** (tel. 612/156-8947, www.rancholaventa.com, US$75) offers a few *casitas* for rent, meals included. Owners Bob and Liz Pudwell ran a popular fish taco restaurant in Alaska before moving permanently to Baja. Now they grow organic vegetables on their ranch.

In Santiago, **Palomar Restaurant-Bar** (tel. 624/130-2019) offers six plain but clean rooms with air-conditioning around a shady courtyard for US$45.

INFORMATION AND SERVICES

San Antonio (pop. 800) has a Pemex, post office, and several markets. And there are two options for basic groceries in El Triunfo: **Abarrotes La Escondida** (on Carr. Transpeninsular, no tel.) and the **Tienda Comunitaria** (off Carr. Transpeninsular in the center of town, no tel.).

GETTING THERE AND AROUND

Santiago, at the foothills of the Sierra de la Laguna, is an easy day trip from San José del Cabo or a good place to stretch your legs during the drive between San José and La Paz. Allow 3-5 nights if you want to explore the backcountry of the Sierra de la Laguna.

To get to Santiago, turn west off the Carretera Transpeninsular at the Pemex station at kilometers 84-85 and follow this road

for two kilometers to a boulevard that eventually meets the plaza.

Eight kilometers northeast of Santiago on the Carretera Transpeninsular (around km 93), Las Cuevas marks the exit ramp for La Ribera and El Camino Costero Rural. Services include a mini-super and bus stop.

With high clearance and a sense of adventure, you can drive across the mountains from the Carretera Transpeninsular north of San José del Cabo to Highway 19 on the Pacific side via an ungraded road called Los Naranjos. The road is 42 kilometers long and ends at the village of El Aguaje, near El Pescadero.

From the Los Cabos airport, head north until you pass Santa Anita and go about eight kilometers more. Turn left onto Los Naranjos road, which ascends from the flats up into the sierra.

Bring along a copy of the *Baja California Plant and Field Guide,* by Norman C. Roberts.

Follow the switchbacks to a plateau and then continue west until you glimpse the Pacific Ocean in the distance. At this point, the road frequently washes out and may not be passable. If it's clear, you can continue on to El Pescadero.

If you're driving north along the Carretera Transpeninsular from Los Barriles and want to head over to the coast at Bahía de la Ventana or Bahía de los Muertos, you can take a recently paved shortcut from San Antonio (btwn. km 158 and km 159). The road is 22 kilometers long and meets state highway BCS 286 in San Juan de los Planes. The unsigned road is easy to miss. (Look for an intersection near the school zone.) Once you reach BCS 286, turn left (north) for La Paz and La Ventana, or right (south) for Los Planes, Los Muertos, and the Sea of Cortez coast. There is a Pemex station at this intersection as well.

Buses stop at Santiago, for access to the Sierra de la Laguna, and at La Ribera/Las Cuevas, kilometer 93, for access to Cabo Pulmo (no connecting service).

La Paz

For many travelers, the Baja California Sur state capital achieves the perfect balance of beauty and civilization: Nestled at the southern end of the largest and one of the most beautiful bays along the Gulf coast, it is tropical and picturesque, with a five-kilometer-long bayside promenade and plenty of opportunities for outdoor adventure. Protected islands offshore entertain paddlers, snorkelers, bird-watchers, and scuba divers. Remote beaches, mountain scenery, and even surf on the Pacific coast are all only a short drive away.

And yet La Paz conveys the feel of a real place with genuine people and a unique history and culture. The first Europeans to set foot on the peninsula arrived at La Paz in the 16th century, and the city was a pearling center long before it became a tourist destination. Today, it is a hub for government, commerce, education, medical services, and environmental conservation. This is not a purpose-built resort town. The locals go about their business, and tourists can take it or leave it. La Paz is ideal for the visitor who wants more than a beach-and-booze vacation; here, you'll experience some history, eco-adventure, and a taste of the real Mexico. And that's exactly why many people fall in love with the city.

Marine biologists on sabbatical from universities in the United States, young professionals from mainland Mexico, vacationers cruising on their yachts, and baby boomers looking to live comfortably in their retirement are all making La Paz their seasonal or year-round home base.

Despite the feverish pace of real estate activity, the city that John Steinbeck described as *antigua* has protected its deep-rooted traditions, many of which came from the mainland along with the earliest immigrants. Then, as now, people who came over from Mexico City and other large cities were searching for a slower pace and a better quality of life.

BEACHES

A series of public beaches line the Bahía de La Paz, from the city center all the way to the tip of the Pichilingue Peninsula. As a general rule, the beaches become prettier as you get farther away from the city. To find them, follow the La Paz-Pichilingue Road (Paseo Obregón becomes this road at the northeast end of the *malecón*), which is paved all the way to El Tecolote at the northern tip of the peninsula.

Palmira, El Coromuel, and El Caimancito

At Playa Palmira, closest to downtown La Paz (km 2.5), resort development has encroached on the sand—so it's best to continue another kilometer to Playa El Coromuel (km 4.3), a small beach with a restaurant, bar, *palapa* structures for shade, and restrooms. Lined with tall palms, this beach also has a water slide park that attracts families in the hot summer months.

Playa El Caimancito, at the La Concha Beach Resort (km 6), has a rock reef close to shore suitable for snorkeling, as well as the (rarely open) Acuario de las Californias. Enjoy a strawberry daiquiri at the resort bar and treat yourself to a pedicure in the salon.

Playa El Tesoro and Punta Colorada

Playa El Tesoro (km 13) has *palapas* and a hit-or-miss restaurant. The dirt road that heads southwest from the beach goes to Playa Punta Colorada, a secluded swimming cove.

Playa Pichilingue

The next beach east of the ferry terminal (km 17-18) has restrooms open 24/7 for visitors who want to camp. Its simple *palapa* restaurant (tel. 612/122-4565, 11am-9pm daily, mains US$5-15) serves Mexican fare, but the real reason to go is the shellfish: clams, lobster, mussels, and

EXCURSIONS

spinner dolphin, Sea of Cortez

crab. A taxi from the *malecón* to the ferry terminal will run about US$20.

Playa Balandra

The best beach for snorkeling along this stretch is Playa Balandra, which came under protection by the La Paz City Council in 2008—a victory for local environmental organizations. Known for Mushroom Rock, which balances offshore, this sometimes-crowded beach usually is protected from the wind (good for calm water and chilly days, but not so good for bugs when camping). The shallow bay is great for kids, who can wade quite far from shore without worrying about currents or sudden drop-offs. Swim out to the coral reef at the south end of the beach for the best underwater scenery. To get the best views, you'll have to scale the rock cliffs behind the beach. Services are limited, but there may be a food stand selling drinks and snacks. Look for an access road about five kilometers past the ferry terminal.

Playa El Tecolote

Continue another three kilometers beyond the road to Playa Balandra and you'll reach Playa El Tecolote, an exposed beach that faces the Canal de San Lorenzo and Isla Espíritu Santo to the north. A handful of *pangas* are moored here, and you can swim in a roped-off area, or anywhere along the beach. The slope is gentle leading into the water and the bottom is sandy, so you can wade quite far from shore before having to swim. Campers often come here to escape the bugs. Two beachfront restaurants, **El Tecolote** (tel. 612/127-9494, mains US$8-20) and **Palapa Azul** (tel. 612/122-1801, mains US$8-15), offer food and drinks as well as rental gear (chairs, umbrellas, fishing equipment) and boat tours (US$40-50). There are pay showers and public *palapas* for shade. Restrooms are free for customers, US$0.80 for everyone else.

The strawberry margaritas at El Tecolote are generously sized for US$8, and the kitchen turns out tasty seafood, such as *pescado*

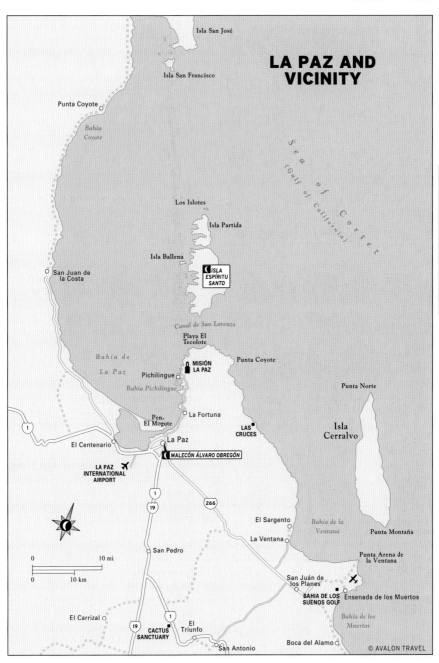

LA PAZ AND VICINITY

Isla San José

Isla San Francisco

Punta Coyote

Bahía Coyote

Sea of Cortez
(Gulf of California)

Los Islotes

Isla Partida

Isla Ballena

ISLA ESPÍRITU SANTO

San Juan de la Costa

Canal de San Lorenzo

Playa El Tecolote

Bahía de La Paz

Punta Coyote

MISIÓN LA PAZ

Pichilingue

Bahía Pichilingue

Punta Norte

Pen. El Mogote

La Fortuna

Isla Cerralvo

El Centenario

LAS CRUCES

La Paz

MALECÓN ÁLVARO OBREGÓN

LA PAZ INTERNATIONAL AIRPORT

1

1

19

266

El Sargento

Bahía de la Ventana

La Ventana

Punta Montaña

San Pedro

Punta Arena de la Ventana

0   10 mi

0   10 km

San Juán de los Planes

BAHÍA DE LOS SUEÑOS GOLF

Ensenada de los Muertos

El Carrizal

19

CACTUS SANCTUARY

1

El Triunfo

Bahía de los Muertos

San Antonio

Boca del Alamo

© AVALON TRAVEL

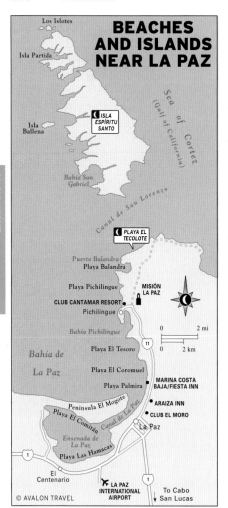

BEACHES
AND ISLANDS
NEAR LA PAZ

Los Islotes

Isla Partida

Isla Ballena

ISLA ESPÍRITU SANTO

Sea of Cortez (Gulf of California)

Bahía San Gabriel

Canal de San Lorenzo

PLAYA EL TECOLOTE

Puerto Balandra
Playa Balandra

Playa Pichilingue

CLUB CANTAMAR RESORT
Pichilingue

MISIÓN LA PAZ

Bahía Pichilingue

Bahía de La Paz

Playa El Tesoro

Playa El Coromuel

Playa Palmira

Peninsula El Mogote

Playa El Comitán

Canal de La Paz

Ensenada de La Paz

Playa Las Hamacas

El Centenario

0   2 mi
0   2 km

MARINA COSTA
BAJA/FIESTA INN

ARAIZA INN
CLUB EL MORO
La Paz

LA PAZ
INTERNATIONAL
AIRPORT

To Cabo
San Lucas

© AVALON TRAVEL

zareandeado (broiled, seasoned fish; US$10) and butterflied cabrilla (US$20). Both of these restaurants are casual affairs with plastic chairs and tables.

Though you are well away from the city, don't leave valuables unattended. Theft is rare, but it happens.

Playa El Coyote

After El Tecolote, a dirt road continues around to the east side of the Pichilingue Peninsula to Punta Coyote. Coves along this stretch are rocky, and sand is gray or brown instead of white. The road effectively ends here, although the most adventurous off-roaders might attempt to find their way through a maze of sand roads to Puerto Mejia and Las Cruces.

Península el Mogote

The closest land you see when standing on the *malecón* is the thumb-shaped Mogote Peninsula. Extending 11 kilometers in an east-west direction, it joins the main Baja Peninsula via a narrow sand spit on the north side of the Ensenada de La Paz. Mangroves grow along the Mogote's southern shore, which faces the city; the opposite shore features a long, sandy beach.

Once the domain of kayakers and other adventure-seekers, the area is now under development as the US$240 million **Paraíso del Mar real estate project** (tel. 612/125-5199, toll-free U.S. tel. 888/207-2825, www.paraisodelmarlapaz.com, stay-and-play packages starting at US$129 and up) takes shape. Plans call for two golf courses, a clubhouse, hundreds of homes, a shopping mall, church, hotels, marina, and park. Necessary infrastructure will include desalination plants, water and sewage treatment plants, and a ferry terminal. (Although there is a dirt road leading out to the peninsula from El Comitá, north of La Paz, primary access for visitors will be by water taxi, since the distance is only 800 meters from the *malecón*.)

The project has encountered criticism from environmentalists, including Greenpeace, for endangering hundreds of acres of mangroves, which provide a habitat and nutrients for thousands of marine species in the Sea of Cortez. But the developers are taking steps to protect the fragile ecosystem—by landscaping the golf courses with native plants, for example.

Accommodations today consist of 90 homes and 5 condo buildings, with more on the way. The golf course is also open. The resort has an office on the *malecón* in the Vista Coral Plaza

© LAUREN SWIFT

Playa Balandra

near Papas and Beer, where guests check in and catch the water taxi to the peninsula. Activities so far are mainly centered around golf tournaments, but you can also walk the beach, borrow a kayak, and play volleyball, tennis, horseshoes, or boccie. Transportation within the resort is via golf cart (US$20 per day). A free shuttle is also provided. The golf course (tel. 612/165-1818) is open 7am-7pm Tuesday-Sunday. A restaurant on the course is open the same hours. La Tiendita, a small convenience store, is open 11am-7pm daily.

ISLANDS

You haven't fully experienced La Paz until you've explored the undeveloped barrier islands that guard the entrance to the bay. Along the shores of Isla Espíritu Santo and Isla Partida, protected coves in shallow bays provide a safe environment for swimming, rock and coral reefs attract abundant marine life, and steep cliffs lead to stunning bay views.

🅲 Isla Espíritu Santo

Closest to the Pichilingue Peninsula, Isla Espíritu Santo is 22.5 kilometers long. Its southwest side is scalloped with a series of narrow bays, each with one or more fingers reaching deep into the interior of the island. The shoreline on the northeast side is smoother, with fewer protected places to land small boats and snorkel or swim.

Formerly owned by a local *ejido,* this island was "sold" to the Mexican government in 2003 through the cooperative efforts of several nonprofits, which raised US$3.3 million to compensate *ejido* members for the land. For the traveler in search of outdoor adventure, this means the island has a good chance of remaining undeveloped, even as large real estate projects take shape on the peninsula.

Due to the presence of numerous reefs and underwater rock formations, this island is a popular stop for snorkeling and scuba diving tours. Bahía San Gabriel near the southwest

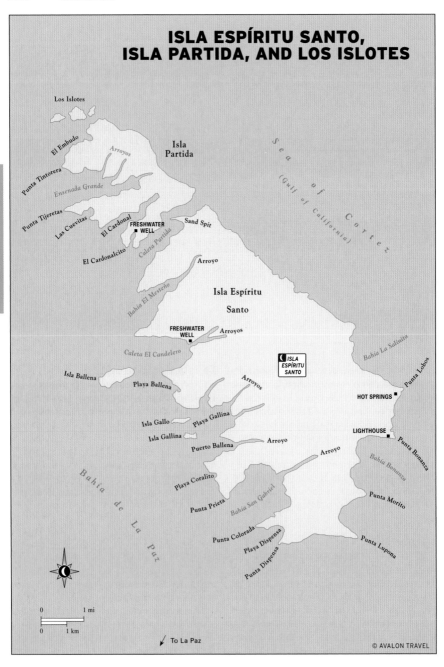

ISLA ESPÍRITU SANTO, ISLA PARTIDA, AND LOS ISLOTES

Los Islotes

El Embudo

Arroyos

Isla Partida

Punta Tintorera

Ensenada Grande

Punta Tijeretas

Las Cuevitas

El Cardonal

FRESHWATER WELL

Sand Spit

El Cardonalcito

Caleta Partida

Arroyo

Bahía El Mestino

Isla Espíritu Santo

Sea of Cortez (Gulf of California)

FRESHWATER WELL

Arroyos

Caleta El Candelero

ISLA ESPÍRITU SANTO

Isla Ballena

Bahía La Salinita

Punta Lobos

Playa Ballena

Arroyos

HOT SPRINGS

Isla Gallo

Playa Gallina

Isla Gallina

LIGHTHOUSE

Punta Bonanza

Puerto Ballena

Arroyo

Arroyo

Bahía Bonanza

Bahía de La Paz

Playa Coralito

Punta Prieta

Bahía San Gabriel

Punta Morito

Punta Colorada

Playa Dispensa

Punta Lupona

Punta Dispensa

0   1 mi

0   1 km

To La Paz

© AVALON TRAVEL

tip of the island features ruins from a former pearl-fishing operation.

For a good hike, begin at the beach at Caleta El Candelero on the northwest side of the island. Find the arroyo and follow it inland, where a deep canyon is carved into the volcanic bluffs. Along the way are wild fig and plum trees; keep your eyes peeled for the rare black jackrabbit.

Isla Partida

The next major island heading north from Pichilingue is the much smaller Isla Partida, which has more beaches, dive sites, and opportunities for hiking and views. Fish camps at either end of the island sometimes have freshwater, but it isn't guaranteed. Plan to bring your own drinking water. If you are navigating your own boat, beware the sandbar that almost connects Isla Partida with Isla Espíritu Santo. The channel is extremely narrow.

Los Islotes

Hundreds of playful sea lions live on and around this group of small jagged rock islands north of Isla Partida. Roughly a one-hour boat ride from Pichilingue, they are a popular destination for snorkeling, scuba diving, kayaking, and sportfishing.

Camping

Because the islands near La Paz are protected by the Mexican government, a permit (US$4/day) is required to camp on them. Visit the local **SEMARNAT office** (2nd floor, Ocampo 1045 btwn. Rubio and Verdad, tel. 612/123-9300, www.semarnat.gob.mx, 8am-1:30pm Mon.-Fri.) before you head out to sea. Pets are prohibited, as is harvesting wood for campfires. The availability of freshwater limits camping options on the larger islands, and camping is not allowed on Ensenada Grande or Playa Ballena.

Two of the bays, Caleta El Candelero on Isla Espíritu Santo and El Cardonalcito on Isla Partida, have freshwater wells where you can bathe. You'll need a bucket and five meters of rope to reach the water level. Purify the water if you must use it for drinking. (Plan to bring your own purified water; only use the well water in an emergency.) It's also a good idea to bring multi-fuel stoves for camping to increase your chances of finding the canisters you need while in Baja.

Getting to the Islands

There are several ways to reach the islands. Most visitors book a daylong kayak, snorkeling, or scuba diving tour. You can also join a guided multiday kayak/camping trip, or arrive by private yacht. Experienced paddlers can rent a kayak in La Paz and paddle the 6.5 kilometers across the channel from Pichilingue (Playa El Tecolote is the closest launch point) to the islands. Wind, current, and tides make this a challenging trip, even though the distance is relatively short. At Playa El Tecolote, you can also hire a *panga* for an excursion to the island. Rates are around US$150 per boat, including lunch. A one-way shuttle out to the island costs about US$75.

WATER SPORTS
Snorkeling and Scuba Diving

La Paz has one of the largest scuba diving communities anywhere in Mexico. The islands offshore from the city present divers of all skill levels with some of the most interesting underwater topography in the Sea of Cortez as well as opportunities to spot some of the largest pelagics in the sea. Sea lions frolic at Los Islotes, while hammerhead sharks school around El Bajo and giant mantas cruise against the current. From the surface, you may see flying rays, schools of bottlenose and spinner dolphins, and giant bait balls.

Unlike the reef and wall diving in Cabo Pulmo and Cabo San Lucas, where dive sites are a 5- to 15-minute boat ride from shore, long, choppy boat rides (45-60 minutes) are the norm here—hence the higher rates. Remember to take your seasickness medicine the night before. (Many divers swear by Bonine, found over the counter in the United States and Mexico.)

A day of diving typically begins 7am-8am and finishes in the late afternoon. Lunch is usually included at no extra cost.

Most operators require a minimum of at least two divers to send a boat out to the islands. Some require four divers to visit the more remote sites.

DIVE SITES

Most boats frequent about a dozen different sites around the islands offshore from La Paz. A sea lion colony at Los Islotes (7-15 meters) provides loads of underwater entertainment. Also suitable for beginners, the *Salvatierra* wreck (18 meters) presents an opportunity to explore the remains of a cargo ferry that sank in 1976. If conditions permit, advanced divers might request a trip to El Bajo, a seamount that peaks at 18-30 meters below the surface, in hopes of encountering a school of hammerhead sharks as well as giant mantas, whale sharks, and towers of schooling amberjacks and tuna.

DAY TRIPS

In business since 1992, **Buceo Carey** (Legaspy and Topete, tel. 612/128-4048, toll-free U.S. tel. 877/239-4057, www.buceocarey.com) is one of the more respected dive centers in town. Local captains and international dive guides lead one-day and multiday dive trips to Espíritu Santo sites for US$85 a day, and to El Bajo and Isla Cerralvo for US$95. The cost includes lunch, transportation, guide, unlimited sodas and beer, weight belt, and two tanks. Rental equipment includes regulators, BCDs, wetsuits, masks, snorkels, fins, tanks, weight belts, booties, and portable air compressors. The company has a second office at Marina de La Paz. Inquire about accommodations packages.

The largest dive operation in La Paz is Fernando Águilar's **Baja Diving and Service** (BCS 11/Carr. a Pichilingue, past the ferry terminal, tel. 612/122-7010, www.clubcantamar. com). Based at the Club Cantamar Resort and Sports Centre on the Pichilingue Peninsula, the company operates a fleet of eight vessels, including some of the largest dive boats on the Sea of Cortez, holding more than 20 divers. Its custom-built 53-foot *Liberación* features air-conditioning and hot water, two heads, and a pleasant sundeck for warming up after each

dive. The boat accommodates 30 divers for day trips and 10 divers as a live-aboard. They also run *pangas* for divers who consider the larger boats to be too much like cattle cars. Besides the sheer scale of the operation, shorter boat rides are a significant advantage of diving with the Cantamar staff. Boats typically depart at 8:30am and return by 5pm. For divers who aren't staying at the resort, a shuttle service is provided at no additional cost.

Dive rates are US$115 per person per day for two or three tanks, depending on conditions. Day trips include transportation, boat ride, lunch, and drinks. The resort has an ultralight plane used for spotting whale sharks (extra charge of US$20 pp). Shorter boat rides also make the more distant dive sites, like Las Animas and the San Diegito Reef, more accessible for day-trippers (extra charge of US$25 per diver for trips to these sites).

Dive packages for 3-14 nights, lunch and breakfast included on dive days, cost US$400-1,705; Nitrox and rebreather dive packages are also available at additional cost. Round-trip airport transfers are also included.

Rental gear is available (snorkel set US$7/day, dive gear US$23/day). Certified divers can also get nitrox refills for US$8-12 and rent rebreathers for US$65. New divers can get certified in the resort's own pool (US$420, includes two days of open-water dives) or try an introductory Discover Scuba course (US$152). Advanced certification costs US$370. Nitrox certification is US$220. In case of a dive emergency, the Cantamar has the only recompression chamber in La Paz. For more information or to make a reservation, drop in at the Cantamar's downtown sales office (Paseo Obregón 1665-2, Plaza Cerralvo, near the Hotel Perla, tel. 612/122-1826, 9am-8pm daily).

Another multiboat operation is based at the La Concha Beach Resort. The **Cortez Club Dive Center** (Carr. a Pichilingue km 5, tel. 612/121-6120, www.cortezclub.com) has 12 dive boats, its own classroom for dive instruction, and a private jetty and ramp. Rates are a little higher than at other shops.

Day excursions aboard **Baja Expeditions'**

© LAUREN SWIFT

scuba diving with Baja Diving and Service, based at the Club Cantamar resort

(tel. 612/125-3828, toll-free U.S. tel. 800/843-6967, www.bajaex.com) 45-foot *Don Cano* or 48-foot *Pez Sapo* cost US$125 per day (Mar.-Dec.), which covers three dives, breakfast, lunch, snacks, and happy hour.

SNORKEL TOURS

Most dive and kayak outfitters also run snorkel tours. Less-expensive trips visit the beaches along the Pichilingue Peninsula; the more expensive ones go to the islands for the day. If you have the opportunity to go snorkeling in the bay when the whale sharks are around, sign up immediately. While there is no guarantee of encountering them on any given day, the guides will tell you if they've seen any activity lately; seeing these enormous baleen creatures up close is like starring in your own private National Geographic film.

Buceo Carey (Legaspy and Topete, tel. 612/128-4048, toll-free U.S. tel. 877/239-4057, www.buceocarey.com) offers snorkeling trips for US$65 to Playa Encantada and the sea lion colony. Baja Diving and Service (tel.

612/122-7010, www.clubcantamar.com) at the Cantamar does local snorkel trips for US$65.

One of the best values among organized trips is the snorkeling trip to Espíritu Santo run by **Azul Tours** (Paseo Obregón 774, tel. 612/125-2596, www.azultourslapaz.com). The staff is knowledgeable, well equipped, and safety-conscious. The adventure takes the better part of a day and includes a delicious lunch, prepared by its sister restaurant, Palapa Azul, for US$65 per person.

El Tecolote Restaurant/Bar/Playa (tel. 612/127-9494) transports snorkelers to Espíritu Santo in *pangas* for US$40 per person. The price includes gear and lunch. Boats depart between 10 and 11am for a four-hour tour. Stop by the booking office, just off the plaza next to the Hotel Miramar, for more information. El Tecolote also offers WaveRunners, kayaks, banana boats, and waterskiing.

Marlin Adventures (Obregón 460, at Ocampo, tel. 612/125-7842, cell 612/137-4495, www.marlinadventures.net, 8am-7pm daily) offers snorkeling tours as well as diving, instructor certification, whale-shark tours, fishing, and kayak rentals at Playa Tecolote (US$66 for a four-hour tour, including lunch and gear). It has three 28-foot *pangas,* which are fully insured and have oxygen and first aid on board.

Mar y Aventuras (Topete 564, btwn. 5 de Febrero and Navarro, tel. 406/522-7596, toll-free U.S. tel. 800/355-7140, www.kayakbaja. com) specializes in kayaking but also leads snorkeling trips. We snorkeled with juvenile whale sharks in La Paz Bay on a recent visit.

Whale-Watching

There are several ways to observe gray and blue whales near La Paz, and several dive and kayak outfitters offer special whale-watching tours. Some tours go to the Sea of Cortez, while others go to Laguna San Ignacio or Magdalena Bay on the Pacific side of the Baja Peninsula. Some trips involve snorkeling and paddling; others are just boat cruises. You can go for one day or eight, depending on your budget and how much time you want to spend with the mammals.

Baja Outdoor Activities (tel. 612/125-5636, toll-free U.S. tel. 888/217-6659, www.kayakin-baja.com) offers a package with two three-hour boat trips plus an overnight stay and all meals for US$250 per person.

Johnny Friday and Maldo Ficher lead eco-tours in the area through **Baja Adventure Company** (tel. 612/125-9081, toll-free U.S. tel. 877/506-0557, www.bajaecotours.com), a division of Mar de Cortez sports. Its marine biologists, zoologists, and other professionally trained guides lead whale-watching trips.

A pioneer in environmental education and sustainable tourism, **Baja Expeditions** (tel. 612/125-3828, toll-free U.S. tel. 800/843-6967, www.bajaex.com) offers multiday whale-watching trips to Magdalena Bay and Laguna San Ignacio and in the Sea of Cortez.

Kayaking and Stand-Up Paddling

The islands near La Paz are some of the best places in the world to kayak, and several companies provide highly recommended tours. Day trips are possible, but given the amount of gear and transportation logistics involved, many day-trippers end up feeling rushed and wish they had chosen a multiday tour instead. Most trips fall into one of two categories: a four-day paddle along the west side of Isla Espíritu Santo (usually north to south) and a seven-day (or more) paddle all the way around Isla Espíritu Santo and Isla Partida (56 km).

Overnight package trips usually include the first and last nights in hotel accommodations, with camping on the nights in between. Meals, transportation to the islands, and airport transfers are also typically covered by the price. Some trips return to a base camp every night, while others move to a new place each day. Some have motorized support boats to move camping gear from place to place and shuttle paddlers to the best snorkeling sites for the particular conditions each day. Some outfitters supply camping gear; others ask that you bring your own.

Many companies book kayak tours, but often they are brokers for the actual outfitter. In general, it's better to book directly so you can get complete information about the itinerary and equipment before you sign up for a trip. Two of the most popular operators are Mar y Aventuras and Baja Outdoor Adventure.

Owned by a friendly La Paz native, **Mar y Aventuras** (Topete 564, btwn. 5 de Febrero and Navarro, tel. 406/522-7596, toll-free U.S. tel. 800/355-7140, www.kayakbaja.com), near La Marina Don José and Marina de La Paz, leads one-day and multiday trips and rents kayaks and gear to experienced paddlers (reserve well in advance if you want to rent). Its boats are a mix of doubles and singles made of fiberglass and some plastic. All have rudders.

If you want to explore El Mogote or the islands on your own, you'll have to convince the staff that you know what you're doing. For safety reasons, they are reluctant to rent to novice and intermediate paddlers. Single sea kayaks rent for US$45 a day, with a PFD (personal flotation device), paddle, bilge pump, and spray deck. Double kayaks cost US$65 a day. You can also rent snorkeling gear and camping equipment. Boat shuttles out to Isla Espíritu Santo cost US$200-400 round-trip for one or two people; a truck shuttle to Playa El Tecolote for launching from the beach to Espíritu Santo costs US$25 one-way for one or two people. You can pay the US$4-per-day camping fee at the Mar y Aventuras office. Many guests book their first and last nights in the attached inn. The accommodations are very authentically Baja, and staying with other eco-minded travelers makes for a great way to start and finish an adventure trip.

Baja Outdoor Activities (BOA) (tel. 612/125-5636, www.kayakinbaja.com) is another option for kayak trips.

Baja Expeditions (tel. 612/125-3828, toll-free U.S. tel. 800/843-6967, www.bajaex.com) has been running seven-day trips to Espíritu Santo (US$1,125) since 1985. Other destinations include Loreto to the La Paz coast (10 days) and Magdalena Bay (eight days). An aggressive 10-day, open-water kayak trip hops among the islands of Espíritu Santo,

© CARMEL TSABAR

bottlenose dolphins swimming in a boat wake

Los Islotes, San José, Santa Cruz, and Santa Catalina (Oct.-Apr. only).

Stand-up paddling has come to La Paz, and there is a company right on the *malecón* that provides gear and lessons. Experienced paddlers with enough time can head out to the mangrove on the Mogote Peninsula.

Boating

With the largest bay along the Gulf coast, La Paz is far and away the frontrunner in all of Baja when it comes to boating services and supplies. Even Cabo San Lucas pales in comparison. There are numerous public and private marinas, boatyards, and marine supply stores, with new businesses opening and old ones upgrading all the time.

BOAT CHARTERS

If you like the idea of cruising but don't have your own boat or any experience on the water, you might book a trip with **Baja Coast SeaFaris** (Dock B, Marina de La Paz, tel. 612/111-7335, www.bajaseafaris.com). This company offers full-service charters with a bilingual crew aboard *Tesoro del Mar,* a Beneteau 50 that has space for six adults. Privacy is the distinguishing factor with this outfitter. All trips are private, whether for a party of two or six; pricing varies with the size of the group. Multiday trips (3-5 days or longer) include stops at Espíritu Santo, Isla Partida, and Los Islotes for swimming with sea lions, scuba diving, kayaking, tubing (for kids), sailing, beachcombing, whale-watching, bird-watching, snorkeling, or fishing. Rates are US$795 per night for two persons and US$165 additional per night for additional adults, US$115 additional per child. The price covers all meals, snacks, and cocktails while on board the yacht; a night of lodging on the final evening; and round-trip airport transfers. The boats are fully equipped with kayaks and other gear. Scuba diving and rental gear are also arranged upon request. Book well ahead (several months) for peak travel times. Miscellaneous taxes, permits, and island and port fees will add about 15 percent to the total trip cost.

The owner of Baja Coast SeaFaris has compiled a thorough list of FAQs for novice and experienced sailors that covers topics related to cruising in Baja at www.bajaseafaris.com/cruise.html.

Baja Expeditions (tel. 612/125-3828, toll-free U.S. tel. 800/843-6967, www.bajaex.com) offers custom-designed sailing charters aboard *El Mechudo,* a catamaran with four en suite cabins, which can accommodate up to eight adults for US$2,250 per day.

Fishing

The best fishing near La Paz takes place May-November, and the typical catch includes wahoo, dorado, and tuna as well as sailfish and blue, black, and striped marlin. A seamount called El Bajo is exposed to the wind but has developed a legendary reputation for some of the biggest marlin, tuna, and dorado.

The waters around the far side of the Pichilingue Peninsula near Isla Cerralvo, Punta Arena de la Ventana, and Bahía de los Muertos have more consistent fishing than the bay and islands closer to La Paz. For this reason, many fishers choose the relative ease of a one-hour van ride and launch at Punta Arena de la Ventana over the *panga*-pounding journey by sea to the same fishing grounds.

If the wind is blowing too hard to get to the pelagics offshore, you can try for inshore species such as barred *pargo,* snapper, mackerel, sea bass, and grouper. Ceviche made from fresh mackerel is a fine consolation prize for getting blown off the big water. The norm for inshore fishing is live sardines with a few thrown in around your bait as chum.

Roosterfish (*pez gallo*) are available in the Punta de la Ventana area and can reach world-record size. The all-tackle world record, weighing 51.7 kilograms, was landed off La Paz in 1960. In 2007 an angler caught an estimated 54-kilogram roosterfish, but it was never weighed. Whether you are fishing or not, there is nothing more exciting than the moment when the spiked comb of the *pez gallo* breaks the surface of the turquoise waters and tears across a shallow bay on Isla Espíritu Santo. Your first instinct might be to run.

CHARTERS

The fishing charter business in La Paz is well developed, with many professional operations, experienced captains, and well-appointed boats. Here are a few of the most popular choices. Owned by Jonathan Roldan, who has lived in La Paz since 1996, **Tailhunter International** (Obregón 755 btwn. Salvatierra and Torre Iglesias, cell 612/125-3311, U.S. tel. 626/638-3383, www.tailhunter-international.com) has a loyal clientele. He often guides fly-fishing clients who want to catch roosterfish and dorado. Jonathan has two fleets: The La Paz boats head to Espíritu Santo and El Bajo; a separate Punta Arena fleet fishes the waters around Isla Cerralvo, Banco 88, and Bahía de los Muertos. Anglers gather at the adjoining **Tailhunter Bar & FUBAR Cantina** (Obregón 755 btwn. Salvatierra and Torre Iglesias, cell 612/125-3311, U.S. tel. 626/638-3383, toll-free U.S. tel. 877/825-8802, www.tailhunter-international.com, mains US$6-14) on the *malecón* to check for their trips, and then again to trade stories over drinks at the bar afterwards.

Jay Murakoshi's **C&J Fishing Adventures** (Flies Unlimited, U.S. tel. 559/449-0679, www.fliesunlimited.com) specializes in saltwater fly-fishing in tropical destinations around the world and leads charter trips to Bahía de la Ventana. Jay also sells his own saltwater and surf-zone flies.

Baja Pirates (toll-free U.S. tel. 866/454-5386, www.bajapiratesoflapaz.com) has a fleet of eight boats, from a standard 22-foot *panga* up to cruisers and a 26-foot Bay Liner. Boats are equipped with life jackets, marine heads (on 210 or larger), tackle, gear, and ice chests (with ice), along with breakfast and lunch. This company has package deals that include airfare out of Los Angeles.

HIKING, BIKING, AND HORSEBACK RIDING

Co-located in the **Baja Outdoor Activities (BOA)** office next to the El Moro hotel,

Mexican-owned Katún (tel. 612/125-8522, www.katuntours.com) runs guided mountain-biking day trips and multi-day tours of the Sierra de la Laguna. A six-hour tour runs $US60.

Baja Challenge (Obregón 460-1, btwn. Ocampo and Degollado, tel. 612/128-6089, www.bajachallengetours.com, 9am-11pm daily; US$2-4 per hour) rents mountain bikes, cruisers, tandems, and Rollerblades and operates a five-kilometer mountain biking course across from the Hotel Marina.

ADVENTURE SPORTS AND TOURS

Travel companies and outfitters offer a variety of guided tours and organized activities, from island kayak trips and whale-watching to language immersion and cooking classes. A number of the newer ones are committed to promoting environmentally aware tours and trips. Since each outfitter may partner with others to offer unique trips, it's difficult to keep up with all the options. Aside from the activity-specific outfitters mentioned earlier in this chapter, **Espíritu & Baja Tours** (Obregón 774-A, btwn. Allende and Juárez, tel. 612/122-4427, www.espiritubaja.com) runs professional and reasonably priced trips, such as snorkeling at Espíritu Santo (US$75 pp), whale-watching trips to Bahía Magdalena (US$140 pp), sportfishing (US$255 per boat), kayaking along the Pichilingue Peninsula (US$95 pp), and airport transfer services (airport to hotel US$30, hotel to airport US$15).

Readers have reported pleasant outings with **Eduardo's Tours** (tel. 612/166-1657 or 612/152-1213, www.eduardostours.com). Eduardo Gomez provides ground transportation and leads guided trips to Los Cabos (US$115 pp), Todos Santos (US$95 pp), and El Triunfo (US$95 pp). A La Paz city tour costs US$32 per person, and a tour of several beaches along the Pichilingue Peninsula is US$32. Whale-watching tours (US$130 pp, includes two hours of whale-watching but is a full-day trip with a long drive to Bahía Magdalena and back) and snorkeling (US$85 pp, US$100 pp

with kayaks) are also possible. Travelers with more time can arrange multiday trips to the missions in Loreto and Mulegé or to see nearby cave paintings in the mountains.

In addition to hiking and horseback riding tours, **Antonio Moller** (tel. 612/123-1370) offers guided trips to El Triunfo and the nearby cactus sanctuary. Tours cost US$40 per person, with a minimum of three people, and last approximately six hours (8am-3pm).

Besides catering to divers and kayakers, **Baja Expeditions** (tel. 612/125-3828, toll-free U.S. tel. 800/843-6967, www.bajaex.com) offers wildlife cruises, open-water swim clinics, and a wide variety of custom-designed group trips that usually blend an element of adventure with a conservation-minded approach.

SIGHTS
Malecón Álvaro Obregón

The most defining feature of downtown La Paz is the five-kilometer promenade that parallels Paseo Álvaro Obregón and hugs the shoreline from Calle 5 de Febrero at the southwest end to Playa Caimancito at the northeast end. Along the way are a couple of marinas, numerous restaurants, shops, car rental agencies, hotels, a tourist pier, *panga* boats, and a small beach area. A fixture since the early days of the city, the *malecón* is looking better than ever these days. Decorative paving, whimsical aquatic-themed sculptures, and wrought-iron benches invite visitors and residents to take a sunset stroll along the Bahía de La Paz, just as the afternoon breeze kicks up. At Parque de la Amistad (Friendship Park), you can walk under the arch onto a pier and look back at the cityscape. Water quality has improved, too, making it possible to swim once again (though most people continue northeast to the beaches along the Pichilingue Peninsula).

Museo Regional de Antropología e Historia

As Southern Baja's cultural center, La Paz has a wonderful anthropology and history museum, the **Museo Regional de Antropología e Historia** (5 de Mayo and Altamirano, tel.

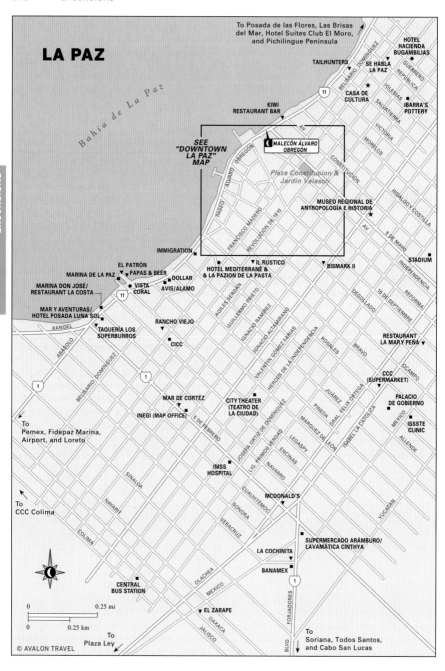

LA PAZ

Bahía de La Paz

To Posada de las Flores, Las Brisas
del Mar, Hotel Suites Club El Moro,
and Pichilingue Peninsula

HOTEL
HACIENDA
BUGAMBILIAS

TAILHUNTERS
SE HABLA
LA PAZ

CASA DE
CULTURA

IBARRA'S
POTTERY

KIWI
RESTAURANT BAR

SEE
"DOWNTOWN
LA PAZ"
MAP

MALECÓN ÁLVARO
OBREGÓN

Plaza Constitución &
Jardín Velasco

MUSEO REGIONAL DE
ANTROPOLOGÍA E HISTORIA

IMMIGRATION

IL RUSTICO

EL PATRÓN
PAPAS & BEER

HOTEL MEDITERRANE &
& LA PAZION DE LA PASTA

BISMARK II

STADIUM

MARINA DE LA PAZ

DOLLAR

MARINA DON JOSÉ/
RESTAURANT LA COSTA

VISTA
CORAL

AVIS/ALAMO

MAR Y AVENTURAS/
HOTEL POSADA LUNA SOL

RANCHO VIEJO

RANGEL

TAQUERÍA LOS
SUPERBURROS

CICC

RESTAURANT
LA MARY PEÑA

CCC
(SUPERMARKET)

PALACIO
DE GOBIERNO

MAR DE CORTÉZ

CITY THEATER
(TEATRO DE
LA CIUDAD)

ISSSTE
CLINIC

To
Pemex, Fidepaz Marina,
Airport, and Loreto

INEGI (MAP OFFICE)

IMSS
HOSPITAL

To
CCC Colima

MCDONALD'S

SUPERMERCADO ARÁMBURO/
LAVAMÁTICA CINTHYA

LA COCHINITA

BANAMEX

CENTRAL
BUS STATION

EL ZARAPE

To
Soriana, Todos Santos,
and Cabo San Lucas

0   0.25 mi

0   0.25 km

© AVALON TRAVEL

To
Plaza Ley

612/122-0162, 9am-6pm daily). Its three floors contain exhibits that depict life in Baja California before the Europeans arrived—including photos and replicas of prehistoric cave paintings—and progress all the way up through the Mexican-American War of the 19th century. Fossils and minerals tell the story of the geologic past of the peninsula. The knowledgeable and enthusiastic staff speaks limited English, and exhibit signs for the permanent exhibits are only in Spanish. The on-site gift shop has replicas of Amerindian pottery and other souvenirs for sale as well as books, music, and guides focused on the history, geology, and anthropology of Mexico. On a visit in 2012, galleries were under renovation and the artist who masterminded several of the exhibits was at work on a new display. Admission is by donation, US$2 suggested.

Plaza Constitución and Jardín Velasco

La Paz's central plaza and garden take up a full block between Avenida Independencia and Calle 5 de Mayo and between Calles Revolución de 1910 and Madero. With its gazebo and wrought-iron benches, this is a good place to get your bearings and begin a walking tour. Note the fountain with a representation of the Mushroom Rock that stands just offshore in Balandra Bay. In the evening you might catch a live performance, a game of Mexican bingo, or a formal event at the church.

On the southwest side of the plaza (Revolución de 1910 btwn. 5 de Mayo and Independencia) stands the 1871 Catedral de Nuestra Señora de La Paz, built by the Dominicans as a replacement for the original Jesuit mission church.

La Unidad Cultural Profesor Jesús Castro Agúndez

This cultural center (Navarro btwn. Altamirano and Independencia, tel. 612/125-0207, 8am-3pm Mon.-Fri.) has art exhibits, classes, and the 1,500-seat city theater, which stages dance performances, concerts, and plays year-round. In the complex, **Galería de Arte**

Carlos Olochea (tel. 612/122-9196) hosts temporary and permanent exhibitions by renowned national artists. The city's central library and historical archives are also located here.

NIGHTLIFE AND ENTERTAINMENT
Bars

La Paz nightlife is more diverse and vibrant than that of San José del Cabo, but not as crazy and tourist-oriented as what you'll find in Cabo San Lucas. Many Baja expats who live in surrounding towns come to La Paz for live concerts and other performances. A former journalist and Canadian expat maintains an up-to-date website (www.rozinlapaz.com) that describes all the venues and lists most of the goings on around town. Most venues are open nightly until at least midnight or later on weekends.

One of the oldest watering holes in town is **Tequilas Bar and Grill** (Ocampo 310 E. at Mutualisimo, tel. 612/121-5217), with simple decor, pool tables, and a cigar bar. It has a full kitchen and will happily cook your fresh catch for you for US$3. Bar Salsipuedes (Obregón 2130, btwn. Allende and Juárez, tel. 612/128-5594) seems to attract a concentration of the city's marine biologists. Besides serving drinks, it shows films, arts exhibits, and sports events.

The Hotel Perla's **Nightclub La Cabaña** (Obregón 1570, tel. 612/122-0777, 9pm-3am daily) hosts *norteña* bands, usually on Thursday and Sunday.

On the *malecón,* sportfishing outfitter Jonathan Roldan runs the three-level **Tailhunter Bar & FUBAR Cantina** (Obregón 755 btwn. Salvatierra and Torre Iglesias, cell 612/125-3311, U.S. tel. 626/638-3383, toll-free U.S. tel. 877/825-8802, www.tailhunter-international.com, mains US$6-12). Watch your step on the spiral stairs as you climb up to find nine flat-screen TVs showing all the major sporting events. Battery-powered candles on the tables change colors throughout the night. Enjoy a margarita or cold beer on tap while you work out the details of your fishing trip. The kitchen will prepare and serve your

EXCURSIONS

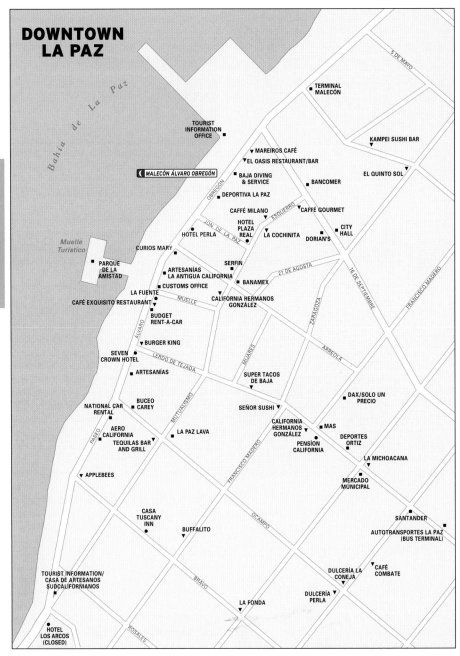

DOWNTOWN LA PAZ

Bahía de La Paz

TERMINAL MALECÓN

5 DE MAYO

TOURIST INFORMATION OFFICE

KAMPEI SUSHI BAR

▼ MAREIROS CAFÉ

▼ EL OASIS RESTAURANT/BAR

EL QUINTO SOL ▼

MALECÓN ÁLVARO OBREGÓN

■ BAJA DIVING & SERVICE

BANCOMER

OBREGÓN

■ DEPORTIVA LA PAZ

CAFFÉ MILANO ■

ESQUERRO

CAFFÉ GOURMET ■

HOTEL PLAZA REAL

CITY HALL ■

Muelle Turístico

JDN. DE LA PAZ

HOTEL PERLA ■

LA COCHINITA ■

DORIAN'S ■

CURIOS MARY ■

PARQUE DE LA AMISTAD

SERFIN ■

ARTESANÍAS LA ANTIGUA CALIFORNIA

21 DE AGOSTA

16 DE SEPTIEMBRE

FRANCISCO MADERO

■ CUSTOMS OFFICE

■ BANAMEX

LA FUENTE ■

MUELLE

CAFÉ EXQUISITO RESTAURANT ▼

CALIFORNIA HERMANOS GONZÁLEZ ■

ÁLVARO

BUDGET RENT-A-CAR ■

ZARAGOZA

▼ BURGER KING

SEVEN CROWN HOTEL ●

LERDO DE TEJADA

ARREOLA

■ ARTESANÍAS

MIJARES

SUPER TACOS DE BAJA ▼

BUCEO ● CAREY

NATIONAL CAR RENTAL ■

DAX/SOLO UN PRECIO ■

SEÑOR SUSHI ▼

MUTUALISMO

AERO CALIFORNIA

CALIFORNIA HERMANOS GONZÁLEZ ▼

■ MAS

PASEO

TEQUILAS BAR AND GRILL ▼

LA PAZ LAVA ■

PENSIÓN CALIFORNIA ●

DEPORTES ORTIZ ■

LA MICHOACANA ▼

▼ APPLEBEES

FRANCISCO MADERO

MERCADO MUNICIPAL ■

CASA TUSCANY INN ●

OCAMPO

SANTANDER ■

BUFFALITO ▼

AUTOTRANSPORTES LA PAZ (BUS TERMINAL) ■

TOURIST INFORMATION/ CASA DE ARTESANOS SUDCALIFORNIANOS ■

BRAVO

DULCERÍA LA CONEJA ▼

CAFÉ ● COMBATE

DULCERÍA ▼ PERLA

HOTEL LOS ARCOS (CLOSED) ●

ROSALES

LA FONDA ▼

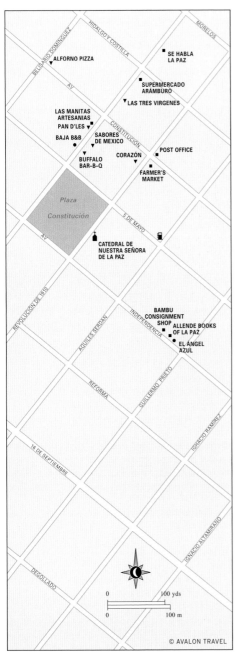

Map labels:
HIDALGO Y COSTILLA
MORELOS
BELISARIO DOMINGUEZ
ALFORNO PIZZA
SE HABLA LA PAZ
AV.
SUPERMERCADO ARÁMBURO
LAS TRES VIRGENES
LAS MANITAS ARTESANIAS
PAN D'LES
CONSTITUCIÓN
BAJA B&B
SABORES DE MEXICO
POST OFFICE
BUFFALO BAR-B-Q
CORAZÓN
FARMER'S MARKET
Plaza Constitución
5 DE MAYO
AV.
CATEDRAL DE NUESTRA SEÑORA DE LA PAZ
REVOLUCIÓN DE 1910
AQUILES SERDÁN
INDEPENDENCIA
BAMBU CONSIGNMENT SHOP
ALLENDE BOOKS OF LA PAZ
EL ÁNGEL AZUL
REFORMA
GUILLERMO PRIETO
IGNACIO RAMÍREZ
16 DE SEPTIEMBRE
IGNACIO ALTAMIRANO
DEGOLLADO
0   100 yds
0   100 m
© AVALON TRAVEL

fresh catch or vacuum-seal it to go. You can also order from a menu of traditional Mexican dishes with a Hawaiian flair. For example, the Hawaiian burger comes with teriyaki sauce, cheese, pineapple, mushrooms, lettuce, and tomato. Guacamole comes garnished with radicchio, and the teriyaki rice bowl (US$6.50) is a refreshing change from the standard Mexican meal.

Festivals and Events
CARNAVAL
La Paz is known throughout Mexico for its all-out celebration of Carnaval, a six-day festival held throughout the world in mid-February or early March on the days leading up to Ash Wednesday. Like Mardi Gras in New Orleans, Oktoberfest in Munich, or Burning Man in the Nevada desert, this is a destination event—something every traveler should consider experiencing at least once. There are daily parades along the *malecón,* brightly colored costumes, the crowning of a queen, amusement rides, fireworks, music, and food stands—with tequila and cerveza flowing freely all the while.

The Carnaval tradition came to Mexico from Spain and is believed to have evolved as the last chance for Christians to party before the fasting time of Lent. Some interpret the name Carnaval as deriving from the Latin *carne vale,* which means "farewell to meat."

FIESTA DE LA PAZ
The Fiesta de La Paz (officially known as Fiesta de la Fundación de la Ciudad de La Paz) takes place on May 3, the anniversary of the city's founding. Contact the **state tourism office** (tel. 612/124-0100, turismo@correro.gbcs. gob.mx), between kilometers 5 and 6 on the Carretera Transpeninsular (Avenida Abasolo), for festival venues and events.

BAJA 1000
The Baja 1000 off-road race comes to town in mid-November. Produced by **SCORE International** (U.S. tel. 818/225-8402, www. score-international.com), the event is the sixth and last in a series of desert races that take place

in the southwestern United States and Mexico each year. The Baja 1000 attracts more than 400 pro contestants who drive trucks, motorcycles, ATVs, and every imaginable variation of off-road vehicle. They start in Ensenada and cruise at breakneck speeds through the desert to the outskirts of La Paz. Only about half of the race entrants complete the challenging 1,000-mile (1,600-kilometer) course.

In its 46th year in 2013, the race draws thousands of support crew and spectators to the most remote parts of the peninsula. The course opens for pre-running approximately three weeks before the race start. Travelers on the Carretera Transpeninsular during this time will often see vehicles kicking up a cloud of dust in the distance, moving at speeds faster than highway drivers go. This is one of the few times a year you may encounter traffic on the more remote stretches of the Carretera Transpeninsular. Watch the 2005 documentary *Dust to Glory* for a fascinating inside look at the sport.

SHOPPING

La Paz serves as a vital commerce center for all of Southern Baja. Its many shops and department stores cater not only to local residents but also to those of towns as far away as Todos Santos and the East Cape. The result is a greater variety of items at competitive prices. Two large shopping centers were in the works at press time, which promise to bring high-end department stores and boutiques similar to the Puerto Paraíso mall in Cabo San Lucas.

Home Furnishings

One of 28 **Segusino** furniture stores (Álvaro Obregón 2140, Loc.1, tel. 612/125-1703, www. segusino.com) has opened in La Paz, selling beautiful contemporary and rustic Mexican furniture. With headquarters in Puebla on the mainland, the company advocates a fair trade approach in choosing its materials.

Art Galleries

La Paz has about 20 up-and-coming fine-art galleries, representing mostly contemporary

Mexican artists working in a variety of media and styles. Housed in a restored colonial building, **Galería Galería** (Revolución 590, at Juárez, tel. 612/125-6973, 9am-4pm Mon.-Sat.) is both a working studio for local artists and an interior design store. Attend a workshop or simply browse the shelves for the perfect something to accent your home. Next door is a new children's library. Both are reportedly funded by Christy Walton of Walmart.

Near the post office, **Galería de Arte Tonantzin** (Constitución 320 btwn. Serdán and Revolución, 10am-2pm and 5pm-8:30pm Mon.-Sat., cell 612/154-8136) has contemporary works from Latin American artists. Call or stop by for a schedule of music concerts.

Artesanías (Crafts)

Several tourist-oriented shops line the *malecón* between the bus terminal and the Applebee's. They sell handicrafts, T-shirts, jewelry, and postcards. **La Antigua California** (Obregón 220, tel. 612/125-5230) has a good selection of arts and crafts made primarily in mainland Mexico. **México Lindo** (Álvaro Obregón at 16 de Septiembre) is another option.

Next to Pan D'Les bakery, the baker's wife, Diane Carmona, has opened a gallery/gift shop called **Las Manitas ARTesanias** (Madero 1235 btwn. 5 de Mayo and Constitución, tel. 612/135-1539, lasmanitaslapaz@gmail.com, Mon.-Sat. 10am-2pm or by appointment). She carries some high-end museum-quality pieces created by the masters of Mexican handicrafts, as well as a selection of ceramics, apparel, artwork, and other keepsakes.

The government-run **Casa de Artesanos Sudcalifornianos** (Paseo Obregón at Bravo, tel. 612/125-8802), next to the Tourist Information/Tourist Police office and skate park, stocks *artesanías* from all over Southern Baja.

You can watch artists at work when you visit **Ibarra's Pottery** (Prieto 625 btwn. Iglesias and República, tel. 612/122-0404, 9am-3pm Mon.-Fri., 9am-2pm Sat.) The outdoor store contains several aisles of plates, mugs, pitchers, vases, pots, and the like—mostly in bold patterns

© NIKKI GOTH ITOI

patio dining at Las Tres Virgenes

and colorful designs. **Artesanía Cuauhtémoc** (Abasolo btwn. Jalisco and Nayarit, no tel.), in a white building near the Chedraui, has Oaxacan-style textiles, including rugs, blankets, and table linens.

Artesanías Colibri (Paseo Obregón btwn. Muelle and Arreola, tel. 612/128-5833, 10am-1pm and 3pm-8:30pm Mon.-Sat.) carries a good selection of *artesanías,* rustic furniture, and decorating accessories, plus cute clothes for babies and kids.

Bookstores

La Paz has a wonderful English-language bookstore, **Allende Books of La Paz** (Independencia 518, btwn. Serdan and Prieto, tel. 612/125-9114, www.allendebooks.com, 10am-6pm Mon.-Sat.). Open since 2007, it's located in the same historic building as El Ángel Azul bed-and-breakfast and carries maps, dictionaries, cookbooks, history books, and contemporary fiction. The store also holds occasional events such as book signings, children's story time, and book club meetings.

FOOD

La Paz has become a culinary destination of sorts, with outstanding meals to be found in every price category, from street-side tacos to fresh seafood and gourmet cuisine.

Mexican

A new generation of chefs up and down the peninsula is working hard to define a distinct identity for Baja regional cuisine, which centers around fresh seafood prepared with a Mediterranean influence. La Paz enjoyed its first such restaurant debut with the opening of 【 **Las Tres Virgenes** (Madero btwn. Constitución and Hidalgo, tel. 612/123-2226, 1pm-11pm Tues.-Sun., mains US$10-30) in 2006. Its name refers to three mountains, one of which is a dormant volcano, visible in the distance on the drive from San Ignacio to Santa Rosalía. Think tuna *tataki,* rose-petal quesadillas, roasted bone marrow, and damiana crème brûlée, and you'll have a good idea of what culinary delights the menu holds in store. Tables are arranged around a large garden patio. Wines are reasonably priced. In 2010 the chef/owner began serving a lunch menu from 1 to 4:45pm.

Corazón Café (formerly El Aljibe, Revolución 385 at Constitución, tel. 612/128-8985, 8am-11pm Mon.-Sat., mains US$15) specializes in *comida mexicana,* or traditional fare. The play chalkboard and kitchen in one corner of the restaurant provide entertainment for little ones. Sit indoors under open-sky seating or out in the courtyard. Walmart's Christy Walton, who lives in town, has provided funding for the business as well as the restoration of the small park across the street.

Seafood

Mariscos Los Laureles (Obregón s/n, corner of Salvatierra, tel. 612/128-8532, daily 10am-10pm, mains US$5-15) is a family-run gem on the *malecón.* The raw bar is piled high with all kinds of shellfish. Order the shrimp and scallop *aguachile* (ceviche in a watery, chile-based broth) or the fish ceviche

© LAUREN SWIFT

generous serving of *ceviche* at Mariscos Los Laureles

as a large starter or standalone lunch. Both were generously portioned and exceptionally fresh on a recent visit (US$12). The open-air ambience is cheerful and comfortable, with colorful seascape murals on the walls, bright yellow tablecloths, and heavy wooden chairs. Plates come with a green salad, potato salad, and side of Mexican rice. Kids can order from their own menu.

Long ago a well-kept secret, **Bismark II** (Degollado at Altamirano, tel. 612/122-4854, 8am-10pm daily, mains US$10-20) has become a mainstay within the local expat crowd. Lobster, abalone, and carne asada are its hallmark dishes, but the ceviche is also worth a try. On the *malecón,* Bismarkcito (Paseo Obregón, near Constitución, tel. 612/128-9900, lunch and dinner daily, mains US$10-15) is a waterfront offshoot of its parent restaurant and appeals more to visitors. The menu includes all manner of seafood cocktails, and fish and shellfish entrées; Peñafiel brand Mexican sodas are a treat.

The owners of Rancho Viejo have expanded with **Mariscos La Palapa** (Pineda at Obregón, tel. 612/126-1886, 7am-midnight daily, lunch/dinner mains US$8-20), a two-story restaurant that overlooks Marina de La Paz. Order ceviche or a seafood cocktail to start, followed by a plate of *arrachera* (skirt steak) tacos. Enjoy patio seating in the second-level bar, where a pitcher of margaritas costs US$35.

The secret to the tacos at **Taco Fish La Paz** (Márquez de León at Héroes de Independencia, 8:30am-4pm Tues.-Sun.) is a tempura batter. See if you can tell the difference.

Italian

Owned and run by an Italian-Chinese husband-and-wife team, **Caffé Milano** (Esquerro 15, btwn. Callejón de la Paz and 16 de Septiembre, tel. 612/125-9981, www.caffemilano.com.mx, 1pm-11pm Mon.-Sat., mains US$6-18) prepares traditional Italian fare such as fried oysters with caviar, homemade pasta, and *frutti di mare.* Homemade *limoncello* (a lemon liqueur) is a fitting way to end the meal. Look for the tall, light blue wooden doors.

Decorated in pastel colors and original artwork, **La Pazion de la Pazta** (Allende, adjacent to Hotel Mediterrané, tel. 612/125-1195, 7am-11pm Wed.-Mon., 7am-3pm Tues., mains US$10-15) prepares a mix of Italian and Swiss dishes, including pastas, pizzas, and fondues. Choose from an impressive list of wines from Italy, the United States, Chile, and Baja.

Two blocks from the *malecón*, **Il Rustico** (Revolución de 1910 btwn. Rosales and Bravo, tel. 612/157-7073, www.ilrusticolapazmx.com, 2pm-11pm Wed.-Sat. and Mon., 2pm-9pm Sun.) serves tasty thin-crust pizzas with creative toppings.

American

Near the plaza and across from Baja Bed and Breakfast, **Buffalo BAR-B-Q** (Madero 1420, tel. 612/128-8755, www.buffalolapaz.com, 6pm-midnight Mon.-Fri., 2pm-10pm Sat.-Sun., mains US$10-20) continues to earn praise from locals and visitors for its steaks and burgers, made of Angus and Sonora beef. Owner Carlos Valdez is passionate about wine, and the restaurant's wine list shows it. But by the end of his first year in business, Carlos's little brother had proved with **Buffalito Grill** (Madero btwn. Ocampo and Nicholas Bravo, tel. 612/140-1142, buffalitogrill@gmail.com, 2pm-11pm Tues.-Sun., 6pm-11pm Mon.) that he has the chops to live up to his older brother's establishment. Locals now rave about the little brother's fries, juicy burgers, and casual ambience.

Organic

Owner/chef Chiara Abente is leading the local organic food scene with **Sabores de México** (Madero 389, btwn. 5 de Mayo and Constitución, tel. 612/122-1192, www.sabores-demexico.mx). She keeps a small retail store open in La Paz for loyal customers but is extremely busy fulfilling orders for Walmart and other supermarkets throughout the country. You can pick up a picnic to go, order gluten-free pizza to eat at the tables outside, or buy a few gifts to bring home. The possibilities include squid ink pasta, chipotle sea salt harvested from

San Juan de Los Planes, homemade jams, and honey from nearby San Antonio.

El Quinto Sol (Domínguez and Independencia, tel./fax 612/122-1692) prepares vegetarian *tortas* (Mexican sandwiches), *comida corrida* (fixed-price lunch), pastries, salads, granola, fruit and vegetable juices, and yogurt. You can also stock up on healthy foods in the attached store.

Antojitos and Fast Food

It's easy to find **Rancho Viejo** (Legaspy, a half block from the Marina de La Paz, tel. 612/128-4647, 24 hours daily, dinner mains US$12-17) from the smell of the grill wafting up the street. Sit at a picnic table on the sidewalk or in either of two dining rooms inside to get away from the smoke. *Tacos de arrachera* (skirt steak), carne asada, or *al pastor* (marinated pork) arrive with the usual tray of fresh condiments. You can also order by the kilo. Service is prompt and friendly, and you can't beat the prices. Rancho Viejo has expanded to include a new space next door and has also opened a satellite location on the *malecón,* near the Thrifty Ice Cream shop. Instead of staying open 'round the clock, this one closes at 3am-4am.

Street vendors open in the afternoons around the plaza and along Calle 16 de Septiembre. They typically sell hot dogs, tacos, stuffed baked potatoes *(papas rellenas),* burgers, and seafood cocktails.

Cafés

The espresso business is booming in La Paz. Several chains now have multiple locations, and new ones seem to open every month. Starbucks look-alike **5th Avenida Coffee** has wireless Internet in various locations, including 5 de Mayo on the plaza and Avenida Abasolo near the Marina de La Paz. **Café Exquisito** has a *malecón* location with sidewalk tables (Paseo Obregón, south of La Fuente, 6:30am-11:30pm Mon.-Sat., 8am-11pm Sun., drinks US$1-3), plus two drive-through espresso stands north and south of town on the Carretera Transpeninsular and one more at the airport.

Café Combate has at least two locations in town: Serdán between Calles Ocampo and Degollado, and on Calle Bravo at the southeast entrance to Mercado Bravo.

Aside from these chains, air-conditioned **Caffé Gourmet** (Esquerro and 16 de Septiembre, tel. 612/122-6037, 8am-10pm Mon.-Sat.) has a counter full of sweets to go with your coffee, plus a selection of smoothies, Italian sodas, cigars, and liquors. Breakfast is served until 3pm. There is a nonsmoking section in the back and a newer second location on the *malecón*.

Groceries

Vendors in the **Mercado Municipal Francisco E. Madero** (Revolución de 1910 at Degollado) sell fresh fish, meats, fruit, vegetables, and baked goods, and there is a *tortillería* at the corner of Revolución de 1910 and Bravo.

La Paz has two large **Chedraui** (formerly Centro Comercial California/CCC) stores (Abasolo at Colima s/n, tel. 612/146-2263, Isabel La Católica 1915 at Bravo, tel. 612/129-3810). They stock U.S. and Mexican brands, but prices are relatively high. **Supermercado Arámburo** also has three branches in town: 16 de Septiembre at Altamirano, Madero at Hidalgo y Costilla (tel. 612/122-1599), and Durango 130 Sur (btwn. Ocampo and Degollado), plus another on Boulevard Forjadores at Cuauhtémoc (tel. 612/123-9210).

For big-box stores with groceries and more, head to **Plaza Ley** on the eastern edge of town (Las Garzas at Teotihuacán), **Walmart** (Lázaro Cárdenas 2200, tel. 686/568-0579), or **Soriana** (Forjadores de Sudcalifornia at Luis Donaldo Colosio s/n, tel. 612/121-4771) and **City Club** (Forjadores de Sudcalifornia at Luis Donaldo Colosio s/n, tel. 612/165-4990), which are in a shopping plaza on Boulevard Forjadores at the corner of Luis Donaldo Colosio. Comercial Mexicana opened a Mega supermarket in the Punto La Paz shopping center on Abasolo in 2011.

Sabores de México (Madero btwn. Constitución and 5 de Mayo, tel. 612/122-1231 www.saboresdemexico.mx) specializes in organic foods made only in Mexico, such as pure vanilla extract, sea salt, olive oil, and the like.

On Tuesday and Saturday a recently established **farmers market** takes place 9:30am-noon in the small park at the corner of Constitución and Revolución, across from the post office and Corazón Café. Enjoy fresh produce and organic foods at the twice-weekly local food fest. In addition to seasonal fruits and veggies from El Pescadero, you can find fresh mozzarella, eggs, young chickens, jams, shrimp, and flavored sea salts (without the added fluoride and iodine).

Breads and Sweets

A day in La Paz isn't complete without an icy treat, and the downtown area has lots of options for *nieves* (Mexican-style ice cream), *paletas* (popsicles), and the like. **La Michoacana** (no tel.) is a chain with branches on Paseo Obregón and Calle Madero. But the most popular stand in town by far is ◖ **La Fuente** (Paseo Obregón

Pan D'Les Bakery

btwn. Degollado and Muelle, no tel.), known for its long list of flavors, some of which are quite unusual. Look for a polka-dot tree in front of the entrance.

Run by an accomplished pastry chef from California known in La Paz as "the bread guy," **Pan D'Les Bakery** (Madero btwn. Ocampo and Degollado, tel. 612/119-8392, loaves US$3 and other treats US$1-2 each) combines domestically sourced flours, yeast, salt from the Sea of Cortez, and local water to make handcrafted artisan breads that reflect the colonization period in Mexico's history. Each day of the week brings a different special loaf (US$3 each)—rustica and ciabatta on Monday, multigrain and sourdough on Tuesday, and so on. For a sugar fix, order muffins, cookies, scones, cinnamon buns, and other irresistible treats.

ACCOMMODATIONS

In general, rooms in La Paz are more affordable than their counterparts in Los Cabos, but they aren't the same bargains you might have found a decade ago. There are hotels in all budget categories, many with kitchenettes, plus bed-and-breakfasts, condo complexes, and private vacation rental homes. Rates do not include tax or service fees, but many places offer discounts for stays of a week or longer.

Despite the planned construction of several large luxury hotels, most rooms in La Paz still fall in the US$50-125 range. Some of the older establishments could use a makeover, but the time warp is also part of their charm. You'll pay a bit more to stay right on the water rather than along the *malecón*. And none of the bay-front hotels are within easy walking distance of the *malecón* or downtown La Paz, although taxis are always available.

Most times of year, you can wing it and find a room when you arrive. But if you plan to visit during mid-November, check the Baja 1000 event schedule and make reservations well in advance.

Under US$100

Above the Mar y Aventuras offices and adventure center is ◖ **Hotel Posada Luna Sol**

(Topete 564, btwn. 5 de Febrero and Navarro, tel. 612/122-7039, www.posadalunasol.com, US$65-75). Eco-minded travelers gravitate to 14 authentically Baja rooms, all with local TV, air-conditioning, private baths, and hot water; some also have bay views. Brew your own coffee in the communal kitchen any time of day, and enjoy a sunset cocktail under the rooftop *palapa*. In recent years, the property has added a new top-floor suite and a room with a small kitchen. Rates include tax. The location is a short walk to the start of the *malecón*.

The historic **Hotel Perla** (Paseo Obregón 1570, tel. 612/122-0777, toll-free Mex. tel. 800/716-8799, toll-free U.S. tel. 888/242-3757, www.hotelperlabaja.com, US$75-100) has been hosting foreign and domestic visitors since 1940. The building and 110 guest rooms (28 with bay views) have been well cared for over the years, but the overall impression is more business hotel than vacation destination. And rates seem to be climbing without substantial renovations in recent years. Rooms are small but very clean; decor is minimal, which means noise carries in hallways. High ceilings at least create the illusion of more space. Amenities include air-conditioning, TVs, Wi-Fi, and phones. A small pool on the mezzanine level may not be heated in winter months; the rooftop playground entertains young kids.

You can't beat the Perla's location right in the middle of the action on the *malecón*. In fact, the hotel's La Terraza restaurant is a great place to grab breakfast or lunch and watch the city life stream by. Bottom line: Stay here if a central, waterfront location and secure indoor parking are important and the price is acceptable.

Under Swiss ownership, ◖ **Hotel Mediterrané** (Allende 36, tel./fax 612/125-1195, www.hotelmed.com, US$65-95) has nine immaculate rooms in a blue and white stucco building just steps from the *malecón*. In keeping with the Mediterranean theme, its large and pleasant guest rooms are named for the various Greek islands. They come with air-conditioning, refrigerators, and TVs; some have bay views, but these are also the closest to the street and pick up a little more noise than those at the back of the hotel. A rooftop sundeck with lounge chairs invites visitors to catch a breeze and enjoy the bay views. The owners have loaner kayaks, canoes, and bikes available. **Restaurant La Pazion** (4pm-11pm Wed.-Mon., mains US$10-20) and the **Hotel Mediterrané Café** are downstairs; the café opens at 7am daily and has wireless Internet.

At the northeast end of the *malecón,* on the way to Pichilingue, the **Club El Moro** (Carr. a Pichilingue km 2, tel./fax 612/122-4084, www.clubelmoro.com, US$80-130) is a popular choice for families and travelers planning to take the ferry across to Mázatlan. A Moorish design and nicely landscaped pool and bar area are highlights of the property. Both rooms and suites come with air-conditioning, satellite TV with HBO, reliable wireless Internet, and a private terrace. Standard rooms are a little small for the price, but at US$120, the large junior suites are a great value. There is off-street and gated parking. The adjoining **Café Gourmet** serves great espresso as well as breakfast and lunch every day. Hotel guests receive free coffee and a coupon for US$2.50 per day. Friendly staff and an attractive frequent-guest program bring repeat visitors back year after year. You can easily catch a city bus during daylight hours to cover the two kilometers to the downtown area. In the evening, you'll have to walk or take a cab.

US$100-200

La Concha Beach Resort and Condos (Carr. a Pichilingue km 5, tel. 612/121-6160, toll-free Mex. tel. 800/716-8603, toll-free U.S. tel. 800/999-2252, www.laconcha.com, US$115) has the closest beachfront location to town, but the beach itself is much less attractive than those found farther out along the Pichilingue Peninsula, and the accommodations are in need of some serious attention. There are hotel rooms as well as condos with lovely bay views, and there have been some improvements such as new air-conditioners in some units; however, for the most part, the property is run-down. Part of the new 500-acre **CostaBaja Resort**

& Marina (www.costabajaresort.com), the **Fiesta Inn La Paz** (Carr. a Pichilingue km 7.5, tel. 612/123-6000, www.fiestainn.com, US$85-145) is popular with families as well as boaters, who can anchor at the on-site marina. The resort has 120 guest rooms, including some that are wheelchair accessible; amenities include wireless Internet and a separate lap-swimming lane in addition to the main pool. The location far from town and near an oil refinery may disappoint some travelers. To find the hotel, look for a signed entrance on a rise on the seaside of the road to Pichilingue.

Over US$200

Some of the classiest accommodations in town are found at the ◖ **Posada de las Flores** (Paseo Obregón 440 btwn. Militar and Guerrero, tel. 612/122-7463, www.posadadelasflores.com, US$150-290). With its signature coral-colored building and beautiful landscaping, this property looks out on the bay from the west side of the *malecón.* Rooms are designed in a rustic Mexican style, with tile floors and marble baths. Amenities include air-conditioning, wireless Internet, cable TV, and small refrigerators. Guests can also rent a larger *casa* next door. Bikes and kayaks are complimentary, and rates include breakfast. Posada de las Flores also has sister properties in Loreto and Punta Chivato.

Bed-and-Breakfasts

If you like cozier accommodations and the opportunity to socialize with your host, bed-and-breakfast-style accommodations can be a wonderful way to meet Mexican and expat families during your stay in La Paz.

In ◖ **El Ángel Azul** (Independencia 518, tel./fax 612/125-5130, www.elangelazul.com, US$100-165), Esther Ammann has converted an abandoned 19th-century courthouse into a modern-day bed-and-breakfast, with guidance from the National Institute of Anthropology and History (INAH). The result is a living piece of La Paz history with a contemporary flair. Nine rooms and one suite are arranged around a lush and private courtyard garden.

EXCURSIONS

© LAUREN SWIFT

El Ángel Azul is a historic bed-and-breakfast in La Paz.

Brightly colored rooms have queen or twin beds, private baths with showers, air-conditioning, and a radio. Locally created artwork adds to the ambience in common areas. The inn creates an ideal setting to relax and gather your thoughts after a busy day of outdoor or city activities. A multicourse breakfast begins each day with freshly squeezed juice and strong coffee. The adjoining consignment boutique, also run by Esther, has become a gathering place for style-savvy women in town.

Casa Tuscany Bed and Breakfast (Bravo 110A, tel. 612/128-8103, www.tuscanybaja.com, US$85-145, tax included) has a new proprietor, Carol Dyer. Four colorful guest rooms overlook a garden courtyard behind the main house. Each room has a comfortable queen bed, private bath, ceiling fan, and remote-control air-conditioning. Prices include tax and full hot breakfast that varies each day. The new owner has remodeled one room, the Firenze Suite. Two dedicated parking spots in front of the inn are not enclosed.

INFORMATION AND SERVICES
Tourist Assistance

Baja California Sur's state tourism office, **Fideicomiso de Turismo Estatal de BCS** (Carr. Transpeninsular km 5.5, tel. 612/124-0100, www.explorebajasur.com, 8am-8pm Mon.-Fri.) is a few kilometers north of downtown on the Carretera Transpeninsular (Abasolo), opposite the Grand Plaza Resort. Also here is the Attorney for the Protection of Tourists. More convenient is the **information booth** on the *malecón,* near the Applebee's, which has maps and brochures (Paseo Obregón at Allende, 8am-8pm Mon.-Fri.).

Banks

Unlike in the Los Cabos area, you will need pesos for making cash purchases at many businesses in La Paz. Three banks with ATMs are clustered near the intersection of Calle 16 de Septiembre and the *malecón.* They provide currency-exchange service 9am-noon

Monday-Friday. If you need to exchange money in the afternoon or on a Saturday and you can't use an ATM, **Tony Money Exchange** (Mutualismo, near La Perla, and nearby on 16 de Septiembre near the *malecón,* 9am-9pm Mon.-Sat.) usually has acceptable rates. On Sundays the larger hotels are the only option.

Postal Services

The main **La Paz post office** is at the intersection of Revolución de 1910 and Constitución, one block northeast of the cathedral. It's open 8am-3pm Monday-Friday, 9am-1pm Saturday. **DHL** (Abasolo at Nayarit, tel. 612/122-8282) offers domestic and international shipping.

Internet

Most hotels and cafés now offer high-speed wireless Internet access for free. The **5th Avenida Coffee** and **Café Exquisito** chains offer wireless access, as do most of the marinas. Hotels with wireless connections include the **Mediterrané, Fiesta Inn, Seven Crown, El Moro,** and **Posada de las Flores.** Air-conditioned **Hotel Mediterrané Café** (Allende 36, tel. 612/125-1195, 7am-11pm daily) has a desktop computer set up for customer use; wireless access is free if you bring your own computer.

Immigration

La Paz has an **immigration office** on Paseo Obregón between Allende and Juárez (tel. 612/125-3493, 8am-8:30pm daily). Another immigration office at the airport also is open daily, and a third office, at the Pichilingue ferry terminal, opens about an hour before each ferry departure.

Emergency Services

La Paz has two hospitals: **Hospital Fidepaz** (Carr. Transpeninsular km 5.5, tel. 612/124-0400), on the Transpeninsular Highway near the tourist office, and **Hospital Juan María de Salvatierra** (tel. 612/175-0503), off Boulevard Forjedores. Dial 066 for emergencies and call 612/122-5939 for information and the tourist police.

GETTING THERE AND AROUND

La Paz is a bit far from Los Cabos for a day trip. It takes about two hours to get there from Cabo San Lucas on Highway 19 and up to four hours from San José del Cabo on the Carretera Transpeninsular via Los Barriles. It's best to plan this as an overnight excursion. Allow two to three days to explore the city and surrounding beaches—a week or more if you plan to fish, snorkel, dive, or kayak around the islands just offshore. If you're coming to learn Spanish, local schools recommend a minimum stay of two weeks and up to a month if you can swing it. Travelers planning to take the ferry to Mazatlán should allow an extra day or two to arrange permits and reservations.

February is La Paz's busiest month for tourists. But even then, hotel rooms are usually easy to find. One exception is when the Baja 1000 off-road race comes to town in mid-November. With the race finish just outside the city limits, every room, condo, and vacation rental books up months in advance. If you roll into La Paz without reservations, you'll likely have to continue south to Los Barriles to find a place to crash for the night.

Getting Around

Except on the hottest of days, downtown La Paz is best explored on foot. Narrow one-way streets filled with people and vehicles can be intimidating to navigate for the first-time visitor, but if you stick to the perimeter streets—Avenida Abasolo, Paseo Obregón, Boulevard Forjadores, etc.—it's fairly easy to get around by car as well. City buses and taxis are readily available, too.

If you are driving into La Paz from the south and want to head directly to the Pichilingue Peninsula and the ferry terminal, you can take a shortcut just after the university on Boulevard Forjadores. Look for a sign for *Libramiento Norte* heading off to the right. If you get to Soriana and Office Depot, you've missed the turn and it's best to continue on into the city and make your way to the waterfront.

BY BUS

Municipal buses and *colectivo* shuttles congregate around the Mercado Municipal on Calle Degollado and head out in all directions from there. Routes may be indicated by the name of the street the bus will follow (e.g., G. Prieto) or the district to which it is heading (e.g., El Centro). To get to the Soriana mall on Boulevard Forjadores, look for buses labeled Soriana.

Frequent Aguila buses connect the downtown area to the Pichilingue Peninsula. Catch them at the **Terminal Malecón** (Paseo Obregón 125, tel. 612/122-7898). Buses to Playa Balandra and Playa El Tecolote depart at noon and 2pm on weekends only.

BY TAXI

Taxis are easily found along the west end of Calle 16 de Septiembre and in front of the La Perla hotel. Fare for rides within the downtown area should be under US$5, about US$5 to Soriana, US$15 to the airport, and US$20 to the ferry terminal. There are no meters, so be sure to agree on a price before you hop in.

BY CAR

A handful of international car rental agencies have airport and downtown locations in La Paz. Rates start around US$25 per day for unlimited kilometers, not including tax and insurance.

La Paz has numerous Pemex stations, all selling *magna sin* (unleaded), premium, and diesel.

Construction is under way to widen Highway 19 to a four-lane highway connecting La Paz and Cabo San Lucas. So far, the entire stretch between La Paz and Todos Santos is complete. On the other side of the city, the government is working on another stretch of highway, to create a four-lane bypass around La Paz, from El Centenario to the Carretera Transpeninsular south and on to Highway 19.

Bahía de la Ventana and Bahía de los Muertos

Two scenic bays southeast of La Paz—Bahía de la Ventana and Bahía de los Muertos—are joined to the city via paved BCS 286, which departs the Carretera Transpeninsular at kilometer 211 and extends 43 kilometers to the farming town of San Juan de los Planes. In between, the peaks of the Sierra de la Laguna range rise to more than 1,200 meters. (The mountains here are also called the Sierra de las Cruces on the north side of the highway and the Sierra el Novillo and Sierra la Trinchera on the south side.) The descent affords stunning views of the sea and Isla Cerralvo just 16 kilometers (10 miles) offshore.

Combine the culture and history of La Paz with a more rustic outdoor experience along one of these bays and you have a near-perfect Baja itinerary.

In winter green sea turtles nest along the bay, and lucky visitors might catch the hatch on a full moon. Leatherback turtles nest later in the spring. Nesting areas are marked with hand-painted signs that give a zone number and read *Cuida Los Nidos* (Protect the Nests). Nests are marked with tape. Needless to say, do not disturb them.

BEACHES
Bahía de la Ventana

Once a pair of quiet fishing villages, Bahía de la Ventana and neighboring El Sargento were discovered by windsurfers in the 1990s and kiteboarders soon after. In winter months when the powerful El Norte winds blow through the narrow Canal de Cerralvo, sailboards fill the bay—as well as the campgrounds that surround it.

Other times of year, the towns attract scuba divers/free divers, beachgoers, and sportfishing enthusiasts.

BAHÍA DE LA VENTANA

LIGHTHOUSE

El Sargento

Punta Arena de la Ventana

La Ventana

LIGHTHOUSE

SEE "LA VENTANA AND EL SARGENTO" MAP

266

San Juán de los Planes

Bahia de los Muertos

0   2 mi

0   2 km

To El Triunfo

© AVALON TRAVEL

Though it's still relatively undeveloped compared to nearby La Paz or the Los Cabos corridor, the word is out on La Ventana; the area has been experiencing a real estate boom for the last few years, with dozens of properties for sale and many new buildings taking shape each year.

Expats here support the local community through annual fundraising contests, English-language instruction, and other events. The result is an integrated community that gives a warm welcome to its visitors.

Isla Cerralvo

Less than 16 kilometers offshore from Bahía de la Ventana is Isla Cerralvo, one of the largest islands in the gulf and once a key destination in the historic pearl-oyster trade. Few travelers make their way out to this island because it is a long boat ride from the charters in La Paz and the whole land mass is privately owned, but it has several good dive and sportfishing sites around its shores. Scuba divers can explore rock reefs, coves, and wrecks. Presently, Palapas Ventana (www.palapasvenana.com) is the only PADI-certified dive operation in La Ventana and leads trips to Cerralvo when conditions are favorable. Along the way, you might see

spinner dolphins, sea lions, humpback whales, and more.

Bahía de los Muertos

BCS 286 ends at Los Planes, but if you follow the graded road that continues east, you'll end up at the Bay of the Dead. The dark name of this pretty bay dates back to the 18th century, but its exact origins are unknown. At least two later incidents in history validated the name: In 1885 a Chinese ship landed and lost a crew of 18 to yellow fever after port authorities in La Paz refused to admit the ship. And in the early 1900s, when a group of farmers from the United States attempted to cultivate the land around the bay, the effort for some ended in starvation. Another possible explanation is that an El Triunfo Mining company named the bay after burying train axles underwater to provide moorings for its barges.

Long-abandoned Ensenada de los Muertos dates back to the 1920s, when it was used for transporting ore from mines in the Sierra de la Laguna.

Panga boats still line the shore, but the bay is changing little by little each year as a massive luxury real estate development takes shape to the south.

Bahía de los Sueños

When complete, the Bahía de los Sueños (Bay of Dreams, toll-free U.S. tel. 866/202-0789) project is supposed to encompass 1,700 hectares with an 18-hole golf course designed by Tom Doak, 432 homes, and 192 villas and condos. Inside the Bay of Dreams development, Gran Sueños (www.gransueno.com) sits on 25 landscaped acres with tennis courts, a nine-hole golf course, multiple swimming pools, a fitness facility, and a long list of luxury amenities—including an on-site chef service and concierge. Its seven villas have king-size beds, rain showers, Viking barbecues, satellite TV, wireless Internet, private or shared pool and spa, and complimentary Internet calling to the United States. One-bedroom villas range US$350-750 per night; two-bedrooms are US$650-1,050 per night.

shore of Isla Cerralvo

EXCURSIONS

WATER SPORTS

Though the area is best known for wind sports, there is an activity for just about every weather condition: Calm seas mean short boat rides and good visibility for snorkeling or diving; windy days are good for sails—or a hike. Big swells are an excuse to head to the Pacific side to catch some waves.

Windsurfing and Kiteboarding

Windsurfers discovered the ideal conditions at La Ventana in the 1990s, but in recent years, the rising popularity of kiteboarding has brought many more adventure-seeking travelers to the area. Kiteboarders say La Ventana is one of the best places in the world to learn the sport, because the shoreline of the bay curves around to catch those who drift downwind on white-sand beaches. Experienced windsurfers say the wind at La Ventana isn't as strong as at Los Barriles but it tends to be more consistent. The wind typically picks up around 11am and holds steady until just before sunset.

Several schools certified by the International Kiteboarding Organization (IKO) rent gear and offer lessons for windsurfing and kiteboarding. (They'll also come get you if you have trouble staying upwind.) Radio-assisted lessons are a great way to get minute-by-minute coaching. The student wears a waterproof helmet system, and the instructor gives directions from the shore. Watercraft-assisted lessons are another option for beginners. "Downwinders," offered by many of the schools, eliminate the need to worry about staying upwind. Take a shuttle ride to the north end of the bay and enjoy a two-hour sail back to camp.

One of the first to set up shop in the early 1990s was **Captain Kirk's Windsurfing** (U.S. tel. 310/833-3397, www.captainkirks.com), with headquarters in San Pedro, California. The shop also rents several vacation homes, ranging US$60-300 per night. For example, options include a two-bedroom home with kitchen (US$275/night) and a *casita* with two double beds and bath (US$160/night). Rentals come with free use of mountain bikes, sea kayaks, and snorkeling equipment.

Breakfast is included. A windsurfing or kiteboarding gear package is US$65 per person per day. Other activities include stand-up paddling and yoga.

With headquarters in Hood River, Oregon, the **New Wind Kite School** (U.S. tel. 541/387-2440, www.newwindkiteboarding.com, Nov. 15-Mar. 15) offers lessons for new and experienced kiteboarders (US$216-280/day, depending on the number of students; US$85 for a 1.5-hr session). Custom instruction runs US$89 per hour for one person, with a two-hour minimum. Board rentals cost US$39 per day, kite-only rentals are US$70 per day, kite and bar rentals are US$89 per day, and a full setup goes for US$119 per day. This school also has a beach house next door, Casa del Sol (beachfront suite US$150/night, courtyard room US$105/night, rates include tax). Store your gear and use the air compressor to inflate your kite for free.

British Columbia-based **Elevation Kiteboarding School** (Canada tel. 604/848-5197, www.elevationkiteboarding.com) offers private lessons for CDN$115 per hour (two-hour minimum), a full day (about four hours) for CDN$325 per person, and multiday kiteboarding camp packages. The school is located at Baja Joe's Resort. Sheldon Kiteboarding (U.S. tel. 707/374-3053, www.sheldonkiteboarding.com) maintains summer headquarters in Rio Vista, California, and winter headquarters at La Ventana. Owner Bruce provides beds and mattresses for camping, plus a shared kitchen, and bath with a hot-water shower. Bring your own sleeping bag. Bruce offers lessons, equipment, and repairs.

Baja Adventures at Ventana Bay Resort (tel. 612/114-0222, www.ventanabaykiteboarding.com) is a full-service operation that provides equipment rentals and lessons. It replaces its rental gear each season, selling the previous year's equipment at reduced prices. Kiteboarding equipment is the latest lines from North Kites. You can also rent K2 full-suspension mountain bikes from the shop.

South of the campground, **Kitemasters** (www.kitemasters.com) offers six hours of lessons for US$600 or US$85/hour. Student use radio helmets and NAISH gear.

New in winter 2010, **Playa Central** (www.laventanakiteboarding.net) aims to create a much-needed gathering place for the kiteboarding community. Run by the twentysomething children of a Mexican family from Cozumel, the business occupies a former shrimp factory near the arroyo in La Ventana. A small patch of grass in front of the yellow building makes it easier to pump up and wrap kites.

Snorkeling, Scuba Diving, and Spearfishing

Palapas Ventana (tel. 612/114-0198, www.palapasventana.com) has a certified PADI dive shop on-site that leads guided trips to Isla Cerralvo year-round. The 26-foot super-*panga* has a four-stroke engine and takes up to six divers per trip. Trips cost US$125 for a two-tank dive, including all gear and lunch. Snorkelers pay US$50, including all gear and lunch. Boats depart at 7:45am and return at 3pm. Scuba certification packages are available (six days/five nights for US$679 pp, min. three people). Captain Tavo is a shark fisherman and dive instructor. Several of the windsurfing and kiteboarding resorts dabble in scuba trips as well.

The small reef in La Ventana Bay provides a good introduction to the underwater life in the area. Watch for urchins during entry/exit and keep an eye out for the local frogfish on the reef. The best snorkeling from shore is at Las Arenas reef, a 20-minute drive. Follow BCS 286 east through Los Planes and turn left at the airstrip, before you reach Bahía de los Muertos. Follow this road less than two kilometers, past several guard stations, until you reach an abandoned hotel at the coast.

For a more adventurous day of snorkeling, accompany researchers on a day of whale-shark observation in La Paz Bay (US$75 pp). Boats depart from the Costa Baja Marina near Pichilingue, north of La Paz. The drive along BCS 286 and the bypass around La Paz takes about 45 minutes from La Ventana. Palapas Ventana can arrange your trip.

For those who want to catch their dinner,

Palapas Ventana offers spearfishing instruction and guided trips. Students learn to identify edible fish and test their aim on an underwater target (US$50 pp from shore, US$85 pp by *panga*).

Stand-Up Paddling

Stand-up paddling has come to La Ventana, and you can rent or borrow gear at several shops along the bay, including **Captain Kirk's, Casa Verde,** and **Palapas Ventana,** where rentals cost US$10 per hour or US$30 all day. Guided tours cost US$40 for three hours.

Fishing

The waters surrounding Isla Cerralvo, Bahía La Ventana, Punta Arena de la Ventana, and Bahía de los Muertos offer more consistent fishing than Bahía de La Paz and the islands near the city. Many charters will drive BCS 286 from La Paz and launch at Punta Arena or Los Muertos, rather than traveling by boat across the choppy water. The Canal de Cerralvo is known for roosterfish and *pargo colorado* January-July and for marlin and dorado in the summer months. It is also a world-class spearfishing destination. The 88 bank area off Cerralvo is known for marlin, dorado, and yellowfin tuna.

Sportfishing with Lalo (tel. 612/114-0335, cell 612/151-9921, www.fishlalo.com) offers fly-fishing, live bait, and trolling services. Run by Captain Nono, **HOOKUP** offers trips aboard a 22-foot (US$250) or 26-foot *panga* (US$300). Boats depart at 6:30am and return at 3pm, or earlier upon request. Contact Palapas Ventana (tel. 612/114-0198, www.palapasventana.com) for reservations.

You can launch small boats easily from the beaches at Bahía de la Ventana, Punta Arena, and Bahía de los Muertos. Fishing licenses cost US$15 per day.

EVENTS

The **La Ventana Classic** is a fundraising kiteboarding race held in January every year. Participants start at Isla Cerralvo and finish on the shore of Bahía de la Ventana. Proceeds are donated to the town for schools and other

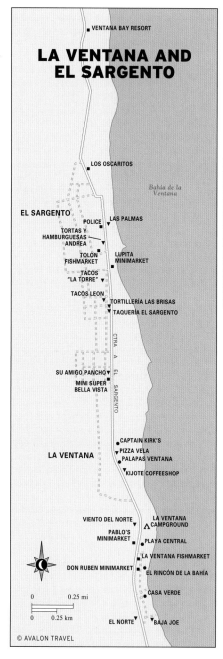

LA VENTANA AND EL SARGENTO

EXCURSIONS

© AVALON TRAVEL

community needs. Contact **Palapas Ventana** (tel. 612/114-0198, www.palapasventana.com) for information.

La Ventana and El Sargento celebrate their annual town festival in late October with three days of live music, carnival rides, and street food.

FOOD
La Ventana
Each winter season brings a new wave of eateries to these sleepy bayside towns. Expect to find several small minisupers (no supermarkets), a few traditional Mexican restaurants, several newer gringo establishments, a number of *taquerías* (casual taco restaurants), and a *tortillería* (on the paved part of the road in El Sargento). Prices are generally low, and the atmosphere is casual. If you plan to cook most of your own meals, stock up on supplies in La Paz.

Playa Central (www.laventanakiteboarding.net) is a gathering place for the kiteboarding community, but it also has a bakery and pizzeria. The not-yet-renovated interior of the warehouse is large enough to host music events during the high season.

On the way to El Sargento, before the pavement ends, **El Amigo Pancho** (no tel., 8am-10pm daily, breakfast mains US$2-5, dinner mains US$4-7) is one of a few eateries that stay open late. Follow the smell of meat sizzling on the grill to a simple *palapa* structure next to Minisuper Belle, where you can order Mexican specialties, including chicken mole, burgers, enchiladas, and fish prepared various ways, such as *al mojo de ajo* (in garlic sauce), *a la veracruzana* (Veracruz style), or *al diablo* (spicy). During breakfast hours, the restaurant offers *licuados* (fruit smoothies), *chilaquiles* (salsa or mole over crisp tortilla triangles), and various egg dishes.

About 200 meters south of the public campground, **Rincón del Bahía** (no tel., hours vary, mains US$7-13) serves tasty seafood and Mexican fare on the beach. Owner Joaquin will serenade you while you dine. The stuffed fish with shrimp has been popular since the restaurant opened in the 1990s. Just south of Palapas

Ventana, **Tacos Rafa** (no tel., hours vary) grills fish tacos for US$6-13. The restaurant at **Palapas Ventana** (tel. 612/114-0198, www.palapasventana.com, breakfast and lunch daily, plus dinner Fri.-Sat. and live music in winter, mains US$8-13) prepares lasagna, steaks, barbecued ribs, fresh grilled fish (all of it caught by the staff themselves). Try the coconut wahoo. Enjoy local wines, an icy margarita, or a Negra Modelo on tap (the only draft beer available in La Ventana) with your meal. Reservations are recommended.

Look for **Tacos en la Torre** ("Tower Tacos," no tel., hours vary, mains US$4-7) at the base of the radio tower in El Sargento, with a menu of *chilaquiles* (salsa or mole over crisp tortilla triangles), *tortas cubanas* (extra-stuffed sandwiches), and *flautas* (fried, stuffed, and rolled tortillas). On the west side of the road in El Sargento, behind Mini Super Corona, Tacos Leon (no tel., hours vary) has hot dogs, *papas rellenas* (stuffed potatoes), and enchiladas for US$4-10. Long a favorite among campers, Viento del Norte (mains US$4-9) serves hearty breakfasts, enchiladas, and jumbo margaritas.

In a yellow two-story building on the beach, **Las Palmas** (no tel., 8am-10pm daily, dinner mains US$5-8) prepares omelets, *flautas* (fried, stuffed, and rolled tortillas), *machaca* (dried beef), and espresso drinks for breakfast and a menu of enchiladas, tacos, *mariscos,* and pastas for lunch and dinner. The fish tacos, made of freshly caught cabrilla, come with an exceptionally fresh medley of avocado, lettuce, cucumber and tomato. There are tables on both levels. Head upstairs for the bar and the best views. The restaurant is located at the end of the pavement, about a kilometer or so past La Ventana and across from the police station.

Pizza Vela (500 meters north of Palapas Ventana on the beach side of the road, no tel., hours vary, mains US$5-15) offers an alternative to Mexican fare; you can order a fresh salad and a glass of wine to go with your pie. Wine bottles are stored in a wine refrigerator, ensuring the right temperature on the hottest of days. At Mariscos El Cone (beach side of the road in El Sargento, diagonally across from MiniSuper

Los Delfines, no tel., breakfast, lunch, and dinner), start with the raw scallop or shrimp *aguachile* (ceviche) plate, and then move on to the *pescado al mojo de ajo* (fish in garlic sauce).

ACCOMMODATIONS AND CAMPING
Under US$100

Located about 800 meters past El Sargento, the **Ventana Bay Resort** (tel. 612/114-0222, www. ventanabay.com, US$60-85 pp) has clubhouse rooms on the beach or private bungalows set back from the beach. Amenities include tiled floors and showers, rustic wooden furniture, ceiling fans, private patios, and hammocks strung between palms on the beach. The resort offers a variety of packages that combine accommodations, meals, and windsurfing/kiteboarding or other activities. For example, a seven-day kiteboarding package includes accommodations, two meals per day, and unlimited use of kiteboarding gear for US$875-1,050. A sports package for US$575-795 includes unlimited use of mountain bikes, sea kayaks, snorkeling gear, and Hobie Cats. Wireless Internet is available at additional cost. The resort also manages a few private homes as vacation rentals. Its Cisco Restaurant serves breakfast, lunch, and dinner. Fresh fruit margaritas are a popular way to pass the afternoon.

Mokie's (tel. 612/114-0201, U.S. tel. 541/478-2199, www.mokies.com, US$650/wk. or US$2,000/mo., payment via PayPal) rents studio and one-bedroom *casitas* on 1.4 fenced hectares fronting the beach. Both *casitas* come with full-size bed, kitchen (including margarita glasses), two full-size futons, bath with large shower, mountain and sea views, and an outdoor terrace. Guests store their gear in a beachfront loft just 10 meters from the water's edge, or walk to shops that rent gear and offer lessons. When not on the water, you can enjoy a partially shaded beachfront terrace that has a glass wall for shelter from the wind.

Kurt-n-Marina (tel. 612/114-0010, U.S. tel. 509/590-1409, www.kurtnmarina.com) offers several *casitas* with *palapa* roofs and tiled baths (US$70) as well as camping (RV spaces US$16, tent camping US$8) and a spacious outdoor kitchen area for guests to share.

Steps from the sea, **Baja Joe's** (tel. 612/114-0001, www.bajajoe.com) has several *palapa*-roof cabins for rent (US$50-110). Some share a bath; others have their own. All have air-conditioning and a small refrigerator. RV cabanas have private kitchens, while economical bunkhouse rooms (US$40/50 s/d) have use of a shared outdoor kitchen and one of six baths on the property. Rates include use of mountain bikes, sea kayaks, snorkel equipment, and a storage area for gear. No children under age four. Discounts for long-term stays. Baja Joe's rents windsurfing and kiteboarding equipment, or you can stop by its store to buy new or consigned gear. Its instructors use WaveRunners and helmet radios to facilitate faster learning.

Playa Central's (www.laventanakiteboarding.net) accommodations consist of a bunkhouse with four beds, hostel style, for US$14 a night, and two basic apartments, each with a king-size bed and loft area, for US$65 a night.

US$100-200

Between La Ventana and El Sargento, **Palapas Ventana** (tel. 612/114-0198, www. palapasventana.com) has two types of newly constructed *palapa*-roof *casitas*. Regular ones sleep two in a king or in two twin beds with shared shower and bath and air-conditioning (US$60 pp double occupancy). Specialty *casitas* sleep four (in one room) with private tiled bath and air-conditioning (US$77.50 pp double occupancy). Extra touches include high ceilings (with fans), Mission-style furnishings, hammocks, purified water dispensers, and rain showers. Also on-site are a dive shop, gated parking area, Internet café, and restaurant. The resort offers kiteboarding lessons, stand-up paddle surfing lessons and rentals, kayaks, fishing/spearfishing, whale-shark research trips, and surf trips to the West Cape as well as guided hikes to local cave paintings. Stay-and-dive packages include five days/four nights of accommodations; three days of diving (two tanks per day); breakfast every day and lunch on dive days; and free use of kayaks,

EXCURSIONS

snorkeling gear, and sailboats (US$655 pp, min. three people).

Lush gardens, comfortable beds, and seven stylish rooms (called *casitas*) are a plus in relatively new ⓒ **Casa Verde** (tel. 612/114-0214, U.S. tel. 509/228-8628, www.bajmahal.com, US$110, tax included). Enjoy natural light, private baths, small refrigerators, and sea views in each one. Two stand-alone houses on the property rent for US$150 per night. Three Native American lodges are set up for camping (US$35/50 s/d); guests may use a main kitchen or garden kitchen and shared bath with hot showers. Bikes, kayaks, stand-up paddle boards, and wireless Internet are included as well. The resort has teamed up with Kitemasters to offer seven-night, all-inclusive packages that cover accommodations, all meals, and eight hours of lessons for two people, plus the use of kayaks and mountain bikes (US$1,800, including tax). Tee Pee Camping (US$55) in one of the resort's three Native American lodges is a unique option for budget travelers. These are simply furnished with beds, and guests use shared bath and kitchen facilities. The on-site espresso stand is a plus while you're waiting for the wind to pick up. RV camping and a new spa are great additions to the guest experience at this property.

INFORMATION AND SERVICES

There are no visitor centers or banks in this area. Withdraw cash in Los Barriles or La Paz before you go.

You can get gas and supplies in Los Planes; there are also a few convenience stores in El Sargento.

Internet

Many local resorts and campgrounds now have wireless Internet; most offer it for free. Across from the main beachfront campground, **El Norte Restaurant** has satellite Internet for US$3 for 30 minutes. You can use the restaurant's computers or bring your own. Mobile phones work here but get spotty signals. There

are public pay phones as well; pick up a Ladatel card at one of the mini-supers.

Near the end of the pavement in El Sargento you'll find a hardware store, mechanic, pharmacy, and Internet café, as well as mini-market Miscellania Lupita.

Emergency Services

La Paz has the closest hospital and other emergency services, but there is a **BlueMedicalNet clinic** (tel. 624/104-3911, 24/7 daily) at kilometer 55, on the road from La Paz to Los Planes. El Sargento also has a Centro de Salud (Public Health Clinic) and a place where you can buy barrel gas.

GETTING THERE AND AROUND

Most people reach La Ventana and Los Muertos by car from Los Cabos or La Paz. It takes about 35 minutes to get to La Ventana from downtown La Paz and about 45 minutes from the airport. Once on BCS 286, look for the La Ventana turnoff at kilometer 38—it's a paved road that branches northeast. Follow this road along the edge of the bay about eight kilometers to La Ventana and 11 kilometers to El Sargento.

Shuttles from La Paz to La Ventana cost around US$120 (US$350 from Los Cabos). Public transportation is an option, albeit a complicated one. It's about a US$15 taxi from the airport to the La Ventana bus stop. From there, a bus leaves daily at 2pm for US$5.

If you are on the East Cape heading to Bahía de los Muertos, you have two options: Follow the 47-kilometer dirt road between Los Barriles and Los Planes, or follow the Transpeninsular Highway north and use the now-paved connector between the Carretera Transpeninsular and BCS 286. The dirt road begins with a relatively smooth ride, but after El Cardonal (13 km into the drive), the road narrows and ascends into the sierra, where the going gets pretty rough. You don't need four-wheel drive, but this is not a drive for those prone to vertigo or anyone in a hurry. Many of the curves have steep drop-offs, and you'll have to take it slow.

If you are coming from the south on the

Carretera Transpeninsular, a paved route connects BCS 286 and Los Planes to the town of San Antonio. This road is straight and flat, and its east end begins on BCS 286 about 3.5 kilometers south of the turnoff for La Ventana and El Sargento. The road is not marked when approaching the turnoff from northbound Carretera Transpeninsular. Look for a few handmade signs pointing the way to kiteboarding schools.

EXCURSIONS

BACKGROUND

The Land

GEOLOGY

The Baja Peninsula separated from mainland Mexico and opened up the Sea of Cortez some 5-10 million years ago in the Cenozoic Age, as the result of a gradual shifting of landmasses called plates. The process, called plate tectonics, began as far back as the Mesozoic Age (63-230 million years ago), when the North American and Pacific Plates began to collide, pushing up mountains from Alaska to the tip of Baja. As the collision took place, the thicker North American Plate rode over the thinner Pacific Plate, forming a new landmass prone to volcanic activity along volatile faults such as the San Andreas, which runs through the middle of the Sea of Cortez. Over a period of tens of millions of years, the Pacific Plate drifted northward, tearing Baja from the mainland of Mexico. About five million years ago, Baja pulled far enough away from the mainland to open up the Sea of Cortez. Many of the islands we see today were formed during the last ice age, when low-lying valleys filled with water, leaving only the highest points along the coast exposed.

Baja continues to drift northward today as part of the Pacific Plate, and geologists predict

it will eventually become an island, proving the early Spanish explorers right.

GEOGRAPHY

The lower California peninsula stretches 1,300 kilometers (806 miles) from top to bottom. It begins at Tijuana at the border with the United States and extends 193 kilometers (120 miles) east to Mexicali and south to the cape at San Lucas below the Tropic of Cancer. Baja lies 250 kilometers (155 miles) west of mainland Mexico at its greatest distance. In between is the Golfo de California (Gulf of California), more commonly known as the Mar de Cortés (Sea of Cortez). On the west coast of the peninsula is the Pacific Ocean. At its narrowest point, between Bahía de La Paz and the Pacific Ocean, the peninsula measures just 45 kilometers (28 miles) across.

Numerous mountain ranges (23 to be exact) run the length of the interior, from northwest to southeast, with the highest peak, Picacho del Diablo, rising more than 3,000 meters (10,000 feet). The longest and highest ranges include the **Sierra de Juárez** and **Sierra de San Pedro Mártir** in the north, the **Sierra de la Giganta** in the central peninsula, and the **Sierra de la Laguna** in the south.

At the foot of the sierras are vast desert areas comprising about 65 percent of the peninsula. The San Felipe Desert covers much of northeastern Baja, while the Gulf Coast Desert extends from Bahía de Los Angeles to San José del Cabo in the south. The Vizcaíno Desert, in the west-central part of the peninsula, is Baja's largest desert area and has been designated a protected biosphere reserve by the United Nations. South of this area, the Magdalena Plains (Llano Magdalena) border Bahía Magdalena, the largest bay on either side of the peninsula. Together, these two desert areas are often called the Desierto Central.

In addition to these extremes, the peninsula features coastal wetlands, sandy beaches, more than 100 islands (most of them located along

© NIKKI GOTH ITOI

Sierra de la Laguna

ENDANGERED SEA

In 2005 the United Nations Educational, Scientific and Cultural Organization (UNESCO) added the Gulf of California (referred to in this book as the Sea of Cortez) to its World Heritage List of areas with outstanding natural and cultural value. Citing its striking beauty and critical role as a natural laboratory for the study of thousands of marine species, UNESCO identified a site of 244 islands, islets, and coastal areas within the Gulf of California. Also important was the fact that all major oceanographic processes occurring in the planet's oceans take place in this body of water.

Environmental conservation groups heralded the designation as a critical step forward in curbing severe damage wrought by commercial fishing and bottom trawling, which destroy eelgrass beds and shellfish that sustain many other species in the sea. But World Heritage status is only the beginning of a long and costly battle. Several international organizations, including Conservation International (www.conservation.org), the Environmental Defense Fund, and the World Wildlife Fund (www.worldwildlife.org), are funding projects in the area in an effort to protect the fragile ecosystem for generations to come. Meanwhile, the Mexican government is stepping up its commitment to fund marine parks and conservation activities throughout the region.

the Gulf coast), and deep canyons filled with palms.

The Sea of Cortez

The Mar de Cortés (Sea of Cortez) was originally named for the legendary Spanish explorer, Hernán Cortés, in the 16th century, and was sometimes also called the Mar Vermejo (Vermillion Sea) on early maps—a name that referred to the massive schools of pelagic red crabs that float on the water's surface in the spring. The Mexican government changed the official name to the Golfo de California (Gulf of California) in the early 20th century. Both names are used on maps today.

The sea is 1,077 kilometers (669 miles) long, extending from the mouth of the Colorado River to the cape at San Lucas. The northern section of the sea is shallow, the result of silt deposits from the river. Tidal fluctuations are extreme, as much as six meters near San Felipe.

Around the Midriff Islands near Bahía de los Angeles, the sea gets deeper and colder, and strong currents bring more nutrients, which sustain a phenomenal diversity of life—more than 900 species of marine vertebrates and more than 2,000 invertebrates. It's an environment that Jacques Cousteau once called the aquarium of the world.

South of La Paz, the gulf becomes more like an ocean, with deep trenches, submarine canyons, and towering seamounts.

The Sea of Cortez meets the Pacific Ocean below the tip of the Baja Peninsula, offshore from the rocky point known as Finisterra (Land's End).

ENVIRONMENTAL ISSUES

Many books, articles, and websites are now dedicated to the communication of Baja's environmental challenges. Travelers should understand that the rapid growth of tourism and real estate development, especially in the Los Cabos area, has strained fragile ecosystems up and down the peninsula. Coastal development threatens the mangrove habitat on the Mogote Peninsula near La Paz and the Estero San José. The delicate coral reef offshore from Cabo Pulmo could deteriorate rapidly if the water gets polluted from ongoing beachfront development. Even the pristine islands offshore from La Paz are showing signs of stress from the increase in camping and organized trips.

On both sides of the peninsula, endangered sea turtles face poaching and loss of habitat for laying eggs. Commercial fishing has taken a toll on other species as well, with prized billfish

© NIKKI GOTH ITOI

Recycling is now standard in Cabo Pulmo.

reportedly now much smaller in size than in the early years of Baja's fishing camps. Desperate to make ends meet, poachers take illegal reef fish, flying mobula rays, lobsters, and desert pronghorn. At the same time, aggressive international corporations negotiate with the Mexican government for licenses to use harmful longline fishing techniques in the Sea of Cortez, which destroy all manner of marine life. Conservationists are routinely called to help rescue whales, whale sharks, and dolphins from these nets.

In the long term, the scarcity of freshwater and the ability of municipalities to keep up with water and sewage treatment needs pose other concerns. Communities from Los Cabos to La Paz have banded together to fight the potential of open-pit gold-mining in the Sierra de la Laguna, which could contaminate drinking water with arsenic.

On the bright side, gray whales have made a remarkable comeback, and reefs are showing signs of recovery as local groups team up with the government to provide education and

training so that fishers can earn a living as ecotour guides instead of poaching.

Residents and visitors, both Mexican and foreign, are getting involved to help conserve the environment for years to come. For example, Grupo Tortuguero (www.grupotortuguero.org) runs a turtle conservation program in Baja, and Pro Peninsula (www.propeninsula.org) publishes an informative website and quarterly newsletter about Baja's environmental concerns.

Comunidad y Biodiversidad A.C. (COBI, www.cobi.org.mx) is a Mexican nongovernmental organization (NGO) that promotes marine conservation throughout Baja California Sur. Another NGO, Rare Conservation (www.rareconservation.org), uses grassroots methods to promote sustainable fishing within marine parks in the Gulf of California.

In a landmark victory in 2012, international and local agencies worked together to block development of the planned Cabo Cortez resort in the East Cape near Cabo Pulmo. Hopefully, this decision by the federal government will

LEAVE NO TRACE

Visitors intent on setting foot on the delicate islands of the Sea of Cortez should heed the recommendations proffered by Conservation International as follows:

- Check your equipment and provisions thoroughly before landing to avoid the introduction of rats, mice, insects, or seeds from other islands or from the mainland. Check your shoes and cuffs.

- Don't bring cats, dogs, or any other animals to the islands.

- Don't take plants, flowers, shells, rocks, or animals from the islands.

- The animals and plants that live on the islands are not used to human presence. Keep this in mind during your visit.

- Keep a minimum distance of 45 meters from all seabird and sea lion colonies, and keep at least 300 meters away from pelicans during their nesting period (Apr.-May).

- Don't cut cacti or shrubs. Don't gather wood; plants take a long time to grow on these arid islands. Dry trunks are the home of many small animals. If you need to cook, take your own stove and avoid making fires.

- Don't make new walking paths. Don't remove stones or dig holes; you will cause erosion.

- Don't camp on the islands unless you are familiar with low-impact techniques. Conservation International Mexico can provide you with that information.

- Help keep the islands clean. Don't throw or leave garbage on the islands or in the sea. Help even more by bringing back any garbage you find.

- To camp or even land for any activity on the islands of the Sea of Cortez you need a permit from the Secretaría de Medio Ambiente y Recursos Naturales (SEMARNAT). To obtain a permit, contact Instituto Nacional de Ecología, Dirección de Aprovechamiento Ecológico, Periférico 5000, Col. Insurgentes Cuicuilco, C.P. 04530, Delegación Coyoacán México D.F. 01049, México, www.ine.gob.mx.

For more information, contact Conservation International in Mexico (Calle Banamichi Lote 18 Manzana 1, Lomas de Cortés, Guaymas, Son. 85450, México, tel./fax 622/221-1594 or 622/221-2030, www.conservacion.org.mx) or at its main U.S. office (1919 M St., NW Suite 600, Washington, DC 20036, tel. 202/912-1000 or 800/406-2306, www.conservation.org).

lead to increased awareness and environmental protection throughout the region.

CLIMATE

The most important feature of Baja's climate for most travelers is its abundance of warm, sunny, dry days. In fact, your chances of enjoying a winter beach vacation without rain are higher here than in Hawaii or Florida. (Wind is another matter, however.) Across the entire peninsula, the climate ranges from Mediterranean to desert to tropical. In general, the mountains are cooler than the coast, the Pacific coast is cooler than the Gulf coast in summer (but can be warmer than the Gulf coast in winter), and the northern part of the peninsula is cooler than the southern part. But within these guidelines are numerous microclimates, caused by the interplay of mountains, bays, currents, fog, and winds.

In summer and fall, tropical storms called *chubascos* can bring rain and high winds for a few hours to a few days at a time. Hurricanes are less common, but they do occur every few years. One if the most severe systems to strike Baja in recent history was Hurricane John in 2006, which made landfall at Cabo Pulmo, bringing heavy rains and 150-mph winds all the way to Mulegé and Santa Rosalía. Five deaths were attributed to the storm.

Flora

According to botanist estimates, the unique ecosystems of the Baja Peninsula and its islands support more than 4,000 varieties of plants. For an introduction to about 550 of them, consult the *Baja California Plant Field Guide,* by Norman C. Roberts.

CACTI

Scientists have identified 120 species of cactus here, and the majority of them live only on this peninsula or its offshore islands. Many of them flower after summer and fall rains, painting the desert in splashes of bright color for a few weeks of the year. One of the most common cacti in Baja is the *cardón (Pachycereus pringlei),* the tallest of them all, which is especially prevalent in the Valle de los Gigantes (Valley of the Giants) south of San Felipe. They can grow to heights of 18 meters (60 feet) and weights of 12 tons (not counting the roots), and they live for hundreds of years.

Less common but also unique to Baja, the *biznaga (Ferocactus),* or barrel cactus, lives only on a few islands in the Sea of Cortez. It has red-tinged spines and blooms yellow and red flowers in the spring.

The indigenous Pericú treasured the *pitahaya dulce,* or organ pipe cactus, for its watermelon-like fruit. During the late summer and early fall harvest, the Pericú ate the abundant fruit until they fell asleep, waking only when they were ready to eat some more. The species lives south of the Sierra de San Borja in Central Baja and on a few islands in the Sea of Cortez. A related species, *pitahaya agria* (galloping cactus), has a less sweet but still edible fruit.

Multiple kinds of cholla and nopal (prickly pear), both part of the *Opuntia* species, grow throughout the region. The nopal is an edible cactus, common on menus up and down the peninsula.

AGAVES

Nineteen types of agave are found in Baja, including several varieties of yucca. Agaves are pollinated most commonly by bats and flower only after several years. Many of them are edible. The tree yucca, or *datilillo* (little date), looks a lot like a date palm and thrives on the west side of the Vizcaíno Desert, among other places. You can eat its fruit and flowers, boil its roots to soften soap or leather, and weave the leaves into sandals, baskets, or mats. Maguey, or century plant, flowers only once in its lifetime, sending up a tall, slender stalk after maturation. It was another major source of food and fiber for the indigenous people that inhabited the peninsula.

FOUQUIERIACEAE

The most striking plant in this family of succulents is easily the most distinctive in all of Baja. Indeed, the tall and lanky *cirio* (candle)

© NIKKI GOTH ITOI

cardón on the East Cape

© NIKKI GOTH ITOI

vibrant flora of the desert

are clinging to the walls of a deep canyon high in the sierras. Seven varieties live in the Baja California wilderness. Besides providing shade and an overall tropical aesthetic, they are used to make woven baskets, thatched roofs, and construction materials such as roof beams or rails for fences.

The endemic blue fan palm (also called the Mexican blue palm, and in Spanish *palma ceniza* or *palma azul*) has bluish-colored leaves and grows from the canyons and arroyos of the Sierra de Juárez in the north to San Ignacio in the south, reaching heights of 24 meters (79 feet).

The smallest palm found in Baja is the *tlaco* palm (also called the *palma palmia* and the *palma colorado*). It's found south of Loreto. The tallest palm in Baja, also with fan-shaped leaves, is the Mexican fan palm (Baja California fan palm, skyduster, or *palma blanca*). It tops out at 27-30 meters (90-100 feet).

Spanish Jesuit missionaries brought the feather-leaf date palm to Baja, and it continues to thrive near Loreto, Comondú, Mulegé, San Ignacio, and San José del Cabo. And the coconut palm *(cocotera),* the only other feather-leaf palm in Baja, grows south of Mulegé.

or boojum tree looks like an upside-down carrot—something right out of a Dr. Seuss book. Almost as tall as the *cardón,* it grows about three centimeters a year and lives for hundreds of years. In order to see this unusual plant, you have to venture into central Baja. It only grows between the southern end of the Sierra de San Pedro Mártir and the Sierra Tres Vírgenes and on Isla Ángel de la Guarda, near Bahía de los Angeles. If you're driving the Transpeninsular Highway south, your first glimpse of the species comes as you enter the desert below El Rosario.

Also part of the same family, the *ocotillo* and *palo adán* (Adam's tree) are found throughout the peninsula and often used to make fences.

TREES
Palms
A universal symbol of the tropics around the globe, palm trees are used as landscaping in warm climates all over North America. But there is something spectacular about seeing them grow in the wild, especially when they

Elephant Tree
Part of the sumac family of trees that emit a milky sap, the *Pachycormus discolor* (*copalquín* or *torote blanco* in Spanish) has a gnarled trunk and branches covered in a gray-white outer layer that peels off, exposing a smooth blue-green inner bark. It's most common in the Desierto Central. This tree is often confused with *Bursera odorata* (*pachycormus,* also called *torote blanco* in Spanish), a member of the torchwood family, which has a yellow inner bark and grows south of Bahía Concepción.

Conifers
An unexpected delight when exploring the interior of the peninsula is the wide variety of conifers that grow in the high sierras. Cypress, cedar, juniper, white fir, and lodgepole pine are just a few examples. The Tecate cypress grows on the western slopes of the Sierra de

Juárez and north to Orange County in Alta California, while the San Pedro Mártir cypress lives on the eastern escarpment of the Sierra de San Pedro Mártir. Cedros Island in the Pacific Ocean has its own endemic conifer, the Cedros Island pine, as does Isla Guadalupe, with the Guadalupe Island pine.

Ironwood

If you browse any of Baja's arts and crafts markets, you'll often see shelves filled with animals carved out of wood. The raw material for these crafts comes from the ironwood tree (*palo fierro* or *tesota* in Spanish). A hard, hot-burning wood, it has been logged extensively on the peninsula and is no longer as common as it once was.

Mimosas

Mimosas are a subfamily of the pea family *(Leguminosae),* all of which have linear seed-pods and double rows of tiny leaves. Within this subfamily, mesquite and acacia occur throughout the peninsula. Baja's indigenous people had many uses for mesquite wood, from construction materials to herbal remedies, and the traditions are carried on today by those who live in the most rural parts of the peninsula.

When it blooms in the spring, the small white blossoms of the *palo blanco* tree are a sight to behold. The Sierra de la Giganta, near Loreto, is one of the best places to find it.

Wild Figs

Even figs grow wild in Baja. Called *zalates,* they tend to prefer the rocky areas of Southern Baja, below La Paz.

HERBS

A number of herbs used in cooking and alternative medicine thrive in the hot, dry Baja climate. For example, white sage is found on the rocky hillsides in Northern Baja. Another type of sage, the rare chia, grows only in the desert areas of Baja, Sonora, and the southwestern United States. But the herb most commonly associated with Baja California is damiana *(Turnera diffusa),* consumed either as a tea or in a liqueur and believed to be a powerful aphrodisiac. When you see a Baja margarita on the menu, it usually contains damiana liqueur instead of triple sec. This shrub prefers the rocky areas of Southern Baja, near the capes.

Fauna

LAND MAMMALS

Baja's marine and animal life is just as diverse as its plant life. More than 100 mammals inhabit the peninsula, two dozen of which are considered endemic. The extreme terrain and climate has made for some interesting adaptations. Among the list of carnivores that live in the wilderness are coyotes, mountain lions, foxes, bobcats, and raccoons. Mule deer live below 1,500 meters (5,000 feet), while fewer white-tailed deer live in the higher elevations.

Desert bighorn sheep *(borrego cimarrón)* have yet to recover from excessive big-game hunting of the early 20th century. And the endangered peninsular pronghorn *(berrendo)* survives only in the protected preserve of the Vizcaíno Desert. Also on the endangered species list is the endemic black jackrabbit.

GRAY WHALES

Before it was overhunted by Dutch, British, and American whalers in the 19th century, the gray whale inhabited the Atlantic Ocean, Baltic Sea, and North Sea, as well as the Pacific Ocean. Today it lives only in the Pacific. The object of many organized trips to Baja, gray whales migrate around 19,300 kilometers (12,000 miles) a year from the Arctic Circle, where they feed, to the shallow lagoons on the west side of Baja California, where they give birth to their calves. Adults measure 10-15 meters (35-50 feet) long and weigh 20-40 tons. Their skin is almost black at birth, but the growth and scarring of barnacles over the years makes them look more gray than black.

There are three lagoons along the central Pacific coast of Baja where visitors can observe the gray whales up close: Laguna Ojo de Liebre near Guerrero Negro, Laguna San Ignacio, and Bahía Magdalena.

OTHER MARINE MAMMALS

Besides the social gray whale, Baja's Pacific and Gulf waters host two dozen species of whales and dolphins, including the endangered vaquita dolphin, which once thrived in the northern Sea of Cortez near San Felipe.

The elephant seal and Guadalupe fur seal have made a recent comeback on Isla Guadalupe and nearby islands, where they were hunted nearly to the point of extinction in the 19th century. More common California sea lions, or *lobos marinas,* live on and around several islands in the Sea of Cortez, including Isla

Ángel de la Guarda near Bahía de los Ángeles and Isla Espíritu Santo near La Paz.

FISH

Marine biologists have labeled the Sea of Cortez the richest body of water in the world. Diverse marine environments along both sides of the Baja Peninsula support thousands of species of fish. There are sailfish and marlin (collectively called billfish); corvinas and croaker, including the protected totuava; yellowtail, amberjack, pompanos, and roosterfish; dorado (mahimahi), wahoo, and bluefin, albacore, and yellowfin tuna, which can grow to sizes exceeding 180 kilograms (400 pounds); various types of sea bass, including *garropa* (grouper) and cabrilla (sea bass); flounder and halibut; and snappers (*pargo,* including the red snapper, which is called *huachinango* in Spanish). More than 60 types of sharks live here, among them the hammerhead, thresher, bonito (mako), bull, whitetip, sand, blue, blacktip, and whale

a trio of dolphins in the Sea of Cortez

© LAUREN SWIFT

a whale shark in the Bay of La Paz

shark—the world's largest fish at 18 meters (59 feet) and 3,600 kilograms (almost four tons).

Eagle rays, guitarfish, stingrays, and other rays often rest on the sandy bottom of the sea, offshore from the southern part of the peninsula. Divers and snorkelers are sometimes lucky enough to see the Pacific manta ray glide by. With a wingspan of up to seven meters (23 feet), it can weigh nearly two tons.

The Humboldt squid is another unusual deepwater creature. It grows to 4.5 meters (15 feet) long and weighs up to 150 kilograms (330 pounds).

Barracuda are found in both the Pacific and the Sea of Cortez. And in Southern Baja, the flying fish puts on a good show as it leaps out of the water offshore.

Abundant shellfish, including clams, oysters, mussels, scallops, and shrimp, are found all along the coast, along with spiny lobster.

BIRDS

With this great variety of plant and fish life comes an equally fantastic bird population. Ornithologists have identified at least 300 species, but unfortunately no one has published a Baja-specific field guide to date, though several Mexican bird guides include the species found on the peninsula and its islands.

Baja California Sur Birds (BCS Birds, www.bcsbirds.com) is dedicated to raising awareness of the area's potential as a world-class bird-watching destination. The BCS Birds website is designed as a reference for naturalists and birders who wish to identify what they have seen here and who wish to learn what species are regularly observed in Baja California Sur.

Coastal Birds

The Midriff Islands in particular provide habitat for many rare and endangered species, and the Mexican government protects 49 of these islands as wildlife preserves. Well known among birders, Isla San Pedro Mártir has the blue-footed booby as well as the brown booby and masked booby. Tiny Isla de Raza is another popular birding destination.

Brown pelicans are common in Baja but

gone from the coastal islands of California and the U.S. shores of the Gulf of Mexico. Other noteworthy birds include the frigate, fisher eagle, cormorant, egret, gull, heron, loon, osprey, plover, sandpiper, and tern.

Boaters sometimes see pelagic birds such as the albatross, black-legged kittiwake, red phalarope, shearwater, surf scoter, south polar skua, storm petrel, black tern, and red-billed tropic bird.

Freshwater Birds

The inland ponds, springs, lakes, streams, and marshes of Baja support two species of bittern, the American coot, two species of duck, the snow goose, the northern harrier, six species of heron, the white-faced ibis, the common moorhen, two species of rail, five species of sandpiper, the lesser scaup, the shoveler, the common snipe, the sora, the roseate spoonbill, the wood stork, three species of teal, the northern waterthrush, and the American wigeon.

Birds of the Sierra

The golden eagle, western flycatcher, lesser goldfinch, black-headed grosbeak, red-tailed hawk, pheasant, yellow-eyed junco, white-breasted nuthatch, mountain plover, acorn woodpecker, and canyon wren live in the peaks and valleys of the sierras, along with two species of hummingbird, four species of vireo, and eight species of warbler.

Desert Birds

Falcons, flycatchers, hawks, hummingbirds, owls, sparrows, and thrashers live in the hot, dry desert environment, along with the American kestrel, merlin, greater roadrunner, vernon, turkey vulture, ladder-backed woodpecker, and cactus wren.

The largest bird in North America is the endangered California condor *(Gymnogyps californianus),* which weighs up to 11 kilograms (24 pounds), with a wingspan of nearly 3.6 meters (12 feet). A group of U.S. and Mexican scientists plans to release captive-bred condors in Baja's Sierra de San Pedro Mártir in hopes that the more limited human presence will permit the bird to survive in the wild.

REPTILES AND AMPHIBIANS

Thirty types of lizards live on the Baja Peninsula, including the large chuckwalla, which inhabits several islands in the Sea of Cortez and can grow to one meter (three feet) long. The desert iguana and the endemic coast-horned lizard are also noteworthy species. With lots of color photos, *Amphibians and Reptiles of Baja California,* by Ron McPeak, can help you identify the many frogs, toads, salamanders, snakes, and lizards of the peninsula.

Turtles

Five sea turtles live in Baja waters: the leatherback, green, hawksbill, western ridley, and loggerhead, which swims 10,460 kilometers (6,500 miles) between the island of Kyushu in Japan and the Sea of Cortez. All these turtles are endangered, and it's illegal to hunt any of them or collect their eggs, but enforcing the law has been a challenge.

Many organizations are involved in turtle conservation efforts in Baja. One of the largest is Grupo Tortuguero (www.grupoturtuguero. org), which holds its annual meeting in late January-early February in Loreto. A who's who of Baja influencers usually attends.

Snakes

There are 35 species of snakes *(serpientes)* in Baja, about half of which are poisonous, although they rarely come into contact with people.

Nonvenomous kinds *(culebra)* include the western blind snake, rosy boa, Baja California rat snake, spotted leaf-nosed snake, western patch-nosed snake, bull snake, coachwhip, king snake, Baja sand snake, and California lyre snake.

Among the poisonous types *(víbora)* are the yellow-bellied sea snake, which resembles a floating stick in the water, and 18 species of rattlesnake *(serpiente de cascabel* or *cascabel),* including the common Baja California rattler, red diamondback, and western diamondback, which is the largest and most dangerous of Baja's snakes and lives in the canyons of the northern sierras.

The only rattler that's endemic to Baja California is the rattleless rattlesnake *(Crotalus catalinensis),* which lives only on Isla Santa Catalina in the Sea of Cortez.

History

PRE-CORTESIAN HISTORY

The Asians who crossed the Bering Strait land bridge beginning around 50,000 BC most likely migrated as far south as the Baja Peninsula, but relatively little archaeology has been done to test the theory. About 7,000 years ago, a group called the San Diegito moved south into Northern Baja and lived near the peninsula's freshwater sources. Next came the Yumanos, around 2,500 years ago, who painted much of the peninsula's rock art—the only aspect of the culture that survives today. Yumano tribes included the Cucapá, Tipai, Paipai (or Pa'ipai), Kumyai, and Kiliwa.

Historians believe that the indigenous people who lived in Central and Southern Baja at the time of the Spanish conquest were more primitive than the Yumanos, who engaged in more advanced hunting, fishing, and cultivation. But it is difficult to know for sure because the missionary histories—the only documentation available—were written with a strong bias against the indigenous people, whom they sought to convert. According to the missionaries, the Cochimís inhabited the central peninsula and Comondú, while Guaycuras (consisting of the Pericú, Huchiti, and Guaicura tribes) lived in Southern Baja near the capes.

THE SPANISH CONQUEST

Following its conquest of Mexico and Central America in the early 16th century, Spain turned its attention farther west. Early explorers believed the Baja Peninsula was an island and that the present-day Sea of Cortez was a northwest passage to the Atlantic. Legendary conquistador Hernán Cortés directed four voyages into the Sea of Cortez beginning in 1532.

In 1534 the first Europeans set food on the peninsula, landing at La Paz, but most were promptly killed by the indigenous inhabitants. A few survivors returned to the mainland with stories of rich pearl-oyster beds on a big island.

Cortés himself landed in the Bahía de La Paz in 1535, but he failed to establish a permanent colony. He sponsored a fourth voyage in 1539, led by Captain Francisco de Ulloa, who explored the entire perimeter of the Gulf of California and then continued north along the Pacific coast, as far as Isla Cedros. Ulloa is credited with naming the Mar de Cortés.

Cortés returned to Spain in 1541 and was replaced by a Portuguese explorer named Juan Rodríguez Cabrillo, whose expedition explored the Pacific coast as far north as Oregon.

Manila Galleons

When the Portuguese conquered the Philippines, they quickly established a trade route from Manila to the New World, following the Japanese Current across the Pacific Ocean. The ships that made this arduous journey were called the Manila galleons; in order to make it safely to Asia, their crews needed a place to stop for freshwater and a protected harbor to hide their treasure from enterprising pirates like the famous Sir Francis Drake. Baja's fate as a target for European colonization was sealed.

As English and Dutch privateers began to raid Spanish ships with increasing frequency and success, the Spanish got more serious about settling Baja. Sebastián Vizcaíno landed in Bahía de La Paz in 1596, encountered friendly indigenous inhabitants, and named the place La Paz. From there, he traveled north along the Gulf coast and then returned to mainland

© NIKKI GOTH ITOI

church ahead

at about 50,000 at the time of Salvatierra's arrival.

Over the next 70 years, the Jesuits established 22 settlements and supporting *visitas* (visiting missions), creating a mission trail south to the cape at San José and north to Cataviña in the Desierto Central. The missionaries introduced the indigenous people to the "civilized" Spanish way of life and offered food and water in exchange for labor. The indigenous people planted crops, dug waterways, and built churches. But they did not always welcome the missionary efforts to change their ways, particularly when it came to the decree against polygamy.

Uprisings were a frequent occurrence during the missionary period. The Pericú rebellion of 1734 caused extensive damage, destroying four missions in the southern part of the peninsula and killing two of the padres. Through the rest of the 18th century, the indigenous population decreased rapidly due to epidemics of European-borne diseases such as smallpox and measles. By 1748 more than 80 percent of the population estimated at Salvatierra's arrival had perished. With no one left alive to convert, the missions began to close. By 1767 only one member of the entire Huchiti branch of the Guaycura nation had survived.

In the wake of disease and death, the missionaries pressed northward, always seeking more "neophytes" for their religious activities.

On June 15, 1767, King Charles III of Spain issued the Jesuit Expulsion Decree, requiring the 16 missionaries left in Antigua California to return to the mainland, where they were shipped back to Europe and imprisoned or exiled. Historical accounts of the reason for the expulsion differ. One theory says the Jesuits were accused of stealing the hidden treasures of Antigua California from the crown; others believe the Jesuits were punished for speaking out against government corruption. In any case, they were replaced immediately by the Franciscan Order.

Mexico. He returned in 1602 and sailed around the cape and up the Pacific coast to Mendocino, California, renaming the islands, bays, and points along the way. But the Spanish would not prevail in Baja for another 80 years.

The next expedition, led by Admiral Isidor Atondo y Antillón and Jesuit priest Eusebio Francisco Kino, landed first at La Paz and later at San Bruno to the north, where they established a mission that lasted less than two years. Lack of food and freshwater forced the colonists to head home to the mainland.

THE MISSION ERA
The Jesuits (1697-1767)

Padre Juan María Salvatierra established Antigua California's first permanent Spanish mission in 1697. He landed in San Bruno but promptly found a more reliable source of freshwater 24 kilometers (15 miles) south of the original mission, and proceeded to establish the mission that would become "the mother of all California missions," Nuestra Señora de Loreto. Historians estimate the indigenous population

The Franciscans and Dominicans

Fourteen Franciscan padres landed in Loreto in

1768, including Padre Junípero Serra, who carried the mission torch north to Alta California. The Franciscans established one mission in Northern Baja, San Fernando Velicatá, before crossing into the present-day U.S. state of California to establish a mission at San Diego and a new mission trail that would extend as far north as Sonoma.

With his attention on Alta California, Serra transferred the Baja missions to the Dominican Order in 1772, and the first of nine Dominican missions (and one *visita*) was established at El Rosario in 1774, which became the official boundary between Alta and Baja California in 1777. In 1776 Monterey replaced Loreto as the capital of the two Californias.

By 1800 only 5,000 indigenous people survived on the peninsula, and the Spanish government could no longer justify support of the missions.

THE 19TH CENTURY

Mexico's revolt against the Spanish crown began on September 16, 1810, a date celebrated annually as Día de la Independencia, or Mexican Independence Day, in a climate of social and economic instability. In an attempt to regain control over the powerful Catholic Church, the Spanish government had seized all church funds, which left the local economy in turmoil. Padre Miguel Hidalgo y Costilla issued the call for independence from the mainland city of Dolores, Guanajuato. It would take more than a decade, but Mexico would finally emerge independent from Spain in 1821. According to the Plan de Iguala treaty, the Catholic Church would remain the dominant force in Mexico, a constitutional monarchy would rule, and mestizos and Mexican-born Spaniards would gain equal rights under the new regime. Former viceroy Agustín de Iturbide became emperor of the new republic but only for two years. In its first 30 years of independence, Mexico would weather 50 changes in government.

In 1830 the capital of Baja California moved from Loreto to La Paz following a severe hurricane, and in 1834 the last Dominican mission in Baja was established at Guadalupe, northeast of Ensenada.

The Mexican-American War

In 1833, Antonio López de Santa Anna, a powerful general who had enforced the expulsion of Spain's troops from Mexico, seized power, revoked the Constitution of 1824, and set in motion the chain of events that would lead to independence for Texas, war with the United States, and the loss of vast territories in the north.

The United States declared war on Mexico in 1846, following a series of skirmishes over the border with the newly established U.S. state of Texas. In Baja, Mexican and U.S. forces confronted each other at Santo Tomás, Mulegé, La Paz, and San José del Cabo. Mexico City surrendered to the United States in March 1847, and the two countries signed the Treaty of Guadalupe Hidalgo in 1848, in which Mexico conceded the Rio Grande area of Texas as well as part of New Mexico and all of Alta California in exchange for US$25 million and the cancellation of all Mexican debt. The treaty moved the border between Baja California and Alta California from El Rosario to Tijuana, establishing a new international border zone.

In 1849 many Baja California residents left the peninsula to pan for gold in the California gold rush. As Baja's population dwindled, it became a land of bandits, pirates, outlaws, and misfits.

The latter part of the 19th century brought more turbulence for Mexico. In 1853 Mexico sold Arizona and southern New Mexico to the United States for US$10 million, and American military "freebooter" William Walker invaded La Paz with 45 mercenaries and declared himself president of the Republic of Lower California. The American fled when he heard that Mexican troops were en route to La Paz. Walker was tried and acquitted in the United States for violating neutrality laws, but he was subsequently executed for a similar attempt in Nicaragua two years later.

The War of Reform
The Mexican people overthrew General Santa Anna in 1855, and he was replaced by a Zapotec lawyer named Benito Juárez. In 1858 a civil war called the War of Reform broke out on the mainland, with the wealth of the church at the root of the conflict. The liberals, led by Juárez, drafted a new constitution to limit the powers of the church, while the opposition seized control of Mexico City. The liberals declared victory in 1861, and Juárez became president.

The French invaded Mexico the following year, after Mexico failed to pay its debts to France. Napoleon III captured Puebla and then Mexico City, where he placed Austrian Ferdinand Maximilian as emperor of Mexico. The United States pressured France to withdraw, Maximilian was executed by a Juarista firing squad, and Juárez resumed control of the nation in 1867.

The end of the decade brought a series of reforms to strengthen the Mexican economy and its educational system. Juárez died in 1872, and his political opponent, Porfirio Díaz, took over, continuing the program of reform but with a much more authoritarian approach. Díaz ran the country for nearly three decades, and during this time, he improved its transportation and education systems, but at the expense of political freedom.

Foreign Investment
Díaz promoted aggressive foreign investment in Baja, selling large tracts of land to U.S. and European corporations. The peninsula's gold- and silver-mining era began in 1878, with the arrival of the American Progreso Mining Company. In 1883 the International Company of Mexico, a joint venture among U.S., British, and Mexican investors, bought the rights to develop more than seven million hectares (18 million acres) of land south of Tijuana. The British would build a pier and flour mill near San Quintín, but colonization efforts would end without success. A French mining company named Boleo & Cie commenced mining operations and built the town of Santa Rosalía beginning in 1885. In 1889 the discovery of gold near Ensenada triggered a rush to Santa Clara.

The Territory of Baja California was divided into two districts, north and south, at the 28th parallel, in 1885.

THE 20TH CENTURY
The Mexican Revolution
Several decades of political oppression under Díaz and an ever-widening gap between rich and poor sowed the seeds for a full-scale revolution. The country's underrepresented workers and peasants—led by liberal Francisco Madero and aided by a bandit named Pancho Villa and a peasant named Emiliano Zapata—rose up against Díaz. The rebels prevailed, but through the course of the conflict, they divided into factions, one of which, the Magonistas, took control of Tijuana in 1911. Madero was executed in 1913.

Following several more years of instability, revolutionary Venustiano Carranza became president and drafted the Constitution of 1917, which returned lands to the peasants as cooperatively owned *ejidos*. Three years later, supporters of Carranza's political opponent, Álvaro Obregón, overthrew Carranza.

Obregón stayed in office four years and initiated more educational reforms. Plutarco Elías Calles, who succeeded him in 1924, redistributed three million hectares (7.5 million acres) of land and helped establish the National Revolutionary Party (Partido Nacional Revolucionario, PNR), a regime that would maintain a tight grip on the country for the next 70 years.

U.S. Prohibition
Northern Baja began to develop a tourism-driven economy around the time of the U.S. Prohibition, in 1920. With alcoholic beverages illegal north of the border, U.S. residents flocked to Tijuana and Mexicali to drink and gamble in newly opened casino resorts. Flush with cash, the cities began to invest in manufacturing and agricultural infrastructure. Building of the Transpeninsular Highway began in 1927.

The repeal of Prohibition in 1933 caused a deep recession just a few years later.

Nationalist Reforms and World War II

In 1938, PNR candidate Lázaro Cárdenas, a mestizo, became president of Mexico and enacted far-reaching social reforms. He redistributed 18.6 million hectares (46 million acres) to the *ejidos* and established Petróleos Mexicanos (Pemex), a government-owned oil monopoly. Foreign investors fled the country as a result. Under Cárdenas, the PNR became the Partido Revolucionario Institucional (PRI), which would control the Mexican government until 2000.

In 1942 the United States allowed Mexican citizens to work north of the border for short periods of time under the Bracero Program, which stayed in place until 1962 and contributed to rapid urban development along the international border.

Statehood

Following World War II, Mexico enjoyed steady growth in its manufacturing and agricultural sectors. Northern Baja became Mexico's 29th state in 1952, with a population of 80,000 (the minimum required for statehood). Southern Baja remained a sparsely populated territory of isolated ranches and fishing settlements. A small number of Mexicans from the mainland visited La Paz to shop in the duty-free zone. But commerce by land was difficult because it took 10 days to drive the rough road from Tijuana to La Paz. A paved highway was needed to link the prosperous border zone with the rest of the peninsula. Construction of the 1,700-kilometer (1,054-mile) Carretera Transpeninsular (Transpeninsular Highway, or Mexico 1) was completed in 1974, opening the door to greater commerce and tourism. Baja California Sur became Mexico's 30th state less than one year later. In 1975 the government decided to invest in tourism infrastructure along the corridor between San José del Cabo and Cabo San Lucas, setting the stage for the destination resort we know today as Los Cabos.

Baja California (Norte) and Baja California Sur (BCN and BCS) are socially more progressive than the majority of mainland states. In 1989 BCN elected a National Action Party candidate as governor, becoming the first state in the nation to vote in an opposition party to the PRI. For its part, BCS voted in a leftist coalition party consisting of the PRD (Partido Revolucionario Democrático, or Democratic Revolutionary Party) and the PT (Partido Trabajadores, or Workers Party). These victories represented major milestones in Mexican politics, long notorious for election fraud and corruption.

From Devaluation to Democracy

Mexico experienced another period of instability under President Ernesto Zedillo when the North American Free Trade Agreement (NAFTA) took effect in 1994. Indigenous uprisings in Chiapas on the mainland, the assassination of PRI presidential candidate Luis Donaldo Colosio in Tijuana, and the exposing of systemic corruption at the highest level of government scared investors out of the country, triggering a currency crisis and severe recession in early 1995.

But in the final years of the century, a grassroots movement succeeded in gradually and peacefully transforming the country into an open, multiparty democracy. In July 2000 the Mexican people elected the first non-PRI candidate in 70 years to the presidency, Vicente Fox of the National Action Party. *Opening Mexico: The Making of a Democracy,* written by *New York Times* reporters Julia Preston and Samuel Dillon, chronicles this period of change in an engaging, narrative format.

With its close ties to the U.S. economy, Baja California emerged from the currency crisis stronger in many ways than the mainland. But it faces grave challenges today in the form of organized crime, human trafficking, and corruption among law enforcement officials.

In July 2006 Felipe Calderón (PAN) was elected president of Mexico in a contentious election by a margin of only 0.56 percent over López Obrador (PRD). Amid allegations of voting irregularities by the losing party, the initial election results were challenged. The ghosts of Mexico's past civil unrest hung in the air during the months it took to confirm the initial results.

During his term, Calderón took on the drug cartels and corruption at the city level. The Tijuana city police force had its guns confiscated and officers temporarily armed themselves with slingshots. Narco-violence rages on in the border region and a few mainland states, but Baja Sur has been unaffected by the violence.

In 2012, Enrique Peña Nieto won the presidential election, bringing the PRI back into power for the first time in 12 years. His term will expire in 2018.

Government and Economy

GOVERNMENT
Political Boundaries
The 28th parallel divides the Baja California peninsula into two states, Baja California (BC) north of the parallel and Baja California Sur (BCS) to the south. The northern state is sometimes called Baja California (Norte) or BCN to distinguish the state from the entire peninsula.

Mexicali is the capital of Baja California (Norte), and the state consists of five *municipios* that are similar to U.S. counties: Tijuana, Rosarito, Ensenada, Mexicali, and Tecate. The state shares an international northern border with the United States.

2012 G-20 MEXICO SUMMIT

The Group of Twenty (G-20) heads of government met to discuss international economic and financial issues at the Los Cabos Convention Center in June 2012. Notable guests included U.S. president Barack Obama and former president of Mexico Felipe Calderón. The event brought thousands of visitors to the region and put Southern Baja in the spotlight as a travel destination and a venue for leaders to debate such hot topics as the future of international finance, sustainable development, and security of the global food system.

Baja California Sur also consists of five *municipios:* La Paz, Los Cabos, Mulegé, Loreto, and Comondú. La Paz is the state capital.

Political System
The 31 United Mexican States form a representative democracy, which functions according to a constitution that was ratified in 1917. There are three branches: executive, legislative, and judicial. Presidents serve for six-year terms with no reelection. The legislature consists of two houses, the Senate and the Chamber of Deputies. States and municipalities (counties) have some independence, but each one must follow a republican form of government based on a congressional system.

Three parties dominate Mexican politics today: the National Action Party (PAN), the Party of the Democratic Revolution (PRD), and the Institutional Revolutionary Party (PRI), which was the single reigning party through most of the 20th century.

The present governor of Baja California Sur is Marcos Alberto Covarrubias Villaseñor (PAN), who assumed office in 2011.

ECONOMY
Tourism, commercial fishing, large-scale agriculture, and manufacturing in the border zone drive the economy of the Baja Peninsula. The mining of salt and other minerals plays a lesser role in the state of BCS. Organic agriculture is on the rise, with peppers, tomatoes, mangoes, basil, asparagus, and oranges among the crops that are being grown without the use of pesticides.

In the border region, hundreds of maquiladoras produce airplanes, electronics, automobiles, and medical devices. This part of the Baja economy is inseparably tied to that of the County of San Diego in the United States. People on both sides of the border regularly cross to the other side to work, shop, and travel.

Income and Employment

People who live in Baja are well-off compared to the majority of their fellow citizens on the mainland. Per-capita income in both states ranks higher than the national average, while unemployment is the lowest in the country. Workers employed by the in-bond plants earn higher wages than at comparable jobs elsewhere in the country, though the pay is far less than what their U.S. counterparts would make on the other side of the border.

Recent Economic Conditions

Former president Calderón spent his term fighting the drug cartels and ridding the government of corrupt officials at every level. Upon entering the office, his successor, Enrique Peña Nieto, pledged to reduce the violence by half by the end of his term, even it means backing down from the assault on the drug cartels. Immigration, corruption, and narco-terrorism continue to pose grave challenges to the Mexican economy.

People and Culture

The people of Baja California are a diverse mix of farmers, anglers, laborers, entrepreneurs, students, and professionals. Some belong to families that have lived on the peninsula for generations; others arrived more recently from mainland Mexico, the United States, Canada, or Europe. But regardless of their line of work and heritage, Baja's residents tend to share a common outlook on life: Somewhere along the line, they decided to search for—and found—a better way of life, albeit one that requires resourcefulness. Mainland Mexicans tend to regard Baja California in the same way that Americans view Hawaii or Alaska—as a faraway place that captures the imagination.

POPULATION

The current population of the Baja Peninsula is between three and four million people, most of whom reside above the 28th parallel in Baja California (Norte). More than half the population lives in Mexicali or Tijuana. The rest of the peninsula is sparsely populated, with an average density of less than one person per 26 square kilometer (one person per 10 square miles).

Mexico's population growth rate is estimated at 1.1 percent per annum for 2011. The average for Baja California is probably somewhat higher than the national average because of immigration. Baja California Sur is Mexico's least-populated state.

Origins

When the Spanish missionary period began in 1697, historians estimate the indigenous population of Baja was about 50,000. Less than 100 years later, only 20 percent of the population survived. Today very few people of the central and northern Cochimí and Yumano tribes live in the valleys and sierras of Northern Baja.

True *bajacalifornianos* are a multicultural lot, with a much more diverse heritage than Mexican people from the mainland. Many are a mix of the Spanish and Indian cultures, but others descend from British, French, German, Dutch, Chinese, Russian, and other roots.

In addition to the families that have been in Baja since the early days of colonization, the peninsula has attracted a sizable population of U.S. and Canadian retirees as well as increasing numbers of younger professionals from Mexico City and groups of migrant workers from Oaxaca.

IS WATER WORTH MORE THAN GOLD?

Los Cabos-area residents have defeated, for the moment, a potentially disastrous international gold-mining venture at Picacho Blanco in the Sierra de la Laguna near El Triunfo. Two Canadian companies have been in discussions with the Mexican government to excavate a 422-square kilometer (163-square-mile) site using cyanide and arsenic in an open-pit mining operation. Environmentalists have raised concerns that the mine could poison the water supply of Los Cabos, further harm the health of local fisheries, and deepen unemployment in the region. The area surrounding the mine is a buffer zone of the UNESCO-designated Sierra de la Laguna Biological Reserve and is the sole source of drinking water for Los Cabos and Baja California's East Cape.

BajaSurViva (www.soscabo.com) and Human SOS are among the environmental groups fighting the mine. Residents from Cabo San Lucas to Todos Santos to La Paz have organized to vocally oppose the mine, and in January 2011 they made some progress when Mexico's two main environmental agencies, SEMARNAT and CONANP, denied the companies the required federal land-use permit.

Religion

The Spanish missionaries first introduced Catholicism to Baja California, and it remains the dominant religion today. As in the rest of Mexico, Baja's Catholics celebrate Our Lady of Guadalupe as an icon of the Virgin Mary on December 12. Baja has fewer churches per capita than the mainland, so in order to accommodate demand for worship services, some churches *(iglesias)* hold a dozen or more masses a day.

Language

Latin-American Spanish is the primary language spoken in Baja California. People who work in the tourism industry tend to speak at least some English, especially in the larger cities, but a little Spanish goes a long way in day-to-day interactions with the local residents. Learning and using the basic greetings and a few essential phrases will show respect and build trust with the people you meet, which will likely result in a better overall travel experience.

FOOD

Fresh seafood, hearty ranch-style foods, organic produce, and the fusion of culinary influences from around the world are some of the delights of eating your way through Baja California.

Where to Eat

Travelers generally have many choices at mealtimes in Baja, although in more remote areas or off-peak seasons, you may have to settle for any place that's open. Restaurants vary from traditional Mexican establishments that seat a dozen patrons in plastic chairs around metal tables on a raked sand floor to culinary destinations that offer creative dishes in a white-linen and candlelight setting. You could make your way down the peninsula searching for the best *taquería* (casual restaurant) in every town. Or plan an itinerary around the top five or ten chefs that are defining contemporary Baja California cuisine. Serious foodies find some of the most exciting options in Tijuana (La Diferencia), Ensenada and the Valle de Guadalupe wine country (Laja), La Paz (Tres Vírgenes), San José del Cabo (Don Emiliano), and Cabo San Lucas (Nick-San Sushi).

To find the best *taquería* in any given town, stroll near the plaza in the evening and look for the longest line. Locals eat tacos for the evening meal *(cena),* not for lunch *(comida).* Casual places may be called *loncherías,* cafés, *cenadurías,* or restaurants. Most will serve a variety of Mexican *antojitos,* such as tacos, burritos, enchiladas, quesadillas, tamales, *flautas* (fried, stuffed, and rolled tortillas), and the like, plus main dishes emphasizing meat and/or seafood.

BAJA MIDNIGHT

Outside of Cabo San Lucas and La Paz, Baja is not a late-night kind of place. In most of its sleepy coastal communities, early to bed, early to rise is the mantra. Full days of water sports, beachcombing, and sunset cocktails, combined with a dependence on the sun for electricity, mean most places shut down soon after dark. When you hear a local refer to Baja midnight, they usually mean 10pm, or as early as 9pm in winter.

Some offer *comida corrida,* affordable multi-course meals for a fixed price of US$5-7. In more remote places, restaurants serve whatever they happen to have on hand.

Aside from these eateries, one of the real pleasures of traveling around Baja is the chance to shop in local markets and create your own meals using the variety of fresh ingredients on hand, including tortillas, shellfish and seafood, chiles, avocados, mangoes, cheese, limes, and more.

What to Eat

Centuries ago, Spanish, Asian, French, and indigenous foods met in Mexico to form a distinctive—if varied—cuisine. Far removed from the culinary traditions of such mainland states as Oaxaca Puebla, Veracruz, and Yucatán, Baja California was known only for its fish tacos, until the turn of the 21st century, when celebrated chefs from the mainland and overseas began bringing their talents to the Los Cabos Corridor, La Paz, and the Valle de Guadalupe wine country. The Baja California cuisine that is emerging today blends fresh seafood from the coast with ranchero staples from the interior and organic produce from the fertile valleys in between. The flavors are fresh and unique, reflecting influences from around the world.

ANTOJITOS

The majority of menus in Baja feature a long list of *antojitos* ("little whims"), or traditional Mexican fast-food fare such as tacos, *tortas* (sandwiches), *flautas* (stuffed and fried corn tortilla rolls), chiles rellenos (stuffed, breaded, and fried poblano peppers), enchiladas, and quesadillas.

When ordered as main dishes, these items typically come with rice and beans on the side.

MEATS

Beef appears in many forms on Baja menus, including as steak *(bistec),* carne asada (in tacos), and hamburgers *(hamburguesas).* Chicken *(pollo)* and pork *(puerco)* are the next most common meats. Worth seeking out in Rosarito, La Paz, or San José del Cabo, *carnitas* (sold by the kilo) are a slow-braised pork dish originally from the mainland state of Michoacán.

SEAFOOD

A trip to Baja isn't complete without a sampling of fresh fish and shellfish. Order the *pescado del día* and enjoy the fresh catch of the day, which may be mahimahi *(dorado),* sea bass *(corvina),* or red snapper *(pargo).* Huachinango is a whole red snapper cooked over an open flame. Mackerel (sierra) is commonly used in ceviche (raw fish "cooked" in lime juice). Puerto Nuevo, between Rosarito and Ensenada, is the self-proclaimed lobster capital of the region, although these days, most of its lobsters come from Southern Baja. Oysters, shrimp, scallops, and clams also make their way onto many seafood menus.

But the simplest and tastiest seafood delight in Baja is the fish taco—small filets of white fish breaded and fried, topped with shredded green cabbage, raw onion, fresh cilantro, and a squeeze of fresh lime and then wrapped in a tortilla and devoured. The variations are infinite, but the result is always delicious.

FRUITS AND VEGETABLES

Given the dry climate, Baja does not have the same variety and abundance of fresh produce as mainland Mexico. In fact, most of what you'll find in the larger grocery stores is imported from the mainland. However, in Southern Baja, a handful of boutique growers are farming organic produce and supplying it to local restaurants. The Saturday farmers market in San José del Cabo is a good place to buy from these growers.

True vegetarian cuisine is difficult but not impossible to find; you'll often find a restaurant or two, plus a few natural foods stores, in the larger cities.

SALSAS AND CONDIMENTS

Many restaurants in Baja distinguish themselves by the variety and presentation of condiments that accompany their meals. Trays of ceramic dishes containing half a dozen salsas, plus guacamole and *crema* (thinned sour cream), are common. Most places make their own original salsa recipes, with varying levels of spiciness, so no two will taste alike.

BEVERAGES

Soft drinks like Coca-Cola tend to taste better in Mexico because they contain cane sugar instead of high-fructose corn syrup, which is what is used in the U.S. versions, and the beer in Mexico is a bit stronger than in the United States. Tecate in the north and Pacífico in the south are the local beers of choice. When you've had enough cerveza and tequila, try some of the local nonalcoholic treats: Refreshing *agua de jamaica* (hibiscus) is an iced-tea-like drink served from large glass jars; other flavors of *agua fresca* include strawberry *(fresa),* watermelon *(sandia),* and lime *(limón).* A *limonada natural* is freshly squeezed lime juice mixed with sparkling water and a simple syrup.

If you're particular about coffee, you may want to bring your own; the larger towns have decent coffeehouse chains with beans from Chiapas on the mainland, but the stuff you get in ordinary hotels and restaurants is pretty weak; oftentimes it's instant.

Buying Groceries

If you're traveling on a tight budget or you have dietary restrictions, preparing your own food will be easier and more economical. You can shop at large supermarkets, smaller *abarrotes* stores, or municipal markets called *mercados.*

You'll find a mix of familiar international brands as well as local Mexican foods, which generally cost less. For the most interesting, authentic, and cost-effective food-shopping experience, seek out the *mercados,* which typically have a butcher, fish market, and several produce stands.

FESTIVALS AND EVENTS

In addition to celebrating Mexico's national holidays as well as the major Catholic religious holidays, every town in Baja that is named after a Catholic saint holds an annual fiesta on the feast day of its namesake. Add to this seasonal festivals that celebrate lobster, gray whales, wine, etc., and you stand a pretty good chance of happening upon an event of one sort or another on your trip. Here are some of the highlights.

January

- **New Year's Day,** January 1, is a national holiday.

- **Día de los Santos Reyes** (Day of the King-Saints), January 6, is a Catholic religious holiday, the conclusion of Las Posadas.

February

- **Constitution Day,** February 5, is a national holiday.

- **Carnaval** takes place in late February or early March before Lent. La Paz and Ensenada put on the biggest celebrations in Baja.

- **Flag Day,** February 24, is a national holiday.

- The **Festival Internacional de Ballena Grís** takes place in Puerto López Mateos.

March

- The **Birthday of Benito Juárez,** March 21, is a national holiday.

- **Spring Break** is not a Mexican festival, but a time when U.S. college students invade Rosarito, Ensenada, San Felipe, and Cabo San Lucas to party.

- The **Ironman Los Cabos** triathlon brings elite endurance athletes to the destination for an all-day event.

April
- **Semana Santa** (Holy Week) takes place during the week leading up to Easter. After Christmas, it's the most important holiday of the year for Mexicans, and a time when many popular resorts are likely to fill up with visitors from the mainland.

May
- **International Workers' Day,** May 1, is a national holiday.

- **Cinco de Mayo,** May 5, honors the defeat of the French at the mainland city of Puebla, in 1862.

June
- **Día de la Marina** (Navy Day), June 1, is a national holiday, celebrated most enthusiastically in La Playita near San José del Cabo.

September
- **Fiesta Patria de la Independencia** (Mexican Independence Day), September 16, is also called Diez y Seis, referring to the date. This is Mexico's celebration of independence from Spain, which dates back to 1821. Mexicali and La Paz put on fireworks, parades, *charreadas,* music, and folk-dance performances.

October
- **Día de la Raza,** October 12, commemorates the arrival of Christopher Columbus in the New World and the subsequent founding of the Mexican race.

November
- **Día de los Muertos** (Day of the Dead), November 1-2, is Mexico's third-most important holiday after Christmas and Easter. It is similar to the European All Saints Day.

- The **Baja 1000** off-road race takes place during the second or third week of November

Day of the Dead art

between Ensenada and La Paz. On alternate years, the course is shorter and limited to Northern Baja only. The event is sponsored by SCORE International (U.S. tel. 818/225-8402, www.score-international.com).

- The **Anniversary of the 1910 Revolution,** November 20, is a national holiday.

December
- The Virgin of Guadalupe, also called Our Lady of Guadalupe, is one of the most important religious and cultural symbols in Mexico. The feast day for this patron saint, **Día de Nuestra Señora de Guadalupe,** takes place on December 12.

- **Las Posadas,** December 16-January 6, are nightly candlelight processions to local nativity scenes.

- **Día de la Navidad** (Christmas Day), December 25, is the most important holiday period in Mexico, as well as the United

States. Resorts book well in advance around this time, and rates go up accordingly.

THE ARTS
Working artists open their studios and galleries in the **historic art district** *(distrito del arte)* **of San José.** There are also a few fine art galleries in Cabo San Lucas. The **Pabellón Cultural de la República** (Cultural Pavilion) in Cabo San Lucas hosts music and theater performances, as well as weekly movie screenings.

ESSENTIALS

Getting There and Around

BY AIR

The **Los Cabos International Airport (SJD)** has flights originating in Atlanta, Chicago, Dallas, Denver, Houston, Los Angeles, New York, Oakland, Phoenix, San Diego, San Francisco, and San Jose. You can also get to Los Cabos via connections on the mainland. **La Paz (LAP)** offers limited direct connections to the United States but also has flights to and from the mainland. Alaska Airlines is the only U.S. carrier that has offered direct service consistently from the United States to these airports in recent years, though beginning in April 2013, Alaska will no longer serve the La Paz airport. American, United, and Delta have offered on-again, off-again connections. Virgin America introduced direct service from San Francisco to SJD at competitive prices in 2010.

Flying out of **Tijuana International Airport (TIJ)** is an economical way to get to Southern Baja. A discount carrier called Volaris offers luxury bus service from downtown San Diego to the Tijuana airport and competitively priced flights on new planes to La Paz. Volaris and Southwest Airlines have announced a partnership to coordinate service to popular destinations in Mexico, but they have yet to provide a date for extending the partnership to Baja.

DRIVING WASHBOARD ROADS

Whether you rent a car or drive your own, exploring Baja's back roads takes a toll on vehicle and driver alike. Follow these tips to enjoy a safe and smooth ride:

- **Less is more:** Lower the air pressure in your tires for driving on softer sand.

- **Stay to the side:** You can often find a smoother track on the far left or right side of the road.

- **Pick up the pace:** Faster speeds often smooth out the bumps, but be sure to slow down when approaching turns to avoid skids and unexpected obstacles.

- **Know your clearance:** Watch for large rocks and deep potholes that can wreak havoc on low-hanging oil pans.

- **Travel with tools:** At a minimum, a spare tire and jack are essential. Old carpet remnants work well for getting traction on soft sand.

- **Ask around:** For less-traveled routes, inquire when the road was last graded and what kind of vehicle you need to pass through safely.

General Aviation

Pilots can fly their own aircraft over the border to remote destinations all over the peninsula. The majority of landing fields in Baja are unattended dirt strips. The process for crossing the border is straightforward and well documented, but allow a few weeks for the paperwork from the Federal Communications Commission and U.S. Customs and Border Protection to arrive in the mail after you submit your applications and fees. Contact **Bush Pilots International** (formerly Baja Bush Pilots, U.S. tel. 480/730-3250, www.bajabushpilots.com) and the **Aircraft Owners and Pilots Association** (toll-free U.S. tel. 800/872-2672, www.aopa.org) for up-to-date information about destinations, entry requirements, insurance policies, airport fees, runway conditions, and fuel availability.

BY CAR

Most Los Cabos visitors navigate the peninsula by car—either their own vehicle or a rented one. If you stay at a large resort and don't want to venture far from it, you may be able to rely on shuttles and taxis to get around.

Driving the Carretera Transpeninsular (Transpeninsular Highway, or Highway 1) and the few other paved routes in Baja is fairly straightforward. Road conditions can vary, though—with potholes, speed bumps *(topes),* livestock, construction, rock slides, and other unexpected obstacles possible around every bend. In Southern Baja, road crews have been busy building bridges over arroyos that flood in the rainy season. Watch for *Desviación* (Detour) signs and slow down. There may or may not be a worker flagging vehicles to stop, and workers take few precautions to protect themselves from oncoming traffic. Drive carefully through any construction zones. Among the greatest challenges are the deep *vados,* dry river beds that fill with water after heavy rains; the narrow width of the road, and the fact that it has no shoulder in many places; and the 18-wheelers that barrel along at high speeds, often passing cars on blind turns.

Other than the four-lane toll roads between La Paz and Todos Santos, and between San José del Cabo and Cabo San Lucas, these highways are two-lane roads.

Off-Highway Travel

The condition of Baja's unpaved roads varies widely, from smooth graded paths to heavy washboard, soft sand, and steep grades with frequent washouts. Good road maps categorize dirt roads to give you an idea of what to expect, but it's best to ask about current road conditions before embarking on an off-highway excursion.

the streets of Todos Santos

Travelers who aren't intending to venture into the backcountry often get stuck in the sand the moment they pull off the coastal road to check the surf or park at the beach. Carry a shovel for digging yourself out, plus something to put under the wheels to provide traction, like a piece of wood or ribbed plastic. It also helps to let some of the air out of your tires, but bring a compressor for pumping the tires back up.

Driving Precautions

Common sense and a few additional precautions will get you safely from one town to the next in Baja. Wherever you go, plan the driving so that you are not on the road at night. The biggest danger after dark is animals—cows, burros, and dogs, which appear in the road more frequently than you'd think. Other concerns include local vehicles without headlights, brake lights, or tail lights; drivers under the influence of alcohol; and the lack of lighting or reflectors on most of these roads.

Follow the speed limits, even though the locals often drive much faster (they know the road, you don't). Taking it slow gives you a little extra time to react in an emergency situation and also reduces the chance that you'll inadvertently commit a traffic offense. Plus, it's a better way to enjoy the scenery.

Note that *topes* (bumps) and *vados* (dips) are not always marked, so pay attention and be ready to slow down immediately upon spotting them. We've seen cars take particularly bad speed bumps at full speed and launch themselves in the air to reveal the undercarriage of the vehicle. Measure the depth of water in any *vado* before driving through.

Highway Signs

Highway signs in Baja are usually self-explanatory, with symbols or pictures as well as words. Some of the more useful road signs include:

- *Curva Peligrosa* (Dangerous Curve)
- *Despacio* (Slow)
- *Zona de Vados* (Dip Zone)
- *Desviación* (Detour)

PAY ATTENTION AT THE PUMP

Refueling at the Pemex stations continues to be the most unpleasant part of traveling around Southern Baja. Corruption at the pump seems to be on the rise in these hard economic times, and motorists need to stay alert to prevent fraud.

On a recent road trip, 9 out of 10 attendants attempted one kind of scam or another. One attendant tried the familiar trick of short-changing the driver by 100 pesos when giving back change for a 500 peso bill. Another attempted to convince us that we had given him a 50-peso bill when we knew for a fact that it was a 500-peso bill. And there was the convenient miscalculation of the exchange rate when we paid in dollars and received change in pesos.

But the most blatant example happened at a station near Los Cabos International Airport in December 2010. We were on a roll catching Pemex scams in the making and felt especially on guard by this point in the trip. The pump was on the passenger side of the car, and I was the designated "pump watcher" for this Pemex adventure. I was prepared to pay exact change in pesos. I saw the pump register 180 pesos worth of fuel and knew the tank was almost full. Just as the pump was about to switch off, a second attendant came over to the driver side and said to my husband, "Excuse me, you will pay in cash?"

That was a strange question because you have to pay cash for fuel in Mexico. Suspecting foul play, I whipped my head back around to see the final reading on the pump. Sure enough the dial now showed 283 pesos. The two attendants had staged the distraction so they could add 100 pesos to the cost. We had caught them in the act, and they knew it. I said firmly in Spanish, *"Ciento ochenta y tres,"* paid the correct amount, and we drove off, incredulous.

I can only imagine how often this trick works on visiting motorists. Follow these guidelines and you'll avoid losing money at the Pemex: Take your time when refueling. Get out of the car and watch the pump closely. Pay in pesos and count your change before you go. Use a calculator if necessary to check your math. When paying in large bills, tell the attendant what denomination you are handing over and make sure he or she acknowledges the amount; then count your change carefully.

On a brighter note, attendants we've encountered in El Pescadero, Santiago, and other out-of-the-way places have been exceptionally polite, honest, and helpful.

- *No Tire Basura* (Don't Throw Trash)
- *Conserve Su Derecha* (Keep to the Right)
- *Conceda Cambio de Luces* (Dim Your Lights)
- *No Rebase* (No Passing)
- *No Hay Paso* (Road Closed)

Kilometer Markers

Baja's major highways feature kilometer markers that count up or down between cities, depending on which direction you are heading. People often use these markers when measuring distances and giving directions (e.g., "Turn off at kilometer 171."). In Baja California (Norte), the markers start at zero (km 0) in Tijuana and ascend heading south. Starting at the state line with Baja California Sur, the markers descend as you continue south, beginning with kilometer 220 in Guerrero Negro.

Traffic Offenses

In the larger cities, it can be difficult to navigate busy streets and unfamiliar intersections; foreign motorists do get pulled over for running hard-to-see (or nonexistent) stop signs and other legitimate (though understandable) violations. The best way to prevent this kind of incident is to drive slowly and assume you must stop at every urban intersection, whether you see a sign or not.

If you're stopped, respond kindly and

respectfully and you may be let go without a ticket. If the officer persists, you'll need to proceed to the nearest police station to pay the fine. If the officer asks you to pay on the spot, you're being targeted for *la mordida,* a minor bribe.

In Southern Baja these incidents rarely if ever happen in Los Cabos, but they are happening with increasing frequency in La Paz, especially on the roads near the airport. If you get pulled over, you should insist on going to the nearest station to pay the fine, and when you pay, ask for a receipt. You might also ask for the tourist police to explain the charges.

Something many drivers don't know that could invite trouble with the police is that in Mexico, it's illegal to display any foreign national flag over an embassy or consulate—this includes small flags flying from the antenna of your vehicle.

Fuel

Motorists fill their tanks in Mexico at government-owned Pemex stations, which are common in the larger towns and less prevalent as you get into the more remote parts of the peninsula. Barrel gas is sometimes available in rural settlements. You can choose among regular unleaded fuel (*magna sin,* octane rating 87), a.k.a. *verde* (green); a high-test unleaded (premium, octane rating 89), a.k.a. *roja* (red); and diesel. Rates are the same from station to station (but exchange rates offered may vary if you pay in dollars). At press time, a gallon of *verde* in Baja was US$3.24 (MEX$10.83 per liter), and *roja* was US$3.38 per gallon (MEX$11.31 per liter). Price increases are expected for 2013, to bring the cost in line with international prices. The price should always be marked in pesos (MEX$ per liter) on the pump.

Most Pemex stations are full-serve (though Los Cabos now has the first self-serve station on the peninsula), and a visit begins with two questions: How much and what type of gas do you want? *"Lleno con premium (roja)/magna (verde), por favor"* is the usual answer. Leave a small tip (up to US$1) for window washing or other extra services. Baja Insider maintains an up-to-date webpage with current Pemex prices: www.bajainsider.com/driving-baja/gasprices-mexico.htm.

Mexico's Pemex attendants are notorious for "adjusting" the size of a legal liter and adjusting exchange rates to their advantage. Follow these steps to prevent corruption at the pump:

- Check to make sure the pump is zeroed before the attendant starts pumping your gas.

- Get out of your vehicle to watch the pumping procedures.

- Carry a handheld calculator to check currency conversions.

- When paying in large bills, tell the attendant what denomination you are handing him and make sure he acknowledges the amount; then count your change carefully. A common scam happens when you hand over a 500-peso bill, expecting change, and the attendant comes back to say you only gave him a 50.

Cash is the only way to pay for gas in Mexico. Some stations near the border and in the Los Cabos Corridor will accept U.S. dollars, but they are notorious for offering below-market exchange rates. At press time, many were following the old 10:1 rule, while the exchange rate was closer to 12:1.

Parts and Repairs

Just about every town has a *llantera* (tire repair shop). Experienced mechanics are harder, but not impossible, to come by. Try any of the larger towns and cities. For those used to the systematic process of a large U.S. auto shop, the Baja approach might seem haphazard, but they do seem to get the job done most of the time. For extensive driving in remote areas, bring your own spare parts.

Roadside Assistance

If you have a breakdown while traveling

in Mexico, chances are one of the **Angeles Verdes** (Green Angels) will come to the rescue. Sponsored by the Secretaría de Turismo, these green trucks patrol the highways in Baja twice a day and offer roadside assistance to anyone with car trouble. The service is free, but tips are appreciated. Trucks are equipped with first-aid kits, shortwave radios, fuel, and spare parts. Drivers can do minor repairs for the cost of the parts and/or provide towing for distances up to 24 kilometers (15 miles). If they can't solve your vehicle's problem or tow it to a mechanic, they'll arrange for other assistance. They can also radio for emergency medical assistance if necessary. Visit www.sectur.gob.mx/wb2/sectur/sect_9454_rutas_carreteras to see a map of the roads that are patrolled by the Green Angels.

Recreational Vehicles

Baja has long been popular with RV travelers because it offers so many beautiful and accessible places to camp; however, driving a big rig along the narrow and winding stretches of the Carretera Transpeninsular can be a white-knuckle experience for first-timers. One way to learn the ropes is to join an organized caravan, which leads a group of RVers along a set itinerary down the peninsula and back. These trips cost around US$100 a day, not including meals and fuel.

Car Rental

You can rent cars in Tijuana, Rosarito, Mexicali, Ensenada, Loreto, La Paz, Los Barriles, Todos Santos, San José del Cabo, and Cabo San Lucas. In general, larger cities offer the least-expensive rentals. Most of the international chains offer economy/compact cars for around US$30-45 a day with unlimited kilometers or US$60-75 for an SUV or Jeep. Rates in La Paz are slightly lower than in Los Cabos. Mexican liability insurance costs an additional US$25 a day with these companies, and deductibles are often high (US$1,000 and up). It pays to shop around. Book ahead online or comparison shop when you arrive.

Online discount car rental services, such as Hotwire (www.hotwire.com), offer substantially lower rates than the major brands by selling excess inventory for their partner companies. Rentals through Hotwire come from names like Avis, Hertz, or Budget, but you won't know which company until you agree to purchase the rental. The other difference is that you prepay for the rental at the time of reservation, so you won't be able to change your mind once you get to Baja. Prepaying is a risky strategy in Baja because the rental car companies frequently overbook and they tend to give cars on a first-come, first-serve basis regardless of whether you have a reservation or have prepaid for the vehicle. The agency will do its best to get you a car, but it could be a full 24 hours later than you the date you reserved.

Independent agencies are another option, sometimes at lower cost but often with per-kilometer charges in addition to the daily rate.

Rentals out of San Diego are sometimes a bit cheaper, but most agencies that allow their cars into Mexico won't allow them any farther south than Guerrero Negro. Some only allow travel 40 kilometers (25 miles) into Baja. If you drive beyond these limits, you won't be covered. They often add mandatory collision damage waivers to the cost as well. If you're planning to rent in San Diego, note that even though Avis and other companies allow you to drive across the border, Hotwire's contracts with its partners stipulate no cross-border travel. Go directly to the rental car provider if you want to rent from San Diego.

California Baja Rent-A-Car (9245 Jamacha Blvd., Spring Valley, CA 91977, U.S. tel. 619/470-7368 or 888/470-7368, www.cabaja.com) specializes in vehicle rentals for driving the Baja Peninsula. Internet discount rates start at about US$50 a day plus US$0.35 per mile beyond 100 miles per day for a subcompact. A Wrangler rents for US$110 a day plus US$0.35 per mile (100 free miles per day), while a Suburban costs US$130 daily plus US$0.39 per mile (100 free miles per day). Mexican insurance is included in these discounted rates. Drop-offs in Cabo San Lucas can be arranged for an extra charge. Optional accessories include satellite phones, Sirius satellite radio, and coolers. Note: This agency is located about 20 minutes from the San Diego airport and did not have a shuttle at press time, so customers need to take a US$40-45 cab to the pickup location.

Insuring Your Rental Car

The Mexican proof of financial responsibility law applies to drivers of rental cars in Mexico, except in this case, you don't get to choose a specific policy—rather, you agree to pay an additional US$25-40 per day for whatever coverage the rental car company provides. The exact amount depends on the size of the rental car and how far into Baja you drive it (if you rent from San Diego). Terms and coverage limits vary among the various agencies, and they don't make it easy to see the fine print before you arrive at the counter. To learn about the policy before you agree to rent the car, call the local office for the company you are considering. Read the contract carefully at the rental car counter, and be sure you understand the terms. If you drive farther than the contract permits, fail to report an accident within the time specified, or violate other clauses, your coverage may be nullified.

There is a lot of confusion and misinformation in travel circles about why and how to insure a vehicle when driving in Mexico. Whether you are driving your own vehicle into Mexico, renting a car to drive over the border, or renting within Mexico, read this section carefully.

Mexican law requires drivers to have proof of financial liability (a minimum of US$50,000 worth) for any property damage or bodily injury they cause to other parties in an accident. Unless you have a bond with a Mexican bank or cash in hand at the time of an accident, the only practical way to comply with the law is to purchase an insurance policy underwritten by a Mexican company. Without it, a minor traffic accident can turn into a nightmare, involving jail time and steep financial penalties. *No matter what your own insurance company may tell you, Mexican authorities do not recognize foreign insurance policies for private vehicles in Mexico.*

If you are planning to drive your own vehicle, you can purchase short-term insurance—as little as one day's worth—from one of 20 or so online vendors of Mexican Tourist Auto Insurance. Simply request a quote, complete an application, pay by credit card, and print a certificate from home before you leave for your trip. (You can purchase a policy in advance and set it to begin on the day you plan to cross the border.) Policy terms and quality of service vary significantly, so be sure you are dealing with a reputable broker before you buy. A good way to tell is to call and speak to a live person and then complete the process online.

If you're not the plan-ahead type or you prefer to speak in person, you can stop in at several agencies found in nearly every border town between the Pacific Ocean and the Gulf of Mexico. Again, read the terms carefully before paying.

The first decision you'll need to make is between a liability-only policy (to comply with the law) or full coverage (to protect your vehicle). Liability-only policies typically cover third-party liability from a minimum of US$50,000, up to US$300,000, plus legal expenses (levels range widely from US$500 to US$30,000), medical payments for you and your passengers (US$2,000-5,000 per person; US$19,000-25,000 per accident), and some form of roadside assistance. Higher-end policies may include medical evacuation and a flight home if your car is stolen or not drivable. Standard deductibles begin at US$500 and scale to 2-10 percent of the value of the vehicle, or a flat US$5,000 for motorcycles.

Full coverage adds physical damage and theft coverage to the list. Since the cost of upgrading from liability-only to full coverage amounts to a few dollars more per day, it usually makes sense to add the theft coverage and enjoy the peace of mind. Theft coverage typically carries a higher deductible than just liability.

In business since 2001, Santa Cruz, California-based **Adventure Mexican Insurance** (U.S. tel. 831/477-0599 or 800/485-4075, www.mexadventure.com) provides daily, monthly, and annual Mexican auto insurance to individual travelers as well as travel organizations. The company's website clearly explains Mexican insurance options and allows you to compare various policies from its three underwriters; well armed with information, you can then purchase online in a matter of minutes. For a long weekend trip to Baja, you'll pay around US$30 for liability only and US$40 for full coverage (both at the minimum liability level of US$50,000). Full coverage monthly rates range US$200-350, depending on the value of the vehicle. Its policies cover repairs in the United States and include a bundled travel assistance package for medical evacuation of up to four passengers and plane tickets home if your vehicle is not drivable. Call toll-free for detailed information about insuring an RV, trailer, or for other special circumstances. Short-term policies cover travel in all of Mexico, but for long-term policies, customers have the option of a regional northwest policy covering Baja as well as the mainland states of Sonora, Chihuahua, and Sinaloa at a reduced rate.

Several travel clubs offer discounted rates to members: For example, **Discover Baja Travel Club** (3264 Governor Dr., San Diego, tel. 619/275-4225, toll-free U.S. tel. 800/727-2252, www.discoverbaja.com, 9am-5pm Mon.-Fri., 10am-1pm Sun.) offers liability insurance for only US$83 per year and full coverage starting at US$152. AAA members can purchase Mexican auto insurance through the travel club website (www.aaa.com) or by phone.

If you forget to purchase insurance before you leave or prefer to purchase your policy in person, try **Instant Mexico Insurance Services** (223 Via de San Ysidro, U.S. tel. 619/428-4714, or 800/345-4701, www.instant-mex-auto-insur.com, 24 hours daily) at the last exit before the San Ysidro/Tijuana border crossing. You can also purchase tourist cards, fishing permits, maps, guidebooks, and other Baja requisites here.

Once you've purchased a policy, make several copies of it and put the originals in a safe place, separate from the copies. You should also carry a copy of the first page—the "declaration" or "renewal of declaration" sheet—of your home country insurance policy, since Mexican law requires drivers to enter the country with at least six months' worth of insurance in their home country.

Temporary Vehicle Import Permits

If you plan to head to the mainland from Southern Baja (via ferry from La Paz), you'll need to obtain a temporary vehicle import permit from a Mexican customs office at any of the border crossings or in La Paz at the ferry terminal. Bring a valid state registration for the vehicle (or similar document certifying legal ownership), driver's license, and major credit card (not debit card) issued outside Mexico.

If you are leasing or renting the vehicle, you'll also need to present the contract you've signed that allows you to bring the vehicle into Mexico. If you are borrowing the vehicle, you'll need a notarized letter from the owner giving you permission to take the vehicle to Mexico.

Once Mexican customs officials have approved your documents, you'll be directed to pay by credit card (issued to the name of the driver of the vehicle) at an adjoining Banjercito office (US$20). If you don't have a credit card, you'll have to post a bond (1-2 percent of the vehicle's blue-book value) issued by an authorized Mexican bond company, a time-consuming and expensive procedure.

Permits are valid for the same period of time shown on your tourist card or visa. You can drive back and forth across the border—at any crossing—as many times as you wish during this time; however, you need to cancel the permit at the completion of your trip or the government will presume that you've permanently imported your vehicle (illegally) in Mexico and forbid you from obtaining another temporary vehicle import permit, should you need one for a future trip. Mexico has implemented a computerized vehicle permit tracking system, so you do not need to return the permit at the same place as you checked it in. You do, however, need to stop at the

Banjercito office on the Mexican side of the border before leaving the country. Mexican border officials will scan your permit before you leave the country and give you a receipt for revoking the permit. For more information on this process, call toll-free U.S. tel. 800/922-8228.

BY FERRY FROM MAINLAND MEXICO

If you are on the Pacific coast of the mainland and want to get to Baja, you can take a modern passenger or car ferry service from Mazatlán or Topolobampo/Los Mochis to La Paz. Routes and schedules change periodically, so double-check the current service offerings a week or so before you want to cross. At last check, **Baja Ferries** (Pichilinque Terminal, tel. 612/123-0208, U.S. tel. 915/833-3107, downtown La Paz office: Allende 1025 at Rubio, tel. 612/123-6600 or 800/122-1414, www.bajaferries.com, 8am-5pm daily) was running two routes: La Paz-Topolobampo (6 hours, US$73 per seat) and La Paz-Mazatlán (12 hours, Tues.-Sun. once daily, US$89 per seat). Cabins (US$64) and cars (US$86-203) cost extra. Baja Ferries has another ticket office at the Mega grocery store in San José del Cabo (Carr. Transpeninsular at the traffic circle). If you're starting from Topolobampo, the local number is 668/862-1003.

Transportación Marítima de California (TMC) (La Paz office tel. 800/744-5050, Mazatlán office tel. 800/700-0433, www.ferrytmc.com) also runs a car ferry between La Paz and Mazatlán (15.5 hours). A car and driver cost about US$200; RVs up to 10 meters (about 33 feet) cost US$650.

BY BUS

Several companies offer connections between Northern and Southern Baja towns. It takes about 30 hours to complete the journey from Tijuana to Cabo San Lucas by bus with **Autotransportes Aguila** (tel. 612/122-4270, www.autotransportesaguila.com, US$155) or **Autotransportes de Baja California** (ABC, tel. 800/025-0220, www.transportes-abc.com,

US$160). Many travelers divide the trip into two parts by stopping overnight in La Paz.

Buses are modern, comfortable, and usually air-conditioned for longer trips. Schedules vary (this is not Switzerland), and prices are reasonable. You don't usually need reservations (stop by the day before just in case), and in many cases, it's not possible to make them.

The Spanish word for ticket is *boleto*. Fares are usually posted on the wall inside the depot.

Cabo San Lucas and San José del Cabo have city bus systems that cost a dollar or two per trip (pesos only). The route or destination (a street name or district) usually is posted on the front of the bus.

BY TAXI

Taxis wait at the larger hotels and designated taxi stands in most of the larger towns along the peninsula. There are no meters; you pay a set fare based on the distance you are traveling. Ask around for the going rate to your destination and negotiate the fare with the driver before you hop in. Even the smaller towns often have a few taxis for hire near the town plaza or bus terminal.

BY MOTORCYCLE

The open roads of Baja have captured the imagination of many a motorcyclist. The **Adventure Rider Motorcycle Forum** (www.advrider.com) has some of the best motorcycle trip reports around.

Motorcycle mechanics are even harder to come by in Baja than auto mechanics, so you'll need to be self-sufficient in handling equipment problems. Midday travel may be impossible in some parts of the peninsula due to intolerably high temperatures. Factor this into your trip planning.

Chris Haines Motorcycle Adventure (P.O. Box 966, Trabuco Canyon, CA 92678, toll-free U.S. tel. 866/262-8635, www.bajaoffroadtours.com) operates four-day rides from Ensenada to Mike's Sky Ranch for US$2,100 and seven-day rides from Ensenada to Cabo San Lucas for US$4,550, including equipment and road support. Custom itineraries are also possible.

BY BICYCLE

It's not unusual to meet cyclists riding their way down the Transpeninsular Highway, often as part of longer coastal journeys from Alaska all the way to Panama. While we understand the attraction of this epic cycling tour, we believe the dangers of riding along the highway have been downplayed for too long. In the early days of the paved road, when traffic was lighter, cycling may have been a safer option, but today motorists, RVers, and truckers drive at faster speeds and in greater numbers. The problem is the width of the road. When two 18-wheelers approach from opposite directions, they pass with inches of pavement between them. If the driver must choose between colliding with an oncoming truck or pushing a cyclist off the road, the cyclist is inevitably going to lose out. Shoulders and guardrails are nonexistent on many of the most dangerous stretches of road.

If your dream is to ride your bike the length of Baja, consider an off-road route à la the Baja 1000. This way, you can enjoy more of the coastal and mountain scenery and avoid putting yourself in danger on the highway.

In Southern Baja, the Camino Rural Costero between San José del Cabo and Cabo Pulmo is a fantastic route along the coast, as is the dirt road between Los Barriles and Bahía de los Muertos.

Equipment and Repairs

Many cyclists have never completed an overnight bike trip before planning a ride through Baja. Though the larger towns in Baja all have bicycle repair shops, here are some of the basics you'll need before starting your trip:

- Camping gear
- Helmet
- Rearview mirror
- Locking cable
- Removable handlebar bag for valuables
- Four one-liter bottles of water per day (puncture resistant)
- Heavy-duty tires (including one spare) and, preferably, slime tubes (2-3 spares)
- Tire gauge
- Complete tire repair kit
- Basic first-aid kit, including duct tape and moleskin
- Spare parts and tools to work on them

Guided Bicycle Trips

Pedaling South (U.S. tel. 707/942-4450 or 800/398-6200, www.tourbaja.com) offers a number of multiday mountain biking tours: Sierra Ridge Ride (nine days, US$1,195) and Sierra Giganta (eight days, US$995). Combo sea kayak/mountain bike trips are also available. If you bring your own bike, Pedaling South deducts US$95 from the tour rates. Included in the price are accommodations, ground transport, meals on tour days, camping gear, tents, guides, tracking vehicles, and first aid.

Visas and Officialdom

ENTRY REGULATIONS
Passports and Tourist Permits

Under the Western Hemisphere Travel Initiative, as of January 2007, anyone traveling by air between the United States, Canada, Mexico, Central and South America, the Caribbean, and Bermuda (including infants) is required to present a valid passport. The same applies to anyone traveling by land or sea as of January 2008.

Citizens of the United States or Canada (or of 42 other designated countries in Europe and Latin America, plus Singapore) who are visiting Mexico as tourists do not need a visa. They must, however, obtain validated tourist cards, called *formas migratorias turistas,* or FMTs, available at any Mexican consulate or Mexican tourist office, on flights to Mexico and at any border crossing. The tourist card is valid for 180 days and must be used within 90 days of issue. It expires when you exit the country. If you are planning to enter and leave Mexico more than once during your trip, you can ask for a multiple-entry tourist card, which is available at Mexican consulates.

To validate the tourist card, you need to present proof of citizenship to a Mexican immigration officer, either at the border or in the airport. Acceptable documentation includes a birth certificate (or certified copy), voter's registration card, certificate of naturalization, or passport. Your driver's license won't suffice.

In 1999 the Mexican government instituted a tourist fee (currently around US$25), which is factored into your airfare if you fly but must be paid separately at a bank in Mexico if you cross the border by land or sea. The immigration office you visit will direct you to the nearest bank. Once you've paid, you'll get a receipt, which you can bring back to the immigration office in exchange for validation of the tourist card. If you do not plan to travel south of Ensenada or San Felipe, you are not required to pay this fee.

Tourist Visas

Tourists from countries other than the 45 countries referenced earlier must obtain visas before arriving in Mexico. Apply in person at a Mexican consulate and expect about a two-week turnaround. The Mexican Consulate General in San Diego can often issue same-day tourist visas. Required documentation includes a valid passport, valid U.S. visa for multiple entries, form I-94, proof of economic solvency (such as an international credit card), and a round-trip air ticket to Mexico. The visa fee costs about US$40.

Foreign visitors who are legal permanent residents of the United States do not need visas to visit Mexico for tourism. You can get a validated tourist card by presenting your passport and U.S. residence card at the airport or border control.

Pets

Dogs and cats may be brought into Mexico with proof of current vaccinations and a **health certificate** issued within 72 hours before entry into Mexico and signed by a registered veterinarian.

Mexican Consulate in San Diego

San Diego's **Mexican Consulate General** (1549 India St., San Diego, CA 92101, U.S. tel. 619/231-8414, www.consulmex.sre.gob. mx, 7am-11am Mon.-Fri.) is 30-45 minutes by car from the Tijuana border crossing. The office can help with visas, immigration problems, special-import permits, and questions concerning Mexican customs regulations.

CUSTOMS
Entering Mexico

Mexico allows tourists to enter the country with personal items that they will use during their trip and additional merchandise worth less than US$75 per person if arriving by land or US$300 if arriving by air. There are official limits for the number of electronic devices (2 cameras, 2 mobile phones, 1 laptop), musical instruments (2), liters of liquor (3), cartons of cigarettes (20), fishing rods (4), and other recreational sports equipment you may bring. For the most part, as long as it doesn't look like you are sneaking in items that you intend to sell or bringing bags of professional equipment for business instead of tourism, you'll be able to enter without declaring anything. In addition, you may carry up to US$10,000 in cash without paying a duty. Do not under any circumstances attempt to bring firearms without a permit (issued for hunting only) or illegal substances. For the latest information in Spanish, visit www.aduanas.sat.gob.mx.

Returning to the United States
The process of returning to the United States almost always takes longer than leaving. U.S. customs officials may ask to search your luggage, and they'll ask a few routine questions. Sometimes they also use dogs to inspect luggage and/or vehicles for illegal substances and undocumented immigrants.

Many items made in Mexico may be imported duty-free. Adults may bring only one liter (33.8 fluid ounces) of alcohol and 200 cigarettes (or 100 cigars) per person. Remember that it is illegal to import Cuban cigars into the United States. You can bring US$400 worth of purchases within any 31-day period without declaring the goods.

Here is a list of prohibited items. Regulations change occasionally, so check with a U.S. consulate before crossing or visit www.cbp.gov for the latest information:

- Oranges
- Grapefruits
- Mangoes
- Avocados
- Potatoes
- Straw
- Hay
- Unprocessed cotton
- Sugarcane
- Any plants in soil (including houseplants)
- Wild and domesticated birds (including poultry, unless cooked)
- Pork or pork products
- Raw eggs (cooked eggs are okay)

Returning to Canada
Duty-free items for travelers returning to Canada include 200 cigarettes (or 50 cigars or 200 grams of tobacco) and one bottle (1.1 liters) of liquor or wine, 24 cans or bottles (355 ml) of beer or ale, and gifts up to C$60 per gift (other than alcohol or tobacco). Exemptions run C$50-800, depending on how long you've been outside the country. To obtain the maximum exemption of C$800, you must travel outside Canada for at least one week.

LEGAL MATTERS
The Mexican legal system differs from the U.S. system in several ways. It does not provide for trials by jury; rather, a judge decides the fate of the accused. The Mexican system also does not provide the writ of habeas corpus, although it does stipulate that you must be charged within 72 hours of incarceration or set free. Arrested foreigners rarely are granted bail, so once you are in jail, it can be very difficult to get out. You do have the right to notify your consulate if you are detained. You can also contact the local state tourism offices for help in emergencies.

Tips for Travelers

WHAT TO TAKE

Seasoned Baja travelers pride themselves on the detailed nature of their packing lists. Spreadsheets with multiple tabs for each kind of gear are not unheard of. These are some of the items you should consider.

Gadgets: A camera is a must-have for any trip to Baja. A GPS, laptop, cell phone, and portable music player may also come in handy while on the road, but the more electronics you pack, the heavier your bags will be, and the more you'll have to keep track of your belongings. Even if you don't plan to camp, a headlamp is useful in remote places where there are no streetlights for getting around at night.

Toiletries and first aid: You can buy just about anything you need in major cities and larger towns, but bring any favorite specialty items from home, just in case. Tums and

© LAUREN SWIFT

the essentials for a snorkeling trip

Pepto-Bismol come in handy when you OD on the hot sauce. Bug repellent and anti-itch lotion help prevent and soothe insect bites. Hand sanitizer is always a good idea.

Shoes, clothes, and accessories: Bring sturdy footwear for walks and hikes, and Tevas or other water-friendly footwear for the beach. A sunhat, sunglasses, and sunscreen are essential. Layers come in handy. Also pack your reading material of choice—English-language books and magazines are hard to find and more expensive in Baja.

Sports equipment: Consider the size of your vehicle when packing up the sports closet. Camping equipment, fishing rods, scuba gear, and surfboards take up lots of room. Bring straps for securing gear on the roof and repair kits for fixing dings and leaks. Renting equipment is an option in the more developed towns. Even out-of-the-way places sometimes have kayaks and scuba gear available for rent.

TRAVELING WITH CHILDREN

Los Cabos is without question a family-friendly destination. People are warm and inviting toward children, and there are many suitable activities for kids of all ages. With the exception of a few adult-only resorts, most accommodations are happy to have families as their guests, and the bed configurations can usually be adjusted to work for families that want to share a room or suite.

Parents and guardians should take extra precaution to supervise young children. Beaches and swimming pools typically do not have lifeguards. Keep a close eye on kids near the water at all times. From scorpions to cactus thorns in the desert to uneven sidewalks and unmarked construction areas in towns, there are hazards you may not be used to at home. Bring a first-aid kit to treat minor wounds and insect bites and over-the-counter medicines or home remedies in case of illness. Protective clothing such as long-sleeve shirts and pants that can be worn in hot weather will help prevent sunburn, scrapes, and insect bites. Sunhats and sunscreen are essential packing items. You may also want plenty of hand sanitizer to wash up after trips to public restrooms and before eating meals on the go. Remind children not to drink the tap water.

For infants, bring a mosquito netting that can cover your stroller, backpack, or travel crib. A backpack is more convenient than a stroller, unless you are staying at one resort. You can buy infant formula, diapers, toys, and most other baby supplies (including the U.S. brands) at the larger supermarkets in Baja, including Mega and Soriana. These stores also have pharmacies in case you need prescription medication. And they are well stocked with toys, art supplies, and beach gear for older children.

If you venture away from the busiest tourist centers, you may find yourself far from a full-service hospital in case of an emergency. Before leaving home, find the location and contact information for the nearest medical clinics along your itinerary. Bring contact information for your doctor at home, and if you are worried about access to medical care, consider purchasing emergency evacuation insurance from **Aeromedevac** (toll-free Mex. tel. 800/832-5087, U.S. tel. 619/284-7910, toll-free U.S. tel. 800/462-0911, www.aeromedevac.com), **Advanced Aeromedical Air Ambulance Service** (toll-free U.S. tel. 800/346-3556, www.aeromedic.com), or SkyMed (toll-free Mex. tel. 866/805-9624, toll-free U.S. tel. 800/475-9633, www.skymed.com).

TRAVELERS WITH DISABILITIES

Southern Baja can be a difficult place to travel independently if you have mobility needs. Sidewalks are uneven with many sudden drop-offs, and older buildings often do not have elevators or ramps; however, many of the larger resorts do provide wheelchair access, and we are starting to see an occasional Pemex station, campground, vacation rentals, and other facilities built to accommodate travelers with disabilities. Mobility International USA (www.miusa.org) has extensive information and advice for planning and enjoying overseas travel.

LGBTQ TRAVELERS

Gay and lesbian travelers should feel comfortable traveling throughout the Baja Peninsula, and especially in Los Cabos. In fact, the destination has become an increasingly popular place for holidays, commitment ceremonies, and weddings among LGBTQ travelers.

Alyson Adventures (U.S. tel. 800/825-9766, www.alysonadventures.com) is a leader in adventure travel for gay men, lesbians, and "open-minded friends and family who enjoy tours with a gay flair." In recent years, it has offered a guided kayak trip out of La Paz, but it did not have a trip on its calendar at press time due to reduced demand for travel to the region. It's still worth a call to ask about information and advice for planning your own trip.

The more international and cosmopolitan regions of La Paz and Los Cabos will have more options for accommodations, entertainment, and nightlife. The expat community in bohemian Todos Santos also welcomes LGBTQ travelers. Consult the Purple Roofs GLBT Travel Directory (www.purpleroofs.com) for a current listing of accommodations in Mexico that give an especially warm welcome to gay and lesbian travelers.

Here are a few examples of especially welcoming establishments:

- **La Paz:** Casa Tuscany Bed and Breakfast, Casa Verde Inn, and Hotel Mediterrané

- **Cabo San Lucas:** ME Cabo and its Passion Club and Lounge, The Rainbow Bar, Casa Contenta

- **San José del Cabo:** Posada Chabela Bed and Breakfast

- **Todos Santos:** Todos Santos Inn

TYING THE KNOT

Destination weddings are big business in Los Cabos. Inviting your friends and family to a seaside marriage ceremony and wedding reception will create memories to last a lifetime. But the choices can be overwhelming, and there seems to be no upper limit on what you can spend. Consider these tips before you start planning the big day.

HIRE A WEDDING COORDINATOR

Different legal issues, languages, and business norms can make for a difficult planning process. Do yourself a favor and get help early. Dozens of wedding specialists operate from the area and can advise on reception sites, flowers, music, and food. Booking service **Earth, Sea & Sky Vacations** (www.cabovillas.com/weddings.asp) works with a professional coordinator to plan weddings in the area. **Baja Weddings** (www.bajawedding.com) is another reputable service.

CHOOSE YOUR PRIORITIES

When planning from afar, you won't be able to oversee every last detail of the event in person. Decide in advance what matters most and focus your attention there. Leave the other details in the hands of the wedding coordinator.

FIND THE RIGHT SETTING FOR YOU AND YOUR GUESTS

An all-inclusive resort may simplify the logistics for some couples; others will prefer to select food, music, cake, photography, and flowers à la carte.

SET A BUDGET AND STICK TO IT

You may fall in love with the gourmet lunch at the One&Only Palmilla, but it may not be the place to host your 100-person event.

READ THE FINE PRINT BEFORE YOU BOOK

Are you committing to rent all the rooms in the inn? Make sure you know the terms of the deal before you pay a deposit.

DIG FOR DEALS

Join an online group or forum to learn from the experience of others. Brides report finding bands and vendors for as low as half the cost of vendors their coordinator recommended. **Baja.com** and the **Los Cabos Guide** (www.loscabosguide.com) both have wedding-related resources online.

Health and Safety

A trip to Baja California exposes travelers to relatively few health risks compared to mainland Mexico. Driving and recreational activities pose the greatest danger, which you can minimize through common-sense precautions.

FOOD SAFETY

First-time Baja travelers tend to share two concerns about the food in Mexico: 1) Will I get sick from the food? 2) Can I drink the water?

The answer to the first is, most likely not, but the dreaded *turista* does happen. Here's how to avoid overtaxing your system: Go easy at first—lots of heavy, spicy foods combined with alcoholic drinks and desert heat are a recipe for digestive trouble. If you're prone to food illness or especially worried about getting it, avoid street food, raw fruits and vegetables (except the ones you wash and peel yourself), and fresh salsas—at least until your stomach has had a few meals to adjust. (Many of these foods are fine to eat, but if there's going to be trouble, they are a likely source.) Some people swear by Pepto-Bismol tablets as preventative medicine.

If you do get a case of the runs, drink lots of purified water and revert to a diet of bland foods. The symptoms usually go away within a few days. Unfortunately, this can also be the duration of your visit.

As for the water, it's not recommended. Use purified water to brush your teeth and rinse fruits and vegetables before consuming them. Most tourist-oriented restaurants and hotels use only purified water and ice in their kitchens. When buying *licuados* (Mexican-style smoothies), *aguas frescas,* and drinks with ice from street stands, try to do your own inspection first. Many, but not all, use purified water, but asking whether they use *agua purificada* will most likely elicit an affirmative, whether or not it's true. Some hotels and vacation homes are equipped with water filtration systems; most just provide bottled water.

For extended stays, economical 20-liter (approx. 5-gallon) plastic jugs called *garrafones* are sold in most Baja towns. They cost about US$6 for the first container, which includes a deposit on the jug, and then US$2 for each refill.

SUNBURN AND DEHYDRATION

Most people worry about drinking the water in Baja, but the most common afflictions are sunburn and dehydration. Get used to carrying a bottle of water and sunscreen at all times.

Most visitors aren't used to the intensity of the tropical sun in Baja. Use sun protection in all its forms, even if you aren't prone to sunburn. Even mild sunburn can sap your energy and make sleeping and showering painful.

Hats, sunglasses, light long-sleeve shirts, and sunscreen are essential. Apply sunblock of at least SPF 25 to any skin exposed to the sun—especially the face and neck region as well as the scalp if it is exposed. Bring sunblock with you and reapply it after swimming or perspiring.

Familiarize yourself with the signs of heat exhaustion and heat stroke. The symptoms include flushed face, excessive perspiration and then the inability to perspire, headache, and dizziness. If you suspect heat exhaustion, the first priority is to get the victim in the shade and cool him or her with a wet towel and then rehydrate. Heat stroke can be fatal, so if the symptoms persist, get to a doctor.

MOTION SICKNESS

Some say the best views of Baja are found from the gently rocking bow of a *panga.* Unfortunately, that rocking can cause many people to get seasick. If you haven't been on a small boat, it's better to assume that you are one of the 60 percent of people who will experience motion sickness on a rocking boat, even if you've never been carsick.

Preventing seasickness seems to be more art than science, since a drug that works for one person might not work for the next. The main side effect of motion-sickness medications is drowsiness. There are over-the-counter drugs such as Dramamine, Bonine, Meclizine, and Marezine; prescription drugs include Antivert, Phenergan, and Transderm Scopolamine. Transderm Scopolamine, popular with boaters, is a dime-sized patch worn behind the ear for 72 hours. The most important thing is to take the medication well before boarding the boat. These drugs do not work after you have begun to feel sick.

Yawning and drowsiness are the earliest signs of seasickness. Try to stay alert, stand or sit as close to the center of the boat as possible, and get a view of the horizon. Some people swear that lying down and closing their eyes is the best remedy, while others guarantee that will cause the condition to get worse. Stay in the fresh air and avoid exhaust fumes if at all possible.

BITES AND STINGS
Mosquitoes and *Jejenes*

Mosquitoes and *jejenes* (gnats or no-see-ums) can pose a minor or major nuisance, depending on the time of year you travel (times of rain and little wind are the worst), where you go (oasis towns like San Ignacio and Mulegé are the worst), and how susceptible you are to insect bites. Malaria is not a concern, however. Use liberal amounts of insect repellent and wear lightweight clothes that cover your arms and legs. Bring Caladryl or another brand of calamine lotion to relieve itching.

Scorpions

Scorpions are common throughout the

peninsula, especially in thatched-roof shelters and buildings. The sting is rarely dangerous, but it can be painful. Check showers and avoid walking around barefoot or sticking your bare hand in damp, dark, warm places. Shake out your shoes and always check bedding in the desert before climbing in. If you do get stung, lie down to avoid spreading the venom. Use ice packs to prevent swelling. Seek medical attention for small children (under 13 kg/30 lb.). Ultraviolet flashlights can be a fun way to find scorpions at night. When this black light shines on a scorpion, the insect turns fluorescent yellow.

Poisonous Sea Creatures

Jellyfish, Portuguese man-of-war, cone shells, stingrays (in sandy areas), sea urchins (in rocky areas), and fish with poisonous spines present a potential danger when swimming, snorkeling, or diving. Look before you leap, and you'll be able to avoid most of these marine creatures. Scan the surface for jellies before hopping off the dive boat, wear a Lycra dive skin and water shoes even in warm water, and learn to do the stingray shuffle when entering the water to send any rays resting in the sand scurrying away.

If you do get stung, don't scratch the area with your hands, since you'll spread the poison wherever you touch next. Seek immediate medical attention for any allergic reactions.

MEDICAL ASSISTANCE

You can find knowledgeable medical practitioners in just about every sizable town on the peninsula. Facilities range from hospitals (in Tijuana, Mexicali, Ensenada, Guerrero Negro, Ciudad Constitución, San José del Cabo, and La Paz) to Red Cross stations and private and public clinics. There are public IMSS clinics or Red Cross (Cruz Roja, tel. 066) stations in nearly every other town.

Emergency Evacuation

Several companies offer emergency evacuation services from Baja via land or sea, but read the fine print before you buy a policy. Providers include **Aeromedevac** (toll-free Mex. tel. 800/832-5087, U.S. tel. 619/284-7910, toll-free U.S. tel. 800/462-0911, www.aeromedevac. com), **Advanced Aeromedical Air Ambulance Service** (toll-free U.S. tel. 800/346-3556, www.aeromedic.com), and SkyMed (toll-free Mex. tel. 866/805-9624, toll-free U.S. tel. 800/475-9633, www.skymed.com).

SAFETY

Baja California Sur is an extremely safe place to travel. Common sense and keeping a low profile are the best ways to prevent being the victim of crime. Leave valuables at home, and safely stow the ones you must bring. Experts disagree on the relative safety of using in-room hotel safes; in theory, anyone can call the number on the box to get the combination and remove your money. We prefer a strategy of hiding money and electronics in unlikely places, such as hard-to-find luggage compartments or simply the dustiest place in the room. When out and about, keep your belongings close to you, especially in busy tourist areas, to avoid tempting a pickpocket. Use the locks on your hotel room and vehicle, but don't leave any valuables in clear view. Call the **SECTUR** (Secretary of Tourism) hotline (tel. 555/250-0123 or 800/903-9200) for emergencies of all kinds.

IS BAJA SAFE?

If you've read any of the news headlines coming out of Mexico in the past few years, you have to wonder, is it safe to visit Baja right now? It's a fair question that's difficult to answer. Here's the context.

When he took office as president in December 2006, Felipe Calderón vowed to crack down on the country's drug traffickers and refused to negotiate with the cartels. While necessary and admirable, the policy has led to a dramatic increase in violence and corruption throughout the border region. Warring cartels are battling each other for power and testing the government in an unprecedented stand-off that was ongoing as of February 2013. The facts alone are gruesome enough, but when the U.S. media begins to sensationalize them, it can be difficult to uncover the truth.

Visitors need to remember that tourists are not the target in this fight, although they certainly can get caught in the crossfire. The kidnappings and shootouts have taken place primarily in the northern and eastern parts of Tijuana, which are not places tourists frequent. And statistically, Tijuana is safer than several U.S. cities, based on the number of homicides per capita.

That said, there is another, likely related trend playing out: The entire northwestern Baja California region has experienced a rise in armed robberies of a more professional nature than the petty theft that might have occurred in the past. From surfers and RVers to veteran Baja 1000 participants, foreigners have been pulled over, held at gunpoint, and robbed of their possessions. The victims represent a tiny percentage of all the visitors who make their way through Baja, but it's enough of a shift to give cause for concern.

Those who are studying the problem believe the trend is connected with rising drug use within some Baja communities. In the past, drugs flowed through the peninsula but were too expensive for most residents to buy. That apparently has begun to change, and the result is troubling.

For every local and traveler who tells you it's business as usual in Baja, there are others who counter with a well-intentioned warning to take precautions. We can't rule one way or the other, but we do advocate a few basic guidelines that have always applied to travel in this part of the world: Drive only during daylight hours, travel in groups whenever possible, and keep a low profile at all times.

Meanwhile, Los Cabos and Southern Baja remain safe and as peaceful as ever. There have been no violent crimes or threats to visitor safety reported in this area during the narco war years.

Information and Services

TOURIST INFORMATION

Mexico's national **Secretaría de Turismo** (SECTUR, Secretary of Tourism) has an office in La Paz that distributes free brochures, maps, hotel and restaurant lists, and information on local activities (Abasolo or Carr. Transpeninsular km 5-6, tel. 612/124-0100, toll-free Mex. tel. 800/903-9200, toll-free U.S. tel. 800/482-9832, www.sectur.gob.mx). It's located outside town on the way to the airport and the Fidepaz marina.

SECTUR maintains the **Mexican Tourism Board** (www.visitmexico.com) offices in the United States and other countries to market the country's tourist destinations.

MONEY
Currency

The Mexican currency is called the **peso,** which is abbreviated as MXN and uses the same symbol ($) as the U.S. dollar. It's printed in denominations of MEX$20, MEX$50, MEX$100, MEX$200, and MEX$500. There are also 5, 10, 20, and 50 centavo coins and MEX$1,

CHANGING CURRENCY EXCHANGE RATES

For a number of years, the ratio between the Mexican peso (MXN) and the U.S. dollar (USD) hovered near 10:1, making it easy to do the math when reading prices in local currency and paying in foreign denominations. Recently, however, turbulence in global markets has pushed the dollar up in value versus the peso (to approximately 12:1 at press time), which means a hotel room priced at MEX$900 a night should cost US$62 instead of US$90—a significant savings.

But there's a catch: Many businesses in Baja have begun pricing their goods and services in dollars instead of pesos. This has made for some rather steep hikes. Others keep their prices in pesos, but if you pay in dollars, they offer only the old 10:1 conversion. Pemex stations in particular are known for this practice.

There are several steps travelers can take to navigate the more complicated and volatile currency exchange environment:

- Take your time when negotiating prices and making purchases, and be sure you understand the real price of any item or service before you commit.

- Only spend money at places that you believe are charging a fair price relative to the market; if you think it's over-priced, then go elsewhere.

- Carry a calculator for computing exchange rates on the fly.

- Carry some of both currencies to avoid situations in which a merchant might offer a below-market exchange rate.

- Remember that many business owners in Baja are dependent on revenue from tourism to make ends meet, and they are feeling the effects of the global recession just the same as you.

MEX$2, MEX$5, MEX$10, MEX$20, and MEX$100 coins. If you see the abbreviation *m.n.* next to a price, it stands for *moneda nacional* (national money), which is another term for pesos.

Dollars vs. Pesos

U.S. currency is accepted in many places on the peninsula, but you may not always get the current market exchange rate. It's better to bring an ATM card and withdraw pesos from a Mexican bank when you arrive. You can also use a major credit card at many businesses in the larger towns and cities.

If you need to exchange currency, banks offer the best rates but have limited hours (in the mornings only).

Tipping

Tips of 10-15 percent are the norm at restaurants, unless a service charge appears on the bill. Tip bellhops about US$2, maids US$2-5 per day, and Pemex attendants US$1 if they wash your windows or check your oil.

MAPS

The best road map currently available for the Baja Peninsula is the **Baja Almanac** for US$24.95 (www.baja-almanac.com).

National Geographic's **Baja North and Baja South Adventure Maps** (www.natgeomaps.com, US$19.95) are printed on waterproof, tear-resistant paper and feature insets of the larger cities, with most of the popular dive, fishing, sailing, and surfing locations identified. **Guia Roji** (www.guiaroji.com.mx), the largest map publisher in Mexico, publishes a city map (scale 1:20,000) for La Paz (hasn't been updated since 2004), plus state maps for Baja California Sur (scale 1:350,000) and Baja California Norte (scale 1:1,000,000). The complete *2008-09 Mexico Tourist Road Atlas* (English edition, paperback, US$38.95) is invaluable for extended trips that include the mainland.

Topographical Maps

For serious off-road exploration, topographic maps are essential. Order them before your trip, unless you're going to be in the La Paz area, where the **Instituto Nacional de Estadística Geografía e Informática** (INEGI, in Plaza Cuatro Molinos at Altamirano 2790, Col. Centro, tel. 612/123-1545 or 612/122-4146, www.inegi.gob.mx) sells them.

Communications and Media

TELEPHONE SERVICES

You can make local calls from public phones in most towns for just a few pesos. It's almost always more expensive to make local phone calls from your hotel, which adds a surcharge. The larger cities also have public TelMex offices. Private telephone services, often available at Internet cafés and office/business centers, are another place to make calls. Yellow Ladatel pay phones accept TelMex phone cards for local or long-distance calls. You can buy these cards in many grocery stores, pharmacies, bus depots, and airports in 20-, 30-, 50-, and 100-peso denominations. These days, using Skype or another Internet phone service is much cheaper and easier than navigating the public phone system.

Area Codes and Local Numbers

Phone numbers in Mexico follow the same format as U.S. numbers, with a three-digit area code (except for Mexico City, which is 55) followed by a seven-digit local number. The difference is that numbers are not hyphenated according to any standard format. In this book, we've adopted the U.S. convention of a slash after the area code and a dash between the middle three and last four digits. Prior to 2001, numbers followed an older format, which some businesses still use.

To dial long-distance within Mexico, use 01 before the area code. Calling cards from Sprint, AT&T, MCI, Bell Canada, and British Telecom can also be used. Each has its own access code (usually toll-free) in Mexico for direct dialing. To reach toll-free 800 numbers in Mexico, dial 01 first.

Mobile Phones

Most of the Baja Peninsula now enjoys reliable mobile phone access through two competing companies: Telcel and Movistar. Telcel has better coverage and lower rates.

Two U.S. carriers offer North America plans that include calling to and from Mexico and the United States: The AT&T Viva Mexico plan (www.wireless.att.com/learn/international/viva-mexico.jsp) gives you 450 minutes to or from Mexico for US$55 per month, plus 1,000 night and weekend minutes. Data rates are US$5 per MB, US$0.50 per SMS, and US$1.30 per photo message. A better deal is to pay US$30 per month for 120 MB and sign up for global messaging for US$10 per month for 50 SMS messages and US$0.20 per additional message. Just remember to cancel these plans when you are back in the United States.

Verizon (U.S. tel. 800/922-0204, www.verizonwireless.com/international) partners with Movistar to offer North America calling for US$15 per month for 1,000 minutes in Mexico or Canada, and US$0.35 per minute additional. SMS messages cost US$0.50 each to send and US$0.05 to receive. The price is the same for photo messages. The data rate for roaming in Mexico is US$5.12 per MB. Verizon's coverage also is not as good in Southern Baja as AT&T's.

International Calls

To dial an international number from Mexico to the United States or Canada via TelMex, dial 001 and then the area code and number. Rates are about US$0.25 per minute. For international calls to other countries, dial 00 followed by the country code, area code, and number. To make an operator-assisted call, dial 09 before the country code.

Internet Phones

In areas with reliable high-speed Internet

access, voice-over-IP (VoIP) calling has just about replaced the need for satellite phones and Ladatel cards. Skype (www.skype.com) and Google Talk are two of the many service providers out there. Rates are about US$0.01-0.03 per minute, plus an account setup fee of around US$10. Some companies include a free U.S. number for family and friends back home to dial while you are on the road.

Long Distance the Old-Fashioned Way

If you don't have access to the Internet, you can dial access numbers to reach operators from AT&T, MCI, or Sprint for calling-card or credit-card calls. Beware the no-name phone companies that try to get you to call the United States collect or via credit card. They are notorious for overcharging, and some have forged partnerships with hotels that get a cut when guests use their inflated services.

Satellite Phone

For the many areas of Southern Baja where there are no regular telephone lines, no radio phones, no Internet, and no cellular phone service, the only solution is satellite phone—assuming you *have* to stay in phone contact at all times. **California Baja Rent-a-Car** (9245 Jamacha Blvd., Spring Valley, CA 91977, U.S. tel. 619/470-7368 or 888/470-7368, www.cabaja.com) rents GPS-satellite phones, as does **Discover Baja Travel Club** (3089 Clairemont Dr., San Diego, CA 92117, U.S. tel. 619/275-1836 or 800/727-2252, www.discoverbaja.com).

EMAIL AND INTERNET ACCESS

To the surprise of many first-time visitors, high-speed Internet access is almost ubiquitous in Baja these days. Hundreds of kilometers of fiber-optic cable were buried alongside the Transpeninsular Highway in 2002-2003, replacing the need for slow dial-up connections in most towns and connecting Baja residents and visitors to computers and websites around the world.

Reliability is another matter, however. Even the most well-equipped business centers have trouble keeping their connections up 24/7. If all you need to do is check your email now and then, this won't be a problem. But if you intend to run business processes remotely while on the road, it may be difficult to find a good setup.

Five-star resorts, espresso bars, marinas, and RV parks all have set wireless antennas for guests who travel with their own laptop or other Internet-enabled devices. Some charge extra by the hour or day; others throw it in for the price of a latte. In the larger condo complexes, you may be able to find an open (unsecured) Wi-Fi network to use. And for those traveling sans computer, there are dozens of Internet cafés in hotels, real estate offices, and business centers with desktop machines, as well as printers, copiers, and scanners for imaging needs.

Rates vary widely, from free with a food or beverage purchase to US$8 an hour at one of the hotels in San José del Cabo.

In more remote areas of the peninsula, some residents and RV owners have costly satellite Internet service through providers like HughesNet (formerly Direcway) and Starband.

WEIGHTS AND MEASURES

Mexico uses the metric system for measuring weights, volumes, temperature, and distances. Driving directions are given in kilometers (1 kilometer is 0.6 mile), meat is bought by the kilo (1 kg is 2.2 lb.), temperature is measured in degrees Celsius (27°C is 80°F), and Pemex stations sell gas by the liter (1 liter is 0.26 gallon).

In this book, distances are given in kilometers. Most other measurements are given in the metric system, except for boat lengths and fishing-line tests, which are given in feet and pounds in Baja.

Electricity

Mexico uses the same electrical system as the United States and Canada: 110 volts, 60 cycles, and alternating current (AC). U.S.-style outlets work with appliances that have standard double-bladed plugs. This means you can recharge your electronics without bringing an adapter.

Time

Baja California Sur follows U.S. mountain time. Don't forget to adjust your clocks when you cross the state line. Daylight saving time takes effect from the first Sunday in April to the last Sunday in October.

RESOURCES

Glossary

abarrotes: groceries

aduana: customs service

aguachile: style of ceviche; a watery, chili-based broth used to "cook" fresh seafood

a la veracruzana: fish or meat prepared with a mild sauce of tomato, garlic, and green olives (Veracruz style)

al diablo: fish or meat prepared in a sauce of tomato, garlic, and chiles

al mojo de ajo: meat or fish prepared in a garlic sauce

alta cocina mexicana: Mexican food prepared in a "high cuisine," or gourmet, style

antojitos: literally "little whims"; quick Mexican dishes like tacos and enchiladas

aparejo: burro saddle

arrachera: skirt steak, the choice cut of beef for fajitas

bahía: bay

basura: trash or rubbish; a sign saying No Tire Basura means Don't Throw Trash

BCD: buoyancy compensation device (for diving)

BCN: the state of Baja California (Norte)

BCS: the state of Baja California Sur

boca: literally "mouth"; a geographic term describing a break in a barrier island or peninsula where sea meets lagoon

calle: street

callejón: alley or lane

cañon: canyon

cardón: Pachycereus pringlei, the world's tallest cactus

carne asada a la tampiqueña: marinated beef steak grilled over dry heat and served with enchiladas and beans

carne en su jugo: meat and beans served in a meat broth

carnitas: heavily seasoned pork that is braised slowly until it can be pulled apart easily

casa de huéspedes: guesthouse

cerro: mountain peak

cerveza: beer

champurrado: a hot chocolate drink typically made with corn starch and cinnamon

charreada: Mexican-style rodeo

charro/charra: horseman/horsewoman

chilaquiles: green or red salsa or mole poured over fried tortilla triangles and topped with any combination of eggs, pulled chicken, cheese, beans, and Mexican cream

chile en nogada: poblano chiles stuffed with meats, aromatics, fruits, and spices, topped with a walnut-based cream sauce

cochinita pibil: pork marinated in a strongly acidic citrus juice and roasted while wrapped in banana leaves

colectivo: van or taxi that picks up several passengers at a time for a standard per-person fare, much like a bus

comida corrida: a small (usually lunch) meal of several courses served at a fixed price

correo: post office

corrida de toros: "running of the bulls" or bullfight

COTP: captain of the port (capitanía del puerto in Spanish)

curandero: traditional healer

de rajas: served with poblano peppers

Diconsa: Distribuidora Conasupo, S.A., a government-subsidized food distributor

efectivo: cash payment

ejido: collectively owned agricultural lands

ensenada: cove or small bay

flauta: a tortilla that has been stuffed with meat and spices, rolled, and fried

Fonatur: Fondo Nacional de Fomento del Turismo (National Foundation for Tourism Development)

Gral.: abbreviation for General (rank)

hostería: hostelry, inn

IMSS: Instituto Mexicano del Seguro Social (Mexican Social Security Institute)

INAH: Instituto Nacional de Antropología e Historia (National Institute of Anthropology and History)

indígenas: indigenous people (**indigenes** is the less common but more politically correct term)

indios: Mexicans of predominantly Amerindian descent

INEGI: Instituto Nacional de Estadística, Geografía e Informática (National Institute of Statistics, Geography, and Information)

ISSSTE: Instituto de Seguridad y Servicios Sociales para Trabajadores del Estado (Security and Social Services Institute for Government Workers)

laguna: lagoon, lake, or bay

licuados: blended beverages made from fruit, milk and ice

limonada: beverage of lemon or lime juice, sugar, and water

llano: plains

lleno: full

lonchería: a small lunch counter or food stand

machaca: dried beef usually served with eggs, onions, and peppers

malecón: waterfront promenade

maquiladora or maquila: a "twin-bond" or "in-plant" manufacturing enterprise where foreign components may be imported and assembled, then exported to a foreign country, free of customs duties in each direction

mariscos: literally "shellfish," but often used as a generic term for seafood

mercado: market

michelada: a mixture of beer, lime juice, and assorted sauces, spices, and peppers, served in a chilled, salt-rimmed glass

mochila: knapsack or backpack

mochilero: backpacker

mole poblano: a complex Mexican sauce made of more than 20 ingredients, featuring a combination of *ancho, pasilla, mulato,* or chipotle peppers

nopales: cactus, typically served in salads or with eggs or meats

nopalitos: strips of cooked or pickled prickly-pear cactus

PADI: Professional Association of Dive Instructors

palacio municipal: literally "municipal palace," equivalent to city or county hall in the United States

palapa: thatched, umbrella-like shade shelter or roof

PAN: Partido Acción Nacional (National Action Party)

panadería: bakery

panga: aluminum skiff used for fishing and diving in Baja

panguero: captain of a *panga*

papas rellenas: deep-fried potatoes stuffed with meats, spices, chiles, and onions

parrada: bus stop

Pemex: Petroleos Mexicanos (Mexican Petroleum)

pensión: boardinghouse

pescado zareandeado: broiled fish rubbed in a chile and garlic paste and glazed with flavored mayonnaise before grilling

playa: beach

plazuela: smaller plaza

posole: a stew typically made with hominy, pork, chiles, and vegetables

PRD: Partido Revolucionario Democrático (Democratic Revolutionary Party)

pre-Cortesian: a reference to Mexican history before the arrival of Spanish conquistador Hernán Cortés; i.e., before 1518; other terms with the same meaning include pre-Columbian (before Columbus's arrival) and pre-Hispanic (before the arrival of the Spanish)

PRI: Partido Revolucionario Institucional (Institutional Revolutionary Party)

punta: point

ramal: branch road

rancheria: a collection of small ranching households, most often inhabited by *indios*

ranchito: small ranch

salsa verde: salsa made from tomatillos, chili peppers, onion, cilantro, and lime

SECTUR: Secretaría de Turismo (Secretariat of Tourism)

SEDESOL: Secretaría de Desarrollo Social (Secretariat of Social Development)

SEMARNAT: Secretaría de Medio Ambiente y Recursos Naturales (Secretariat of the Environment and Natural Resources)

sopes: meat and toppings in a bowl of fried maize soaked in lime

tacos al pastor: tacos served with marinated and thinly sliced, slow roasted pork

taquería: a small and casual restaurant that serves Mexican staples, particularly tacos

temazcal: type of sweat lodge

tienda: store

tinaja: pool or spring

topes: speed bumps

torta: a sandwich served on a crusty roll with any variety of meat, typically garnished with avocado, poblano, jalapeno, tomato, and onion.

torta cubana: extra-large sandwich stuffed with mixture of meats, spices, and vegetables

ultramarinos: minimarket/delicatessen

ABBREVIATIONS IN ADDRESSES

Av.: Avenida (avenue)

Blvd.: Boulevard

Calz.: Calzada (road, drive)

Carr.: Carretera (highway)

Col.: Colonia (neighborhood)

Fracc.: Fraccionamiento (residential area)

Loc.: locale or locales

nte.: *norte* (north)

ote.: *oriente* (east)

pte.: *poniente* (west)

s/n: *sin número* ("without number;" used for street addresses without building numbers)

Spanish Phrasebook

Your Mexican adventure will be more fun if you use a little Spanish. Mexican folks, although they may smile at your funny accent, will appreciate your halting efforts to break the ice and transform yourself from a foreigner to a potential friend.

Spanish commonly uses 30 letters—the familiar English 26, plus four straightforward additions: ch, ll, ñ, and rr, which are explained in "Consonants," below.

PRONUNCIATION

Once you learn them, Spanish pronunciation rules—in contrast to English—don't change. Spanish vowels generally sound softer than in English. (*Note:* The capitalized syllables below receive stronger accents.)

Vowels

a like ah, as in "hah": *agua* AH-gooah (water), *pan* PAHN (bread), and *casa* CAH-sah (house)

e like ay, as in "may:" *mesa* MAY-sah (table), *tela* TAY-lah (cloth), and *de* DAY (of, from)

i like ee, as in "need": *diez* dee-AYZ (ten), *comida* ko-MEE-dah (meal), and *fin* FEEN (end)

o like oh, as in "go": *peso* PAY-soh (weight), *ocho* OH-choh (eight), and *poco* POH-koh (a bit)

u like oo, as in "cool": *uno* OO-noh (one), *cuarto* KOOAHR-toh (room), and *usted* oos-TAYD (you); when it follows a "q" the **u** is silent; when it follows an "h" or has an umlaut, it's pronounced like "w"

Consonants

b, d, f, k, l, m, n, p, q, s, t, v, w, x, y, z, and ch pronounced almost as in English; **h** occurs, but is silent—not pronounced at all

c like k as in "keep": *cuarto* KOOAR-toh (room), Tepic tay-PEEK (capital of Nayarit state); when it precedes "e" or "i," pronounce **c** like s, as in "sit": *cerveza* sayr-VAY-sah (beer), *encima* ayn-SEE-mah (atop)

g like g as in "gift" when it precedes "a," "o," "u," or a consonant: *gato* GAH-toh (cat), *hago* AH-goh (I do, make); otherwise, pronounce **g** like h as in "hat": *giro* HEE-roh (money order), *gente* HAYN-tay (people)

j like h, as in "has": *Jueves* HOOAY-vays (Thursday), *mejor* may-HOR (better)

ll like y, as in "yes": *toalla* toh-AH-yah (towel), *ellos* AY-yohs (they, them)

ñ like ny, as in "canyon": *año* AH-nyo (year), *señor* SAY-nyor (Mr., sir)

r is lightly trilled, with tongue at the roof of your mouth like a very light English d, as in "ready": *pero* PAY-doh (but), *tres* TDAYS (three), *cuatro* KOOAH-tdoh (four)

rr like a Spanish r, but with much more emphasis and trill. Let your tongue flap. Practice with *burro* (donkey), *carretera* (highway), and Carrillo (proper name), then really let go with *ferrocarril* (railroad)

Note: The single small but common exception to all of the above is the pronunciation of Spanish **y** when it's being used as the Spanish word for "and," as in "Ron y Kathy." In such case, pronounce it like the English ee, as in "keep": Ron "ee" Kathy (Ron and Kathy).

Accent

The rule for accent, the relative stress given to syllables within a given word, is straightforward. If a word ends in a vowel, an n, or an s, accent the next-to-last syllable; if not, accent the last syllable.

Pronounce *gracias* GRAH-seeahs (thank you), *orden* OHR-dayn (order), and *carretera* kah-ray-TAY-rah (highway) with stress on the next-to-last syllable.

Otherwise, accent the last syllable: *venir* vay-NEER (to come), *ferrocarril* fay-roh-cah-REEL (railroad), and *edad* ay-DAHD (age).

Exceptions to the accent rule are always marked with an accent sign: (á, é, í, ó, or ú), such as *teléfono* tay-LAY-foh-noh (telephone), *jabón* hah-BON (soap), and *rápido* RAH-pee-doh (rapid).

BASIC AND COURTEOUS EXPRESSIONS

Most Spanish-speaking people consider formalities important. Whenever approaching anyone for information or some other reason, do not forget the appropriate salutation—good morning, good evening, etc. Standing alone, the greeting *hola* (hello) can sound brusque.

Hello. *Hola.*

Good morning. *Buenos días.*

Good afternoon. *Buenas tardes.*

Good evening. *Buenas noches.*

How are you? *¿Cómo está usted?*

Very well, thank you. *Muy bien, gracias.*

Okay; good. *Bien.*

Not okay; bad. *Mal or feo.*

So-so. *Más o menos.*

And you? *¿Y usted?*

Thank you. *Gracias.*

Thank you very much. *Muchas gracias.*

You're very kind. *Muy amable.*

You're welcome. *De nada.*

Goodbye. *Adios.*

See you later. *Hasta luego.*

please *por favor*

yes *sí*

no *no*

I don't know. *No sé.*

Just a moment, please. *Momentito, por favor.*

Excuse me, please (when you're trying to get attention). *Disculpe or Con permiso.*

Excuse me (when you've made a boo-boo). *Lo siento.*

Pleased to meet you. *Mucho gusto.*

How do you say... in Spanish? *¿Cómo se dice... en español?*

What is your name? *¿Cómo se llama usted?*

Do you speak English? *¿Habla usted inglés?*

Is English spoken here? (Does anyone here speak English?) *¿Se habla inglés?*

I don't speak Spanish well. *No hablo bien el español.*

I don't understand. *No entiendo.*

How do you say... in Spanish? *¿Cómo se dice... en español?*

My name is... *Me llamo...*

Would you like... *¿Quisiera usted...*

Let's go to... *Vamos a...*

TERMS OF ADDRESS

When in doubt, use the formal *usted* (you) as a form of address.

I *yo*
you (formal) *usted*
you (familiar) *tu*
he/him *él*
she/her *ella*
we/us *nosotros*
you (plural) *ustedes*
they/them *ellos* (all males or mixed gender); *ellas* (all females)
Mr., sir *señor*
Mrs., madam *señora*
miss, young lady *señorita*
wife *esposa*
husband *esposo*
friend *amigo* (male); *amiga* (female)
sweetheart *novio* (male); *novia* (female)
son; daughter *hijo; hija*
brother; sister *hermano; hermana*
father; mother *padre; madre*
grandfather; grandmother *abuelo; abuela*

TRANSPORTATION

Where is...? *¿Dónde está...?*
How far is it to...? *¿A cuánto está...?*
from... to... *de... a...*
How many blocks? *¿Cuántas cuadras?*
Where (Which) is the way to...? *¿Dónde está el camino a...?*
the bus station *la terminal de autobuses*
the bus stop *la parada de autobuses*
Where is this bus going? *¿Adónde va este autobús?*
the taxi stand *la parada de taxis*
the train station *la estación de ferrocarril*
the boat *el barco*
the launch *lancha; tiburonera*
the dock *el muelle*
the airport *el aeropuerto*
I'd like a ticket to... *Quisiera un boleto a...*
first (second) class *primera (segunda) clase*
roundtrip *ida y vuelta*
reservation *reservación*
baggage *equipaje*
Stop here, please. *Pare aquí, por favor.*
the entrance *la entrada*
the exit *la salida*
the ticket office *la oficina de boletos*
(very) near; far *(muy) cerca; lejos*
to; toward *a*
by; through *por*
from *de*
the right *la derecha*
the left *la izquierda*
straight ahead *derecho; directo*
in front *en frente*
beside *al lado*
behind *atrás*
the corner *la esquina*
the stoplight *la semáforo*
a turn *una vuelta*
right here *aquí*
somewhere around here *por acá*
right there *allí*
somewhere around there *por allá*
road *el camino*
street; boulevard *calle; bulevar*
block *la cuadra*
highway *carretera*
kilometer *kilómetro*
bridge; toll *puente; cuota*
address *dirección*
north; south *norte; sur*
east; west *oriente (este); poniente (oeste)*

ACCOMMODATIONS

hotel *hotel*
Is there a room? *¿Hay cuarto?*
May I (may we) see it? *¿Puedo (podemos) verlo?*
What is the rate? *¿Cuál es el precio?*
Is that your best rate? *¿Es su mejor precio?*
Is there something cheaper? *¿Hay algo más económico?*
a single room *un cuarto sencillo*
a double room *un cuarto doble*
double bed *cama matrimonial*
twin beds *camas gemelas*
with private bath *con baño*
hot water *agua caliente*
shower *ducha*
towels *toallas*
soap *jabón*
toilet paper *papel higiénico*

blanket *frazada; manta*
sheets *sábanas*
air-conditioned *aire acondicionado*
fan *abanico; ventilador*
key *llave*
manager *gerente*

FOOD

I'm hungry *Tengo hambre.*
I'm thirsty. *Tengo sed.*
menu *carta; menú*
order *orden*
glass *vaso*
fork *tenedor*
knife *cuchillo*
spoon *cuchara*
napkin *servilleta*
soft drink *refresco*
coffee *café*
tea *té*
drinking water *agua pura; agua potable*
bottled carbonated water *agua mineral*
bottled uncarbonated water *agua sin gas*
beer *cerveza*
wine *vino*
milk *leche*
juice *jugo*
cream *crema*
sugar *azúcar*
cheese *queso*
snack *antojo; botana*
breakfast *desayuno*
lunch *almuerzo*
daily lunch special *comida corrida (or el menú del día* depending on region)
dinner *comida* (often eaten in late afternoon); *cena* (a late-night snack)
the check *la cuenta*
eggs *huevos*
bread *pan*
salad *ensalada*
fruit *fruta*
mango *mango*
watermelon *sandía*
papaya *papaya*
banana *plátano*
apple *manzana*
orange *naranja*

lime *limón*
fish *pescado*
shellfish *mariscos*
shrimp *camarones*
meat (without) *(sin) carne*
chicken *pollo*
pork *puerco*
beef; steak *res; bistec*
bacon; ham *tocino; jamón*
fried *frito*
roasted *asada*
barbecue; barbecued *barbacoa; al carbón*

SHOPPING

money *dinero*
money-exchange bureau *casa de cambio*
I would like to exchange traveler's checks. *Quisiera cambiar cheques de viajero.*
What is the exchange rate? *¿Cuál es el tipo de cambio?*
How much is the commission? *¿Cuánto cuesta la comisión?*
Do you accept credit cards? *¿Aceptan tarjetas de crédito?*
money order *giro*
How much does it cost? *¿Cuánto cuesta?*
What is your final price? *¿Cuál es su último precio?*
expensive *caro*
cheap *barato; económico*
more *más*
less *menos*
a little *un poco*
too much *demasiado*

HEALTH

Help me please. *Ayúdeme por favor.*
I am ill. *Estoy enfermo.*
Call a doctor. *Llame un doctor.*
Take me to... *Lléveme a...*
hospital *hospital; sanatorio*
drugstore *farmacia*
pain *dolor*
fever *fiebre*
headache *dolor de cabeza*
stomach ache *dolor de estómago*
burn *quemadura*

cramp *calambre*
nausea *náusea*
vomiting *vomitar*
medicine *medicina*
antibiotic *antibiótico*
pill; tablet *pastilla*
aspirin *aspirina*
ointment; cream *pomada; crema*
bandage *venda*
cotton *algodón*
sanitary napkins use brand name, e.g., Kotex
birth control pills *pastillas anticonceptivas*
contraceptive foam *espuma anticonceptiva*
condoms *preservativos; condones*
toothbrush *cepilla dental*
dental floss *hilo dental*
toothpaste *crema dental*
dentist *dentista*
toothache *dolor de muelas*

POST OFFICE AND COMMUNICATIONS

long-distance telephone *teléfono larga distancia*
I would like to call... *Quisiera llamar a...*
collect *por cobrar*
station to station *a quien contesta*
person to person *persona a persona*
credit card *tarjeta de crédito*
post office *correo*
general delivery *lista de correo*
letter *carta*
stamp *estampilla, timbre*
postcard *tarjeta*
aerogram *aerograma*
air mail *correo aereo*
registered *registrado*
money order *giro*
package; box *paquete; caja*
string; tape *cuerda; cinta*

AT THE BORDER

border *frontera*
customs *aduana*
immigration *migración*
tourist card *tarjeta de turista*
inspection *inspección; revisión*
passport *pasaporte*

profession *profesión*
marital status *estado civil*
single *soltero*
married; divorced *casado; divorciado*
widowed *viudado*
insurance *seguros*
title *título*
driver's license *licencia de manejar*

AT THE GAS STATION

gas station *gasolinera*
gasoline *gasolina*
unleaded *sin plomo*
full, please *lleno, por favor*
tire *llanta*
tire repair shop *vulcanizadora*
air *aire*
water *agua*
oil (change) *aceite (cambio)*
grease *grasa*
My... doesn't work. *Mi... no sirve.*
battery *batería*
radiator *radiador*
alternator *alternador*
generator *generador*
tow truck *grúa*
repair shop *taller mecánico*
tune-up *afinación*
auto parts store *refaccionería*

VERBS

Verbs are the key to getting along in Spanish. They employ mostly predictable forms and come in three classes, which end in *ar, er,* and *ir,* respectively:

to buy *comprar*
I buy, you (he, she, it) buys *compro, compra*
we buy, you (they) buy *compramos, compran*

to eat *comer*
I eat, you (he, she, it) eats *como, come*
we eat, you (they) eat *comemos, comen*

to climb *subir*
I climb, you (he, she, it) climbs *subo, sube*
we climb, you (they) climb *subimos, suben*

Here are more (with irregularities indicated):

to do or make hacer (regular except for hago, I do or make)
to go ir (very irregular: voy, va, vamos, van)
to go (walk) andar
to love amar
to work trabajar
to want desear, querer
to need necesitar
to read leer
to write escribir
to repair reparar
to stop parar
to get off (the bus) bajar
to arrive llegar
to stay (remain) quedar
to stay (lodge) hospedar
to leave salir (regular except for salgo, I leave)
to look at mirar
to look for buscar
to give dar (regular except for doy, I give)
to carry llevar
to have tener (irregular but important: tengo, tiene, tenemos, tienen)
to come venir (similarly irregular: vengo, viene, venimos, vienen)

Spanish has two forms of "to be":

to be estar (regular except for estoy, I am)
to be ser (very irregular: soy, es, somos, son)

Use estar when speaking of location or a temporary state of being: "I am at home." "Estoy en casa." "I'm sick." "Estoy enfermo." Use ser for a permanent state of being: "I am a doctor." "Soy doctora."

NUMBERS
zero cero
one uno
two dos
three tres
four cuatro
five cinco
six seis
seven siete
eight ocho
nine nueve
10 diez
11 once
12 doce
13 trece
14 catorce
15 quince
16 dieciseis
17 diecisiete
18 dieciocho
19 diecinueve
20 veinte
21 veinte y uno or veintiuno
30 treinta
40 cuarenta
50 cincuenta
60 sesenta
70 setenta
80 ochenta
90 noventa
100 ciento
101 ciento y uno or cientiuno
200 doscientos
500 quinientos
1,000 mil
10,000 diez mil
100,000 cien mil
1,000,000 millón
one half medio
one third un tercio
one fourth un cuarto

TIME
What time is it? ¿Qué hora es?
It's one o'clock. Es la una.
It's three in the afternoon. Son las tres de la tarde.
It's 4 a.m. Son las cuatro de la mañana.
six-thirty seis y media
a quarter till eleven un cuarto para las once
a quarter past five las cinco y cuarto
an hour una hora

DAYS AND MONTHS
Monday lunes
Tuesday martes
Wednesday miércoles

Thursday *jueves*
Friday *viernes*
Saturday *sábado*
Sunday *domingo*
today *hoy*
tomorrow *mañana*
yesterday *ayer*
January *enero*
February *febrero*
March *marzo*
April *abril*
May *mayo*
June *junio*

July *julio*
August *agosto*
September *septiembre*
October *octubre*
November *noviembre*
December *diciembre*
a week *una semana*
a month *un mes*
after *después*
before *antes*

(Courtesy of Bruce Whipperman, author of *Moon Pacific Mexico*.)

Suggested Reading

TRAVELOGUES

Amey, Ralph L. *Wines of Baja California: Touring and Tasting Mexico's Undiscovered Treasures.* San Francisco: Wine Appreciation Guild, 2003. A compilation of historical information and winery profiles covering the Valle de Guadalupe and other regions in Northern Baja.

Berger, Bruce. *Almost an Island: Travels in Baja California.* Tucson: University of Arizona Press, 1998. Berger, a pianist, poet, desert aficionado, and keen observer of human behavior, surveys Baja's social landscape, with a special focus on La Paz.

Mackintosh, Graham. *Into a Desert Place.* New York: W. W. Norton & Co., 1995. One of the most widely read accounts of a gringo discovering Baja for the first time. With no wilderness experience, Graham decides to walk the entire coastline of Baja California.

Mayo, C. M. *Miraculous Air: Journey of a Thousand Miles through Baja California, the Other Mexico.* Minneapolis: Milkweed Editions, 2007. Poignant, contemporary memoir by a fiction writer originally from the United States who is now a Spanish/English translator and editor living in Mexico City.

Miller, Max. *Land Where Time Stands Still.* Gleed Press, 2007 (paperback). A classic 1940s travelogue that recounts the author's trip from San Diego to Cabo San Lucas.

Salvadori, Clement. *Motorcycle Journeys Through California and Baja,* 2nd ed. North Conway, NH: Whitehorse Press, 2007. A well-known motorcycling journalist advises kindred spirits on the best way to ride the Baja Peninsula.

Steinbeck, John. *The Log from the Sea of Cortez.* New York: Penguin USA, Viking, 1951. This classic armchair-travel read tells of Steinbeck's journey with marine biologist Ed Ricketts from Monterey, California, down the Pacific coast, around the tip of Baja, and up the Sea of Cortez.

HISTORY AND CULTURE

Crosby, Harry. *Antigua California: Mission and Colony on the Peninsular Frontier, 1697-1768.* Albuquerque: University of New Mexico Press, 1994. A well-written academic account of the Jesuit mission era in Baja California, from planning through expulsion.

Niemann, Greg. *Baja Legends.* San Diego: Sunbelt Publications, 2002. A light read that bring the ghosts of Baja past alive, one town at a time.

Preston, Julia, and Samuel Dillon. *Opening Mexico: The Making of a Democracy.* New York: Farrar, Straus, and Giroux, 2004. An engaging, narrative chronicle of Mexican history in the 20th century.

NATURAL HISTORY AND FIELD GUIDES

Case, T. J., and M. L. Cody, eds. *A New Island Biogeography in the Sea of Cortez,* 2nd ed. New York: Oxford University Press, 2002. An interesting read if you want to learn more about conservation efforts in the Sea of Cortez.

Edwards, Ernest Preston. *The Birds of Mexico and Adjacent Areas.* Austin: University of Texas Press, 1998. This field guide may come in handy but is not Baja-specific, and birders find it frustrating that birds of the same species are illustrated on different color plates.

Gotshall, Daniel W. *Sea of Cortez Marine Animals: A Guide to the Common Fishes and Invertebrates Baja California to Panama.* Gig Harbor, WA: Sea Challengers, 1998. A good reference guide for divers, sailors, and snorkelers.

McPeak, Ron. *Amphibians and Reptiles of Baja California,* Gig Harbor, WA: Sea Challengers, 2000. This is the book to get if you want to identify the many frogs, toads, salamanders, snakes, and lizards of the peninsula. It includes lots of color photos.

Peterson, R. T., and E. L. Chaliff. *A Field Guide to Mexican Birds.* 3rd ed. El Cajon, CA: Sunbelt Publications, 2012. The closest thing to a Baja-specific bird-watching guide lacks Spanish names for the birds.

Roberts, Norman C. *Baja California Plant Field Guide.* La Jolla, CA: Natural History Publishing Co., 1989. The must-have field guide to Baja's desert and sierra flora.

CONSERVATION

Dedina, Serge. *Saving the Gray Whale: People, Politics, and Conservation in Baja California* Tucson: University of Arizona Press, 2000. The author describes the natural history and life cycles of gray whale, its habitat, and the human ecology of Scammon's Lagoon and San Ignacio Lagoon in Baja California.

Dedina, Serge. *Wild Sea: Eco-Wars and Surf Stories from the Coast of the Californias,* Tucson: University of Arizona Press, 2011. The author is an environmental activist who lives in Imperial Beach, California, near the Tijuana border, and has played a key role in fighting major industrial development along the California and Baja coastlines.

Nabhan, Gary Paul. *Gathering the Desert,* Tucson: University of Arizona Press, 1986. A 200-page guide to the history and uses of 12 Sonoran Desert plants, organized into a collection of scholarly essays.

Peterson, Brenda, and Linda Hogan. *Sightings: The Gray Whales' Mysterious Journey.* Washington, D.C.: National Geographic, 2003. A nature writer and a native American poet teamed up to tell the story of the gray whale through the eyes of researchers, fishers, and coastal communities whose past and future are tied to the endangered mammal.

Russel, Dick. *Eye of the Whale: Epic Passage from Baja to Siberia,* New York: Simon & Schuster, 2001. This popular account of threats to the gray whale's habitat along the Pacific coast centers around the thwarted effort by a Japanese corporation to build a salt plant in the gray-whale breeding ground.

SPORTS AND RECREATION

Breeding, Shawn, and Heather Bansmer. *Sea of Cortez: A Cruiser's Guidebook,* Kirkland, WA: Blue Latitude Press, 2009. Spiral-bound

guide with detailed information for boaters, such as nautical mileage tables and charts.

Eckardt, Dave. *The Guide to Baja Sea Kayaking: The Sea of Cortez and Magdalena Bay.* Paddle Publishing, 2008. This resource for kayakers covers San Felipe to Los Cabos and all the islands in between, plus Bahía Magdalena on the Pacific coast. Includes GPS coordinates and color maps.

Kelly, Neil, and Gene Kira. *The Baja Catch: A Fishing, Travel & Remote Camping Manual for Baja California,* 3rd ed. Valley Center, CA: Apples and Oranges, 1997. The undisputed bible of Baja fishing has a lot of information on camping as well.

Lehman, Charles. *Desert Survival Handbook,* rev. ed. Phoenix: Primer Publishers, 1998. Practical information for surviving in the desert—essential for any serious Baja exploration.

Parise, Mike. *The Surfer's Guide to Baja.* Los Angeles: SurfPress Publishing, 2012. A must-have resource for Baja-bound surfers, the guide includes detailed directions to more than 75 breaks along the peninsula, plus maps and wave height charts.

Williams, Jack. *Baja Boater's Guide, Vols. I and II.* Sausalito, CA: H. J. Williams Publications, 2001 (Vol. I, 3rd ed.) and 2003 (Vol. II, 4th ed.). These ambitious guides, one each on the Pacific Ocean and the Sea of Cortez, contain useful aerial photos and sketch maps of Baja's continental islands and coastline.

REAL ESTATE AND LIVING ABROAD

Luboff, Ken. *Living Abroad in Mexico.* Berkeley, CA: Avalon Travel, 2005. This resource gives advice and tips for Americans thinking of moving from the United States to Mexico.

Peyton, Dennis John. *How to Buy Real Estate in Mexico.* San Diego: Law Mexico Publishing, 2006. If you've decided you want a place of your own in Baja, read this book first. It will answer many of your questions, saving time and minimizing frustration in the process.

COOKBOOKS

Hazard, Ann. *Cooking with Baja Magic Dos.* El Cajon, CA: Sunbelt Publications, 2005. A collection of updated recipes drawn from conversations with restaurant owners and other Baja characters, plus the author's own experience of living in La Bufadora and Buena Vista.

Schneider, Deborah M. *Baja! Cooking on the Edge,* Emmaus, PA: Rodale, 2006. More than 250 colorful pages of recipes, stories, and photos. Learn to make clams in tequila butter or homemade *paletas* (popsicles). Well-written anecdotes share the history of Baja foods and the author's culinary experience in Baja.

Szekely, Deborah, and Deborah M. Schneider. *Cooking with the Seasons at Rancho La Puerta,* New York: Harry N. Abrams, Inc., 2008. Try preparing your own spa food using these secret recipes from "The Ranch."

Internet Resources

The Internet remains an invaluable resource for Baja-bound travelers. Even out-of-the-way establishments often have at least a basic website with directions and current pricing. The most technologically savvy ones use the Google Earth application to show visitors exactly where they are located. Some are experimenting with mobile applications and other communication tools. When it comes to directory-type sites, you need to be careful what you read. The vast majority of these sites are advertising engines with unedited and out-of-date information. Here is a short list of some of the most useful all-Baja sites.

Baja Books and Maps
www.bajabooksandmaps.com
Online bookstore with a comprehensive collection of Baja-related titles. This company is also the sole distributor of Baja-related titles to English-language bookstores throughout Southern Baja.

Baja Bound
www.bajabound.com
One of many businesses that offer Mexican auto insurance policies for travelers driving their own vehicles to Baja. Lots of related travel information, too.

Baja.com
www.baja.com
Destination community site with vacation rental listings and regional guides, mainly for Southern Baja.

BajaInsider.com
www.bajainsider.com
Comprehensive online publication for visitors and residents with news, weather, and commentary.

Baja Nomad
www.bajanomad.com
An interactive forum with extremely active participants, many of them veteran Baja travelers and local business owners. If you have the time to read through all the threads, you'll find a wealth of information about border crossings, road conditions, restaurant and hotel reviews, and more. If it's not on Baja Nomad, it probably hasn't happened yet.

Baja Times
www.bajatimes.com
Online version of the biweekly English-language newspaper serving tourists and residents of the main Northern Baja communities with news, real estate, and travel information.

Border Wait Times
http://apps.cbp.gov/bwt
Real-time border crossing times from the U.S. Customs and Border Protection. Scroll down to find the list of Mexican Border Ports of Entry.

Bush Pilots International
www.bajabushpilots.com
A must-read for pilots interested in flying a private aircraft to Baja. It costs US$50 a year to access the forums, which might be worth it even if you're not a pilot.

Instituto Nacional de Antropología e Historia (INAH)
www.inah.gob.mx
INAH is the government institution responsible for protection of Baja's cultural sights, including the historic Jesuit missions and ancient cave paintings. It runs museums in La Paz and Loreto and issues visitor permits for trips to the cave paintings and other protected areas.

Instituto Nacional de Estadística, Geografía e Informática (INEGI)
www.inegi.org.mx
INEGI is a Mexican government agency that publishes statistics on population and economics for the entire country as well as topographical

maps. It also has an interactive map of Mexico, including Baja California. Spanish only.

iWindsurf.com and iKitesurf.com
www.iwindsurf.com, www.ikitesurf.com
Daily Baja wind forecast and reports for windsurfers, plus a whole range of consumer weather delivery services, from the parent company WeatherFlow.

Los Cabos Guide
www.loscabosguide.com
Relatively up-to-date, advertiser-driven listings of hospitality and tourism businesses in the Los Cabos area, with some coverage of the East Cape and Todos Santos. Useful restaurant reviews and hotel listings. Fairly comprehensive.

Mexico Fishing News
www.mexfish.com
Weekly fishing report that covers the entire peninsula with conditions, regulations, catches, and photos.

Sunbelt Publications
www.sunbeltbook.com
This book publisher specializing in upper and lower California has an online catalog of its Baja titles.

U.S. Embassy
http://mexico.usembassy.gov
Visit the U.S. Embassy in Mexico City online, with information on services for U.S. citizens, plus current State Department travel warnings.

XE Currency Converter
www.xe.com/ucc
This online tool for currency conversions comes in handy now that the dollar-to-peso exchange rate is no longer an easy 1:10 ratio.

Index

List of Maps

Acknowledgments

This edition of *Moon Los Cabos* was written while:

- snorkeling with a school of mobulas in Los Frailes Bay
- sipping carrot and beet margaritas at Flora Farms
- diving with spinner dolphins near Isla Cerralvo
- shopping for jewels at Amber Gallery
- getting caffeinated at Baja Beans
- watching the sun set over La Poza in Todos Santos
- having a run-in with the *policia* in La Paz
- watching my four-year-old learn to body surf at Playa Los Arbolitos
- taking my six-year old on his first deep-sea fishing adventure
- eating street food on the plaza in San Jose del Cabo

But more than the experiences, it is the people who make Los Cabos a special place. Many local friends and new acquaintances shared their love of all things Baja and called attention to exciting new developments in the region. A sincere thanks to Pablo, Carmel, Lucas, and Lola on the East Cape; the Hatler family at Palapas Ventana; Sergio and Bryan at Todos Santos Eco-Adventures; Esther Amman at El Angel Azul in La Paz; Patricia and Eric at The Bungalows in Cabo San Lucas; Carla White, Chris Sands, Lisa Green, Sheri Guardi, and Jim Pickell at Baja.com.

Traveling with Gretchen and Ryan Boehm was a joy and helped me see Los Cabos through the eyes of first-time visitors. On another scouting trip, travel companion Lauren Swift shared her own observations, photos, and more to help complete the edition. And as always, Paul Itoi led the charge for an action-packed family trip, during which our two sons discovered the joys of surfing, scorpions, and *limonadas*.

A number of professionals offered their time, contacts, and marketing support to arrange tours, verify facts, and contribute photos. In particular, Rose Capasso at Carolyn Izzo Integrated Communications (CIIC) and Gabriela Barron at the Hilton Los Cabos went out of their way to assist.

The team at Avalon Travel—Erin Raber, Albert Angulo, and Darren Alessi—offered expertise and patience as the new *Moon Los Cabos* took shape.

Thanks to all for these invaluable contributions.

www.moon.com

MOON.COM is ready to help plan your next trip! Filled with fresh trip ideas and strategies, author interviews, informative travel blogs, a detailed map library, and descriptions of all the Moon guidebooks, Moon.com is all you need to get out and explore the world—or even places in your own backyard. While at Moon.com, sign up for our monthly e-newsletter for updates on new releases, travel tips, and expert advice from our on-the-go Moon authors. As always, when you travel with Moon, expect an experience that is uncommon and truly unique.

KEEP UP WITH MOON: f 🐦 📌

MAP SYMBOLS

▬▬▬	Expressway	**(**	Highlight	✈	Airport	⚓	Golf Course
▬▬▬	Primary Road	○	City/Town	✕	Airfield	**P**	Parking Area
▬▬▬	Secondary Road	◉	State Capital	▲	Mountain	⛩	Archaeological Site
┄┄┄	Unpaved Road	⊛	National Capital	✛	Unique Natural Feature	⚲	Church
- - -	Trail	★	Point of Interest			⛽	Gas Station
··········	Ferry	•	Accommodation	🏳	Waterfall	🐦	Dive Site
-·-·-·	Railroad	▼	Restaurant/Bar	⚑	Park		Mangrove
▬▬▬	Pedestrian Walkway	▪	Other Location	⬚	Trailhead		Reef
▮▮▮▮	Stairs	Λ	Campground	☀	Lighthouse		Swamp

CONVERSION TABLES

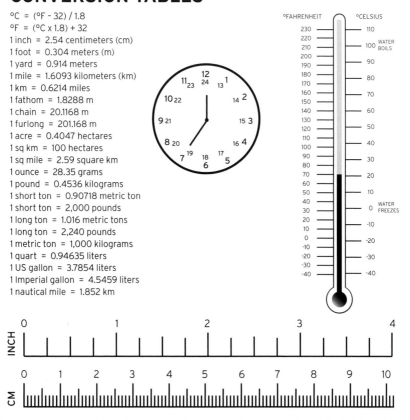

°C = (°F - 32) / 1.8
°F = (°C x 1.8) + 32
1 inch = 2.54 centimeters (cm)
1 foot = 0.304 meters (m)
1 yard = 0.914 meters
1 mile = 1.6093 kilometers (km)
1 km = 0.6214 miles
1 fathom = 1.8288 m
1 chain = 20.1168 m
1 furlong = 201.168 m
1 acre = 0.4047 hectares
1 sq km = 100 hectares
1 sq mile = 2.59 square km
1 ounce = 28.35 grams
1 pound = 0.4536 kilograms
1 short ton = 0.90718 metric ton
1 short ton = 2,000 pounds
1 long ton = 1.016 metric tons
1 long ton = 2,240 pounds
1 metric ton = 1,000 kilograms
1 quart = 0.94635 liters
1 US gallon = 3.7854 liters
1 Imperial gallon = 4.5459 liters
1 nautical mile = 1.852 km

MOON LOS CABOS

Avalon Travel
a member of the Perseus Books Group
1700 Fourth Street
Berkeley, CA 94710, USA
www.moon.com

Editor: Erin Raber
Series Manager: Kathryn Ettinger
Copy Editor: Deana Shields
Graphics Coordinator: Darren Alessi
Production Coordinator: Darren Alessi
Cover Designer: Darren Alessi
Map Editor: Albert Angulo
Cartographers: Chris Henrick, Brian Shotwell,
    Stephanie Poulain
Indexer: Greg Jewett

ISBN-13: 978-1-61238-629-4
ISSN: 1082-5169

Printing History
1st Edition – 1995
9th Edition – December 2013
5 4 3 2 1

Text © 2013 by Nikki Goth Itoi.
Maps © 2013 by Avalon Travel.
All rights reserved.

Photos on pages 1–24 © Nikki Goth Itoi except page
5 © Paul Itoi; page 9 (top) © Carmel Tsabar; page
15 (top left) © Pablo Nobili; page 13 Courtesy
of Secrets Marquis Los Cabos; page 15 (bottom
left) © Lauren Swift; page 16 © Paul Itoi; page 17
(top left) © Carmel Tsabar; page 19 (top left) ©
Gary718/123rf.com, (top right) © Lauren Swift;
page 20, page 21 (right) © Kaia Thomson; page 22
Courtesy of Pueblo Bonito Sunset Beach; page 23
Courtesy of ME Cabo; page 24 Courtesy of Cultural
Pavilion of the Republic

Printed in China by RR Donnelley

KEEPING CURRENT

If you have a favorite gem you'd like to see included in the next edition, or see anything
that needs updating, clarification, or correction, please drop us a line. Send your com-
ments via email to feedback@moon.com, or use the address above.